DATE DUE 7/97

DEMCO 38-297

Contemporary Issues in Educational Psychology

Fifth Edition

HARVEY F. CLARIZIO
ROBERT C. CRAIG
WILLIAM A. MEHRENS

Michigan State University

RANDOM HOUSE
New York

*This book was developed for
Random House by Lane Akers, Inc.*

Fifth Edition

987654321

Library of Congress Cataloging-in-Publication Data

Clarizio, Harvey F., 1934–
  Contemporary issues in educational psychology.

  Includes bibliographies and index.
  1. Educational psychology.   I. Craig, Robert C.
II. Mehrens, William A.   III. Title.
LB1055.C556   1986   370.15   86-20324
ISBN 0-394-35642-X

Manufactured in the United States of America

Contributing Authors

Dr. Marshall Arlin
Faculty of Education
University of British Columbia

Dr. Albert Bandura
Department of Psychology
Stanford University

Dr. Wesley C. Becker
Professor of Education
University of Oregon

Dr. Camilla R. Benbow
Associate Professor of Psychology
Iowa State University

Dr. Carl Bereiter, Professor
Centre for Applied Cognitive Science
Ontario Institute for Studies in Education

Dr. James H. Block, Professor
University of California
Santa Barbara

Dr. Gordon Bower
Professor
Stanford University

Dr. Jere Brophy, Professor
Michigan State University

Susan Burland
Department of Psychology
University of Waterloo, Ontario

Don Cameron
Executive Director
National Education Association

Dr. C. M. Charles
Professor of Teacher Education
San Diego State University

Christiane Hyde Citron
Assistant Attorney General, Education Unit
Office of the Attorney General
of the State of Colorado

Dr. Gary Cooke
Professor, Elementary & Early Childhood
Education
University of Toledo

Dr. Arthur L. Costa
Professor, Education
California State University, Sacramento

Dr. Edward De Bono, Director
Cognitive Research Trust
Cambridge, England
L2, Albany, Piccadilly, London, W.1V 9RR.

Dr. Marcy Perkins Driscoll
Associate Professor of Instructional Systems
Florida State University

Dr. Robert Ebel (deceased)
Professor, Educational Psychology
Michigan State University

Stephen Garger, Director
Issaquah (Washington) Alternative School
Issaquah, Washington

Dr. Milton Goldberg, Director
Programs for the Improvement of Practice
U.S. Department of Education

Pat Guild, President
Pat Guild Associates and
Coordinator of Learning Styles
Seattle Pacific University

Dr. Andrew Hacker
Professor, Political Science
Queens College
City University of New York

Dr. James Harvey
Executive Director
National Commission on Jobs and Small
Business

Dr. Ernest R. Hilgard
Emeritus Professor of Psychology and
Education
Stanford University

Dr. Ronald Hyman
Professor of Education
Graduate School of Education
Rutgers University

Dr. Arthur R. Jensen
Professor of Educational Psychology
University of California, Berkeley

Dr. Janet Kiersted, Consultant
Educational Research and Staff Development
Westlake Village Schools, California

Dr. Gilah C. Leder
Senior Lecturer
Monash University, Australia

Dr. Jerre Levy
Professor
University of Chicago

Dr. Cherie Lohr, Chairman
Department of Curriculum and Instruction
Texas Christian University

Dr. Wilbert J. McKeachie
Emeritus Professor of Psychology
University of Michigan

Dr. Donald H. Meichenbaum
Department of Psychology
University of Waterloo, Ontario

Dr. John F. Mesinger
Professor in Education
Director of the Education Program
Curry School
University of Virginia

Stephen O'Brien
Social Studies Teacher
Hamilton-Wenham Regional High School
Hamilton, Massachusetts

Dr. Richard Podemski
Associate Dean for Instructional Programs
University of Alabama

Dr. W. James Popham, Professor
University of California, Los Angeles

Dr. Lauren B. Resnick
Professor of Psychology and Director
Learning Research and Development Center
University of Pittsburgh

Dr. Carl M. Rogers
Center for Studies of the Person
LaJolla, California

Dr. Barak Rosenshine
Professor of Educational Psychology
University of Illinois

Barbara Rosoff
Doctoral Candidate
Rutgers University

Dr. Cliff Schimmels
Professor of Education
Wheaton College

Dr. Lawrence J. Schweinhart, Director
Voices for Children Project
High/Scope Educational Research Foundation
Ypsilanti, Michigan

Albert Shanker, President
American Federation of Teachers

Dr. B. F. Skinner
Professor Emeritus
Psychology and Social Relations
Harvard University

Dr. Robert E. Slavin
Principal Research Scientist
Johns Hopkins University

Dr. Michele Geslin Small
Professor of English and French
Northland College
Ashland, Wisconsin

Dr. Susan Stainback
Professor, Special Education
University of Northern Iowa

Dr. William Stainback
Professor, Special Education
University of Northern Iowa

Dr. John Stammer
Professor, Elementary and Early Childhood
Education
University of Toledo

Dr. Julian C. Stanley
Professor of Psychology and Codirector,
Study of Mathematically Precocious Youth
Johns Hopkins University

Dr. David P. Weikart, President
High/Scope Educational Research Foundation
Ypsilanti, Michigan

Preface to Fifth Edition

Instructors in educational psychology, like other college teachers, usually encourage their students to read materials in addition to the basic textbook for the course. With the varied and numerous demands on their time, however, instructors frequently find it difficult to provide students with a list of current articles that deal with meaningful concerns of the field. Moreover, even when such reading lists are made available, library facilities are often so limited that broadly based reading among students is commonly frustrated. It was with such difficulties in mind that we developed a collection of readings based on major concerns of a polemical nature. Altogether too frequently students are presented with tentative findings as "truths," with little or no mention of contrasting or incompatible stances. We hope to offer a realistic and sophisticated perspective of educational psychology by making students aware of divergent positions assumed by established professionals on fundamental questions. We believe this appropriate for all students, but expect the instructor of beginning students to help them find a personally satisfying resolution to those questions which would affect their teaching practices—thus avoiding a premature dashing of their hopes for certitude. On the other hand, more advanced students may take the differing views of authorities as a point of departure for further independent study and investigation.

Special Features of the Book

This book of readings in educational psychology differs from others in that all selections attempt to deal with significant issues of current concern and controversy. Consistent with this objective, we have included twenty-one issues and classified them into four broad areas. The issues, for the most part, are presented in a pro and con format. Introductions and thought questions prepared by the editors precede each issue. Introductions to those few research articles which might be difficult for beginning students to comprehend include technical notes to explain statistical terms and procedures.

We have updated many of the issues retained from the fourth edition by selecting current articles. Moreover, we have added several new issues such as matching learning and teaching styles, how to teach thinking, sex differences among the gifted in mathematical achievement, right brain–left brain functioning, and competency testing for teachers.

While all of the issues deal with present concerns, some of them are not of recent origin. In these cases, the contemporary issues are byproducts of major problems that have existed in education and psychology over a long period of time. For example, grade retention versus social promotion, and the effectiveness of direct instruction, which have long been of concern to educators, have gained importance as a result of increased responsibilities placed on the school to provide an appropriate education.

The primary purpose of this volume is to introduce students to the range and variety of the concerns of the field and to stimulate further study of these concerns. Hence, we chose to include a rather large number of issues rather than to treat several in great detail. The highly polemical nature of these issues should serve to encourage discussion and investigation of today's major controversies in educational psychology. Thus, we hope that this book will prove a valuable pedagogical tool, not only in small college classes but also at megaversities where large lecture sections are typically accompanied by discussion sections designed to promote critical thinking.

Another distinctive aspect of this volume is that it is education centered. Bearing in mind that the book is intended for prospective or practicing educators, we have drawn most of the articles—written by major theorists and practitioners—from education–oriented journals.

Since this reader deals with issues of a controversial nature, it will often be used to stimulate the student toward additional reading. For this reason, related references have been provided at the end of each of the four major units.

Criteria for Selection

In selecting papers for this volume, we kept the following criteria foremost in mind:

1. READABILITY. The articles had to be intelligible to students with little or no background in statistics and research design.
2. RELEVANCE. The articles had to deal with meaningful controversies related to educational practice.
3. AUTHORITY. Preference was given, whenever possible, to articles written by established theorists and experienced practitioners.
4. RECENTNESS. Preferences were given to articles published within the past five years.

The editors of this anthology are deeply appreciative to the authors for granting permission to reproduce their articles. We would also like to thank the many anonymous reviewers for their helpful suggestions regarding the selection of articles and their organization.

H.F.C.
R.C.C.
W.A.M.

Contents

UNIT 4

Classroom Dynamics

DISCIPLINE: SELF-GUIDANCE VERSUS EXTERNAL CONTROL

1

Psychological Views
of Children and Schools

Educators have two main tasks confronting them: (1) to decide what to teach, and (2) to decide how to teach most effectively. Since the tasks of deciding what to teach and how to teach are basic, it is quite appropriate to commence this book with articles that discuss very generally the purposes and practices of education.

The authors of the following three readings are not taken completely opposing views on the role of the school in society. Nevertheless, they do emphasize different aspects. Ebel suggests that "schools are for learning, and that what ought to be learned mainly is useful knowledge." He would give moral education a higher priority than affective education, but would give highest priority to cognitive competence.

Rogers wants people to learn to be free. Freedom, according to Rogers, is "the quality of courage which enables a person to step into the uncertainty of the unknown as he chooses himself." Rogers suggests that to facilitate this type of learning teachers need to have a profound trust in the human organism. This trust allows students to choose both their own goals and the procedures in reaching those goals.

Skinner believes that the free and happy student is imaginary. He argues that educators "should be willing to say what we believe students will need to know. . . ." Further, he states that "the natural, logical outcome of the struggle for personal freedom in education is that the teacher should improve his control of the student rather than abandon it. The free school is no school at all."

All the questions about alternative purposes and practices of the schools could not be considered in a whole book of readings, let alone in three articles. However, the viewpoints of Ebel, Rogers, and Skinner, and reflective thinking about questions such as those that follow, will alert you to the kinds of decisions educators must make. The stand you take on such questions will influence which side you choose on several of the issues discussed later in the book. Conversely, the research that educational psychologists present on later issues will help you take a firmer stand on the value questions posed here.

Thought Questions

Which of the following goals should receive the most emphasis in school: Teaching the three Rs, developing character, or instilling good self-concepts in pupils? Defend your answer.

3

Should schools strive for excellence, as Ebel suggests, or for equality among students? Should they strive for diversity or conformity in school programs? What advantages do you see in each approach? What disadvantages do you see?

Should schools attempt to be a vital force in promoting social change? If so, can they also be completely accepting of all the various value systems held by different American subcultures? Explain your answer. Is it more or less democratic to expend more time, money, and energy on those who come to school from impoverished environments?

How free should students be? Should there be diminished authority for the teacher coupled with increased freedom for the student? Should increased freedom for the student include both freedom in determining objectives and freedom in determining how to reach those objectives?

What Are Schools For?

Robert L. Ebel

When the history of our times is written, it may designate the two decades following World War II as the golden age of American education. Never before was education more highly valued. Never before was so much of it so readily available to so many. Never before had it been supported so generously. Never before was so much expected of it.

But in this eighth decade of the twentieth century public education in this country appears to be in trouble. Taxpayers are revolting against the skyrocketing costs of education. Schools are being denied the funds they say they need for quality education. Teachers are uniting to press demands for higher pay and easier working conditions.

College and high school students have rebelled against what they call "the Establishment," resisting and overturning regulations, demanding pupil-directed rather than teacher-directed education, and turning in some cases to drink, drugs, and delinquency. Minorities are demanding equal treatment, which is surely their right. But when integration makes social differences more visible, and when equality of opportunity is not followed quickly by equality of achievement, frustration turns to anger which sometimes leads to violence.

Surely these problems are serious enough. But I believe there is one yet more serious, because it lies closer to the heart of our whole educational enterprise. We seem to have lost sight of, or become confused about, our main function as educators, our principal goal, our reason for existence. We have no good answer that we are sure of and can agree on to the question, What are schools for?

It may seem presumptuous of me to suggest that I know the answer to this question. Yet the answer I will give is the answer that an overwhelming majority of our fellow citizens would also give. It is the answer that would have been given by most educators of the past who established and operated schools. Indeed, the only reason the question needs to be asked and answered at this time is that some influential educators have been conned into accepting wrong answers to the question. Let me mention a few of these wrong answers.

- Schools are not custodial institutions responsible for coping with emotionally disturbed or incorrigible young people, for keeping nonstudents off the streets or out of the job market.
- Schools are not adjustment centers, responsible for helping young people develop favorable self-concepts, solve personal problems, and come to terms with life.

From *Phi Delta Kappan* 54, no. 1 (1972): 3–7. Reprinted with permission.

- Schools are not recreational facilities designed to entertain and amuse, to cultivate the enjoyment of freedom, to help young people find strength through joy.
- Schools are not social research agencies to which a society can properly delegate responsibility for the discovery of solutions to the problems that are currently troubling the society.

I do not deny that society needs to be concerned about some of the things just mentioned. What I do deny is that schools were built and are maintained primarily to solve such problems. I deny that schools are good places in which to seek solutions, or that they have demonstrated much success in finding them. Schools have a very important special mission. If they accept responsibility for solving many of the other problems that trouble some young people, they are likely to fail in their primary mission, without having much success in solving the rest of our social problems.

Then what is the right answer to the question, What are schools for? I believe it is that schools are for learning, and that what ought to be learned mainly is useful knowledge.

Not all educators agree. Some of them discount the value of knowledge in the modern world. They say we ought to strive for the cultivation of intellectual skills. Others claim that schools have concentrated too much on knowledge, to the neglect of values, attitudes, and such affective dispositions. Still others argue that the purpose of education is to change behavior. They would assess its effectiveness by examining the pupil's behavior or performance. Let us consider these three alternatives in reverse order.

If the schools are to be accountable for the performance of their pupils, the question that immediately arises is, What performance? A direct answer to this question is, The performance you've been trying to teach. But that answer is not as simple or as obviously correct as it seems at first glance. Many schools have not been primarily concerned with teaching pupils

to perform. They have been trying to develop their pupils' knowledge, understanding, attitudes, interests, and ideals; their cognitive capabilities and affective dispositions rather than their performances. Those who manage such schools would agree that capabilities and dispositions can only be assessed by observing performances, but they would insist that the performances themselves are not the goals of achievement, only the indicators of it. A teacher who is concerned with the pupil's cognitive capabilities and affective dispositions will teach quite differently, they point out, than one whose attention is focused solely on the pupil's performances. And, if performances are not goals but only indicators, we should choose the ones to use in assessment on the basis of their effectiveness as indicators. Clearly we cannot choose them in terms of the amount of effort we made to develop them.

But, if we reject performance goals, another question arises: What should be the relative emphasis placed on affective dispositions as opposed to cognitive capabilities? Here is another issue that divides professional educators. To some, how the pupil feels—his happiness, his interest, his self-concept, his yearnings—are what should most concern teachers. To others the pupil's cognitive resources and capabilities are the main concern. Both would agree that cognition and affect interact, and that no school ought to concentrate solely on one and ignore the other. But they disagree on which should receive primary emphasis.

In trying to resolve this issue it may be helpful to begin by observing that the instructional programs of almost all schools are aimed directly at the cultivation of cognitive competence. Pupils are taught how to read and to use mathematics, how to write and to express perceptions, feelings, ideas, and desires in writing, to be acquainted with history and to understand science. The pupil's affective dispositions, his feelings, attitudes, interests, etc., constitute conditions that facilitate or inhibit cognitive achievement. They may be enhanced by success or impaired by failure. But they are by-products, not the main products, of the instructional effort. It is almost impossible to find any school that has planned and successfully operated an instructional program aimed primarily at the attainment of affective goals.

That this situation exists does not prove that it ought to exist. But it does suggest that there may be reasons. And we need not look too far to discover what they probably are.

Feelings are essentially unteachable. They cannot be passed along from teacher to learner in the way that information is transmitted. Nor can the learner acquire them by pursuing them directly as he might acquire understanding by study. Feelings are almost always the consequence of something—of success or failure, of duty done or duty ignored, of danger encountered or danger escaped. Further, good feelings (and bad feelings also, fortunately) are seldom if ever permanent possessions. They tend to be highly ephemeral. The surest prediction that one can make when he feels particularly good, strong, wise, or happy is that sooner or later he is going to feel bad, weak, foolish, or sad. In these circumstances it is hardly surprising that feelings are difficult to teach.

Nor do they need to be taught. A new-born infant has, or quickly develops, a full complement of them—pain, rage, satiety, drowsiness, vitality, joy, love, and all the rest. Experience may attach these feelings to new objects. It may teach the wisdom of curbing the expression of certain feelings at inappropriate times or in inappropriate ways. And while such attachments and curbings may be desirable, and may be seen as part of the task of the school, they hardly qualify as one of its major missions.

The school has in fact a much more important educational mission than affective education, one which in the current cultural climate and educational fashion is being badly neglected. I refer to moral education—the inculcation in the young of the accumulated moral wisdom of the race. Some of our young people have been allowed to grow up as virtual moral illiterates. And as Joseph Junell points out, we are paying a heavy price for this neglect as the youth of our society become alienated, turn to revolt, and threaten the destruction of our social fabric.

This change in our perception of the func-

tion of the school is reflected in our statements of educational objectives. A century ago Horace Mann, Herbert Spencer, and most others agreed that there were three main aspects of education: intellectual, moral, and physical. Today the main aspects identified by our taxonomies of objectives are cognitive, affective, and psychomotor. The first and third elements in these two triads are essentially identical. The second elements are quite different. The change reflects a shift in emphasis away from the pupil's duties and toward his feelings.

Why has this come about? Perhaps because of the current emphasis in our society on individual liberty rather than on personal responsibility. Perhaps because we have felt it necessary to be more concerned with civil rights than with civic duties. Perhaps because innovation and change look better to us than tradition and stability. Perhaps because we have come to trust and honor the vigor of youth more than the wisdom of age.

In all these things we may have been misled. As we view the contemporary culture in this country it is hard to see how the changes that have taken place in our moral values during the last half century have brought any visible improvement in the quality of our lives. It may be time for the pendulum to start swinging back toward an emphasis on responsibility, on stability, on wisdom. Older people are not always wiser people, but wisdom does grow with experience, and experience does accumulate with age.

Schools have much to contribute to moral education if they choose to do so, and if the courts and the public will let them. The rules of conduct and discipline adopted and enforced in the school, the models of excellence and humanity provided by the teachers, can be powerful influences in moral education. The study of history can teach pupils a decent respect for the lessons in morality that long experience has gradually taught the human race. Schools in the Soviet Union today appear to be doing a much more effective job of moral education than we have done in recent years. This fact alone may be enough to discredit moral education in some eyes. But concern for moral education has also been expressed by educational leaders in the democracies.

Alfred North Whitehead[1] put the matter this way at the end of his essay on the aims of education:

> "The essence of education is that it be religious."
> "Pray, what is religious education?"
> "A religious education is an education which inculcates duty and reverence. Duty arises from our potential control over the course of events. Where attainable knowledge could have changed the issue, ignorance has the guilt of vice. And the foundation of reverence is this perception, that the present holds within itself the complete sum of existence, backwards and forwards, that whole amplitude of time which is eternity."

If these views are correct, moral education deserves a much higher priority among the tasks of the school than does affective education. But it does not deserve the highest priority. That spot must be reserved for the cultivation of cognitive competence. Human beings need strong moral foundations, as part of their cultural heritage. They also need a structure of knowledge as part of their intellectual heritage. What schools were primarily built to do, and what they are most capable of doing well, is to help the student develop cognitive competence.

What is cognitive competence? Two distinctly different answers have been given. One is that it requires acquisition of knowledge. The other is that it requires development of intellectual skills. Here is another issue on which educational specialists are divided.

To avoid confusion or superficiality on this issue it is necessary to be quite clear on the meanings attached to the terms *knowledge* and *intellectual skills*. Knowledge, as the term is used here, is not synonymous with information. Knowledge is built out of information by thinking. It is an integrated structure of relationships among concepts and propositions. A teacher can give his students information. He cannot give them knowledge. A student must earn the right to say "I know" by his own thoughtful efforts to understand.

Whatever a person experiences directly in living or vicariously by reading or listening can become part of his knowledge. It will become part of his knowledge if he succeeds in integrating that experience into the structure of his knowledge, so that it makes sense, is likely to be remembered, and will be available for use when needed. Knowledge is essentially a private possession. Information can be made public. Knowledge cannot. Hence it would be more appropriate to speak of a modern-day information explosion than of a knowledge explosion.

The term *intellectual skills* has also been used with a variety of meanings. Further, those who use it often do not say, precisely and clearly, what they mean by it. Most of them seem not to mean skill in specific operations, such as spelling a word, adding two fractions, diagramming a sentence, or balancing a chemical equation. They are likely to conceive of intellectual skills in much broader terms, such as observing, classifying, measuring, communicating, predicting, inferring, experimenting, formulating hypotheses, and interpreting data.

It seems clear that these broader intellectual skills cannot be developed or used very effectively apart from substantial bodies of relevant knowledge. To be skillful in formulating hypotheses about the cause of a patient's persistent headaches, one needs to know a considerable amount of neurology, anatomy, and physiology, as much as possible about the known disorders that cause headaches, and a great deal about the history and habits of the person who is suffering them. That is, to show a particular intellectual skill a person must possess the relevant knowledge. (Note well at this point that a person cannot look up the knowledge he needs, for knowledge, in the sense of the term as we use it, cannot be looked up. Only information can be looked up. Knowledge has to be built by the knower himself.) And, if he does possess the relevant knowledge, what else does he need in order to show the desired skill?

Intellectual skill that goes beyond knowledge can be developed in specific operations like spelling a word or adding fractions. But the more general (and variable from instance to instance) the operation becomes, the less likely it is that a person's intellectual skills will go far beyond his knowledge.

Those who advocate the development of intellectual skills as the principal cognitive aim of education often express the belief (or hope) that these skills will be broadly transferrable from one area of subject matter to another. But if the subjects are quite different, the transfer is likely to be quite limited. Who would hire a man well trained in the measurement of personal characteristics for the job of measuring stellar distances and compositions?

Those who advocate the cultivation of knowledge as the central focus of our educational efforts are sometimes asked, "What about wisdom? Isn't that more important than knowledge?"

To provide a satisfactory answer to this question we need to say clearly what we mean when we speak of wisdom. In some situations wisdom is simply an alias for good fortune. He who calls the plays in a football game, who designs a new automobile, or who plays the stock market is likely to be well acquainted with this kind of wisdom—and with its constant companion, folly. If an action that might turn out badly in fact turns out well, we call it an act of wisdom. If it turns out badly, it was clearly an act of folly.

But there is more than this to the relation of knowledge to wisdom. C. I. Lewis of Harvard has expressed that relation in this way:

> Where ability to make correct judgments of value is concerned, we more typically speak of wisdom, perhaps, than of knowledge. And "wisdom" connotes one character which is not knowledge at all, though it is quality inculcated by experience; the temper, namely, which avoids perversity in intentions, and the insufficiently considered in actions. But for the rest, wisdom and knowledge are distinct merely because there is so much of knowledge which, for any given individual or under the circumstances which obtain, is relatively inessential to judgment of values and to success in action. Thus a man may be pop-eyed with correct information and still lack wisdom, because his information has little bearing on those judgments of relative value which he is called upon to make, or

because he lacks capacity to discriminate the practically important from the unimportant, or to apply his information to concrete problems of action. And men of humble attainments so far as breadth of information goes may still be wise by their correct apprehension of such values as lie open to them and of the roads to these. But surely wisdom is a type of knowledge; that type which is oriented on the important and the valuable. The wise man is he who knows where good lies, and how to act so that it may be attained.[2]

I take Professor Lewis to mean that, apart from the rectitude in purpose and the deliberateness in action that experience must teach, wisdom in action is dependent on relevant knowledge. If that is so, the best the schools can do to foster wisdom is to help students cultivate knowledge.

Our conclusion at this point is that schools should continue to emphasize cognitive achievements as the vast majority of them have been doing. Some of you may not be willing to accept this conclusion. You may believe some other goal deserves higher priority in the work of the school, perhaps something like general ability to think (apart from any particular body of knowledge), or perhaps having the proper affective disposition, or stable personal adjustment, or simply love of learning.

If you do, you ought to be prepared to explain how different degrees of attainment of the goal you would support can be determined. For if you cannot do this, if you claim your favored goal is intangible and hence unmeasurable, there is room for strong suspicion that it may not really be very important (since it has no clearly observable concomitants or consequences to render it tangible and measurable). Or perhaps the problem is that you don't have a very concrete idea of what it is you propose as a goal.

Let us return to the question of what schools are for, and in particular, for what they should be accountable. It follows from what has been said about the purposes of schooling, and about the cooperation required from the student if those purposes are to be achieved, that the school should not accept responsibility for the learning achievement of every individual pupil. The essential condition for learning is the purposeful activity, the willingness to work hard to learn, of the individual learner. Learning is not a gift any school can give. It is a prize the learner himself must pursue. If a pupil is unwilling or unable to make the effort required, he will learn little in even the best school.

Does this mean that a school should give the student maximum freedom to learn, that it should abandon prescribed curricula and course content in favor of independent study on projects selected by the pupils themselves? I do not think so. Surely all learning must be done by the learner himself, but a good teacher can motivate, direct, and assist the learning process to great advantage. For a school to model its instructional program after the kind of free learning pupils do on their own out of schools is to abandon most of its special value as a school, most of its very reason for existence.

Harry Broudy and John Palmer, discussing the demise of the kind of progressive education advocated by Dewey's disciple William H. Kilpatrick, had this to say about the predecessors of our contemporary free schools and open classrooms:

> A technically sophisticated society simply does not dare leave the acquisition of systematized knowledge to concomitant learning, the by-products of projects that are themselves wholesome slices of juvenile life. Intelligence without systematized knowledge will do only for the most ordinary, everyday problems. International amity, survival in our atomic age, automation, racial integration, are not common everyday problems to which common-sense knowledge and a sense of decency are adequate.[3]

Like Broudy and Palmer, I believe that command of useful knowledge is likely to be achieved most rapidly and most surely when the individual pupil's effort to learn is motivated, guided, and assisted by expert instruction. Such instruction is most likely to occur, and to be most efficient and effective, when given in classes, not to individuals singly.

If the school is not held to account for the success of each of its pupils in learning, for what should it be accountable? I would say that it should accept responsibility for providing a favorable learning environment. Such an environment, in my view, is one in which the student's efforts to learn are:

1. guided and assisted by a capable, enthusiastic teacher,
2. facilitated by an abundance of books, films, apparatus, equipment, and other instructional materials;
3. stimulated and rewarded by both formal and informal recognition of achievement; and
4. reinforced by the example and the help of other interested, hard-working students.

The first two of these aspects of a favorable learning environment are unlikely to be seriously questioned. But perhaps a word or two needs to be said in defense of the other two. First, what of the need for formal recognition and reward of achievement as a stimulus of efforts to achieve?

In the long run learning may be its own reward. But the experience of generations of good teachers has shown that in the short run learning is greatly facilitated by more immediate recognition and rewards. This means words of praise and of reproof, which good teachers have used from ancient times. It means tests and grades, reports and honors, diplomas and degrees. These formal means and occasions for recognizing and rewarding achievement are built into our system of education. We will do well to retain them, to disregard the perennial advice of educational reformers that such so-called extrinsic incentives to achievements be abandoned—unless, of course, we are also willing to abandon excellence as a goal for our efforts.

Next, what of the influence of classmates in either stimulating, assisting, and rewarding efforts to achieve, or disparaging and ridiculing those efforts? In the experience of many teachers these positive or negative influences can be very strong. Of course a teacher's attitudes and behavior can tend to encourage or discourage learning. But much also depends on the attitudes the students bring with them to the class. If they are interested and prepared to work hard, learning can be productive fun. If not, learning is likely to be listless and unproductive.

There may be some teachers with a magic touch that can convert an uninterested, unwilling class into a group of eager learners. I myself have encountered such teachers only in movies or novels. Surely they are too rare to count on for solving the problems of motivation to learn, especially in some of the more difficult situations. For the most part, motivation to learn is an attitude a student has or lacks well before a particular course of instruction ever begins.

Going to school is an opportunity, and ought to be so regarded by all pupils. The good intentions which led us to enact compulsory schooling laws have trapped us. School attendance can be made compulsory. School learning cannot be. So some of our classrooms are loaded with youth who have no wish to be there, whose aim is not to learn but to escape from learning. Such a classroom is not a favorable learning environment.

The remedy is obvious. No upper grade or high school young person ought to be allowed in a class unless he wants to take advantage of the opportunity it offers. Keeping him there under compulsion will do him no good, and will do others in the class harm. Compulsory school attendance laws were never intended to create such a problem for teachers and school officials. Have we the wit to recognize the source of this problem, and the courage to act to correct it?

Let me now recapitulate what I have tried to say about what schools are for.

1. Public education in America today is in trouble.

2. Though many conditions contribute to our present difficulties, the fundamental cause is our own confusions concerning the central purpose of our activities.

3. Schools have been far too willing to accept responsibility for solving all of the problems of young people, for meeting all of their immediate needs. That schools have failed to discharge these obligations successfully is clearly evident.

4. Schools are for learning. They should bend most of their efforts to the facilitation of learning.

5. The kind of learning on which schools should concentrate most of their efforts is cognitive competence, the command of useful knowledge.

6. Knowledge is a structure of relationships among concepts. It must be built by the learner himself as he seeks understanding of the information he has received.

7. Affective dispositions are important by-products of all human experience, but they seldom are or should be the principal targets of our educational efforts. We should be much more concerned with moral education than with affective education.

8. Intellectual skills are more often praised as educational goals than defined clearly enough to be taught effectively. Broadly general intellectual skills are mainly hypothetical constructs which are hard to demonstrate in real life. Highly specific intellectual skills are simply aspects of knowledge.

9. Wisdom depends primarily on knowledge, secondarily on experience.

10. Schools should not accept responsibility for the success of every pupil in learning, since that success depends so much on the pupil's own efforts.

11. Learning is a personal activity which each student must carry on for himself.

12. Individual learning is greatly facilitated by group instruction.

13. Schools should be held accountable for providing a good learning environment, which consists of (a) capable, enthusiastic teachers, (b) abundant and appropriate instructional materials, (c) formal recognition and reward of achievement, and (d) a class of willing learners.

14. Since learning cannot be made compulsory, school attendance ought not to be compulsory either.

Schools ought to be held accountable. One way or another, they surely will be held accountable. If they persist in trying to do too many things, things they were not designed and are not equipped to do well, things that in some cases cannot be done at all, they will show up badly when called to account. But there is one very important thing they were designed and are equipped to do well, and that many schools have done very well in the past. That is to cultivate cognitive competence, to foster the learning of useful knowledge. If they keep this as their primary aim, and do not allow unwilling learners to sabotage the learning process, they are likely to give an excellent accounting of their effectiveness and worth.

ENDNOTES

1. Whitehead, Alfred N. The *Aims of Education*. New York: The Macmillan Company, 1929.
2. Lewis, C. I. *An Analysis of Knowledge and Valuation*. LaSalle, Ill.: Open Court, 1946.
3. Broudy, Harry S., and Palmer, John R. *Exemplars of Teaching Method*. Chicago: Rand McNally, 1965.

Learning to Be Free

Carl R. Rogers

To some, it must seem strangely out of tune with the modern world to speak of learning to be free. The growing opinion today is that man is essentially unfree. He is unfree in a cultural sense. He is all too often a pawn of government. He is molded by mass propaganda into being a creature with certain opinions and beliefs, desired and preplanned by the powers that be. He is the product of his class—lower, middle, or upper—and his values and his behavior are shaped to a large extent by the class to which he belongs.

He is unfree in a scientific sense. The behavioral sciences have made great strides in showing that all his actions and thoughts are determined, being simply the result of previous conditioning. Hence it seems increasingly clear that the individual is formed and moved by forces—cultural forces without, and unconscious forces within—which are beyond his control. He is in all these ways, unfree.

However, the freedom I want to discuss is essentially an inner thing, something which exists in the living person, quite aside from any of the outward choice of alternatives which we

so often think of as constituting freedom. It is the quality of courage which enables a person to step into the uncertainty of the unknown as he chooses himself. It is the burden of being responsible for the self one chooses to be. It is the recognition by the person that he is an emerging process, not a static end product.

The individual who is thus deeply and courageously thinking his own thoughts, becoming his own uniqueness, responsibly choosing himself, may be fortunate in having hundreds of objective outer alternatives from which to choose, or he may be unfortunate in having none, but his freedom exists regardless.

Further, this experience of freedom exists not as a contradiction to the picture of the psychological universe as a sequence of cause and effect but as a complement to such a universe. Freedom, rightly understood, is a fulfillment, by the person, of the ordered sequence of his life.

It is a freedom in which the individual chooses to fulfill himself by playing a responsible and voluntary part in bringing about the destined events of the world he lives in.

It seems at least a possibility that in our schools and colleges, in our professional schools and universities, individuals could learn to be free in this sense. I say this in full recognition of the fact that the current trend in

From Seymour M. Faber and Roger H. L. Wilson, *Conflict and Creativity: Control of the Mind, Part 2* (New York: McGraw-Hill, 1963) as reprinted in *NEA Journal* 52 (1963): 28–30. Reprinted with permission.

education is away from freedom. There are tremendous pressures today—cultural and political—for conformity, docility and rigidity. The demand is for technically trained students who can beat the Russians—and none of this nonsense about education which might improve our interpersonal relationships! The demand is for hardheadedness, for training of the intellect only, for scientific proficiency.

For the general public and for many educators, the goal of learning to be free is not an aim they would select. Yet if a civilized culture is to survive and if the individuals in that culture are to be worth saving, it appears to be an essential goal of education.

So I would like to abstract, from various educational experiments and from pertinent research in psychotherapy, those conditions which appear to be essential if we are to inculcate in students this quality of inward freedom. I should like to describe these conditions as I see them.

In the first place, if self-initiated learning is to occur, it seems essential that the individual be faced by a real problem. Success in facilitating such learning often seems directly related to this factor. Professional persons who come together in a workshop because of a concern with common problems are a good example. Almost invariably, when they are given the facilitating climate I will describe, they at first resist the notion of being responsible for their own learning, but then they seize upon this as an opportunity and use it far beyond their expectations.

On the other hand, students in a required course expect to remain passive and may find themselves extremely perplexed and frustrated at being given freedom. "Freedom to do what?" is their quite understandable question.

It is thus necessary for self-initiated learning that the student, of whatever level, be confronted by issues which have meaning and relevance for him. In our culture we tend to try to insulate the student from too many of the actual problems of life, and this constitutes a difficulty. If we desire to have students learn to be free and responsible individuals, we must be willing for them to confront life, to face problems. Whether we are speaking of the inability of the small child to make change or the problem of his older brother in constructing a hi-fi set or the problem of the college student in formulating his views on international policy, some real confrontation by a problem seems necessary for this type of learning.

Thus far I have spoken of the essential conditions which involve the student. I come now to those conditions which only the teacher can provide. Experience indicates that the teacher who would facilitate this type of learning needs, first of all, a profound trust in the human organism. If we distrust the human being, then we *must* cram him with information of our own choosing lest he go his own mistaken way. On the other hand, if we trust the capacity of the human individual for developing his own potentiality, then we can permit him the opportunity to choose his own way in his learning.

Another requisite for the teacher is sincerity—realness, absence of a facade. He is a real person in his relations with his students. Because he accepts his feelings as his own, he has no need to impose them on his students. The teacher can dislike a student product without implying that it is objectively bad or that the student is bad. It is simply true that he, as a person, dislikes the product. Thus he is a *person* to his students, not a faceless embodiment of a curricular requirement or a sterile tube through which knowledge is passed from one generation to the next.

Teachers who have been successful in promoting this type of learning value their students, prize them, feel acceptant of the feelings and opinions of their students. Such a teacher can accept the fear and hesitation the student feels as he approaches a new problem as well as the satisfaction he experiences in resolving it. Such a teacher can accept the student's occasional apathy and his desire to explore byroads of knowledge as well as his disciplined efforts to achieve major goals. He can also accept personal feelings which both disturb and promote learning—rivalry with a sibling, hatred of authority, concern about personal adequacy.

In other words, the teacher is able to accept the whole student—to prize him as an imperfect human being with many feelings, many potentialities. This prizing or acceptance is an operational expression of the teacher's genuine confidence in the capacity of the human organism.

Another essential teacher attribute is the ability to understand the student's reactions from the inside, an empathic awareness of the way the process of education and learning seems to the student. This is a kind of understanding too seldom exhibited in the classroom; yet when the teacher is emphatic, it adds an extremely potent aspect to the classroom climate.

When a child says, in a discouraged voice, "I can't do this," that teacher is most helpful who naturally and spontaneously responds. "You're afraid that you can never learn it, aren't you?" The usual denial of the child's feeling by the teacher who says, "Oh, but I'm *sure* you can do it" is not nearly so helpful.

In addition to having the essential attitudes described above, the teacher who facilitates learning to be free provides many resources. Instead of organizing lesson plans and lectures, such a teacher concentrates on providing all kinds of relevant raw material for use by the students, together with clearly indicated channels by which students can avail themselves of these resources. I am thinking not only of books, workspace, tools, maps, movies, recordings, and the like but also of human resources—persons who might contribute to the students' knowledge.

Most important of these human resources is the teacher himself. He makes himself and his special knowledge and experience clearly available to the students, but he does not impose himself on them.

The teacher thus concentrates on creating a facilitative climate and on providing resources. He may also help to put students in contact with meaningful problems. But he does not set lesson tasks or assign readings. He does not lecture or expound (unless requested to). He does not evaluate and criticize unless the student wishes his judgment on a product. He does not give examinations. He does not set grades.

Such a teacher is not simply giving lip service to a different approach to learning; he is giving his students the opportunity to learn to be responsibly free.

When the teacher establishes an attitudinal climate of the sort I have described, when he makes available resources which are relevant to problems which confront the student, then a typical process ensues.

First, for students who have been taught by more conventional means, there is a period of tension, frustration, disappointment, disbelief. Students turn in such statements as "I felt completely frustrated by the class procedure," "I felt totally inadequate to take part in this kind of thing." "The class seems to be lacking in planning and direction," "I keep wishing the *course* would start."

One mature participant-observer, Samuel Tenenbaum, in my book, *On Becoming a Person* (Houghton-Mifflin, 1961), describes the way one group struggled with the prospect of freedom after an initial session in which opportunities and resources had been set forth:

Thereafter followed four hard, frustrating sessions. During this period, the class didn't seem to get anywhere. Students spoke at random, saying whatever came into their heads. It all seemed chaotic, aimless, a waste of time. A student would bring up some aspect of the subject; and the next student, completely disregarding the first, would take the group away in another direction; and a third, disregarding the first two, would start fresh on something else.

At times there were faint efforts at a cohesive discussion, but for the most part the classroom proceedings seemed to lack continuity and direction. The instructor received every contribution with attention and regard. He did not find any student's contribution in order or out of order.

The class was not prepared for such a totally unstructured approach. They did not know how to proceed. In their perplexity and frustration, they demanded that the teacher play the role assigned to him by custom and tradition; that he set forth for us in authoritative language what was right and wrong, what was good and bad.

The statement above is a good description of the bafflement and chaos which is an almost inevitable initial phase of learning to be free.

Gradually, students come to various realizations. It dawns on them that this is not a gimmick; that they are really unfettered; that there is little point in impressing the teacher, since the student will evaluate his own work; that they can learn what they please; that they can express, in class, the way they really feel; that issues can be discussed in class which are real to them, not simply the issues set forth in a text. When these elements are recognized, there is a vital and almost awe-inspiring release of energy.

As the learning continues, personal changes take place in the direction of greater freedom and spontaneity. Here is a report given by a student at the end of a course conducted in this way:

> Your way of being with us is a revelation to me. In your class I feel important, mature, and capable of doing things on my own. I want to think for myself and this need cannot be accomplished through textbooks and lectures alone, but through living. I think you see me as a person with real feelings and needs, an individual. What I say and do are significant expressions from me, and you recognize this. You follow no plan, yet I'm learning. Since the term began, I seem to feel more alive, more real to myself. I enjoy being alone as well as with other people. . . .

I believe the story of this kind of classroom experience is incomplete without some mention of the effect upon the instructor when he has been the agent for the release of such self-initiated learning. One such teacher says:

> To say that I am overwhelmed by what happened only faintly reflects my feelings. I have taught for many years but I . . . never have found in the classroom so much of the whole person coming forth, so deeply involved, so deeply stirred. . . . I can only . . . say that I'm grateful and I am also humbled by the experience.

Although empirical investigations of the sort of teaching I have described are neither large in number nor noteworthy for their research sophistication, they do indicate that improvement in personal psychological maturity is significantly greater in student-centered classes than in conventional ones. There is also evidence of a greater amount of self-initiated extracurricular learning and of greater creativity and self-responsibility.

As to the factual and curricular learning, this seems roughly equal to that achieved in conventional classes. Some studies report slightly more, others slightly less. The fairest summary seems to be that if we are solely concerned with the teaching of teacher-selected content material, this approach is probably no better or worse than the ordinary class. If we are concerned with the development of the person—with initiative, originality, and responsibility—such an approach produces greater changes.

In closing, I would like to say that it is my opinion that for the most part modern culture—in its two main streams, Western and communist—does not, operationally, want persons to be free, and is extremely fearful and ambivalent of any process which leads to inner freedom. Nevertheless, it is my personal conviction that individual rigidity and constricted learning are the surest roads to world catastrophe.

It seems clear that if we prefer to develop flexible, adaptive, creative individuals, we have a beginning knowledge as to how this may be done. We know how to establish, in an educational situation, the conditions and the psychological climate which initiate a process of learning to be free.

The Free and Happy Student

B. F. Skinner

His name is Emile. He was born in the middle of the eighteenth century in the first flush of the modern concern for personal freedom. His father was Jean-Jacques Rousseau, but he has had many foster parents, among them Pestalozzi, Froebel, and Montessori, down to A. S. Neill and Ivan Illich. He is an ideal student. Full of goodwill toward his teachers and his peers, he needs no discipline. He studies because he is naturally curious. He learns things because they interest him.

Unfortunately, he is imaginary. He was quite explicitly so with Rousseau, who put his own children in an orphanage and preferred to say how he would teach his fictional hero; but the modern version of the free and happy student to be found in books by Paul Goodman, John Holt, Jonathan Kozol, or Charles Silberman is also imaginary. Occasionally a real example seems to turn up. There are teachers who would be successful in dealing with people anywhere—as statesmen, therapists, businessmen, or friends—and there are students who scarcely need to be taught, and together they sometimes seem to bring Emile to life.

And unfortunately they do so just often enough to sustain the old dream. But Emile is a will-o'-the-wisp, who has led many teachers into a conception of their role which could prove disastrous.

The student who has been taught *as if he were Emile* is, however, almost too painfully real. It has taken a long time for him to make his appearance. Children were first made free and happy in kindergarten, where there seemed to be no danger in freedom, and for a long time they were found nowhere else, because the rigid discipline of the grade schools blocked progress. But eventually they broke through—moving from kindergarten into grade school, taking over grade after grade, moving into secondary school and on into college and, very recently, into graduate school. Step by step they have insisted upon their rights, justifying their demands with the slogans that philosophers of education have supplied. If sitting in rows restricts personal freedom, unscrew the seats. If order can be maintained only through coercion, let chaos reign. If one cannot be really free while worrying about examinations and grades, down with examinations and grades! The whole Establishment is now awash with free and happy students.

From *New York University Education Quarterly* 4, no. 2 (Winter 1973): 2–6. Reprinted with permission.

Dropping Out of School, Dropping Out of Life

If they are what Rousseau's Emile would really have been like, we must confess to some disappointment. The Emile we know doesn't work very hard. "Curiosity" is evidently a moderate sort of thing. Hard work is frowned upon because it implies a "work ethic," which has something to do with discipline.

The Emile we know doesn't learn very much. His "interests" are evidently of limited scope. Subjects that do not appeal to him he calls irrelevant. (We should not be surprised at this, since Rousseau's Emile, like the boys in Summerhill, never got past the stage of knowledgeable craftsman.) He may defend himself by questioning the value of knowledge. Knowledge is always in flux, so why bother to acquire any particular stage of it? It will be enough to remain curious and interested. In any case the life of feeling and emotion is to be preferred to the life of intellect; let us be governed by the heart rather than the head.

The Emile we know doesn't think very clearly. He has had little or no chance to learn to think logically or scientifically and is easily taken in by the mystical and the superstitious. Reason is irrelevant to feeling and emotion.

And, alas, the Emile we know doesn't seem particularly happy. He doesn't like his education any more than his predecessors liked theirs. Indeed, he seems to like it less. He is much more inclined to play truant (big cities have given up enforcing truancy laws), and he drops out as soon as he legally can, or a little sooner. If he goes to college, he probably takes a year off at some time in his four-year program. And after that his dissatisfaction takes the form of anti-intellectualism and a refusal to support education.

Are there offsetting advantages? Is the free and happy student less aggressive, kinder, more loving? Certainly not toward the schools and teachers that have set him free, as increasing vandalism and personal attacks on teachers seem to show. Nor is he particularly well disposed toward his peers. He seems perfectly at home in a world of unprecedented domestic violence.

Is he perhaps more creative? Traditional practices were said to suppress individuality; what kind of individuality has now emerged? Free and happy students are certainly different from the students of a generation ago, but they are not very different from each other. Their own culture is a severely regimented one, and their creative works—in art, music, and literature—are confined to primitive and elemental materials. They have very little to be creative with, for they have never taken the trouble to explore the fields in which they are now to be front-runners.

Is the free and happy student at least more effective as a citizen? Is he a better person? The evidence is not very reassuring. Having dropped out of school, he is likely to drop out of life too. It would be unfair to let the hippie culture represent young people today, but it does serve to clarify an extreme. The members of that culture do not accept responsibility for their own lives; they sponge on the contributions of those who have not yet been made free and happy—who have gone to medical school and become doctors, or who have become the farmers who raise the food or the workers who produce the goods they consume.

These are no doubt overstatements. Things are not that bad, nor is education to be blamed for all the trouble. Nevertheless, there is a trend in a well-defined direction, and it is particularly clear in education. Our failure to create a truly free and happy student is symptomatic of a more general problem.

The Illusion of Freedom

What we may call the struggle for freedom in the Western world can be analyzed as a struggle to escape from or avoid punitive or coercive treatment. It is characteristic of the human species to act in such a way as to reduce or terminate irritating, painful, or dangerous stimuli, and the struggle for freedom has been directed toward those who would control others with stimuli of that sort. Education has had a long and shameful part in the history of that struggle. The Egyptians, Greeks, and Romans all whipped their students. Medieval sculpture showed the carpenter with his hammer and the schoolmaster with the tool of his trade too, and it was the cane or rod. We are not yet in the clear. Corporal punishment is still used in many schools, and there are calls for its return where it has been abandoned.

A system in which students study primarily to avoid the consequences of not studying is neither humane nor very productive. Its by-products include truancy, vandalism, and apathy. Any effort to eliminate punishment in education is certainly commendable. We ourselves act to escape from aversive control, and our students should escape from it too. They should study because they want to, because they like to, because they are interested in what they are doing. The mistake—a classical mistake in the literature of freedom—is to suppose that they will do so as soon as we stop punishing them. Students are not literally free when they have been freed from their teachers. They then simply come under the control of other conditions, and we must look at those conditions and their effects if we are to improve teaching.

Those who have attacked the "servility" of students, as Montessori called it, have often put their faith in the possiblity that young people will learn what they need to know from the "world of things," which includes the world of people who are not teachers. Montessori saw possibly useful behavior being suppressed by schoolroom discipline. Could it not be salvaged? And could the environment of the schoolroom not be changed so that other useful behavior would occur? Could the teacher not simply guide the student's natural development? Or could he not accelerate it by teasing out behavior which would occur naturally but not so quickly if he did not help? In other words, could we not bring the real world into the classroom, as John Dewey put it, or destroy the classroom and turn the student over to the real world, as Ivan Illich has recommended?

All these possibilities can be presented in an attractive light, but they neglect two vital points:

1. No one learns very much from the real world without help. The only evidence we have of what can be learned from a nonsocial world has been supplied by those wild boys said to have been raised without contact with other members of their own species. Much more can be learned without formal instruction in a social world, but not without a good deal of teaching, even so. Formal education has made a tremendous difference in the extent of the skills and knowledge which can be acquired by a person in a single lifetime.

2. A much more important principle is that the real world teaches only what is relevant to the present; it makes no explicit preparation for the future. Those who would minimize teaching have contended that no preparation is needed, that the student will follow a natural line of development and move into the future in the normal course of events. We should be content, as Carl Rogers has put it, to trust

> the insatiable curiosity which drives the adolescent boy to absorb everything he can see or hear or read about gasoline engines in order to improve the efficiency and speed of his "hot rod." I am talking about the student who says, "I am discovering, drawing in from the outside, and making that which is drawn in a real part of me." I am talking about my learning in which the experience of the learner progresses along the line: "No, no, that's not what I want"; "Wait! This is closer to what I'm interested in, what I need." "Ah, here it is! Now I'm grasping and comprehending what I need and what I want to know!"[1]

Rogers is recommending a total commitment to the present moment, or at best to an immediate future.

Formal Education as Preparation for the Future

But it has always been the task of formal education to set up behavior which would prove useful or enjoyable *later* in the student's life. Punitive methods had at least the merit of providing current reasons for learning things that would be rewarding in the future. We object to the punitive reasons, but we should not forget their function in making the future important.

It is not enough to give the student advice— to explain that he will have a future, and that to enjoy himself and be more successful in it, he must acquire certain skills and knowledge now. Mere advice is ineffective because it is not supported by current rewards. The positive consequences that generate a useful behavioral repertoire need not be any more explicitly relevant to the future than were the punitive consequences of the past. The student needs current reasons, positive or negative, but only the educational policy maker who supplies them need take the future into account. It follows that many instructional arrangements seem "contrived," but there is nothing wrong with that. It is the teacher's function to contrive conditions under which students learn. Their relevance to a future usefulness need not be obvious.

It is a difficult assignment. The conditions the teacher arranges must be powerful enough to compete with those under which the student tends to behave in distracting ways. In what has come to be called "contingency management in the classroom," tokens are sometimes used as rewards or reinforcers. They become reinforcing when they are exchanged for reinforcers that are already effective. There is no "natural" relation between what is learned and what is received. The token is simply a reinforcer that can be made clearly contingent upon behavior. To straighten out a wholly disrupted classroom something as obvious as a token economy may be needed, but less conspicuous contingencies—as in a credit-point system, perhaps, or possibly in the long run merely expressions of approval on the part of teacher or peer—may take over.

The teacher can often make the change from punishment to positive reinforcement in a surprisingly simple way—by responding to the student's success rather than his failures. Teachers have too often supposed that their role is to point out what students are doing wrong, but pointing to what they are doing *right* will often make an enormous difference in the atmosphere of a classroom and in the efficiency of instruction. Programmed materials are helpful in bringing about these changes, because they increase the frequency with which the student enjoys the satisfaction of being right, and they supply a valuable intrinsic reward in providing a clear indication of progress. A good program makes a step in the direction of competence almost as conspicuous as a token.

Programmed instruction is perhaps most successful in attacking punitive methods by allowing the student to move at his own pace. The slow student is released from punishment which inevitably follows when he is forced to move on to material for which he is not ready, and the fast student escapes the boredom of being forced to go too slow. These principles have recently been extended to college education, with dramatic results, in the Keller system of personalized instruction.[2]

The Responsibility of Setting Educational Policy

There is little doubt that a student can be given nonpunitive reasons for acquiring behavior that will become useful or otherwise reinforcing at some later date. He can be prepared for the future. But what *is* that future? Who is to say what the student should learn? Those who have sponsored the free and happy student have argued that it is the student himself who should say. His current interests should be the source of an effective educational policy. Certainly they will reflect his idiosyncrasies, and that is good, but how much can he know about the world in which he will eventually play a part? The things he is "naturally" curious about are of current and often temporary interest. How many things must he possess besides his "hot rod" to provide the insatiable curiosity relevant to, say, a course in physics?

It must be admitted that the teacher is not always in a better position. Again and again education has gone out of date as teachers have continued to teach subjects which were no longer relevant at any time in the student's life. Teachers often teach simply what they know. (Much of what is taught in private schools is determined by what the available teachers can teach.) Teachers tend to teach what they can teach easily. Their current interests, like those of students, may not be a reliable guide.

Nevertheless, in recognizing the mistakes that have been made in the past in specifying what students are to learn, we do not absolve ourselves from the responsibility of setting educational policy. We should say, we should be *willing* to say, what we believe students will need to know, taking the individual student into account wherever possible, but otherwise making our best prediction with respect to students in general. Value judgments of this sort are not as hard to make as is often argued. Suppose we undertake to prepare the student to produce his share of the goods he will consume and the services he will use, to get on well with his fellows, and to enjoy his life. In doing so are we imposing *our* values on someone else? No, we are merely choosing a set of specifications which, so far as we can tell, will at some time in the future prove valuable to the student and his culture. Who is any more likely to be right?

The natural, logical outcome of the struggle for personal freedom in education is that the teacher should improve his control of the student rather than abandon it. The free school is no school at all. Its philosophy signalizes the abdication of the teacher. The teacher who understands his assignment and is familiar with the behavioral processes needed to fulfill it can have students who not only feel free and happy while they are being taught but who will continue to feel free and happy when their formal education comes to an end. They will do so because they will be successful in their work (having acquired useful productive repertoires), because they will get on well with their fellows (having learned to understand themselves and others), because they will enjoy what they do (having acquired the necessary knowledge and skills), and because they will from time to time make an occasional creative contribution toward an even more effective and enjoyable way of life. Possibly the most important consequence is that the teacher will then feel free and happy too.

We must choose today between Cassandran and Utopian prognostications. Are we to work to avoid disaster or to achieve a better world? Again, it is a question of punishment or reward. Must we act because we are frightened, or are there positive reasons for changing our cultural practices? The issue goes far beyond education, but it is one with respect to which education has much to offer. To escape from or avoid disaster, people are likely to turn to the punitive measures of a police state. To work for a better world, they may turn instead to the positive methods of education. When it finds its most effective methods, education will be almost uniquely relevant to the task of setting up and maintaining a better way of life.

ENDNOTES

1. Carl R. Rogers, *Freedom to Learn.* Columbus: Merrill, 1969.

2. *P.S.I. Newsletter,* October 1972 (published by Department of Psychology, Georgetown University, J. G. Sherman, Ed.).

Compensatory Education
Twenty Years Later:
Does It Work?

Since its inception in 1965 as an eight-week summer preschool program, Head Start has served more than 9,000,000 children and families. With only one out of every five preschool children living in poverty being served, there is constant pressure to include more children in the program.

On the occasion of the twentieth anniversary of compensatory education, various authorities have reflected upon the accomplishments of these programs. In the opening article, Lawrence J. Schweinhart and David P. Weikart summarize the major findings of seven of the best-designed investigations of preschool programs for the poor. They conclude that good preschool programs have both short- and long-term beneficial effects on poor children. Arthur R. Jensen, however, holds a far less optimistic view regarding the positive impacts of compensatory education. While acknowledging the beneficial effects of Head Start and similar intervention programs on children's health care, social competence, and attitudes towards school, he charges that these intervention efforts have made their least impressive impact on precisely those variables that they were originally intended to improve the most—namely, IQ and achievement. The plain truth, he argues, is that compensatory programs have not resulted in any appreciable durable gains. He contends that Head Start is judged to be a success only because its advocates have retroactively changed its goals.

Thought Questions

Was the original expectation that relatively brief educational experiences in the preschool years would lead to lasting beneficial effects on general intelligence both naive and unwarranted?

In your opinion, what are the main benefits of compensatory education?

Should the criterion for inclusion in a compensatory program be income level (poverty) or a lack of educational readiness? What difference, if any, would it make if the entrance criterion were one of educational disadvantage instead of economic disadvantage?

Can we generalize from the seven exemplary programs reviewed by Schweinhart and Weikart to the more than 2,000 autonomous, locally administered Head Start programs of varying quality?

While parents are their children's best advocates, does it follow that parents should have the primary authority in determining the nature of local programs?

In what directions, if any, should compensatory programs evolve? Should compensatory efforts expand in the direction of a general family support program?

If compensatory programs are expanded to include more poor children, do we run the risk of having intervention programs becoming little more than a token effort?

Would making preschool mandatory for *all* four-year-olds (poor as well as rich) introduce equity into early childhood programs? Or would the costs of doing so outweigh potential benefits?

READING 4

Evidence That Good
Early Childhood Programs Work

Lawrence J. Schweinhart and David P. Weikart

In the early 1960s, many leading educators and social scientists expressed hopes that preschool education programs for poor children could help break the cycle of poverty. They assumed that a chain of cause and effect linked family poverty to the scholastic failure of children and to their subsequent poverty as adults.

These educators and social scientists speculated that preschool education would enhance the intelligence of poor children. This theory received support from early reports that several experimental preschool programs were in fact raising I.Q.s.[1]

However, two well-publicized events in 1969 undermined the popular credibility of the scientific basis for claims about the beneficial effects of preschool education for poor children. The first was a negative evaluation, by the Westinghouse Learning Corporation and Ohio University, of the first years of Head Start; the second was Arthur Jensen's article in the *Harvard Educational Review*, in which he argued that "compensatory education has been tried and it apparently has failed."[2]

As the years passed, however, evidence of the effectiveness of preschool began to mount.

From *Phi Delta Kappan* 66 (1985): 545–551. Reprinted with permission.

Evidence from several evaluations demonstrated that good preschool programs have both short- and long-term positive effects on low-income youngsters. Many studies bear on these issues, but we will consider only seven of these evaluations here. The ones we chose, though not perfect, are among the most scientifically rigorous, and reviewing them provides a clear picture of the long-term effectiveness of early childhood education, as well as an overview of some of the problems that researchers face in conducting such studies.

Seven Studies

The seven studies listed in Table 1 have followed subjects at least to age 9 and at most to age 21. They have been conducted in locales that represent a cross section of America's urban communities, in both northern and southern states, though all were conducted in areas east of the Mississippi River. Six of the seven studies evaluated programs that operated in a single location.

These seven studies and most of the other recent research on the effects of early childhood education have focused on children liv-

Table 1
The Seven Studies

Study	Year Study Began	Place	Age of Subjects at Last Report
Early Training Project	1962	Murfreesboro, Tenn.	21
Perry Preschool Project	1962	Ypsilanti, Mich.	19
Mother-Child Home Program	1965	Long Island, N.Y.	9–13
Harlem Study	1966	New York, N.Y.	13
Rome Head Start Program	1966	Rome, Ga.	20
Milwaukee Study	1968	Milwaukee, Wis.	10
New York Pre-K Program	1975	New York State	9

ing in poverty. The concern of the 1960s for righting the wrongs of poverty was closely tied to the struggle of blacks to obtain civil rights. Thus the response to this concern tended to focus on the needs of the black population, combining compensatory education programs with new policies to insure equal rights in voting, housing, employment, and education. It is not surprising, then, that in most of the studies reviewed here, at least 90% of the subjects are black.[3]

The size of the samples and any special characteristics of the populations are listed in Table 2. The sample sizes varied from a low of 40 in the Milwaukee Study to 2,058 in the New York Prekindergarten Program. The Perry Preschool Project focused on children whose tested I.Q.s at age 3 were between 60 and 90.* The Milwaukee Study focused on children whose mothers had tested I.Q.s of 75 or below. The Harlem Study focused exclusively on males. The New York Prekindergarten Program was open to the public in selected school districts, so the sample more nearly represents the racial mix of low-income families in the population at large.

---

*The data for the Perry Preschool Project are included in the tables, but we will limit our discussion here. For a more detailed description of the evaluation of the Perry Preschool Project, see "The Promise of Early Childhood Education," by Lawrence J. Schweinhart, John R. Berrueta-Clement, W. Steven Barnett, Ann S. Epstein, and David P. Weikart, *Phi Delta Kappan* 66 (1985): p. 548.

Attrition is a major threat to the validity of longitudinal studies. As more subjects are lost, both internal and external validity are at risk. The investigators who carried out these seven studies fared well in locating subjects for their follow-up studies: they found at least 71% of the original subjects. The Perry Preschool Project found 100% of its original subjects and interviewed 98% of them. The median percentage of subjects located in the follow-ups was 80%. Moreover, differential attrition across groups within the subject populations was not large enough to constitute a major problem.

Four of the seven studies used the standard experimental design; their treatment and control groups were selected from the same population by procedures designed to insure equivalent groups. In the study of the Early Training Project and in the Milwaukee Study, students were randomly assigned to groups. In the Harlem Study, treatment groups were selected by applying the same simple procedures to children born in different months. By chance, one of the two experimental groups had an average I.Q. at age 3 that was six points higher than the average I.Q. of the control group at age 2 years and eight months. This difference was controlled for in the analysis of group differences.

Three of the seven studies used a quasi-experimental design; their treatment and control groups were selected from different populations. One such study, that of the Rome Head Start Program, began in 1966 by identifying all first-graders in the Rome, Georgia, public

Table 2
Design Information

Study	Selection Procedure	Special Sample Characteristics*	Original Sample Size	Subjects Included in Most Recent Follow-up %
EXPERIMENTAL DESIGN				
Early Training Project	Random assignment	—	90	80
Harlem Study	Selections from same population	Boys only	315	81
Milwaukee Study	Random assignment	Mothers' IQs 75 and below	40	80
Perry Preschool Project	Assignment of matched pairs	Children's IQs 60–90	123	98
QUASI-EXPERIMENTAL DESIGN				
Mother-Child Home Program	Assignment by site	—	250	74
New York Pre-K Program	Some assignment by site	42% white; 42% black; 16% other	2,058	75
Rome Head Start	Self-selection	Blacks and whites	218	71

*All samples were selected on the basis of family poverty. Unless otherwise noted, 90% or more of the subjects are black.

schools who qualified for federal funds for the economically disadvantaged. Some of these students had attended Head Start and some had not. In the absence of data to the contrary, we cannot rule out the possibility that Head Start participants and nonparticipants in this study differed in important ways before the study began. Because of such doubts, this study cannot stand alone. However, in combination with other studies, it bears examination because of its extraordinary duration.

In the study of the Mother-Child Home Program—a quasi-experimental effort for the years reviewed here—treatment was offered to all willing participants within a given geographic area. This group was then compared to a demographically similar control group in a nearby geographic area. The groups thus selected were generally equivalent on important background factors, though some risk of unmeasured group differences may affect the outcomes of the study.

The third quasi-experimental study, that of the New York Prekindergarten Program, compared two control groups to an experimental group of approximately 1,800 youngsters who took part in the program in 1966. The control group for comparisons of test scores consisted of 87 children on the program's waiting list. This group may or may not have differed from the program participants, depending on the original procedures for selecting participants. For comparisons of scholastic placement, the control group consisted of both the waiting-list group and a group of 171 children of slightly higher socio-economic status who came from neighboring school districts. Thus some between-group differences certainly exist, but they tend to favor the control group. For example, mothers in the treatment group reported 10.9 years of schooling, while control-group mothers from other districts reported 12.0 years of schooling.

The seven programs varied in size, design, and presumably cost. The Milwaukee program was the most extensive, providing full-time, year-round developmental child care for children ranging in age from a few months to 6 years. It also provided an educational and vocational program for mothers. The Perry Preschool Project provided one home visit per week and a morning classroom program five days a week for two school years (at ages 3 and 4). Its classroom component was equivalent in scope to the one-year programs of the New York Prekindergarten Program for 4-year-olds and the Rome Head Start Program for 5-year-olds. The latter two programs also included several home visits during the school year and offered parents the chance to become involved in the classrooms. The Early Training Project featured part-time classroom experiences five days a week in the summer and weekly home visits during the school year for either three years (for children starting at age 3) or two years (for children starting at age 4). The Mother-Child Home Program consisted of twice-weekly home visits for one to two years, and the Harlem Study provided one-to-one sessions between a child and a tutor twice weekly for eight months.

In reviewing the findings of these studies, we will also mention corroborating findings from the Consortium for Longitudinal Studies. The Consortium was an association of a dozen educators and psychologists each of whom had initiated a longitudinal study of an early childhood program during the 1960s and had agreed to collaborate in a follow-up assessment during the late 1970s. The Consortium was formed in 1975 by Irving Lazar of Cornell University and Edith Grotberg of the U.S. Administration for Children, Youth, and Families. As investigators for the Perry Preschool Project, we belonged to the Consortium, and our review of the seven studies in this article is the better for our experience with that group. The Consortium based its conclusions on careful review of the methodology of each longitudinal study, and we maintain that tradition here.[4]

Findings

The documented effects of early childhood education may be organized according to the major outcomes for participants at each period of their lives. These outcomes and the ages at which they occurred are: improved intellectual performance during early childhood; better scholastic placement and improved scholastic achievement during the elementary school years; and, during adolescence, a lower rate of delinquency and higher rates of both graduation from high school and employment at age 19.

Early Childhood

The best-documented preschool effect is an immediate improvement in intellectual performance as represented by intelligence test scores. Of the studies reviewed here, the six that collected such data all attest to the immediate positive effect of early childhood education on I.Q. Four studies reported a maximum effect of between one-half and one standard deviation (16 points on the Stanford-Binet test); however, statistically significant group differences disappeared by age 8. The intensive Milwaukee Study had a maximum effect of two standard deviations; the difference when the children were last tested (at age 10) was still greater than one standard deviation.

Two other studies in the Consortium for Longitudinal Studies reported effects on I.Q. of about half a standard deviation, which disappeared by age 8. Craig Ramey and his colleagues recently reviewed 11 experimental studies that included I.Q. data on children between the ages of 1 and 6; eight of these studies had data on children between the ages of 1 and 3. In every study, the average I.Q. of children who participated in preschool was as good as or better than the average I.Q. of children in control groups. I.Q. differences ranged from zero in two studies to 21 points in one; the median difference was six points. Of the eight studies with I.Q. data for children between the ages of 1 and 3, six showed I.Q. differences of up to half a standard deviation, and two showed I.Q. differences between one-half and one standard deviation.[5]

Elementary School Years

In the studies we are reviewing, every single comparison of scholastic placement was favorable to the group that had received early childhood education (Table 3). In four of the five

studies that included data on special education placements, the rate of such placements was usually reduced by half. In the Perry Preschool Project, the overall figure for special education placements (by student-years rather than by students, as reported here) was reduced by half. Two studies report statistically significant reductions in retentions as well. The Harlem Study could not obtain data on placements in special education.

The staff of the Consortium for Longitudinal Studies reported similar findings on scholastic placement. Moreover, their technique of pooling probability estimates confirms the improb-

Table 3
Findings for Scholastic Placement

Study	Program Group %	Control Group %	p*
Rome Head Start (age 20)			
Placed in special education	11	25	.019
Retained in grade	51	63	—
Dropped out of high school	50	67	.042
Perry Preschool (age 19)			
Placed in special education	37	50	—
Retained in grade	35	40	—
Dropped out of high school	33	51	.034
Early Training (age 18)			
Placed in special education	3	29	.004
Retained in grade	53	69	—
Dropped out of high school	22	43	.079
Harlem (age 13)			
Placed in special education	No data	No data	No data
Retained in grade	24	45	.006
Dropped out of high school	No data	No data	No data
New York Pre-K (age 9)			
Placed in special education	2	5	.006
Retained in grade	16	21	.019
Dropped out of high school	No data	No data	No data
Mother-Child Home (age 9)			
Placed in special education	14	39	.005
Retained in grade	13	19	—
Dropped out of high school	No data	No data	No data
Milwaukee	No data	No data	No data

*Two-tailed p-values are presented if less than .1.

ability of obtaining all the findings in Table 3 purely by chance.

Avoiding placement in special education programs was one of the major financial benefits of preschool education to emerge from the cost-benefit analysis of the Perry Preschool Project. The strength and consistency of the finding that participants avoided such placements in these other studies argue persuasively that these other preschool programs, too, would show a favorable cost-benefit ratio.

Most of the experimentally derived evidence for the positive impact of preschool on scholastic achievement comes from the study of the Perry Preschool Project, which found differences consistently favoring the preschool group over the control group at ages 7, 8, 9, 10, 11, 14, and 19. Of the other studies reviewed here, only that of the Early Training Project had sufficient data on achievement (from 70% or more of the subjects) to enable conclusions to be drawn. This study found some positive effects at age 8, but no effects at ages 7, 10, or 11.

The Consortium for Longitudinal Studies analyzed achievement test scores across seven of its studies. The pooled analysis found statistically significant positive effects of preschool on arithmetic scores at ages 10, 11, and 12, but not at age 13. In reading, the Consortium analysis found statistically significant positive effects of preschool at age 10 only.

Adolescence

The studies of the Perry Preschool Project and of the Rome Head Start Program are the only preschool studies we know of that have collected information on delinquency or crime— either from police and court records or from self-reports. Neither study found a difference between participants and nonparticipants in the number of persons referred to juvenile court. But the study of the Perry Preschool program did find reduced delinquency among participants—documented by self-reports at age 15[6] and by official records of either total number of arrests or referrals to juvenile court.

Both the Perry Preschool Project and the Early Training Project collected information

on rates of teenage pregnancy. The Perry Project reported 64 teenage pregnancies per 100 females who had attended preschool and 117 teenage pregnancies per 100 females who had not attended preschool. The Early Training Project found that 38% of the females in the study reported a pregnancy, with no between-group differences. The Early Training Project did find that, after pregnancy and childbirth, 88% of the females who had gone to preschool were likely to complete high school, while only 30% of the females who had not gone to preschool were likely to return to school after pregnancy and childbirth.

In three of the studies reviewed here, youngsters who had attended a preschool program were less likely to drop out of high school than were their peers who had not attended preschool. Table 3 shows that the dropout rates of those who attended preschool as opposed to those who did not were 17% lower in the Rome Head Start Program, 21% lower in the Early Training Project, and 18% lower in the Perry Preschool Project. As far as we know, the Perry Project is the only study of the effects of preschool that includes data on employment after graduation, reporting an employment rate at age 19 of 50% for the preschool group and 32% for the non-preschool group.

From our review of these seven studies and from the data collected by the Consortium for Longitudinal Studies, we feel safe in concluding that *good* early childhood programs are a wise investment of public funds that can benefit children, their families, and all citizens and taxpayers. To what extent is the U.S. making this investment today?

During the past 30 years, the federal government has provided the lion's share of funding for early childhood programs for children from low-income families. For prekindergartners, this funding has taken two forms: the Head Start Program and subsidized child care. Head Start has maintained a modest but steady growth since it began in 1965. Federal funding for child care—now provided primarily through the Social Services Block Grant and the Child Care Food Program—has had its ups and downs, but it is still substantial. The federal government annually provides about a billion dollars each for Head Start and subsidized child care.

Compensatory education, during the past three decades, has essentially been delivered by Title I of the Elementary and Secondary Education Act of 1965, now Chapter 1 of President Reagan's Education Consolidation and Improvement Act of 1981. In deciding who participates in Chapter 1 programs, school districts must give priority to children enrolled in kindergarten through grade 12. Thus only a small portion of Chapter 1 funding has found its way to programs serving very young children. During the 1981–82 school year, Chapter 1 funds served a total of 4,866,108 students; only 332,355 of them (7%) were in kindergarten or prekindergarten programs.

However, there are good reasons for state and local school administrators to use whatever Chapter 1 funds they can for prekindergarten programs for children at risk of scholastic failure. The cost-benefit analysis of the Perry Preschool Project showed that school systems recoup their investment in a one-year prekindergarten program by the time the participants graduate from high school.

But the federal government is only a minor source of education funding in general. Well over 90% of funding for education comes from state and local sources. Furthermore, state and local governments bear the largest burden of paying for juvenile delinquency, teenage pregnancy, and welfare assistance. Therefore, state and local governments stand to profit the most from investment in good early childhood programs for children from low-income families.

California leads the nation in funding for early childhood education and child care, spending $277 million in 1984–85. No other state even comes close. New York spends only $155 million on early childhood programs, with $141 million of that sum coming from the Federal Social Services Block Grant. However, the New York Prekindergarten Program has received a good evaluation, and both the staunch support of that program by Gov. Mario Cuomo and State Education Commissioner Gordon Ambach and the recent increase in funding for that program (from $10 million to $14 million) are largely due to the positive research results. In South Carolina, Gov. Richard Riley made expanded child development programs an integral part of his education reform package, with funding for early childhood programs slated to rise to about $11 million. Texas has authorized $50 million for early childhood programs in the coming years, and Missouri recently passed comprehensive legislation on early childhood education. Funding legislation for early childhood programs is now pending in more than a dozen states.

Yet, despite compelling research findings and despite the recent actions of a number of states, there are still not enough good early childhood programs for children from low-income families. We must all do something about that.

ENDNOTES

1. Rupert A. Klaus and Susan W. Gray, *The Early Training Project for Disadvantaged Children: A Report After Five Years* (Chicago: University of Chicago Press, Society for Research in Child Development. Monograph No. 120, 1968); and David P. Weikart, ed., *Preschool Intervention: Preliminary Results of the Perry Preschool Project* (Ann Arbor, Mich.: Campus Publishers, 1967).

2. Westinghouse Learning Corporation, *The Impact of Head Start: An Evaluation of the Effect of Head Start on Children's Cognitive and Affective Developments*, Vols. *I–II* (Athens: Ohio University, 1969); and Arthur R. Jensen, "How Much can We Boost I.Q. and Scholastic Achievement?," *Harvard Educational Review*, February 1969, pp. 1–123.

3. This focus on early childhood education for low-income blacks has left its mark. In 1980, for 3- and 4-year-olds in families with annual incomes under $15,000, the preschool enrollment figures were 37% for black children but only 25% for

white children. See Gerald Kahn, *School Enroll-ment of 3- and 4-Year-Olds by Race/Ethnic Category* (Washington, D.C.: National Center for Education Statistics, 1982), p. 13.

4. Irving Lazar, Richard Darlington, Harry Murray, Jacqueline Royce, and Ann Snipper, *Lasting Ef-fects of Early Education* (Chicago: Society for Re-search in Child Development, Monograph No. 194, 1982). The investigators of the Early Training Project, the Harlem Study, and the Mother-Child Home Program also belonged to the Consortium.

5. Craig T. Ramey, Donna M. Bryant, and Tanya M. Suarez, "Preschool Compensatory Education and the Modifiability of Intelligence: A Critical Re-view," in Douglas Detterman, ed., *Current Topics in Human Intelligence* (Norwood, N.J.: Ablex, 1984).

6. Lawrence J. Schweinhart and David P. Weikart, *Young Children Grow Up: The Effects of the Perry Preschool Program on Youths Through Age 15* (Yp-silanti, Mich.: High/Scope Press, 1980).

Compensatory Education and the Theory of Intelligence

Arthur R. Jensen

The past 20 years have been a period of unparalleled affluence for public education and educational research in the U.S. When the history of this era is written, two features will stand out prominently: racial desegregation of the schools and large-scale experimentation with compensatory education.

The nation focused its educational resources during this period primarily on extending the benefits of education to every segment of the population—especially to those groups that historically have derived the least benefit from the traditional system of schooling. During the past 20 years more young people have gone to school for more years and have obtained more diplomas, per capita, in the U.S. than in any other nation. Fifty percent of U.S. high school graduates in the 1970s went on to college.

These proud facts are one side of the picture. The other side is much less complimentary and should shake any complacency we Americans might feel. The past 20 years, which have brought the most energetic large-scale innovations in the history of U.S. educa-

From *Phi Delta Kappan* 66 (1985):554–558. Reprinted with permission.

tion, have also brought an accelerating decline in Scholastic Aptitude Test scores. And there are other signs of malaise as well. On objective measures of the average level of educational achievement, the U.S. falls below all other industrialized nations, according to the International Association for the Evaluation of Educational Achievement.[1] In fact, average levels of educational achievement lower than that of the U.S. are found only in the industrially underdeveloped nations of the Third World.

Illiteracy in the U.S. has been grossly underestimated. Until recently, the U.S. Census Bureau routinely estimated the rate of illiteracy as the percentage of Americans with fewer than six years of schooling. The 1980 Census found that only two-tenths of 1% (0.2%) of the U.S. population between the ages of 14 and 24 met this definition of illiteracy—a rate that was the same for both black and white Americans.

Simple tests of actual reading ability reveal a much less rosy picture, however. According to lawyer and psychologist Barbara Lerner, evidence collected by the National Assessment of Educational Progress shows that "the overall rate of illiteracy for cohorts reaching their 18th birthday in the 1970s can safely be estimated to have been at least 20%. . . . [Moreover, the] black-white gap was still dramatic: 41.6% of all black 17-year olds still enrolled in school in 1975 were functionally illiterate."[2] Lerner goes on to emphasize the broad implication of this finding:

> On this basis, it would have seemed reasonable to predict serious shortages of literate workers throughout the 1980s and perhaps beyond, along with high levels of structural unemployment, particularly among younger black workers, and increasing difficulty in meeting economic competition from foreign countries with more literate work forces.[3]

Clearly, those conditions that originally gave rise to the aims and aspirations of compensatory education are as relevant today as they were 20 years ago. Of the many lessons that can be learned from assessments and meta-analyses of the results of 29 years of compensatory education, I intend to dwell in this article on what seems to me to be one of the most important. Because the lesson on which I will dwell is one of the clearest and seemingly least-debatable findings of studies of compensatory education programs of all kinds and because this lesson has important implications for both theory and practice, it is peculiar that this lesson has been soft-pedaled in most published summaries of compensatory education outcomes.

The lesson to which I refer is this: compensatory education has made its least impressive impact on just those variables that it was originally intended (and expected) to improve the most: namely, I.Q. and scholastic achievement. The plain truth is that compensatory programs have not resulted in any appreciable, durable gains in I.Q. or scholastic achievement for those youngsters who have taken part in them. This is an important discovery, and the fact that we do not like this outcome or that it is not what we expected neither diminishes its importance nor justifies downplaying it. Rather, we are challenged to try to understand its theoretical implications for the study of intelligence and its practical implications for the practice of education.

Let us not be distracted from trying to understand the discrepancy between the expected and the actual outcomes of compensatory education programs by the too-easy response of retroactively revising our original expectations. We should gain more from our 20 years of experience than just a list of excuses for the disappointing discrepancy between our expectations and the actual results.

To be sure, Head Start and other compensatory education programs have produced some positive gains. The fact that the bona fide benefits of compensatory education have not been primarily cognitive in nature and are not strongly reflected in academic achievement per se should not detract from the social importance of these gains. The positive outcomes of Head Start and similar programs include such things as the improvement of participants' nutrition and of their medical and dental care. The list of positive outcomes also includes greater involvement of parents in their children's schooling, noticeable improvement in the children's attitudes toward school and in their self-esteem, fewer behavioral problems among participants, fewer retentions in grade, and a smaller percentage of special education placements.[4]

These socially desirable outcomes have not been accompanied by marked or lasting improvement in either I.Q. or academic performance, however. Even the smaller percentage of special education placements may be attributable to teachers' and administrators' knowledge that certain children have taken part in Head Start or other compensatory education programs, because such children are less apt than nonparticipating peers to be labeled as candidates for special education. Gene Glass and Mary Ellwein offer an insightful observation on this point in their review of *As the Twig Is Bent*, a book on 11 compensatory education programs and their outcomes, as assessed by the Consortium for Longitudinal Studies. According to Glass and Ellwein:

> Those whose ideas are represented in *As the Twig Is Bent* see themselves as developmental psychol-

ogists molding the inner, lasting core of the individual—one can almost visualize the cortical wiring they imagine being rearranged by ever-earlier intervention. And yet the true lasting effects of a child's preschool experiences may be etched only in the attitudes of the professionals and in the records of the institutions that will husband his or her life after preschool.[5]

Even studies of those compensatory programs that involve the most intensive and prolonged educational experience show the effects of such programs on I.Q. to be relatively modest and subject to "fadeout" within one to three years. The highly publicized "Miracle in Milwaukee" Study by Rick Heber and Howard Garber appears to be a case in point. In that study, the researchers gave intensive training designed to enhance cognitive development to children who were deemed at risk for mental retardation because of their family backgrounds. The training lasted from birth until the participants entered school. Unfortunately, no detailed account of the conduct of the Milwaukee Study or of its long-term outcomes has yet appeared in any refereed scientific journal. Because the data are not available for full and proper critical review, I cannot legitimately cite this study with regard to the effects of early intervention on subsequent intelligence and scholastic achievement.

Fortunately, a similar study—the Abecedarian Project,[6] currently under way in North Carolina—is being properly reported in the appropriate journals, and the researchers conducting this study promise the kind of evaluation that Heber and Garber have failed to deliver. From infancy to school age, children in the Abecedarian Project spend six or more hours daily, five days a week, 50 weeks a year, in a cognitive training program. Their I.Q. gains, measured against a matched control group at age 3, look encouraging. However, the possibility exists that the program has merely increased participants' I.Q. scores and not the underlying g factor of intelligence that the I.Q. test is intended to measure and upon which its predictive and construct validity depend.[7]

Probably the most scholarly, thorough, and up-to-date examination of the variety of experimental attempts to improve intelligence and other human abilities is *How and How Much Can Intelligence Be Increased*, edited by Douglas Detterman and Robert Sternberg.[8] In a review of this book, I said:

> What this book may bring as something of a surprise to many psychologists who received their education in the 1950s and '60s, in the heyday of what has been termed "naive environmentalism" in American educational psychology, is the evident great difficulty in effecting practically substantial and durable gains in individuals' intelligence. In terms of some conceptions of human intelligence as predominantly a product of cultural learning, this fact should seem surprising. . . . The sum total of the wide-ranging information provided in this book would scarcely contradict the conclusion that, as yet, investigators have not come up with dependable and replicable evidence that they have discovered a psychological method by which they can increase "intelligence" in the sense of Spearman's g.[9]

Thus current claims regarding the plasticity of human intelligence are notably more subdued than were the promises of only 20 years ago. Edward Zigler, one of the founders of the leaders in compensatory education, and his colleague, Winnie Berman, have recently warned that workers in the field "must be on guard never again to make the errors of overpromising and overselling the positive effects of early childhood intervention."[10] It turns out that the prevailing views of most psychologists and educators in the 1960s were largely wrong with regard to such questions as, What is the nature of intelligence? What is it that our I.Q. tests measure primarily? Why is the I.Q. so highly predictive of scholastic performance?

The error lay in believing that the disadvantage with which many poor or culturally different children entered school—and the disadvantage that compensatory education was intended to remedy—was mainly a deficiency in *knowledge*. Implicit in this belief was a view of intelligence as consisting of a general learning ability of almost unlimited plasticity plus the "knowledge contents" of memory, particularly those kinds of knowledge that serve to improve scholastic performance. Holders of this view saw the information content of I.Q. tests as an arbitrary sample of the specific items of knowledge and skill normally acquired by members of the white middle and upper classes.

In this highly behavioristic conception of intelligence, which I have elsewhere termed the *specificity doctrine*,[13] intelligence is erroneously identified with the content of the test items that psychologists have devised for assessing intelligence. These test items cover such things as general information, vocabulary, arithmetic, and the ability to copy certain geometric figures, to make block designs, and to work puzzles. To acquire the knowledge and skills to do these things—or to learn other, similar things that would have positive transfer to performance on I.Q. tests or in coursework—is to become more intelligent, according to this deceptive view of intelligence. As Zigler and Berman have put it, "knowing more" is erroneously translated into "becoming smarter."

Striking findings from two recent lines of research—that on test bias and that on mental chronometry—clearly contradict the view of individual and group differences in intelligence as differences primarily in knowledge.

The research on test bias has shown that the level of difficulty of I.Q. and achievement test items is consistent across all American-born, English-speaking ethnic and social-class groups. Moreover, I.Q. and achievement tests do not differ in their predictive validity for these groups. These findings are highly inconsistent with the hypothesis that cultural differences exist in the knowledge base that these tests sample. Available evidence from studies of test bias makes it extremely implausible that racial and social-class differences can be explained by cultural differences in the knowledge base or by differential opportunity for acquiring the knowledge that existing tests sample.[14] For every American-born social class

and racial group, highly diverse test items maintain the same relative standing on indices of item difficulty, regardless of the culture loadings of the items. This phenomenon requires that we find some explanation for group differences on I.Q. and achievement tests other than cultural differences in exposure to the various kinds of knowledge sampled by the tests.

We must seek the explanation, I believe, at the most basic level of information processing. In recent years, both the theory and the technology of research on cognitive processes have afforded powerful means for analyzing individual and group differences in abilities. Within the framework of cognitive processes research, the kinds of questions that we can investigate are quite different and more basic than those we can study through traditional psychometric tests and factor analysis. Mental chronometry, or measurement of the time required for various mental events in the course of information processing, permits us to investigate individual differences at the level of elementary cognitive processes—those processes through which individuals attain the complex learning, knowledge, and problem-solving skills that I.Q. tests sample.

Researchers devise the tasks used to measure individual differences in various elementary cognitive processes in such a way as to rule out or greatly minimize individual differences in knowledge. These tasks are so simple, and the error rates on them are so close to zero, that individual differences can be studied only by chronometric techniques. For example, the cognitive tasks that we use in our laboratory are so easy that they typically require less than one second to perform.[15] Yet these very brief response latencies, derived from a number of elementary processing tasks, together can account for some 70% of the variance in scores on untimed standard psychometric tests of intelligence. Very little of the true score variance on such tests can be attributed to the knowledge covered by the tests' content per se.

It is important to understand that the items of standardized psychometric tests are mainly vehicles for reflecting the past and present efficiency of mental processes. That these items usually include some knowledge content is only an incidental and nonessential feature. The fact is that individual differences on these content-laden tests correlate with response latencies on elementary cognitive-processing tasks that have minimal intellectual content. This means that our standard I.Q. tests—and the scholastic achievement tests with which these I.Q. tests are highly correlated—reflect individual differences in the speed and efficiency of basic cognitive processes more than they reflect differences in the information content to which test-takers have been exposed. In fact, we can account for a substantial portion of the variance in I.Q. scores by measuring the evoked electrical potentials of the brain, using an electrode attached to the scalp—a measure that is not only free of any knowledge content but that is not even dependent on any voluntary or overt behavior by the subject.[16]

Thus I suggest that the design of compensatory education and the assessment of its effects should be informed by the recent studies on information processing. The variables that have been measured by researchers in this field to date have correlated not only with I.Q., but with scholastic achievement as well.[17] An important question for future research is, What proportions of the variance in I.Q. and in scholastic achievement are associated with elementary cognitive processes and with meta-processes respectively? A second but equally important question is, What possible effects can various types of compensatory training have on these two levels of cognitive processes?

Elementary cognitive processes include such variables as perceptual speed, stimulus scanning, stimulus encoding, mental rotation or transformation of visual stimuli, short-term memory capacity, efficiency of information retrieval from long-term memory, generalization, discrimination, comparison, transfer, and response execution. *Meta-processes* include those planning and executive functions that select and coordinate the deployment of the elementary cognitive processes to handle specific situations, e.g., strategies for problem recognition, for selecting and combining lower-order cognitive processes, for organizing information, for allocating time and resources, for monitoring one's own performance, and the like.

Meta-processes are thought to be more amenable than elementary processes to improvement through training, but no solid evidence currently exists on this question. And, though much is already known about social-class and racial-group differences in I.Q. and scholastic achievement, psychologists have scarcely begun to try to understand the nature and locus of these differences in terms of the cognitive processes and meta-processes involved.[18] As yet, virtually nothing is known about the effect of compensatory education on the various levels of cognitive processing or about the extent to which the levels of cognitive processing can be influenced by training especially designed for that purpose.

I suspect that a substantial part of the individual variance in I.Q. and scholastic achievement—probably somewhere between 50% and 70%, according to the best evidence on the heritability of I.Q.—is not subject to manipulation by any strictly psychological or educational treatment. The reason for this, I assume, is that the main locus of control of that unyielding source of variance is more biological than psychological or behavioral.

At an even more fundamental level, we might ask why variance in intelligence should be so surprisingly resistant to experimental manipulation. As I have suggested elsewhere,[19] this apparent resistance to manipulation seems less surprising if we view human intelligence as an outcome of biological evolution. Genetic variation is the one absolutely essential ingredient to enable evolution to occur. If intelligence has evolved as a fitness characteristic in the Darwinian sense—that is, as an instrumentality for the survival of humankind—it is conceivable that the biological basis of intelligence has a built-in stabilizing mechanism, rather like a gyroscope, that safeguards the individual's behavioral capacity for coping with the exigencies of survival. If that were the case, mental development would not be wholly at the mercy of often erratic environmental happenstance. A too-malleable fitness trait would afford an organism too little protection against the vagaries of its environment. Thus, as humanity evolved, processes may also have evolved to buffer human intelligence from being pushed too far in one direction or another, whether by adventitiously harmful or by intentionally benevolent environmental forces.

ENDNOTES

1. Barbara Lerner, "Test Scores as Measures of Human Capital," in Raymond B. Cattell, ed., *Intelligence and National Achievement* (Washington, D.C.: Cliveden Press, 1983).

2. Ibid., p. 73.

3. Ibid., p. 74.

4. Consortium for Longitudinal Studies, *As the Twig Is Bent . . . Lasting Effects of Preschool Programs* (Hillsdale, N.J.: Erlbaum, 1983); and Edward Zigler and Jeanette Valentine, *Project Head Start* (New York: Free Press, 1979).

5. Gene V. Glass and Mary C. Ellwein, review of *As the Twig Is Bent . . .* , by the Consortium for Longitudinal Studies, in *Science*, 20 January 1984, p. 274.

6. Craig T. Ramey et al., "The Carolina Abecedarian Project: A Longitudinal and Multidisciplinary Approach to the Prevention of Developmental Retardation," in Theordore D. Tjossem, ed., *Intervention Strategies for High Risk Infants and Young Children* (Baltimore: University Park Press, 1976).

7. Craig T. Ramey and Ron Haskins, "The Modification of Intelligence Through Early Experience," *Intelligence*, January/March 1981, pp. 5–19; and Arthur R. Jensen, "Raising the I.Q.: The Ramey and Haskins Study," *Intelligence*, January/March 1981, pp. 29–40.

8. Douglas K. Detterman and Robert J. Sternberg, eds., *How and How Much Can Intelligence Be Increased* (Norwood, N.J.: Ablex, 1982).

9. Arthur R. Jensen, "Again, How Much Can We Boost I.Q.?," review of *How and How Much Can Intelligence Be Increased*, edited by Douglas K. Detterman and Robert J. Sternberg, in *Contemporary Psychology*, October 1983, p. 757.

10. Edward Zigler and Winnie Berman, "Discerning the Future of Early Childhood Intervention," *American Psychologist*, August 1983, p. 897.

11. Ibid., pp. 895–896.

12. Quoted in Peter Skerry, "The Charmed Life of Head Start," *Public Interest*, Fall 1983, pp. 18–39.

13. Arthur R. Jensen, "Test Validity: *g* Versus the Specificity Doctrine," *Journal of Social and Biological Structures*, vol. 7, 1984, pp. 93–118.

14. Arthur R. Jensen, *Bias in Mental Testing* (New York: Free Press, 1980); and Cecil R. Reynolds and Robert T. Brown, *Perspectives on Bias in Mental Testing* (New York: Plenum, 1984).

15. Arthur R. Jensen, "Chronometric Analysis of Intelligence," *Journal of Social and Biological Structures*, April 1980, pp. 103–122 idem, "The Chronometry of Intelligence," in Robert J. Sternberg, ed., *Advances in the Psychology of Human Intelligence* (Hillsdale, N.J.: Erlbaum, 1982); and idem, "Reaction Time and Psychometric *g*," in Hans J. Eysenck, ed., *A Model for Intelligence* (Heidelberg: Springer-Verlag, 1982).

16. Donna E. Hendrickson and Alan E. Hendrickson, "The Biological Basis of Individual Differences in Intelligence," *Personality and Individual Differences*, January 1980, pp. 3–34.

17. Jerry S. Carlson and C. Mark Jensen, "Reaction Time, Movement Time, and Intelligence: A Replication and Extension," *Intelligence*, July/September 1982, pp. 265–74.

18. John G. Borkowski and Audrey Krause, "Racial Differences in Intelligence: The Importance of the Executive System," *Intelligence*, October/December 1983, pp. 379–395; Arthur R. Jensen, "Race Differences and Type II Errors: A Comment on Borkowski and Krause," *Intelligence*, in press; and Philip A. Vernon and Arthur R. Jensen, "Individual and Group Differences in Intelligence and Speed of Information Processing," *Personality and Individual Differences*, in press.

19. Jensen, "Again, How Much Can We Boost I.Q.?," p. 758.

Right Brain—Left Brain: A Half-Brained Idea?

People have long been fascinated and puzzled by the human brain, which is about as large as the average-size cantelope. For 2,400 years, ever since Hippocrates located the seat of intellect inside the skull, we have been forced to admit that humanity's greatest achievements, loftiest thoughts, and deepest emotions all arise form this three-pound glob of matter called the brain. If you look at the human brain from the top, it is split down the middle into halves or hemispheres. Until 1962, the prevailing view was that people had half a thinking brain—the left hemisphere. By the early 1970s, research showed that each side of the brain was a highly specialized organ of thought. Shortly thereafter, some tried to sell the idea that humans have neither the whole brain described by Descartes nor the half brain, but two brains each with its own specialized functions which operate independently. The left brain was said to be in charge of logical abilities such as mathematics, written language, and speech, whereas the right brain was thought to be in control of perception, imagination, creativity, and musical and artistic ability and appreciation. The left side was said to think analytically, taking things apart and dealing with the parts one at a time. The right side was thought to see things as a whole and to look at the overall pattern or gestalt. It was not long before educators sought to base instruction upon the neuropsychology of hemispheric specialization. (See the issue entitled Matching Teaching and Learning Styles in Unit 2.)

In the following article, Jerre Levy traces the history of the two-brain movement and examines neuropsychological evidence underlying this movement, which soon called for hemispheric balance in the public school curriculum. She notes that cognitive functions are not as localized as once thought. On the contrary, just the opposite is true. She concludes by stating that, to the extent that regions are differentiated in the brain, they must integrate their activities. In brief, the focus on right brain/left brain training has been misguided. The successful application to the solution of educational problems will require advances in neuropsychology, a clear understanding of the nature and scope of educational problems, careful translation of neuropsychological data into educational practice, and a curbing of excessive zeal in polemicism (Harris, 1985).

Thought Questions

Have proponents of the right brain misinterpreted psychological evidence and thereby postulated untenable dichotomies about left and right brain specialization, learning styles and the nature of academic subjects?

Even assuming that advocates of the right brain movement are correct, is there any evidence to show that this ambitious goal can be accomplished? That is, are right-brained exercises or training effective?

What activities, exercises, and subject matters would advocates of right brain training like to see in the curriculum?

Is it reasonable to assume that certain subject matters (for example, reading) are beamed only to the left hemisphere? Or that selected mental activities (for example, creative thinking) are most closely associated with the right hemisphere?

Defend the proposition that the right hemisphere gets adequately exercised in the so-called left-brained school environment with its stress on reading, writing, and analytic strategies of problem solving.

Did the advent of television with its right-brained visual input system and its left-brained speech input provide children and youth with information in a hemispherically balanced manner?

What are the implications of research on brain specialization for the testing of intelligence? For example, should intelligence tests be more process-oriented rather than content oriented? If so, what processes should be included in the assessment of intelligence? Would better balanced processing tests of intelligence be more culturally fair to blacks who do better on right hemisphere tests?

Some contend that early learning is done in the right hemisphere because the right hemisphere is preverbal. If this assertion is true, might not the right hemisphere be more vulnerable to early stress and to disadvantaged environments?

How can we have a unified mental experience or world if the brain does not function as a unified whole?

How do such factors as sex, age, culture, socioeconomic level, experience, nature of the subskill of a larger skill being assessed, and type of injury, if any, contribute to lateralization?

Right Brain, Left Brain: Fact and Fiction

Jerre Levy

"I guess I'm mostly a right-brain person . . . my left side doesn't work long enough for me to figure it out," concludes a character in a *Frank and Ernest* cartoon. "It's tough being a left-brained person . . . in a right-brained world," moans a youngster in the cartoon *Wee Pals,* after perusing a tome on the "psychology of consciousness."

The notion that we are "left brained" or "right brained" has become entrenched in the popular culture. And, based on a misinterpretation of the facts, a pop psychology myth has evolved, asserting that the left hemisphere of the brain controls logic and language, while the right controls creativity and intuition. One best-selling book even claimed to teach people how to draw better by training the right brain and bypassing the left. According to the myth, people differ in their styles of thought, depending on which half of the brain is dominant. Unfortunately, this myth is often represented as scientific fact. It is not.

As a researcher who has spent essentially her whole career studying how the two hemispheres relate to one another and to behavior, I feel obliged to set the record straight on what

is known scientifically about the roles of the hemispheres. As it turns out, the brain's actual organization is every bit as interesting as the myth and suggests a far more holistic view of humankind.

People's fascination with relating mental function to brain organization goes back at least to Hippocrates. But it was René Descartes, in the 17th century, who came up with the notable and influential notion that the brain must act as a unified whole to yield a unified mental world. His specific mental mapping was wrong (he concluded that the pineal gland—now known to regulate biological rhythms in response to cycles of light and dark—was the seat of the soul, or mind). But his basic premise was on the right track and remained dominant until the latter half of the 19th century, when discoveries then reduced humankind to a half-brained species.

During the 1860s and 1870s, Paul Broca, a French neurologist, and Karl Wernicke, a German neurologist, reported that damage to the left cerebral hemisphere produced severe disorders of language, but that comparable damage to the right hemisphere did not. Neurology was never to be the same.

Despite their generally similar anatomies, the left and right cerebral hemispheres evidently had very different functions. Language

From *Psychology Today Magazine* 19 (May): 42–44. Copyright © 1984 American Psychological Association. Reprinted with permission.

appeared to be solely a property of the left side; the right hemisphere, apparently, was mute. The scientific world generalized this to conclude that the left hemisphere was dominant not only for language but for all psychological processes. The right hemisphere was seen as a mere relay station. Since each half of the brain is connected to and receives direct input from the opposite side of the body, the right hemisphere was needed to tell the left hemisphere what was happening on the left side of space and to relay messages to muscles on the body's left side. But the right hemisphere was only an unthinking automaton. From pre-19th century whole-brained creatures, we had become half-brained.

From the beginning, there were serious difficulties with the idea that the left hemisphere was the seat of humanity and that the right hemisphere played no role in thinking. In the 1880s, John Hughlings Jackson, a renowned English neurologist, described a patient with right-hemisphere damage who showed selective losses in certain aspects of visual perception—losses that did not appear with similar damage of the left hemisphere. He suggested that the right hemisphere might be just as specialized for visual perception as the left hemisphere was for language.

From the 1930s on, reports began to confirm Hughlings Jackson's findings. Patients with right-side damage had difficulties in drawing, using colored blocks to copy designs, reading and drawing maps, discriminating faces and in a variety of other visual and spatial tasks. These disorders were much less prevalent or serious in patients with left-hemisphere damage.

The investigators, quite aware of the implications of their findings, proposed that although the left hemisphere was specialized for langauge, the right hemisphere was specialized for many nonlinguistic processes. Nonetheless, these were voices in the wilderness, and their views hardly swayed the general neurological community. Until 1962, the prevalent view was that people had half a thinking brain.

Beginning in the early 1960s, Nobel Prize winner Roger W. Sperry and his colleagues and students demonstrated certain unusual characteristics in patients who, to control intractable epileptic seizures, had undergone complete surgical division of the corpus callosum, the connecting bridge between the two sides of the brain. These patients, like split-brain animals that Sperry had studied, couldn't communicate between the cerebral hemispheres. An object placed in the right hand (left hemisphere) could be named readily, but one placed in the left hand (nonverbal right hemisphere) could be neither named nor described. But these same patients could point to a picture of the object the left hand had felt. In other words, the right hemisphere knew what it felt, even if it could not speak.

Outside the laboratory, the split-brain patients were remarkably normal, and within the laboratory, each cerebral hemisphere seemed to be able to perceive, think and govern behavior, even though the two sides were out of contact. In later split-brain studies, a variety of tasks were devised to examine the specialized functions of each hemisphere. These showed that the right hemisphere was superior to the left in spatial tasks but was mute and deficient in verbal tasks such as decoding complex syntax, short-term verbal memory, and phonetic analysis. In brief, the split-brain studies fully confirmed the inferences drawn from the earlier investigations of patients with damage to one hemisphere.

These findings were further expanded by psychologist Doreen Kimura and others, who developed behavioral methods to study how functions of the hemispheres differed in normal people. These involved presenting visual stimuli rapidly to either the left or right visual fields (and the opposite hemispheres). Normal right-handers were more accurate or faster in identifying words or nonsense syllables in the right visual field (left hemisphere) and in identifying or recognizing faces, facial expressions of emotion, line slopes or dot locations in the left visual field (right hemisphere).

Another method was "dichotic listening," in which two different sounds were presented simultaneously to the two ears. The right ear (left hemisphere) was better at identifying nonsense syllables, while the left ear (right hemisphere) excelled at identifying certain nonverbal sounds such as piano melodies or dog barks.

By 1970 or soon thereafter, the reign of the left brain was essentially ended. The large majority of researchers concluded that each side of the brain was a highly specialized organ of thought, with the right hemisphere predominant in a set of functions that complemented those of the left. Observations of patients with damage to one side of the brain, of split-brain patients and of normal individuals yielded consistent findings. There could no longer be any reasonable doubt: The right hemisphere, too, was a fully human and highly complex organ of thought.

It was not long before the new discoveries found their way into the popular media and into the educational community. Some mythmakers sought to sell the idea that human beings had neither the whole and unified brain described by Descartes, nor the half brain of Broca and Wernicke, but rather two brains, each devoted to its own tasks and operating essentially independently of the other. The right hemisphere was in control when an artist painted a portrait, but the left hemisphere was in control when the novelist wrote a book. Logic was the property of the left hemisphere, whereas creativity and intuition were properties of the right. Further, these two brains did not really work together in the same person. Instead, some people thought primarily with the right hemisphere, while others thought primarily with the left. Finally, given the presumed absolute differences between hemispheres, it was claimed that special subject matters and teaching strategies had to be developed to educate one hemisphere at a time, and that the standard school curriculums only educated the "logical" left hemisphere.

Notice that the new two-brain myth was based on two quite separate types of scientific findings. First was the fact that split-brain patients showed few obvious symptoms of their surgery in everyday life and far greater integrity of behavior than would be seen if two regions within a hemisphere had been surgically disconnected. Thus, it was assumed that each

hemisphere could be considered to be an independent brain.

Second, a great deal of research had demonstrated that each hemisphere had its own functional "expertise," and that the two halves were complementary. Since language was the speciality of the left hemisphere, some people concluded that any verbal activity, such as writing a novel, depended solely on processes of the left hemisphere. Similarly, since visual and spatial functions were the specialities of the right hemisphere, some people inferred that any visuospatial activity, such as painting portraits, must depend solely on processes of that hemisphere. Even if thought and language were no longer synonymous, at least logic and language seemed to be. Since intuitions, by definition, are not accessible to verbal explanation, and since intuition and creativity seemed closely related, they were assigned to the right hemisphere.

Based, then, on the presumed independent functions of the two hemispheres, and on the fact that they differed in their specializations, the final leap was that different activities and psychological demands engaged different hemispheres while the opposite side of the brain merely idled along in some unconscious state.

The two-brain myth was founded on an erroneous premise: that since each hemisphere was specialized, each must function as an independent brain. But in fact, just the opposite is true. To the extent that regions are differentiated in the brain, they must integrate their activities. Indeed, it is precisely that integration that gives rise to behavior and mental processes greater than and different from each region's special contribution. Thus, since the central premise of the mythmakers is wrong, so are all the inferences derived from it.

What does the scientific evidence actually say? First, it says that the two hemispheres are so similar that when they are disconnected by the split-brain surgery, each can function remarkably well, although quite imperfectly.

Second, it says that superimposed on this similarity are differences in the specialized abilities of each side. These differences are seen in the contrasting contributions each hemisphere makes to all cognitive activities. When a person reads a story, the right hemisphere may play a special role in decoding visual information, maintaining an integrated story structure, appreciating humor and emotional content, deriving meaning from past associations and understanding metaphor. At the same time, the left hemisphere plays a special role in understanding syntax, translating written words into their phonetic representations and deriving meaning from complex relations among word concepts and syntax. But there is no activity in which only one hemisphere is involved or to which only one hemisphere makes a contribution.

Third, logic is not confined to the left hemisphere. Patients with right-hemisphere damage show more major logical disorders than do patients with left-hemisphere damage. Some whose right hemisphere is damaged will deny that their left arm is their own, even when the physician demonstrates its connection to the rest of the body. Though paralyzed on the left side of the body, such patients will often make grandiose plans that are impossible because of paralysis and will be unable to see their lack of logic.

Fourth, there is no evidence that either creativity or intuition is an exclusive property of the right hemisphere. Indeed, real creativity and intuition, whatever they may entail, almost certainly depend on an intimate collaboration between hemispheres. For example, one major French painter continued to paint with the same style and skill after suffering a left-hemisphere stroke and loss of language. Creativity can remain even after right-hemisphere damage. Another painter Lovis Corinth, after suffering right-hemisphere damage, continued to paint with a high level of skill, his style more expressive and bolder than before. In the musical realm, researcher Harold Gordon found that in highly talented professional musicians both hemispheres were equally skilled in dis-criminating musical chords. Further, when researchers Steven Gaede, Oscar Parsons, and James Bertera compared people with high and low musical aptitude for hemispheric asymmetries, high aptitude was associated with equal capacities of the two sides of the brain.

Fifth, since the two hemispheres do not function independently, and since each hemisphere contributes its special capacities to all cognitive activities, it is quite impossible to educate one hemisphere at a time in a normal brain. The right hemisphere is educated as much as the left in a literature class, and the left hemisphere is educated as much as the right in music and painting classes.

Finally, what of individual differences? There is both psychological and physiological evidence that people vary in the relative balance of activation of the two hemispheres. Further, there is a significant correlation between which hemisphere is more active and the relative degree of verbal or spatial skills. But there is no evidence that people are purely "left brained" or "right brained." Not even those with the most extremely asymmetrical activation between hemispheres think only with the more activated side. Rather, there is a continuum. The left hemisphere is more active in some people, to varying degrees, and verbal functioning is promoted to varying degrees. Similarly, in those with a more active right hemisphere, spatial abilities are favored. While activation patterns and cognitive patterns are correlated, the relationship is very far from perfect. This means that differences in activation of the hemispheres are but one of many factors affecting the way we think.

In sum, the popular myths are misinterpretations and wishes, not the observations of scientists. Normal people have not half a brain nor two brains but one gloriously differentiated brain, with each hemisphere contributing its specialized abilities. Descartes was, essentially right: We have a single brain that generates a single mental self.

Sex Differences in Mathematical Achievement: Nature Versus Nurture

Stereotypes about males and females are commonplace in our society. While these stereotypes do reflect, to some extent, real differences between the sexes, they do not apply uniformly to all males and females. In attempting to sort out real differences from myths, various investigators have addressed such questions as "Are women more empathic and sensitive in interpersonal relations?", or "Are there marked differences between the sexes and their desires to achieve and succeed?", "Are males more aggressive and more autonomous than females?", "Is nurturant behavior more typical of one sex?", and "Do girls really exceed boys in verbal ability?" Psychologists have not always agreed upon the answers.

One aspect of sex differences that has attracted attention and given rise to controversy has to do with mathematical ability and achievement. In years past, it was generally accepted that boys were naturally better at mathematics than girls. The women's movement began to challenge that assumption and the differences observed in math performance came to be accepted as resulting from cultural and environmental factors. Sexual stereotyping was thought to be the major contributing factor. A resultant self-fulfilling prophecy was postulated as a reason for the poor preformance of girls in the area of mathematics. Boys were expected to be better in math. They were given toys, games, and books which encouraged mathematical development. They thought they were better and, hence, they actually performed in a superior fashion.

In 1980, Julian Stanley and Camilla Benbow challenged this cultural environmental explanation and caused a major uproar (Benbow & Stanley, 1980). Their research data came from Johns Hopkins' regional talent search. They tested thousands of gifted and talented seventh and eighth graders on the SAT Mathematics Tests and found that boys consistently scored higher than girls. This was particularly true at the upper extremes of the test scores where high scoring boys far outnumbered high scoring girls. These findings, as well as Stanley and Benbow's comments regarding their implications, reactivated the old nature versus nurture issue. The conclusion drawn from their studies, which is still being debated, was that *ability* was a significant factor in influencing the courses which students take, and not vice versa. They contend that sex differences in mathematics achievement and in attitude towards mathematics result from superior male mathematical ability which may in turn be related to greater male ability in spatial tasks. They believe that this male superiority is, at least in part, an expression of genetic factors.

Gilah Leder, in her article, examines cultural pressures and socialization processes as explanations for the lower achievement of gifted girls and girls in general. She notes that the beliefs, prejudices, and expectations about appropriate behavior and achievement are reflected by parents, peers, school, and society at large. She argues that for many females the attainment of success, especially in an area such as mathematics which is deemed less appropriate for females, might well produce anxiety, which in turn tends to have an adverse effect on mathematics performance. Furthermore, she contends that to succeed at tasks of cognitive complexity one must be able to work independently, persist, and choose. These autonomous learning behaviors are much more strongly reinforced by society for boys than they are for girls. The above factors result in creating internal barriers which prevent females from fully developing their mathematical skills.

Thought Questions

Are the sexes more alike than different with respect to mathematical achievement? Are the differences within each sex greater than the differences between the sexes? Defend your answer. What implications, if any, might sex differences have with respect to equal educational and vocational opportunities? If girls as a group are less skilled in visual-spatial and mathematical tasks, does this mean that fewer of them should be admitted to graduate schools in engineering, math, and architecture?

How would you try to motivate female and male students differently in mathematics courses? Should instructional techniques differ from males and females? How would you design an enriched or accelerated program in mathematics for gifted girls? What can schools do to help those females who experience feelings of guilt or fear of social rejection over their mathematical achievements? Can women achieve at a very high level in mathematics and yet be seen as feminine?

Do boys participate in autonomous learning behaviors to a greater extent than girls, and thus perform better on mathematical tests of high cognitive complexity?

Do biological differences in brain organization help explain why males are superior in mathematical achievements? Is the brain of one sex more specialized? Are men superior at such tasks as mentally picturing mathematical functions rotating in three-dimensional space or reading road maps because of a superior, specialized, spatial relations ability?

Sex Differences in Mathematical Reasoning Ability: More Facts

Camilla Persson Benbow and Julian C. Stanley

In 1980 we reported large sex differences in mean scores on a test of mathematical reasoning ability for 9927 mathematically talented seventh and eighth graders who entered the Johns Hopkins regional talent search from 1972 through 1979[1,2]. One prediction from those results was that there would be a preponderance of males at the high end of the distribution of mathematical reasoning ability. In this report we investigate sex differences at the highest levels of that ability. New groups of students under age 13 with exceptional mathematical aptitude were identified by means of two separate procedures. In the first, the Johns Hopkins regional talent searches in 1980, 1981, and 1982,[3] 39,820 seventh graders from the Middle Atlantic region of the United States who were selected for high intellectual ability were given the College Board Scholastic Aptitude Test (SAT). In the second, a nationwide talent search was conducted for which any student under 13 years of age who was willing to take the SAT was eligible. The results of both procedures substantiated our prediction that before age 13 far more males than females would

score extremely high on SAT-M, the mathematical part of SAT.

The test items of SAT-M require numerical judgment, relational thinking, or insightful and logical reasoning. This test is designed to measure the developed mathematical reasoning ability of 11th and 12th graders.[4] Most students in our study were in the middle of the seventh grade. Few had had formal opportunities to study algebra and beyond.[5,6] Our rationale is that most of these students were unfamiliar with mathematics from algebra onward, and that most who scored high did so because of extraordinary reasoning ability.[7]

In 1980, 1981, and 1982, as in the earlier study,[1] participants in the Johns Hopkins talent search were seventh graders, or boys and girls of typical seventh-grade age in a higher grade, in the Middle Atlantic area. Before 1980, applicants had been required to be in the top 3 percent nationally on the mathematics section of any standardized achievement test. Beginning in 1980, students in the top 3 percent in verbal or overall intellectual ability were also eligible. During that and the next 2 years 19,883 boys and 19,937 girls applied and were tested. Even though this sample was more general and had equal representation by sex, the mean sex difference on SAT-M remained constant at 30 points favoring males (males' $\overline{X}$ = 416, S.D. = 87; females' $\overline{X}$ = 386, S.D. = 74; t = 37; $P <$ 0.001). No important difference in verbal ability as measured by SAT-V was found (males' $\overline{X}$ = 367, females' $\overline{X}$ = 365).

The major point, however, is not the mean difference in SAT-M scores but the ratios of boys to girls among the high scorers (Table 1). The ratio of boys to girls scoring above the mean of talent-search males was 1.5:1. The ratio among those who scored ≥500 (493 was the mean cf 1981–82 college-bound 12th grade males) was 2.1:1. Among those who scored ≥ 600 (600 was the 79th percentile of the 12th-grade males) the ratio was 4.1:1. These ratios are similar to those previously reported[1] but are derived from a broader and much larger data base.

Scoring 700 or more on the SAT-M before age 13 is rare. We estimate that students who reach this criterion (the 95th percentile of college-bound 12th-grade males) before their 13th birthday represent the top one in 10,000 of their age group. It was because of their rarity that the nationwide talent search was created in November 1980 in order to locate such students who were born after 1967 and facilitate their education.[8] In that talent search applicants could take the SAT at any time and place at which it was administered by the Educational Testing Service or through one of five regional talent searches that cover the United States.[9] Extensive nationwide efforts were made to inform school personnel and parents about our search. The new procedure (unrestricted by geography or previous ability) was successful in obtaining a large national sample of this exceedingly rare population. As of September 1983, the number such boys identified was 260 and the number of girls 20 a ratio of 13.0:1.[10] This ratio is remarkable in view of the fact that the available evidence suggests there was essentially equal participation of boys and girls in the talent searches.

The total number of students tested in the Johns Hopkins regional annual talent searches and reported so far is 49,747 (9,927 in the initial study and 39,820 in the present study). Preliminary reports from the 1983 talent search

based on some 15,000 cases yield essentially identical results. In the ten Middle Atlantic regional talent searches from 1972 through 1983 we have therefore tested abut 65,000 students. It is abundantly clear that far more boys than girls (chiefly 12-year-olds) scored in the highest ranges on SAT-M, even though girls were matched with boys by intellectual ability, age, grade, and voluntary participation. In the orig-

Table 1
Number of high scorers on SAT-M among selected seventh graders—19,883 boys and 19,937 girls—tested in the Johns Hopkins regional talent search in 1980, 1981, and 1982, and of scorers of ≥700 prior to age 13 in the national search[9].

Score	Number	Percent	Ratio of boys to girls
JOHNS HOPKINS REGIONAL SEARCH			
420 or more*			
Boys	9119	45.9	1.5:1
Girls	6220	31.2	
500 or more			
Boys	3618	18.2	2.1:1
Girls	1707	8.6	
600 or more			
Boys	648	3.3	4.1:1
Girls	158	0.8	
NATIONAL SEARCH IN JOHNS HOPKINS TALENT SEARCH REGION			
700 or more			
Boys	113	†	12.6:1
Girls	9	†	
OUTSIDE JOHNS HOPKINS TALENT SEARCH REGION			
700 or more			
Boys	147	†	13.4:1
Girls	11	†	

*Mean score of the boys was 416. The highest possible score is 800.
†Total number tested is unknown.[9]

inal study[1] students were required to meet a qualifying mathematics criterion. Since we observed the same sex difference then as now, the current results cannot be explained solely on the grounds that the girls may have qualified by the verbal criterion. Moreover, if that were the case, we should expect the girls to have scored higher than the boys on SAT-V. They did not.

Several "environmental" hypotheses have been proposed to account for sex differences in mathematical ability. Fox *et al.* and Meece *et al.*[11] have found support for a social-reinforcement hypothesis which, in essence, states that sex-related differences in mathematical achievement are due to differences in social conditioning and expectations for boys and girls. The validity of this hypothesis has been evaluated for the population we studied earlier[1] and for a subsample of the students in this study. Substantial differences between boys' and girls' attitudes or backgrounds were not found.[5,6,12] Admittedly, some of the measures used were broadly defined and may not have been able to detect subtle social influences that affect a child from birth. But is it not obvious how social conditioning could affect mathematical reasoning ability so adversely and significantly, yet have little detectable effect on stated interest in mathematics, the taking of mathematics courses during the high school years before the SAT's are normally taken, and mathematics-course grades.[5,6]

An alternative hypothesis, that sex differences in mathematical reasoning ability arise mainly from differential course-taking,[13] was also not validated, either by the data in our 1980 study[1] or by the data in the present study. In both studies the boys and girls were shown to have had similar formal training in mathematics.[5,6]

It is also of interest that sex differences in mean SAT-M scores observed in our early talent searches became only slightly larger during high school In the selected subsample of participants studied, males improved their scores an average of 10 points more than females (the mean difference went from 40 to 50 points). They also increased their scores on the SAT-V by at least 10 points more than females.[6] Previously, other researchers have postulated that profound differences in socialization during adolescence caused the well-documented sex differences in 11th- and 12th-grade SAT-M scores,[11] but that idea is not supported in our data. For socialization to account for our results, it would seem necessary to postulate (ad hoc) that chiefly early socialization pressures significantly influence the sex difference in SAT-M scores—that is, that the intensive social pressures during adolescence have little such effect.

It is important to emphasize that we are dealing with intellectually highly able students and that these findings may not generalize to average students. Moreover, these results are of course not generalizable to particular individuals. Finally, it should be noted that the boys' SAT-M scores had a larger variance than the girls'. This is obviously related to the fact that more mathematically talented boys than girls were found.[14] Nonetheless, the environmental hypotheses outlined above attempt to explain mean differences, not differences in variability. Thus, even if one concludes that our findings result primarily from greater male variability, one must still explain why.

Our principal conclusion is that males dominate the highest ranges of mathematical reasoning ability before they enter adolescence. Reasons for this sex difference are unclear.[15]

REFERENCES AND NOTES

1. C. Benbow and J. Stanley, *Science* **210**, 1262 (1980).

2. Also see letters by C. Tomizuka and S. Tobias; E. Stage and R. Karplus; S. Chipman; E. Egleman *et*

al.; D. Moran; E. Luchins and A. Luchins; A. Kelly; C. Benbow and J. Stanley, *ibid.* **212**, 114 (1981).

3. The Johns Hopkins Center for the Advancement of Academically Talented Youth (CTY) conducts talent searches during January in Delawa.e, the District of Columbia, Maryland, New Jersey (added in 1980), Pennsylvania, Virgina, and West Virginia. In 1983 coverage expanded northeast to include Connecticut, Maine, Massachusetts, New Hampshire, Rhode Island, and Vermont.

4. T. Donlon and W. Angoff, in *The College Board Admissions Testing Program*, W. Angoff, Ed. (College Board, Princeton, N.J., 1971), pp. 24–25; S. Messick and A. Jungeblut, *Psychol. Bull.* **89**, 191 (1982).

5. C. Benbow and J. Stanley, *Gifted Child Q.* **26**, 82 (1982).

6. ———, *Am. Educ. Res. J.* **19**, 598 (1982).

7. We have found that among the top 10 percent of these students (who are eligible for our fast-paced summer programs in mathematics) a majority do not know even first-year algebra well.

8. J. Stanley, "Searches under way for youths *exceptionally* talented mathematically or verbally," *Roper Rev.*, in press.

9. The regional talent searches are conducted by Johns Hopkins (begun in 1972), Duke (1981), Arizona State-Tempe (1981), Northwestern (1982), and the University of Denver (1982). Because there was no logical way to separate students who entered through the regional programs from those who entered through the national channel, results were combined. Most students fit into both categories but at different time points, since the SAT could be taken more than once to qualify or could be retaken in the regional talent search programs. The SAT is not administered by the Educational Testing Service between June and October or November of each year. Therefore, entrants who had passed their 13th birthday before taking the test were included if they scored 10 additional points for each excess month or a fraction of a month.

10. There is a remarkably high incidence of left-handedness or ambidexterity (20 percent), immune disorders (55 percent), and myopia (55 percent) in this group (manuscript in preparation).

11. L. Fox, D. Tobin, L. Brody, in *Sex-Related Differences in Cognitive Functioning*, M. Wittig and A. Petersen Eds. (Academic Press, New York, 1979); J.Meece, J. Parsons, C. Kaczala, S. Goff, R. Futterman, *Psychol. Bull.* **91**, 324 (1982).

12. L. Fox, L. Brody, D. Tobin. *The Study of Social Processes that Inhibit or Enhance the Development of Competence and Interest in Mathematics Among Highly Able Young Women* (National Institute of Education, Washington, D.C., 1982); C. Benbow and J. Stanley, in *Women in Science*, M. Steinkamp and M. Maehr, Eds. (JAI Press, Greenwich, Conn., in press); L. Fox, C. Benbow, S. Perkins, in *Academic Precocity*, C. Benbow and J. Stanley, Eds. (Johns Hopkins Univ. Press. Baltimore, 1983).

13. For example, E. Fennema and J. Sherman, *Am. Educ. Res. J.* **14**, 51 (1977).

14. Why boys are generally more variable has been addressed by H. Eysenck and L. Kamin [*The Intelligence Controversy* (Wiley, New York, 1981)] and others.

15. For possible endogenous influences see, for example, R. Goy and B. McEwen, *Sexual Differentiation of the Brain* (MIT Press, Cambridge, Mass., 1980); J. Levy, *The Sciences* **21** (No. 3), 20 (1981); T. Bouchard and M. McGue, *Science* **212**, 1055 (1981); D. Hier and W. Crawley, Jr., *N. Engl. J. Med.* **306**, 1202 (1982); C. DeLacoste-Utamsing and R. Holloway, *Science* **216**, 1431 (1982); L. Harris, in *Asymmetrical Function of the Brain*, M. Kinsbourne, Ed., (Cambridge Univ. Press, London, 1978); M. McGee, *Psychol. Bull.* **86**, 889 (1979; S. Witelsen, *Science* **193,** 425 (1976); J. McGlone, *Behav. Brain Sci.* **3**, 215 (1980); D. McGuiness, *Hum. Nat.* **2** (No. 2), 82 (1979); R. Meisel and I. Ward, *Science* **213**, 239 (1981); F. Naftolin, *ibid.* **211**, 1263 (1981); A. Ehrhardt and H. Meyer-Bahlburg, *ibid.*, p. 1312; J. Inglis and J. Lawson *ibid.* **212**, 693 (1981); M. Wittig and A. Petersen, Eds., *Sex-Related Differences in Cognitive Functioning* (Academic Press, New York, 1979).

We thank K. Alexander, L. Barnett, R. Benbow, R. Gordon, P. Hines, L. Minor, B. Person, B. Polkes, D. Powers, B. Stanley, Z. Usiskin, and P. Zak. This study was supported by grants from the Spencer and Donner Foundations.

Sex-Related Differences in Mathematics: An Overview

Gilah Leder

Despite the large amount of research attention directed at the issue of sex differences in mathematics achievement and participation, agreement has not been reached either on the extent of such differences, or on the relative importance of the factors contributing to them.

A careful reading of the relevant literature reveals an inconsistency of findings, with boys performing better in some studies and girls in others. Few consistent sex-related differences are found at the primary school level. However, there is a substantial body of evidence to suggest that by the beginning of secondary school, boys frequently perform better than girls at mathematics. Differences in the samples being tested and the nature of the tasks to be performed make cross-study comparisons difficult. Yet findings that have emerged with American samples are frequently replicated in other countries. English and Australian public examination data, for example, also indicate a slightly lower performance for girls. The differences seem to increase as the level of examinations taken increases, and are particularly marked when above average performance is considered. These findings are noteworthy, since retention rates of students in mathemat-

ics courses in England and Australia tend to be higher than in the United States.

A large number of variables are thought to contribute to sex differences in mathematics learning. Those who argue that biological factors are important nevertheless seem to accept that their effective contribution to sex differences in cognitive functioning is small, and far too small to account for the sex differences in mathematics learning reported in the literature. Sex differences possibly due to biological constraints are dwarfed by the far greater pressures imposed by social and cultural stereotypes about cognitive skills and occupations. In the research discussed in this paper, emphasis is, therefore, placed on cultural pressures and socialization processes.

The pervasiveness of the socialization process is highlighted by the findings from the first IEA study (Husen, 1967) that boys performed better in mathematics than girls in each country included in the survey, even though girls in some countries perform better than boys in others. The persistently low participation rates of women in mathematics and mathematics-related careers is noteworthy. According to Rossi (1972) the absolute increase in the number of women attracted to selected professions was outweighed by the much greater increase in the number of men. "The field of mathematics is a good illustration of this: there has been 210 percent increase in the number of women, but the number of men in mathematics increased 428 percent, with the result that the percentage of mathematicians who are women actually declined from 38 in 1950 to 26 percent in 1960" (pp. 72, 73). Comparable data have been provided by Kelly (1974) and Keeves and Read (1974) for England and Australia, respectively. More recently Leder (1984) showed that notions of sex-appropriate behavior and achievements continue to be reinforced and perpetuated by contemporary media reports.

Beliefs and prejudice about sex-appropriate behavior are reflected in the expectations of parents, peers, school, and society. The effect of these expectations on selected cognitive and affective variables will be discussed in some detail.

Parental Factors

Parents influence their children's educational performance, including their performance in mathematics, in a number of ways. Representative of the findings are those of Husen (1967) who found that in the countries participating in his cross-cultural study, student achievement in mathematics was related to parents' education and socio-economic status.

Various studies (Armstrong and Price, 1982; Lantz and Smith, 1981) have shown that students' attitudes towards mathematics and a decision to continue with mathematics are linked with their parents' conception of the educational goals of the school mathematics course, and with the extent of the mathematics education desired for their children by the parents. Other studies (e.g., Fennema and Sherman, 1977; Luchins and Luchins, 1980) have highlighted that parents are perceived as encouraging their sons' mathematical studies more strongly than those of their daughters.

School and Teacher Factors

There are a number of ways in which schools, and teachers within the schools, differentiate between students on the basis of sex. The former do so through their organizational procedures; the latter, through their behavior, expectations, and beliefs.

In countries where sex-segregated education is still reasonably prevalent, it is frequently viewed as an anachronism that reflects the outmoded beliefs that the two sexes have different educational needs. Certainly, single-sex schools provide a clear illustration of sex-linked divisions in education. The degree to which a community provides for education in single-sex schools is an explicit measure of the extent to which it considers that boys and girls receive different preparations for different adult roles. Currently, opinion seems somewhat divided about the effect on girls of education in such an environment. Some writers (Shuard, 1982; Harding, 1981) have argued that girls studying mathematics and science seem disadvantaged in a mixed school setting. Others (such as Dale, 1974) have reported that girls in co-educational schools perform better in mathematics than those in single-sex schools. Care must be taken when subject preferences and performance are compared across different school systems in which equipment available, staffing, and class sizes may not be comparable. In both England and Australia where a section of the school populations is still educated in single-sex schools (though in both countries there is an interesting trend towards co-education for economic as well as educational considerations), many of these schools cater to children from higher socio-economic homes. Studies which have examined the apparent benefits or disadvantages of education in a sex-segregated environment have paid insufficient attention to those confounding factors.

It is appropriate to emphasize the substantial amount of research evidence that indicates that co-education does not signify equality of policy and practice between the sexes. When boys and girls study the same object from the same textbooks, there are often implied differences in the relevance for male and female students. Modern textbooks and tests have been written in ways that minimize sex-role stereotyping. Yet, such stereotyping is still prevalent in fiction book characters, in older textbooks to be found on library shelves, and in the ways some teachers communicate with their students.

Sex-role differentiation through sex-typed leisure activities, subject preferences and career intentions is further perpetuated by the peer group which acts as an important reference for childhood and adolescent socialization.

Peer Group Values

The preference of boys for more active games and pastimes concerned with skills and mastery of objects, and of girls to use play to practice skills related to mastery over people and interpersonal relations, is frequently documented, and conforms with common adult-expectations as well. It has also been argued (e.g., Stein and Bailey, 1975) that females and males differ in the areas in which they strive for achievement. While males tend to aim for achievement in the traditional highly valued areas of intellectual expertise and leadership skills, females are apparently more likely to strive for excellence in areas more congruent with their traditional role, i.e., areas that require social skills. Yet, Simkin (1979) pointed out that sex differences in valuations of success may vary, and depend at least in part on the instruments used to study them.

The sex differences in leisure time activities and particularly in attitudes towards mathematics are reflected in career expectations of males and females. The occupational intentions of boys and girls imply that competence in mathematics is a more important prerequisite for the attainment of the career ambitions of the former than the latter. In some studies, this view is expressed explicitly by boys and girls. The long term effects of early career ex-

pectations on decisions to opt out of mathematics courses are substantial.

Sex-related differences in behavior and expectations are at the same time self-perpetuating and self-promoting. Society's standards, beliefs, and expectations are ultimately reflected in personal beliefs that may affect functioning. Selected psychological explanations of sex differences in mathematics learning are briefly reviewed in the next section.

Psychological Explanations

The most persistent and pervasive finding that emerged from the Fennema and Sherman studies (1977, 1978) was that boys in grades 6 to 12 consistently showed greater self-confidence than girls in their ability to learn mathematics. These differences in confidence about mathematics were not paralleled initially by differences in achievement. However, for the older students, there was a high correlation between mathematics performance and confidence in mathematics score. The latter predicted subsequent performance in mathematics for girls, but not for boys. Other researchers have also found that girls underestimate their level of performance more frequently than boys. Particularly relevant in this context are the studies concerned with the motive to avoid success, or the fear of success (FS) construct.

The fear-of-success construct was postulated by Horner (1968) within the framework of the expectancy-value theory of motivation in an attempt to explain the conflicting sex-related findings of research on achievement motivation. Horner argued that for many females, attainment of success, particularly in areas considered by society to be less appropriate for females, produced anxiety which in turn was likely to have an adverse affect on their performance. Put slightly differently, fear about the consequences that might follow the attainment of success would interfere with optimum performance. FS should be aroused particularly when the tasks involved were generally "considered masculine, such as tasks of mathematical, logical, spatial, etc., ability" (Horner, 1968, p. 24). An unwillingness to pay the price extracted from those who conspicuously contravene cultural norms may help to explain the lower performance of post-primary school girls, compared with boys, in mathematics, as well as the consistency of the findings that boys are over-represented among the top mathematics performers.

Conflict, as described and quantified by the FS construct and experienced by successful females, should be seen in tandem with the lower expectations of performance in mathematics expressed by girls, expectations that in time became self-fulfilling.

Sex differences in achievement motivation have also been linked with sex differences in attribution of success and failure. The few studies that have concentrated on success and failure attributions in a mathematics setting (Gitelson et al., 1982; Leder, 1982; Wolleat et al., 1980; Pedro et al., 1981) have reported less functional attributions of success and failure in mathematics by girls compared with boys. While the effect size of attributional patterns on performance in mathematics may be small, the consistency of findings in this area indicate that sex differences in attributions may provide another useful piece in the jigsaw of factors that contribute to sex differences in mathematics learning.

Factors such as the ones discussed so far can be organized constructively to increase our understanding of sex differences in mathematics learning in a number of different ways.

REFERENCES

Armstrong, J. and Price, R. A. Correlates and Predictors of Women's Mathematics Participation, *Journal for Research in Mathematics Education* 13, 1982, 99–109.

Dale, R. *Mixed or Single-sex Schools?*, Vol. III. London: Routledge & Kegan Paul, 1974.

Fennema, E. and Sherman, J. A. Sex-related Differences in Mathematics Achievement, Spatial Visualization, and Affective Factors, *American Educational Research Journal*, 14, 1977.

Fennema, E. and Sherman, J. A. Sex-Related Differences in Mathematics Achievement and Related Factors: A Further Study, *Journal for Research in Mathematics Education* 9, 1978, 189–203.

Gitelson, I. B., Peterson, A. C., and Tobin-Richards, M. H. Adolescents' Expectations of Success, Self-Evaluations, and Attributions About Performance on Spatial and Verbal Tasks, *Sex Roles* 8, 1982, 411–420.

Harding, J. Sex Differences in Science Examinations, in A. Kelly (ed.): *The Missing Half.* Manchester: Manchester University Press, 1981.

Horner, M. *Sex Differences in Achievement Motivation and Performance in Competitive and Non-competitive Situations*, Unpublished doctoral dissertation, University of Michigan, 1968.

Husen, T. (ed.) *International Study of Achievement in Mathematics: A Comparison* in Twelve Countries, Stockholm: Almquist & Wiksell, 1967.

Keeves, J. P. and Read, A. D. Sex Differences in Preparing for Scientific Occupations, Hawthorn, ACER, 1974.

Kelly, A. *An Unfair Profession: A Review of the Position of British Women in Science*, Edinburgh Centre for Educational Sociology, University of Edinburgh, 1974.

Lantz, A. E. and Smith, G. P. Factors Influencing the Choice of Nonrequired Mathematics Courses, *Journal of Educational Psychology* 73, 1981, 825–827.

Leder, G. C. Learned Helplessness in the Classroom: A Further Look, *Research in Mathematics Education in Australia* 2, 1982, 40–55.

Leder, G. C. What Price Success? The View from the Media, *The Exceptional Child* 31, in press.

Luchins, E. H. and Luchins, A. S. Female Mathematicians: A Contemporary Appraisal, in L. H. Fox, L. Brody, and D. Tobin (eds.), *Women and the Mathematical Mystique*, Baltimore: Johns Hopkins University Press, 1980.

Pedro, J. D., Wolleat, P., Fennema, E., and Becker, A. D. Election of High School Mathematics by Females and Males: Attributions and Attitudes, *American Educational Research Journal*, 1981, 207–218.

Rossi, A. S. Barriers to the Career Choice of Engineering, Medicine, or Science Among American Women, in J. M. Bardwick (ed.), *Readings in the Psychology of Women*, New York: Harper and Row, 1972.

Shuard, H. B. Differences in Mathematical Performance Between Girls and Boys, in W. H. Cockcroft (ed.) London: Mathematics Counts, HMSO, 1982.

Simkin, K. Sex Differences in Pupils' Commitment to School Success, *Australian Association for Research in Education Proceedings*, 1979, 123–131.

Stein, A. H. and Bailey, M. M. The Socialization of Achievement Motivation in Women, in M. T. S. Mednick, S. S. Tangri, and L. W. Hoffman (eds.), *Women and Achievement*, Washington: Hemisphere Publishing Company, 1975.

Wolleat, P. L., Pedro, J. D., Becker, A. D., Fennema, E. Sex Differences in High School Students Causal Attributions of Performance in Mathematics, *Journal for Research in Mathematics Education* 11, 1980, 356–366.

REFERENCES AND ADDITIONAL READINGS FOR UNIT I

Psychological Views of Children and Schools

Bereiter, Carl. "Education: An Affront to Personal Liberty?" *Learning* (October 1973): 16–17.

Brodinsky, Ben. "Back to the Basics: The Movement and Its Meaning." *Phi Delta Kappan* 58 (1977): 522–526.

Davis, E. D. "Should the Public Schools Teach Values?" *Phi Delta Kappan* 65 (1984): 358–360.

Dodd, Anne Westcott, "A New Design for Public Education." *Phi Delta Kappan* 65 (1984): 685–687.

Down, Graham A. "Why Basic Education?" *The Education Digest* (November 1977): 1–5.

Goodlad, John I. "The Great American Schooling Experiment." *Phi Delta Kappan* 67 (1985): 266–271.

Rogers, Carl R., & Skinner, B. F. "Some Issues Concerning the Control of Human Behavior: A Symposium." *Science* 124 (1956): 1057–1066.

Wasserman, Selma, "What Can Schools Become?" *Phi Delta Kappan* 65 (1984): 690–693.

Weinstein, Gerald, & Fantaini, Mario D. *Toward Humanistic Education: A Curriculum of Affect.* Ford Foundation Report, 1970.

Compensatory Education Twenty Years Later: Does It Work?

Bereiter, C. "The Changing Face of Educational Disadvantagement." *Phi Delta Kappan* 66 (1985): 538–541.

Goldring, E., & Schutte, L. "A Meta-Analysis of the Effectiveness of Preschool Intervention Programs." Paper presented at the annual meeting of the American Educational Research Association, New Orleans, 1984.

Jensen, A. "The Nonmanipulable and Effectively Manipulable Variables of Education." *Education and Society* 1 (1983): 51–62.

Rutter, M. "Family and School Influences on Cognitive Development." *Journal of Child Psychology and Psychiatry* 26 (1985): 683–704.

Sommer, R., & Sommer, B. "Mystery in Milwaukee: Early Intervention, IQ and Psychology Textbooks." *American Psychologist* 38 (1983): 982–983.

Zigler, E. "Assessing Headstart at 20: An Invited Commentary." *American Journal of Orthopsychiatry* 55 (1985) 603–609.

Right Brain–Left Brain: A Half-Brained Idea?

Annett, M. *Left, Right, Hand and Brain.* Hillsdale, NJ., Erlbaum, 1985.

Best, C. *Hemispheric Function and Collaboration in the Child.* New York: Academic, 1985.

Geschwind, N. "The Biology of Cerebral Dominance: Implications for Cognition." *Cognition,* 17 (1984): 193–208.

Harris, L. "Teaching the Right Brain: Historic Perspective on a Contemporary Fad." In C. Best (Ed.) *Hemispheric Function and Collaboration in the Child.* New York: Academic, 1985.

Springer, S., & Deutsch, G. *Left Brain, Right Brain.* New York: Springer, 1985.

Sex Differences in Mathematics Achievement: Nature Versus Nurture

Benbow, C., & Stanley, J. *"Academic Precocity: Aspects of its Development."* Baltimore, MD: John Hopkins Press, 1984.

Caplan, P., MacPherson, G., & Tobin, P. Do Sex-related Abilities in Spatial Abilities Exist? *American Psychologist* 40 (1985): 786–799.

Eccles, J., & Jacobs, J. "Gender Differences in Math Ability: The Impact of Media Reports on Parents." *Educational Researcher* 14 (1985): 20–25.

Fennema, E., & Peterson, P. "Autonomist Learning Behavior: A Possible Explanation of Gender-related Differences in Mathematics." In N. C. Wilkenson & C. Marrett (Eds.), *Gender Influences in Classroom Interaction.* New York: Academic, 1985.

Linn, M., & Petersen, A. "Emergence and Characterization of Sex Differences in Spatial Ability: A Meta-Analysis." *Child Development* 56 (1985): 1479–1498.

UNIT 2

Learning and Instruction

Do Learning Theories Aid Classroom Practice?

The Improvement of Instruction: Suggestions
from Behavioral and Cognitive Science

Should We Teach *for* Thinking,
about Thinking, or *of* Thinking?

Is Direct Instruction More Effective Than
Methods that Give Students More Freedom?

Mastery Learning: Effective for Whom?

Alternative Strategies for Modifying
Social and Emotional Behavior

Matching Learning and Teaching Styles

Do Learning Theories Aid Classroom Practice?

For many years, educational psychologists have sought to distill, from psychological theory and research, general guides to learning that may be used to improve instruction. How successful have they been? Are their ideas for improving learning as useful in classroom instruction as they are in the laboratory?

In his Presidential Address to the Division of General Psychology of the American Psychological Association, Dr. Wilbert McKeachie traces the history of psychologists' efforts to develop true laws of learning that will hold for both laboratory animals and school students. He concludes that in the past these efforts have failed because they have not taken into account the unique characteristics of human learners or the complexities of classroom situations. He states that educators have been attracted and misled by the apparent simplicity of the "laws" of learning presented by B. F. Skinner and other psychologists. His remarks help to clarify the seriousness of the challenge psychologists and teachers face in attempting to make education more meaningful and humane.

In the 1980s, Professors Gordon Bower and Ernest Hilgard find learning theorists' advice on classroom applications useful. They present twelve such recommendations as generally useful ideas, not prescriptions for practice. They caution against what they refer to as a "medicine cabinet" approach. A teacher should not expect to be able to take a psychological "principle" and apply it like an ointment to an educational "sore spot." Effective application in particular situations requires greater knowledge, good judgment and experience. Yet these authors believe that classroom application of laboratory findings is not to be entirely rejected, and that students of learning do offer very useful advice for classroom instruction.

Thought Questions

What similarities do you find between Hilgard and Bower's reservations about the direct application of learning principles and McKeachie's rejection of the laws of learning? Can the differences be reconciled to your satisfaction? Explain.

In what respects do the "ideas" or "principles" suggested by Hilgard and Bower differ from the "laws" with which McKeachie takes issue? Will the explication and explanation of principles, like those listed by Hilgard and

Bower, take educators in the "more useful" directions that McKeachie thinks desirable? Why or why not?

Theories of learning differ in the relative emphasis that they place on the learners' behavior and on their inner thoughts and feelings. Which of the principles listed by Hilgard and Bower would you attribute to theories that emphasize behavior, and which to those that emphasize internal processes of the learner? What differences would you expect to find in the practice of teachers who differ in the set of principles they choose to emphasize, the "behavioral" ones, or those concerned with thought and feeling? Which type of principle do you believe McKeachie would be most apt to agree with, and which set would he be most apt to challenge?

The authors of the readings on this issue suggest a considerable gap between knowing the principles of learning that are suggested by research and theory, and being able to apply these theories in real classrooms. After completing the readings and thinking about this problem, prepare your own statement about what is needed to close the gap.

The Decline and Fall of the Laws of Learning

*Wilbert J. McKeachie**

In his book, *Animal Intelligence* (1911), E. L. Thorndike wrote, "Two laws explain all learning." He then went on to document his case that all learning depends on the Law of Effect and the Law of Exercise. Thus appeared the "Laws of Learning," part of the basic tenets of psychological belief from that day on. In the decades following, the laws of learning were added to, restructured, and ornamented by new names, but the basic laws formulated by Thorndike remained at the center of both theoretical and applied formulations of learning. The major systematic attack upon them came from Tolman in his book *Purposive Behavior in Animals and Men* (1932). Hull and his students carried the major burden of the battle against Tolman so that the Laws of Learning recouched in Hullian terms continued to be part of the basic stuff in psychology. Even though Thorndike himself later made the Law of Exercise subordinate, the Law of Effect continued to be defended into the 1950s and 1960s and

From *Review of Educational Research* (March 1974): 7–11. Copyright 1974 American Educational Research Association, Washington, D.C. Reprinted with permission.

*Arthur Melton, John Atkinson, and David Birch read an earlier version of this paper and aided in my education. The remaining fault is in the learner rather than in the teaching they gave me.

one would have been hard put to find the portents of decline in the outpouring of research articles on learning in the late 1940s and 1950s. One such portent surely was Spence's exasperated statement that Hullian theory was only a theory of rat learning, but the basic notion of the fundamental nature of the laws of exercise and effect persisted even after the great debates between Hull and Tolman, Spence and Krechevsky, and their later followers began to decline in intensity.

Only one sturdy defender of faith in the Laws of Learning carried the gospel to the unenlightened with continuing zeal. B. F. Skinner, in "The Science of Learning and the Art of Teaching," said:

> Some promising advances have been made in the field of learning. The Law of Effect has been taken seriously; we have made sure that effects do occur and that they occur under conditions which are optimal for producing the changes called learning—(In the teaching of arithmetic) when is a numerical operation reinforced as right?—In the early stages the reinforcement of being right is usually accorded by the teacher. The contingencies she provides are far from optimal.—The lapse of only a few seconds between response and reinforcement destroys most of the effect—many seconds or minutes intervene between the child's response and the teacher's reinforcement. In many cases—for example when papers are taken

home to be corrected—as much as twenty-four hours may intervene. It is surprising that this system has any effect whatsoever.

After this assertion of the importance of immediacy of reinforcement, a point made by Thorndike in his original statement, Skinner goes on to depict the dire state of modern education due to its failure to use the results of learning research and calls upon psychologists and others to change the schools. He says, "We can no longer allow the urgencies of a practical situation to suppress the tremendous improvements which are within reach. The practical situation must be changed."

Skinner then describes teaching machines incorporating the following principles of learning:

1. Practice of the correct responses (the Law of Exercise)
2. Knowledge of results and reinforcement of the right answer (the Law of Effect)
3. Minimum delay of reinforcement
4. Successive small steps with hints "so that the answers of the average child will almost always be right," an approach having some elements of Thorndike's Law of Associative Shifting, a law proposed by Thorndike somewhat later than Exercise and Effect.

Skinner asserted that teaching machines using these principles would be much more effective than teachers working without them and predicted that teaching machines would be commonplace in all instructional situations (Evans, 1965, p. 59). That prediction seemed well on the road to confirmation in the 1960s as both large corporations and individual entrepreneurs rushed in to capitalize on the Skinner-based technological resolution in education. But today teaching machines seem to have survived less well than hula hoops. Probably the most important thing Skinnerian teaching machines have taught us is that teaching machines are often not very effective teachers.

There are a number of reasons for this— and as psychologists anxious to defend the

value of our field, we are likely to be most critical of the technology of teaching machines— to feel that they simply were inconvenient and poorly designed. My thesis is that the weakness is more fundamental. It is not the teaching machine but the laws of learning themselves which were inadequate (at least when applied to human cognitive learning). The points I shall make are not new to learning theorists. They have been expressed and debated in one form or another for many years. But in our undergraduate teaching, in our advice to educators, in our attempts at applications—the laws of learning have continued to be fundamental. My thesis today is that the laws of learning have *fallen* from preeminence in basic learning theory and that in educational learning and other applications, we must also depose them to a place in more complex structures.

The central law, of course, was the Law of Effect, later dubbed reinforcement. The nature and necessity of reinforcement has long been a major point of theoretical controversy. When I was a graduate student, we eagerly watched for new installments of the debate and for the research on latent learning and other attempts to demonstrate that learning could occur without reinforcement. More recently Walker (1969), Bindra (1969), Leeper (1970), Bolles (1972), Logan (1969), Atkinson and Wickens (1971), Estes (1971), and others [e.g., McKeachie (1957), McKeachie and Doyle (1966)] have not only challenged the idea that reinforcement automatically stamps in stimulus-response connections but in some instances have questioned the notion that any useful function is served by the concept of reinforcement.

I shall not review the research evidence at this point since Bolles' *Psychological Review* article does this well. I know that these experiments (e.g., Harlow's monkeys who were less effective in solving puzzles for a food reward than for no reward) can be interpreted in a reinforcement framework. Nevertheless it seems to me that when, as in some of the human studies I shall cite later, a child does less well in learning when materially rewarded, the Law of Effect can no longer be regarded as the first commandment for education.

Most of the alternatives for reinforcement suggested by other theorists emphasize the information value of reinforcement procedures and at least preserve the principle of knowledge of results. As you recall, one of Thorndike's (1931, p. 9) classic experiments was that in which a subject was asked to draw four-inch lines with his eyes closed. After 3,000 trials he was no better than on the earlier trials, demonstrating that practice without knowledge of results does not produce learning. Even those who denied reinforcement as a law of learning have generally accepted the principle that learning depends upon feedback or knowledge of results, and, as we have seen, this was one of the principles determining the design of teaching machines and programming learning.

If we drop reinforcement, can we fall back to "knowledge of results" as the really fundamental law of learning in human education? Even here the research evidence is not very encouraging. For example, Olson (1972) found that giving college students knowledge of results on quiz items failed to produce generally better final performance than no knowledge of results and Oner (1972) also found no effect of feedback or praise in learning decimals in a programmed lesson. Similarly Pambookian (1972) and Centra (1972) found no overall improvement by teachers given feedback from student ratings of their teaching.

One immediately wonders about immediacy of feedback. Perhaps when knowledge of results was ineffective, it was because it did not occur promptly. Skinner has again and again called attention to the long delays in knowledge of results and reinforcement in most classroom situations and asserted that one of the strengths of programmed learning would be that reinforcement of correct responses would occur immediately. How important is immediate knowledge of results?

As early as 1935, Guthrie, in *The Psychology of Learning*, had cast doubts on the principle of immediacy of reinforcement by pointing out that a child spanked an hour after writing on the living room wall will usually learn not to write on the wall if he is told why he is being punished. Laboratory research on delay of reinforcement is also not consistent nor clear in supporting immediacy. (Atkinson and Wickens, 1971, Bourne, 1966). But here we are concerned about human educational learning. When we examine this arena, research evidence on prompt feedback in programmed learning similarly fails to support Skinner's position. Immediate knowledge of results has seemed in several studies to make little difference in learning or even to be detrimental (e.g., Sturges, 1972, Kulhavy and Anderson, 1972). Programmed instruction proponents were understandably aghast to find that immediate knowledge of the correct response (expected to be a reinforcer) did not facilitate learning in programmed instruction. Anderson, Kulhavy, and Andre (1971) suspected that the reason prompt knowledge of results didn't work was that when knowledge of the correct result is immediately available, students become inattentive and careless in trying to answer the question. Thus Anderson et al. used a computer to give knowledge of correct response only after the student gave an answer. This helped. Moreover, on a test of immediate recall (but not on retention) a group who had been allowed during learning to peek at the correct response, whether or not they had given an answer, scored lower than students who had no feedback of the correct response.

One suspects that in a typical programmed learning situation in which most of the learner's responses are right, the cost of time required to get feedback seems to the learner to be too high for the value of information he receives. We might expect more positive effects of feedback in situations in which the task is more difficult and the information provided thus greater. But the Law of Effect and even the principle of knowledge of results can no longer stand as the major support of learning.

And what about the Law of Exercise? As I indicated earlier, this fell into decline even in Thorndike's own lifetime. His experiment on drawing four-inch lines had convinced him that practice does *not* make perfect, and by 1931 he had relegated exercise to a secondary role. Extinction procedures also demonstrated that practice did not necessarily strengthen learning. Yet active practice done correctly with an attempt to minimize errors has remained as a general practical principle of education. In Skinnerian programmed learning, application of this principle involved constructed responses and small steps. This practice too seems to be of dubious value. Wright (1967) found that paragraphs were better than short frames and that reading the responses was superior to writing them. Such results are not uniformly found but are common enough to suggest that a constructed response and small steps are not uniformly facilitative of learning. The Keller plan (1968), now widely used in college courses, has departed widely from this aspect of programmed learning even though generally based upon Skinnerian concepts.

Thorndike's statement that his two laws would explain all learning is no longer tenable and Skinner's assertion that teaching machines would be vastly superior to teachers is even less supportable. The Laws of Learning have fallen from their central place in our psychological lexicon. Yet we cannot help feeling that they contain much truth. Even though the underlying principles may have been flawed, teaching machines were sometimes effective. Surely we should be able to recycle the cores of the laws of learning into something of use, and in the remainder of this paper I'd like to attempt this.

As I see it, there are two reasons for the failure of the Laws of Learning. Some of the problems in trying to apply the laws of learning to educational situations have been failures to take account of differences between humans and other animals—e.g., Man's greater ability to conceptualize, relate and remember. Other problems have simply derived from failure to take account of important variables controlled in laboratory situations but interacting with independent variables in natural educational settings.

For example, let us look more closely at the Law of Effect. Skinner and his followers have usually taken a fairly pragmatic stance toward reinforcers—often analyzing with great acuity and indefatigability the reinforcers in a particular situation. In many cases they have suc-

ceeded, but as I noted earlier, some of the difficulties encountered in using reinforcement theory could be avoided by conceptualizing the usual "reinforcers" as combining two kinds of feedback—informational and affective. In simple human learning situations the reward tells the individual what the correct answer is and also tells him that getting the answer will have pleasant consequences. Even devoted Skinnerians ruefully admit that Skinnerian learning programs are usually boring—a problem deriving, I contend, from failure to take seriously the research literature on motivation, a construct Skinner would prefer to omit.

If one differentiates informational and affective feedback, some of the complex results of differing effects of reinforcers from elementary school learning seem reasonable. One hypothesis, for example, would be, as I stated earlier, that the value of feedback would depend upon the information it provided. Another hypothesis would be that informational feedback would be helpful for improvement in performance for a motivated student but Thorndike's "satisfiers" would be necessary for improvements in performance for those with little motivation for educational learning.

Studies of social class differences in educational achievement tend to support this hypothesis (if one assumes that low achieving children are less motivated for conventional school learning). A number of studies shows that informing a child of the correctness of his response increases achievement for middle-class normally-achieving children, while other children may learn more effectively when given praise or tangible rewards (Terrell, Durkin and Wesley, 1959; Zigler and DeLabry, 1962; Zigler and Kanzer, 1962). Similarly, Blair (1972) showed that normal achievers in the third grade learned more effectively for informational feedback or praise than for tangible rewards, and Cradler and Goodwin (1971) found that in groups of second and sixth graders, sixth grade middle class subjects were more responsive to praise and symbolic feedback while second grade lower class children were more responsive to candy.

Since teachers are likely to emphasize symbolic and social rewards, differences in educational achievement between social classes may be due in some part to lack of effective rewards for motivating underachieving children. It may well be that some Skinnerian techniques, such as fading or schedules of reinforcement, would be useful if applied to teaching motivation for learning activities rather than being directed solely to input-output relationships (where they are inadequate).

The effect of knowledge of results is also clarified if we introduce motivational constructs. Means and Means (1971), for example, found that low grade point average students who were told that they had done *well* on an aptitude test did better on the mid-term in an adolescent psychology course. For high grade point average students, being told that they had done *poorly* produced better performance. Such results remind one of Jack Atkinson's theory that achievement motivation is highest when probabilities of success are moderate.

If one hopes to use reward or knowledge of results to affect human learning, he needs to know something about what expectancies of reward the learner brings to the situation, both in terms of the incentive value of the reward and the learner's estimate of the probability of achieving the reward. This helps explain why knowledge of results is often ineffective in programmed learning. A model Skinnerian program is written with very low probabilities of error. Thus the learner's probability of success on a given frame is often 90 percent or higher. Obviously knowledge of results provides little information here, and also, in terms of achievement motivation theory, this is a region of low motivation—thus, one becomes bored. Consequently, neither the informational nor the affective component of the feedback are potent in the typical Skinnerian program.

On the other hand, when the feedback is discrepant from expectancies (providing more information and perhaps more motivation), learning may occur. Thus Centra, who found no overall effect of feedback of student ratings on teacher improvement, found that teachers who initially rated themselves more favorably than their students did change the direction suggested by the student ratings. Feedback of student ratings thus helped when it was discrepant from expectancy. And on the motivational side, Pambookian (1972) found that feedback to instructors did not help those who were rated as highly effective or as ineffective, but did help those rated as being moderately effective—again fitting the theory of achievement motivation, i.e., those rated poorly had such low probabilities of success that we would expect discouragement, withdrawal, or defensiveness; but those rated in the middle had a moderate probability of success as teachers and thus were at optimal motivation levels.

Pambookian's results fit nicely with those of Flook and Robinson (1972), who found that among students who were told their intelligence and anxiety test scores, those in the middle range of intelligence were the only group to show achievement during the freshman year superior to that of a control group not told their scores. Similarly, Hammer (1972) showed that teachers' comments on undergraduate physics papers had a positive effect on later performance, expecially when the comments were made with reference to the student's expected grade. These latter comments, from the examples given, seem likely to have moved probability of success to an intermediate level, thus increasing motivation and performance.

But motivation and information about what one has done wrong is not enough. It is fitting that I learned from E. L. Thorndike's grandson, Robert M. Thorndike, what I regard as the best generalization we can currently make. He suggests that knowledge of results eventuates in improved performance when the learner is motivated, when the knowledge of results is informative and when the learner knows or is told what to do to correct his errors.

When we turn to the principle of immediacy of reinforcement, we find once again that our basic law is reusable if we add some complications. Probably the chief reason that immediate reinforcement is often not important for human learning is that human beings can attend to and remember critical features of a learning situation better than many other experimental subjects. Thus Goldstein and Siegel

(1972) found that immediate reinforcement in a task requiring discrimination learning of geometric figures was more effective than delayed reinforcement only when the subjects had no previous exposure to the figures and when they were not present during the delay. This suggests that delayed reinforcement should work as well as (or better than) immediate reinforcement if the relevant stimuli and responses are attended to and the subject can remember what he is being reinforced for. The laboratory research in this area is still not conclusive, but it is clear that what happens during the delay is important. Sturges (1972), for example, suggests that the advantages of delayed feedback found in his own and other studies may be due to the learner's exploration and organization of the material before feedback. Delayed feedback was also superior to immediate feedback in the experiment of Kulhavy and Anderson (1972) and their design provided support for the theory that the delay permits potentially interfering errors to be forgotten as well as contributing to greater attention to the feedback.

It probably appears that this lecture has been rather hard on one of the greatest figures of modern psychology, B. F. Skinner, and I confess that his confident assertions in *The Technology of Teaching* provided the primary stimulus for my choice for this topic. The research evidence, I believe, demonstrates that each point enunciated by Skinner is untrue—at least in as general a sense as he believed. This does not mean that Skinner's attempts to influence education have been bad or that the principles are completely false; rather, his attempt to make a systematic effort at application has revealed that what we psychologists once took to be the verities hold only under limited conditions. As a result, new vistas of needed research have been revealed.

If the laws of learning are inadequate why has Skinnerian psychology been so popular? The answer, I think, lies in its simplicity. Education is ever seeking the philosopher's stone that will transmute stubborn, unmotivated students into learners. Skinner's pitch for his philosopher's stone is persuasive and powerful. Like any good salesman he shows how easy his psychology is to use. Those who buy his approach find that the basic ideas are simple to apply and work often enough to maintain their enthusiasm.

This is no small matter. Anyone who can take discouraged, dispirited teachers, mental health aides, or prison officials and revive their hope and vigor has done a great deal. Probably no one thing is more important in education than the teacher's enthusiasm and energy.

But once hope is revived and a start has been made, we need to take teachers beyond the level of the speeches I used to make to them about the principles of learning. Now I believe that these principles may apply most clearly to the learning of animals in highly controlled artificial situations. It may well be that they also have application to other restricted situations, but meaningful educational learning is both more robust and more complex. This complexity, so frustrating to those who wish to prescribe education methods, is a reminder of the fascinating uniqueness of the learner. Fortunately most educational situations are interactive situations in which a developing, learning human being engages with a situation in ways designed to meet his learning needs. Part of that situation is another human being who has some resources for instruction and some capacity to adapt to the learner. It is this that makes education both endlessly challenging and deeply humane.

REFERENCES

Anderson, R. C.; Kulhavy, R. W.; and Andre, T. "Feedback Procedures in Programmed Instruction." *Journal of Educational Psychology*, 1971, 62: 148–156.

Atkinson, R. C., and Wickens, T. D. "Human Memory and the Concept of Reinforcement." *The Nature of Reinforcement*, R. Glaser, ed. New York and London: Academic Press, 1971, pp. 66–87.

Bindra, D. "The Interrelated Mechanisms of Reinforcement and Motivation, and the Nature of Their Influence on Response." *Nebraska Symposium on Motivation*, 1969, 17: 1–37.

Blair, J. R. "The Effects of Differential Reinforcement on the Discrimination Learning of Normal and Low-achieving Middle-class Boys." *Child Development*, 1972, 43: 251–255.

Bolles, R. C. "Reinforcement, Expectancy, and Learning." *Psychological Review*, 1972, 79: 394–409.

Bourne, L. E. "Information Feedback: Comments on Professor I. McD. Bilodeau's Paper," In E. A. Bolodeau, ed., *Acquisition of Skill* (New York: Academic Press, 1966), 297–313.

Centra, J. A. "The Utility of Student Ratings for Instructional Improvement." Educational Testing Service. 1972, 74 pp.

Cradler, J. D. and Goodwin, D. L. "Conditioning of Verbal Behavior as a Function of Age, Social Class, and Type of Reinforcement," *Journal of Educational Psychology*, 1971, 62: 279–285.

Evans, R. I. *B. F. Skinner: The Man and His Ideas* (New York: Dutton, 1968).

Estes, W. K. "Reward in Human Learning: Theoretical Issues and Strategic Choice Points." *The Nature of Reinforcement*, R. Glaser, ed. (New York: Academic Press, 1971), 16–44.

Flook, A. J. M., and Robinson, P. J. "Academic Performance with and without Knowledge of Scores on Tests of Intelligence, Aptitude, and Personality: A Further Study," *Journal of Educational Psychology*, 1972, 63: 123–129.

Goldstein, and Siegel, 1972. (I've lost this one. If any reader recognizes it, I'd be grateful for the reference, W. McKeachie.)

Guthrie, E. R. *The Psychology of Learning* (New York: Harper, 1935).

Hammer, B. "Grade Expectations, Differential Teacher Comments and Student Performance."

Journal of Educational Psychology, 1972, 63: 505–512.

Keller, F. S. "Good-bye, Teacher." *Journal of Applied Behavioral Analysis*, 1968, 1: 79–89.

Kulhavy, R. W., and Anderson, R. C. "Delay-retention Effect with Multiple-choice Tests." *Journal of Educational Psychology*, 1972, 63: 505–512.

Leeper, R. W. "Cognitive Learning Theory." In M. H. Marx, ed., *Learning Theories* (New York: Macmillan, 1970).

Logan, F. A. *Fundamentals of Learning and Motivation* (Dubuque, Iowa: Brown, 1969).

McKeachie, W. J. "Expectancy Concepts in the First Course." Paper delivered at the symposium "Key Concepts in Elementary Psychology," APA Meeting, 1957.

McKeachie, W. J., and Doyle, C. *Psychology*, 1st ed. (Reading, Mass.: Addison-Wesley, 1966).

Means, R. S., and Means, G. H. "Achievement as a Function of the Presence of Prior Information Concerning Aptitude." *Journal of Educational Psychology*, 1971, 62: 185–187.

Olson, G. H. "A Multivariate Examination of the Effects of Behavioral Objectives, Knowledge of Results, and the Assignment of Grades on the Facilitation of Classroom Learning." Doctoral thesis, *Dissertation Abstract International*, 1972, 32: 6214–6215.

Oner, N. P. "Impact of Teacher Behavior and Teaching Technique on Learning by Anxious Children." *Dissertation Abstract International*, 1972, 32: 6215.

Pambookian, H. S. "The Effect of Feedback from Students to College Instructors on Their Teaching Behavior." Unpublished dissertation, University of Michigan, 1972.

Skinner, B. F. "The Science of Learning and the Art of Teaching." *Harvard Educational Review*, 1954, 24: 86–97.

Skinner, B. F. *The Technology of Teaching*. (New York: Appleton-Century-Crofts, 1968).

Ideas from Learning Theory Useful in Education

Gordon H. Bower and Ernest R. Hilgard

While we do not support the medicine-cabinet view of application, the direct application of knowledge from the laboratory to the classroom is not to be entirely rejected. Very often the laboratory knowledge helps us to understand what some of the important variables and influences are, even before these have been formulated in a more prescriptive form. Such principles permit a better analysis by pointing out where to look and what to expect. Students of learning who have not devoted themselves primarily to problems of instruction can still give some very useful advice. Some of this advice comes from those oriented toward S-R theories, some from those who tend more toward cognitive theories, some from those whose concern is with motivation and personality.

1. *Behavioral objectives.* For the behaviorist, the goals of any educational program must be stipulated in concrete behavioral terms—preferably in behaviors that can be measured. Only then can the teacher begin to know how to design a program that will shape the student's behavior towards those goals, and to evaluate the extent to which they have been met. Specifying educational goals in terms of behavioral objectives goes against tradition, which usually states goals in loftier terms of attitudes, analytical skills, understanding, and appreciation of the subject matter. Mager (1961) was an early proponent of writing behavioral objectives for education and wrote an early guidebook on how to translate vague goals into measurable behaviors (see also, Mager, 1972). The translation process itself has a beneficial effect on the teacher and student alike, in forcing the teacher to reflect upon precisely what he or she believes is most important for the student to know, and what student behaviors will comprise evidence for his or her knowing those things. Writing behavioral objectives has become a popular and widespread practice in many school systems as part of the public's concern for accountability of the teaching system. For instance, the parents whose child is taking fifth-grade reading can be told in detail what specific reading competencies the child can be expected to demonstrate by the end of the course. Often, commercial tutoring agencies for reading or math will advertise their programs in specific terms of advancing behavioral objectives of the learner. These changes in stipulating educational goals have

From Gordon H. Bower and Ernest R. Hilgard, *Theories of Learning* (5th ed.), Englewood Cliffs, N.J.: Prentice-Hall, 1981, pp. 538–545. Reprinted with permission.

largely been brought about by the behaviorists' influence on teaching.

2. *Task or skill analysis.* Implicit in the push for stating educational goals in behavioral terms is the requirement that the educator analyze the criterion task (for example, multiplying two three-digit numbers) into the elementary behavioral components and note how they are organized. This leads, in turn, to assessing the child's initial repertoire and designing an educational program to teach the several components of the criterion skill. For multiplying two 3-digit numbers, the child must be taught, among other things, to write the numbers in column form, to proceed multiplying bottom right to left, to carry the tens digit of one multiplication and add it to the next column, to shift the starting point of the second and third lines of the multiplication over one place, and so on. Such microanalyses reveal just how complex are the skills commonly taught in school. Work by a psychologist, Gagné (1970; Gagné & Briggs, 1974), has been especially helpful in decomposing various educational competencies into a *hierarchy* of subskills, noting how one depends on another. . . . The idea of skill analysis has been widely applied in educational research (see Calfee & Drum, 1978, for a task analysis of elementary reading skills).

3. *Shaping.* The analysis of an educational goal into a hierarchy or series of behavioral components implies an educational program. In particular, the fundamental skills are taught first because, according to task analysis, other parts of the criterion competency depend on these. Thus, two-digit multiplication is not taught until the child already can do one-digit multiplication and can add; addition is not taught until the child can identify and use the numbers themselves discriminatively. Thus, a criterion task analysis sets out the *order* in which the component skills should be taught and mastered. This training progression from simple to complex, from a single behavioral unit to a sequence of units, is most like Skinner's *shaping* procedure in which complex skills are taught to animals. One difference is

that in shaping animals the trainer must wait for an approximation of the desired response to occur before she can reinforce it, whereas for children the teacher (or text) typically instructs by describing the correct response or by demonstrating it with some examples. Of course, if the children have severe language deficits or consistently fail to attend to the teacher, the teacher must use operant conditioning methods (see, e.g., Lovaas, 1976, on teaching language to nonverbal psychotic children).

4. *Active responding.* Behaviorists have a strong belief that people learn best by actively manipulating the learning material, responding to it, and relating one part to another. Guthrie, Thorndike, and Skinner have emphasized active responding. People are most likely to learn from text if they ask questions about it, then search the text for answers, then actively recite the answers to themselves. A number of verbal experiments (e.g., Bobrow & Bower, 1969; Slamecka & Graf, 1978) have shown that adults better remember information that they have had to connect actively in some prescribed way. For example, adults in experiments by Bower and Masling (1979) showed much better memory for a set of fake correlational statements or empirical laws (e.g., "the rate of schizophrenia increases with family size") if subjects were forced to invent a causal explanation of each within a few seconds. Generating one's own explanation proved much more beneficial than reading an explanation generated by someone else. Further, all reading improvement courses emphasize the importance of readers actively outlining in their minds the contents of what they are reading, then quickly jotting down that outline after first skimming the material. The outline is then to be filled out or corrected as students read over the material at a more deliberate pace.

Another example of active responding is in learning mathematics. Math seems to be taught and learned largely by working through many thousands of example problems. The problems exemplify certain mathematical concepts, operations, or rules. In learning mathematics, we practice doing so many of these examples that we achieve a level where we can perform correctly some time later without being able to state the general rules of mathematics that justify our performance (e.g., the detailed algebraic steps in solving two linear equations in two unknowns). The rules have been translated into automatic habits, or "productions," that are carried out largely without verbalization of conscious effort. . . .

5. *Recitation and practice.* For most basic academic skills like reading, writing, and arithmetic, there simply is no substitute for repeated practice. Only with much practice will these habits become automatic and be performed rapidly and effortlessly. Because the habits based on the rules must be general (e.g., multiply *any* three-digit number), one obviously must practice over a variety of specific examples of the rule. The practice is also most beneficial if each response is followed by feedback on whether it is right or wrong, and, if wrong, where the error lies.

Many studies in verbal learning have shown the beneficial influence on later memory of having the subject practice reciting the material to be learned. A classic experiment by Gates (1971) showed that after a necessary minimum time spent passively reading the material to be learned (biographies in one experiment, nonsense syllables in another), students learned more not by reading it over and over again but trying actively to recite the material from memory, prompting or reminding themselves with the text to fill in forgotten details. The findings have held up rather well with other materials over the ensuing years. The value of active recitation is partly motivational, since the subject sets personal recall goals and checks her progress; the value is also partly informative, since her failures in one recitation pinpoint the specific material where learning and retention efforts should be concentrated in the next cycle. Further, it seems that later recall is largely a matter of retrieving the current plan for recitation.

Active recitation is a standard prescription of all guidebooks on study skills, and it is clearly beneficial. After reading a section of her text, the student is urged to outline its main points and to recite that outline and its contents from memory, at several distributed times.

6. *Prescribed study guides.* These rehearse-and-review prescriptions are the last two Rs of the famous SQ3R program for improving study skills (see Robinson, 1961) taught in most schools. The parts of the formula refer to important aspects of reading and assimilating textual material—say, a chapter of a school textbook. The first component is to *Survey* the contents of the chapter by skimming the section headings. The second is to pose some 5 to 10 *Questions* to yourself, questions that can be based on headings in the text. The third is to *Read* the text, seeking answers to the questions posed. The fourth is to *Recite* in your own words the contents of what you have just read and perhaps write it down in outline form. The fifth is to *Review* the outline and reread the chapter to refresh its major points.

The preliminary *Survey* gives the student a framework for organizing the many points about to be read. This outline acts as an *advance organizer* (Ausubel, 1960) that helps the learner categorize, pigeonhole, and interrelate the specific topics of the chapter. The underlying rationale behind advance organizers stems from the early Gestalt psychologists' belief that an array of information is best learned by *understanding* how it fits together, what parts depend upon or support others, and how it is organized. Of course, chapter outlines and lecture outlines do just this. Later research on learning from text (e.g., Meyer, 1975; Kintsch & van Dijk, 1979) has been concerned with the organization of expository texts, how the writer communicates this organization to the reader, and how this communication can be facilitated. . . .

A basic problem with such prescribed study aids is that students find them hard work (more so than passive reading), and so they tend not to take them up nor to continue with them unless some strong incentives (reinforcers) can be built in. Apparently, the student's wish for a high grade is too remote or weak a reinforcer. Most study-improvement programs, therefore, require self-reinforcement contingent on achieving daily study goals.

7. *Reinforcing task-relevant behaviors.*

The issue of reinforcing study behaviors is one example of the more general issue of shaping educationally relevant behaviors. The matter comes up in training students not only in self-directed study habits but also in proper "deportment" in the classroom. In elementary grades this usually means that the pupil is to be on time, sit quietly in his or her seat, attend to the teacher, and follow the teacher's instructions on whatever learning task is to be accomplished. These elemental behaviors seem necessary to promote an environment free of continual disruption and distraction, in which tutoring and learning have a chance to occur. In a later section, we will discuss some behavior modification techniques used in classroom management.

Turning to the learning activities themselves, psychologists have learned how to deal with many academic problems created by poor attention, poor concentration, and poor study habits. If a child finds that he cannot concentrate on his reading, the environment can be altered to minimize distractions; the reading material can also be altered to elicit and maintain a high level of concentration. One method devised by Guthrie is to have the student quit studying and leave his desk as soon as he notices his mind wandering from the task at hand. By this technique the desk and books become associated exclusively with studying, not with competing thoughts and daydreams. A more effective method is to ask the child to answer a question after every sentence or two of the lesson and immediately reward his correct answers in some manner. Over trials the number of sentences read before the quiz is increased, and the quiz questions ask for integration of information from several statements. This method may be supplemented with self-instruction (see Meichenbaum & Asarnow, 1979), where the child is taught to recite silently to herself (and follow) a guidance monologue before and during reading. The monologue emphasizes asking questions about the content of the passage, outlining it as one reads, relating one idea to another in the passage or to something else one knows, and so on. Such simple methods prove very effective in dealing with children who have had severe deficiencies in concentration and reading comprehension.

Adult study skills have also been improved through reinforcement procedures (Wark, 1976; Watson & Tharp, 1977). Typical problems occur with high school and college students who have not learned proper study habits. The usual program asks the student to observe and record her study behaviors for a week. Then a reinforcement training procedure is started in which the student studies in only one or two places that are free from distraction, and reinforces herself with some desired privilege (e.g., watching TV) only if she meets certain minimal study goals (usually time spent, pages read, or problems worked) on a given day. Frequently, the student writes her own "contract," specifying what study goals are to be achieved for what rewards to herself. As the program continues, the amount of work required for reinforcement increases, and the reinforcers become more symbolic (e.g., points earned towards a weekend movie). The student continues to be her own "observer and reinforcer" and usually keeps a graph of her cumulative study time on each academic course. The graph of one's self-induced accomplishments (e.g., pages written per day by an author) is frequently more reinforcing than almost any tangible reward. Along with these reinforcement techniques for increasing study time, the teacher also instructs the students on effective study methods such as SQ3R mentioned earlier, and methods for taking notes (on readings or lectures) and reviewing notes for promoting learning.

These reinforcement techniques are effective in overcoming procrastination, the bane of every student's (and professional's) life. The basic idea is to subdivide a large job into many small steps or subgoals, to set oneself just one subgoal at a time, and to reward oneself with a customary privilege (e.g., morning coffee, a pillow at night, reading the newspaper) only if the daily subgoal has been achieved. Getting support for one's program from a group or one's friends helps too, because of the social reinforcement and motivation.

8. *Test anxiety.* Although educators seldom think about test anxiety, students know it can be a problem. Some students panic during crucial exams, their hearts race, their hands shake, their minds go blank; they interpret exam questions in stupid ways, give answers that they later recognize to be wrong, and waste time worrying over the consequences of their behavior. Psychologists consider test anxiety to be just one example of a learned fear, and like other fears, it may be greatly reduced with the right treatment. One successful technique is *systematic desensitization.* . . . A procedure developed by Wolpe (1958), who followed Guthrie's idea of counterconditioning, desensitization tries to substitute the relaxation response for the tension and fear the student experiences in the test situation. The student is first taught deep-muscle relaxation, and then in imagination he pairs relaxation with visualized scenes that gradually approximate the test situations that evoke the most anxiety. With repeated practice and visualization the student extinguishes his fear, and this behavioral state should transfer to the real-life situation. The relaxation procedure should be supplemented whenever possible by having the student relax in the actual room where the exam will occur, take a mock exam, and so on. The student is instructed to relax consciously while taking the exam, and to recite a stream of coping instructions to himself: "Relax, this isn't so terrible. Concentrate on the problem. Keep cool. Think of alternative problem-solving attacks. Breathe deeply. Let your neck, jaw, and shoulders relax. Work steadily, you'll be done soon" (Meichenbaum, 1977). The student may also be taught specific test-taking skills—how to guess optimally on multiple-choice questions, how to overview a test and budget one's time, how to outline the answer to an essay question before starting to write, and so on. Using these techniques with test-phobic students, psychologists have enabled them to dramatically reduce their anxiety during test-taking and consequently improve their test performances and grades (Osterhouse, 1976).

9. *Goals and interests.* Psychologists have always stressed that learning is best fostered by capturing the learner's *interest* in the subject matter. Interest is a nonanalytic cover term for many factors, but it usually refers either to the reinforcing nature of the material itself (such as cartoon and comic book rewards for children) or to the child's perception that learning the material has a clear instrumental value for attaining some recognizable goal other than a course grade. This linkage of learning and life goals is what is meant by "relevance" in academic subjects. Many school texts and workbooks strongly emphasize the relation between the subject matter and everyday practical problems. Field trips also enhance the relevance of classroom learning. Some university psychology and education classes have students actively apply what they learn by working directly with psychiatric patients, retarded or emotionally disturbed children, drug addicts, and various others. These learning experiences are valuable not only to the students but to the recipients as well. The experiences often significantly increase the students' motivation to learn and use what they are studying in a classroom.

At another level, educators and psychologists have found it most useful to give students more freedom to set their own goals, learn at their own pace, and monitor their own progress (Goodwin & Coates, 1976). However, students can set their own goals only after they have been trained to work responsibly and effectively, and to set goals that correspond to those of the school system—for example, reading at or above a certain level of proficiency. But within this framework, self-directed learners are likely to be happier and better learners; they monitor their work rate, set their subgoals according to what they can realistically demand of themselves, and choose reinforcement schedules or backup rewards that are most satisfying to them. These procedures provide motivation, impart a feeling of success, and increase self-esteem, confidence, and competence. The best feature of self-directed learners, of course, is that they are only minimally dependent on the teacher, and are likely to continue learning when the formal requirements of school are no longer in force. The disadvantage is that self-directed learners create problems with the class schedule, curriculum, and teacher activities. Innovative planning and a change in traditional routines are required to make self-directed learning work.

10. *Perceptual structuring of tasks.*   A common prescription from Gestalt psychologists for designing instructional materials is to make the perceptual display highlight the essential features of the problem. Visual aids such as films, pictures, and diagrams can present information organized in space in a manner resembling its conceptual organization. For example, the information in a text passage describing what people belong to what groups, and which groups belong to which organizations, can be depicted as a tree diagram or a network with nodes representing groups, and arrows between nodes representing the "is a member of" relation. The visual aid materially improves memory for the passage itself. Similarly, in presenting physics problems to students, a helpful text will diagram a corresponding physical model or situation with the relevant factors highlighted. These prescriptions for perceptual emphasis are widely known by curriculum and text writers, although they are not always respected.

In teaching complex concepts to children, a frequently helpful strategy (suggested by learning theorists) is to show many close, contrasting negative instances ("near misses") along with a variety of positive instances. Figure 1 shows clusters of positive and negative instances for teaching children the concept of the handwritten capital letter *A*. Seeing the handwritten variations within the positive instances enables the child to isolate critical features and their allowable range of variation. The set of

near-miss negatives also enables the child to learn which features must be in an *A* (such as a crossbar near the middle of the legs) or must not be there (such as an extra crossbar or vertical line inside the legs). Each near miss highlights a slightly different contrasting feature or relation among parts needed for an *A* pattern, and enables the child to develop a sophisticated rule for this discrimination. These prescriptions, using near misses to teach difficult concepts (e.g., distinguish *tourist* from immigrant), strike us as good common sense and second-nature to teachers, yet the rules were in fact suggested by laboratory research on discrimination learning.

11. *Teaching of understanding.*   Laboratory research, initially by Gestalt psychologists such as Katona (1940), has demonstrated that material learned by understanding the reasons (or the rules) underlying some phenomenon is better retained and more easily transferred than is the same material learned by rote memorization. In mathematics, for example, a student is far better off (for later tests) learning the mechanism underlying the generation of the binomial distribution than he is in just memorizing the final formula for the distribution. Similarly, students must learn the sense of a mathematical derivation, such as differentiation of trigonometric functions, rather than just the formula, because later remembering of the sense will allow the student to rederive the formula long after he would have forgotten it from rote memory. The reasons for the rapid forgetting of meaningless statistical formulas are obvious: the many formulas being remembered are similar and interfere with one another, and there is no rule to help sort them out; whereas the concepts underlying the formulas are meaningful, well differentiated, and interconnected in a logical system of rules.

Teachers usually realize that learning by understanding is preferable (when it is possible), and try to teach pupils to understand concepts, their interrelations, and the basis for operations and rules. Unfortunately, if students fail to understand at the conceptual level, they

POSITIVE (AS)   NEGATIVE (NOT AS)

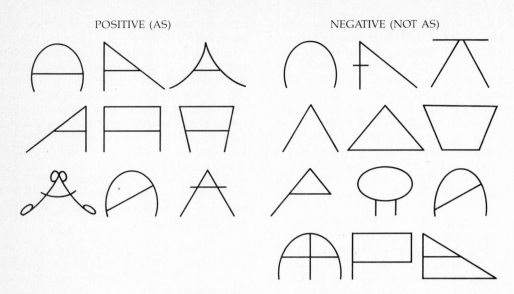

A collection of positive and near-miss negative examples of As.

will often panic and revert to the rote memorization of formulas.

12. *Mnemonic devices.* Over the ages, various showmen as well as teachers have developed a battery of memory aids or mnemonic devices to help themselves or their students learn material of importance to them. A mnemonic device is a method for elaborating some material to be learned, making it more meaningful, relating it to things that are known, and guiding one's recall. The aim is to improve learning and recall. . . .

Mnemonics are attempts to solve practical memory problems. The methods vary with the material to be learned and the way in which memory will be tested. The array of methods is laid out in most of the popular books on memory improvement (Furst, 1958; Lorayne & Lucas, 1974). Laboratory tests show that the methods are usually effective, often dramatically so. Let us briefly mention some of the most helpful mnemonic devices.

One technique for learning numbers (say, telephone numbers) is to break them into small groups of 3 or 4 digits, convert each digit to a stock consonant sound (e.g., all 2's are n's, all 4's are r's, and so on), then add whatever vowels you can to make a meaningful word for each group. The code words are then remembered in association with the person having that phone number. The code words are reconverted to the number when it is needed.

REFERENCES

Ausubel, D. P. (1960). The Use of Advance Organizers in the Learning and Retention of Meaningful Verbal Learning. *J. Ed. Psychol.*, 51: 267–472.

Bobrow, S. A., & Bower, G. H. (1969). Comprehension and Recall of Sentences. *J. Exp. Psychol.*, 80: 445–461.

Calfee, R. C., & Drum, P. A. (1978). Learning to Read: Theory, Research, and Practice. *Curr. Inq.*, 8: 183–249.

Furst, B. (1958). *Stop Forgetting: How to Develop Your Memory and Put it to Practical Use.* Garden City, N.Y.: Doubleday.

Gagné, R. M. (1970). *The Conditions of Learning.* Rev. ed., New York: Holt, Rinehart & Winston.

Gagné, R. M., & Briggs, L. J. (1974). *Principles of Instructional Design.* New York: Holt, Rinehart & Winston.

Gates A. I. (1917). Recitation as a Factor in Memorizing. *Arch. Psychol., N.Y.*, 6 (40).

Goodwin, D. L., & Coates, T. J. (1976). *Helping Students Help Themselves.* Englewood Cliffs, N.J.: Prentice-Hall.

Katona, G. (1940). *Organizing and Memorizing.* New York: Columbia Univ. Press.

Kintsch, W., & VanDijk, T. A. (1979). Toward a Model of Text Comprehension and Production. *Psychol. Rev.*, 85: 363–394.

Lorayne, H., & Lucas, J. (1974). *The Memory Book.* New York: Ballantine Books.

Lovaas, O. I., & Newsom, C. D. (1976). Behavior Modification with Psychotic Children. In H. Leitenberg, ed., *Handbook of Behavior Modification and Behavior Therapy.* Englewood Cliffs, N.J.: Prentice-Hall.

Mager, R. F. (1961). *Preparing Instructional Objectives.* Palo Alto, Cal.: Fearon Publishing.

Mager, R. F. (1972). *Goal Analysis.* Belmont, Cal.: Fearon Publishing.

Meichenbaum, D. (1977). *Cognitive Behavior Modification: An Integrative Approach.* New York: Plenum Press.

Meichenbaum, D., & Asarnow, J. (1979). Cognitive Behavior Modification and Metacognitive Development: Implications for the Classroom. In P. Kendell & S. Hollon, eds., *Cognitve Behavior Interventions: Theory, Research and Procedures.* New York: Academic Press.

Meyer, B. (1975). *The Organization of Prose and Its Effect Upon Memory.* Amsterdam: North-Holland.

Oarwehouse, R. A. (1976). Group Systematic Desensitization of Test Anxiety. In J. D. Krumboltz & C. E. Thoresen, eds., *Counseling Methods.* New York: Holt, Rinehart and Winston: 269–279.

Robinson, F. P. (1961). *Effective Study.* Rev. ed. New York: Harper & Row.

Slamecka, N. J. (1964). An Inquiry into the Doctrine of Remote Association. *Psychol. Rev.*, 71: 61–76.

Wark, D. M. (1976). Teaching Study Skills to Adults. In J. D. Krumboltz and C. E. Thoreson, eds., *Counseling Methods.* New York: Holt, Rinehart & Winston: 454–461.

Watson, D. L., & Thapp, R. G. (1977). *Selfdirected Behavior: Self-Modification for Personal Adjustment* 2nd ed. Monterey, Cal.: Brooks-Cole.

Wolpe, J. (1958). *Psychotherapy by Reciprocal Inhibition.* Stanford: Stanford Univ. Press.

The Improvement of Instruction: Suggestions from Behavioral and Cognitive Science

The National Commission on Excellence in Education (1983) has reported that the achievement of American high school students is at an all-time low. The Commission called for sweeping reforms in the nation's educational system. The proposals included: a longer school day, higher standards for students and teachers, and more emphasis on science and mathematics. Less attention was given to using the suggestions of research scientists for the improvement of instruction.

The authors of the articles on this issue represent scientists with different views of learning. B. F. Skinner represents those who seek to change the behavior of the learner by reinforcing or rewarding the desired responses. Lauren Resnick represents another group who focus on learners' thought processes. They study how learners use their mind to achieve understanding. In the articles for this issue, Skinner and Resnick interpret the meaning of findings in their science for the improvement of instruction.

Skinner begins by reviewing the events leading to a critical need for more effective instruction and what he calls "psychological roadblocks" to acceptance of his suggestions of twenty-five years ago. According to Skinner, the popularity of cognitive science is one of the obstacles. He finds nothing new in suggestions put forward by its proponents.

The heart of Skinner's proposals is the "programming" of the content to be learned. In programming, carefully prepared sequences of tasks lead the learner very gradually to make the correct responses. If programming is well done, each step of the sequence may be easy, no one need fail, and constant reinforcement for correct behavior may generate enthusiasm for continued learning.

According to Resnick, what's "new" in the suggestions of cognitive science is the concept of the learner and what is learned. He reviews the findings that show students invariably construct their own theories about the world and how to solve the problems. Facts and skills must be shown to "fit in" or they will be forgotten and not used. The challenge to instruction is to replace naive and incorrect "personal" theories with those of science to which new knowledge can be related.

Thought Questions

Do you find the suggestions of behavioral and cognitive scientists compatible, contradictory, or complementary? Explain.

Whose proposals do you believe most promising for the improvement of instruction? Does your answer depend upon what is to be taught and who is to be taught? If so, for what learners and objectives would each be most useful?

Whose suggestions do you find most useful for eliciting or prompting the desired response by the learner? Whose for encouraging and strengthening or discouraging and weakening the response after it occurs? Does this suggest a useful synthesis of the two sets?

Skinner's reinforcement strategy has been used by animal trainers to teach rabbits to play basketball, dolphins to jump through hoops, and seals to play tunes. Would you expect Resnick's suggestions to be as useful for training animals to do tricks? What does your answer suggest with respect to when to use the suggestions of each?

Skinner's approach has been criticized as a denial of the value of reasoning in children and as a totalitarian method of manipulating them. What basis is there for such criticisms? Do you believe they are justified? Why or why not?

Computers are expected to play an important role in the education of the future. Whose suggestions appear to be the more adaptable in instruction by computer, those of behavioral or cognitive scientists? Do you believe each will contribute? Why or why not?

What would be the teacher's role in Skinner's instructional approach? In instruction that emphasized cognitive processes? As a teacher, which role do you think you would prefer?

Do you believe Skinner correct when he states that there is nothing new in Resnick's recommendations? Why or why not?

READING 11

The Shame of American Education

B. F. Skinner

ABSTRACT: *Recent analyses of American schools and proposals for school reform have missed an essential point: Most current problems could be solved if students learned twice as much in the same time and with the same effort. It has been shown that they can do so (a) when the goals of education are clarified, (b) when each student is permitted to advance at his or her own pace, and (c) when the problem of motivation is solved with programmed instructional materials, so designed that students are very often right and learn at once that they are. The theories of human behavior most often taught in schools of education stand in the way of this solution to the problem of American education, but the proposal that schools of education simply be disbanded is a step in the wrong direction. Teachers need to be taught how to teach, and a technology is now available that will permit them to teach much more effectively.*

On a morning in October 1957, Americans were awakened by the beeping of a satellite. It was a Russian satellite, Sputnik. Why was it not

From B. F. Skinner, *American Psychologist* (September 1984):947–954. Copyright 1984 the American Psychological Association, Inc., Washington, D.C. Reprinted with permission. An earlier version of this article was given as the Bode Lecture at Ohio State University, April 8, 1981.

American? Was something wrong with American education? Evidently so, and money was quickly voted to improve American schools. Now we are being awakened by the beepings of Japanese cars, Japanese radios, phonographs, and television sets, and Japanese wristwatch alarms, and again questions are being asked about American education, especially in science and mathematics.

Something does seem to be wrong. According to a recent report of the National Commission on Excellence in Education (1983), for example, the average achievement of our high-school students on standardized tests is now lower than it was a quarter of a century ago, and students in American schools compare poorly with those in other nations in many fields. As the commission put it, America is threatened by "a rising tide of mediocrity."

The first wave of reform is usually rhetorical. To improve education we are said to need "imaginative innovations," a "broad national effort" leading to a "deep and lasting change," and a "commitment to excellence." More specific suggestions have been made, however. To get better teachers we should pay them more, possibly according to merit. They should be certified to teach the subjects they teach. To get better students, scholarship standards should be raised. The school day should be extended from 6 to 7 hours, more time should be spent on homework, and the school year should be lengthened from 180 to 200, or even 220, days. We should change what we are teaching. Social studies are all very well, but they should not take time away from basics, especially mathematics.

As many of us have learned to expect, there is a curious omission in that list: It contains no suggestion that teaching be improved. There is a conspiracy of silence about teaching as a skill. The *New York Times* publishes a quarterly survey of education. Three recent issues (Fisk, 1982, 1983a, 1983b) contained 18 articles about the kinds of things being taught in schools; 11 articles about the financial problems of students and schools; 10 articles about the needs of special students, from the gifted to the disadvantaged; and smaller numbers of articles about the selection of students, professional problems of teachers, and sports and other extracurricular activities. Of about 70 articles, only 2 had anything to do with how students are taught or how they could be taught better. Pedagogy is a dirty word.

In January 1981, Frederick Mosteller, president of the American Association for the Advancement of Science, gave an address called "Innovation and Evaluation" (Mosteller, 1981). He began with an example of the time which can pass between a scientific discovery and its practical use. The fact that lemon juice cures scurvy was discovered in 1601, but more than 190 years passed before the British navy began to use citrus juice on a regular basis and another 70 before scurvy was wiped out in the mercantile marine—a lag of 264 years. Lags have grown shorter but, as Mosteller pointed out, are often still too long. Perhaps unwittingly he gave another example. He called for initiatives in science and engineering education and said that a major theme of the 1982 meeting of the association would be a "national commitment to educational excellence in science and engineering for all Americans" (p. 886).

When Mosteller's address was published in *Science,* I wrote a letter to the editor (Skinner, 1981) calling attention to an experiment in teaching algebra in a school in Roanoke, Vir-

ginia (Rushton, 1965). In this experiment an eighth-grade class using simple teaching machines and hastily composed instructional programs went through *all* of ninth-grade algebra in *half* a year. Their grades met ninth-grade norms, and when tested a year later the students remembered rather more than usual. Had American educators decided that that was the way to teach algebra? They had not. The experiment was done in 1960, but education had not yet made any use of it. The lag was already 21 years long.

A month or so later I ran into Mosteller. "Did you see my letter in *Science* about teaching machines?" I asked. "Teaching machines?" he said, puzzled. "Oh, you mean *computers*— teaching machines to *you.*" And, of course, he was right. Computer is the current word. But is it the right one? Computers are now badly misnamed. They were designed to compute, but they are not computing when they are processing words, or displaying Pac-Man, or aiding instruction (unless the instruction is in computing). "Computer" has all the respectability of the white-collar executive, whereas "machine" is definitely blue-collar, but let us call things by their right names. Instruction may be "computer aided," and all good instruction must be "interactive," but machines that teach are teaching machines.

I liked the Roanoke experiment because it confirmed something I had said a few years earlier to the effect that with teaching machines and programmed instruction one could teach what is now taught in American schools in half the time with half the effort. I shall not review other evidence that that is true. Instead I shall demonstrate my faith in a technology of teaching by going out on a limb. I claim that the school system of any large American city could be so redesigned, at little or no additional cost, that students would come to school and apply themselves to their work with a minimum of punitive coercion and, with very rare exceptions, learn to read with reasonable ease, express themselves well in speech and writing, and solve a fair range of mathematical problems. I want to talk about why this has not been done.

The teaching machines of 25 years ago were crude, of course, but this is scarcely an explanation. The calculating machines were crude, too, yet they were used until they could be replaced by something better. The hardware problem has now been solved, but resistance to a technology of teaching survives. The rank commercialism which quickly engulfed the field of teaching machines is another possible explanation. Too many people rushed in to write bad programs and make promises that could not be kept. But that should not have concealed the value of programmed instruction for so many years. There is more than that to be said for the marketplace in the selection of a better mousetrap.

Psychological Roadblocks

I shall argue that educators have not seized this chance to solve their problems because the solution conflicts with deeply entrenched views of human behavior, and that these views are too strongly supported by current psychology. Humanistic psychologists, for example, tend to feel threatened by any kind of scientific analysis of human behavior, particularly if it leads to a "technology" that can be used to intervene in people's lives. A technology of teaching is especially threatening. Carl Rogers has said that teaching is vastly overrated, and Ivan Illich has called for the de-schooling of society. I dealt with the problem in *Beyond Freedom and Dignity* (Skinner, 1971). To give a single example, we do not like to be told something we already know, for we can then no longer claim credit for having known it.

To solve that problem, Plato tried to show that students already possess knowledge and have only to be shown that they possess it. But the famous scene in Plato's *Meno* in which Socrates shows that the slaveboy already knows Pythagoras's theorem for doubling the square is one of the great intellectual hoaxes of all time. The slaveboy agrees with everything Socrates says, but there is no evidence whatsoever that he could then go thorugh the proof by himself.

Indeed, Socrates says that the boy would need to be taken through it many times before he could do so.

Cognitive psychology is causing much more trouble, but in a different way. It is hard to be precise because the field is usually presented in what we may call a cognitive style. For example, a pamphlet of the National Institute of Education (1980) quotes with approval the contention that "at the present time, modern cognitive psychology is the dominant theoretical force in psychological science as opposed to the first half of the century when behavioristic, anti-mentalistic stimulus-response theories of learning were in the ascendance" (p. 391). (The writer means "ascendant.") The pamphlet tells us that cognitive science studies learning, but not in quite those words. Instead, cognitive science is said to be "characterized by a concern with understanding the mechanisms by which human beings carry out complex intellectual activities including learning" (p. 391). The pamphlet also says that cognitive science can help construct tests that will tell us more about what a student has learned and hence how to teach better, but here is the way it says this: "Attention will be placed on two specific topics: Applications of cognitive models of the knowledge structure of various subject matters and of learning and problem solving to construction of tests that identify processes underlying test answers, analyze errors, and provide information about what students know and don't know, and strategies for integrating testing information with instructional decisions" (p. 393). Notice especially the cognitive style in the last phrase—the question is not "whether test results can suggest better ways of teaching" but "whether there are strategies for integrating testing information with instructional decisions."

The Commission on Behavioral and Social Sciences and Education of the National Research Council (1984) provides a more recent example in its announcement of a biennial program plan covering the period 1 May 1983 to 30 April 1985. The commission will take advantage of "significant advances . . . in the cognitive sciences" (p. 41). Will it study learning? Well, not exactly. The members will "direct their attention to studies of fundamental processes underlying the nature and development of learning" (p. 41). Why do cognitive psychologists not tell us frankly what they are up to? Is it possible that they themselves do not really know?

Cognitive psychology is certainly in the ascendant. The word *cognitive* is sprinkled through the psychological literature like salt— and, like salt, not so much for any flavor of its own but to bring out the flavor of other things, things which a quarter of a century ago would have been called by other names. The heading of an article in a recent issue of the APA *Monitor* (Turkington, 1983) tells us that "cognitive deficits" are important in understanding alcoholism. In the text we learn simply that alcoholics show losses in perception and motor skills. Perception and motor skills used to be fields of psychology; now they are fields of cognitive science. Nothing has been changed except the name, and the change has been made for suspicious reasons. There is a sense of profundity about "cognitive deficits," but it does not take us any deeper into the subject.

Much of the vogue of cognitive science is due to advances in computer technology. The computer offers an appealing simplification of some old psychological problems. Sensation and perception are reduced to input; learning and memory to the processing, storage, and retrieval of information; and action to output. It is very much like the old stimulus-response formula patched up with intervening variables. To say that students process information is to use a doubtful metaphor, and how they process information is still the old question of how they learn.

Cognitive psychology also gains prestige from its alignment with brain research. Interesting things are certainly being discovered about the biochemistry and circuitry of the brain, but we are still a long way from knowing what is happening in the brain as behavior is shaped and maintained by contingencies of reinforcement, and that means that we are a long

way from help in designing useful instructional practices.

Cognitive science is also said to be supported by modern linguistics, a topic to which I am particularly sensitive. Programmed instruction emerged from my analysis of verbal behavior (Skinner, 1957), which linguists, particularly generative grammarians, have, of course, attacked. So far as I know they have offered no equally effective practices. One might expect them to have improved the teaching of languages, but almost all language laboratories still work in particularly outmoded ways, and language instruction is one of the principal failures of precollege education.

Psycholinguistics moves in essentially the same direction in its hopeless commitment to development. Behavior is said to change in ways determined by its structure. The change may be a function of age, but age is not a variable that one can manipulate. The extent to which developmentalism has encouraged a neglect of more useful ways of changing behavior is shown by a recent report (Siegler, 1983) in which the number of studies concerned with the development of behavior in children was found to have skyrocketed, whereas the number concerned with how children learn has dropped to a point at which the researcher could scarcely find any examples at all.

There are many fine cognitive psychologists who are doing fine research, but they are not the cognitive psychologists who for 25 years have been promising great advances in education. A short paper published in *Science* last April (Resnick, 1983) asserts that "recent findings in cognitive science suggest new approaches to teaching in science and mathematics" (p. 477), but the examples given, when expressed in noncognitive style, are simply these: (a) Students learn about the world in "naive" ways before they study science; (b) naive theories interfere with learning scientific theories; (c) we should therefore teach science as early as possible; (d) many problems are not solved exclusively with mathematics; qualitative experience is important; (e) students learn more than isolated facts; they learn how facts are related to each other; and (f) students relate what they are learning to what they already know. If these are *recent* findings, where has cognitive science been?

Cognitive psychology is frequently presented as a revolt against behaviorism, but it is not a revolt; it is a retreat. Everyday English is full of terms derived from ancient explanations of human behavior. We spoke that language when we were young. When we went out into the world and became psychologists, we learned to speak in other ways but made mistakes for which we were punished. But now we can relax. Cognitive psychology is Old Home Week. We are back among friends speaking the language we spoke when we were growing up. We can talk about love and will and ideas and memories and feelings and states of mind, and no one will ask us what we mean; no one will raise an eyebrow.

Schools of Education

Psychological theories come into the hands of teachers through schools of education and teachers' colleges, and it is there, I think, that we must lay the major blame for what is happening in American education. In a recent article in the *New York Times* (Botstein, 1983), President Leon Botstein of Bard College proposed that schools of education, teachers' colleges, and departments of education simply be disbanded. But he gave a different reason. He said that schools of that sort "placed too great an emphasis on pedagogical techniques and psychological studies" (p. 64), when they should be teaching the subjects the teachers will eventually teach. But disbanding such schools is certainly a move in the wrong direction. It has long been said that college teaching is the only profession for which there is no professional training. Would-be doctors go to medical schools, would-be lawyers go to law schools, and would-be engineers go to institutes of technology, but would-be college teachers just start teaching. Fortunately it is recognized that grade- and high-school teachers need to learn to teach. The trouble is, they are

not being taught in effective ways. The commitment to humanistic and cognitive psychology is only part of the problem.

Equally damaging is the assumption that teaching can be adequately discussed in everyday English. The appeal to laymanship is attractive. At the "Convocation of Science and Mathematics in the Schools" called by the National Academies of Sciences and Engineering, one member said that "what we need are bright, energetic, dedicated young people, trained in mathematics . . . science . . . or technology, mixing it up with 6- to 13-year-old kids in the classroom" (Raizen, 1983, p. 19). The problem is too grave to be solved in any such way. The first page of the report notes with approval that "if there is one American enterprise that is local in its design and control it is education" (p. 1). That is held to be a virtue. But certainly the commission would not approve similar statements about medicine, law, or science and technology. Why should the community decide how children are to be taught? The commission is actually pointing to one explanation of why education is failing.

We must beware of the fallacy of the good teacher and the good student. There are many good teachers who have not needed to learn to teach. They would be good at almost anything they tried. There are many good students who scarcely need to be taught. Put a good teacher and a good student together and you have what seems to be an ideal instructional setting. But it is disastrous to take it as a model to be followed in our schools, where hundreds of thousands of teachers must teach millions of students. Teachers must learn how to teach, and they must be taught by schools of education. They need only to be taught more effective ways of teaching.

A Solution

We could solve our major problems in education if students learned more during each day in school. That does not mean a longer day or year or more homework. It simply means using time more efficiently. Such a solution is not considered in any of the reports I have mentioned—whether from the National Institute of Education, the American Association for the Advancement of Science, the National Research Council, or the National Academies of Sciences and Engineering. Nevertheless, it is within easy reach. Here is all that needs to be done.

1. Be clear about what is to be taught. When I once explained to a group of grade-school teachers how I would teach children to spell words, one of them said, "Yes, but can you teach spelling?" For him, students spelled words correctly not because they had learned to do so but because they had acquired a special ability. When I told a physicist colleague about the Roanoke experiment in teaching algebra, he said, "Yes, but did they learn algebra?" For him, algebra was more than solving certain kinds of problems; it was a mental faculty. No doubt the more words you learn to spell the easier it is to spell new words, and the more problems you solve in algebra the easier it is to solve new problems. What eventually emerges is often called *intuition*. We do not know what it is, but we can certainly say that no teacher has ever taught it directly, nor has any student ever displayed it without first learning to do the kinds of things it supposedly replaces.

2. Teach first things first. It is tempting to move too quickly to final products. I once asked a leader of the "new math" what he wanted students to be able to do. He was rather puzzled and then said, "I suppose I just want them to be able to follow a logical line of reasoning." That does not tell a teacher where to start or, indeed, how to proceed at any point. I once asked a colleague what he wanted his students to do as a result of having taken his introductory course in physics. "Well," he said, "I guess I've never thought about it that way." I'm afraid he spoke for most of the profession.

Among the ultimate but useless goals of education is "excellence." A candidate for president recently said that he would let local communities decide what that meant. "I am not going to try to define excellence for them," he said, and wisely so. Another useless ultimate goal is "creativity." It is said that students

should do more than what they have been taught to do. They should be creative. But does it help to say that they must acquire creativity? More than 300 years ago, Molière wrote a famous line: "I am asked by the learned doctors for the cause and reason why opium puts one to sleep, to which I reply that there is in it a soporific virtue, the nature of which is to lull the senses." Two or three years ago an article in *Science* pointed out that 90% of scientific innovations were accomplished by fewer than 10% of scientists. The explanation, it was said, was that only a few scientists possess creativity. Molière's audiences laughed. Eventually some students behave in creative ways, but they must have something to be creative with and that must be taught first. Then they can be taught to multiply the variations which give rise to new and interesting forms of behavior. (Creativity, incidentally, is often said to be beyond a science of behavior, and it would be if that science were a matter of stimulus and response. By emphasizing the selective action of consequences, however, the experimental analysis of behavior deals with the creation of behavior precisely as Darwin dealt with the creation of species.)

3. Stop making all students advance at essentially the same rate. The phalanx was a great military invention, but it has long been out of date, and it should be out of date in American schools. Students are still expected to move from kindergarten through high school in 12 years, and we all know what is wrong: Those who could move faster are held back, and those who need more time fall farther and farther behind. We could double the efficiency of education with one change alone—by letting each student move at his or her own pace. (I wish I could blame this costly mistake on developmental psychology, because it is such a beautiful example of its major principle, but the timing is out of joint.)

No teacher can teach a class of 30 to 40 students and allow each to progress at an optimal speed. Tracking is too feeble a remedy. We must turn to individual instruments for part of the school curriculum. The report of the convocation held by the National Academies of

Sciences and Engineering refers to "new technologies" which "can be used to extend the educational process, to supplement the teacher's role in new and imaginative ways" (Raizen, 1983, p. 15), but no great enthusiasm is shown. Thirty years ago educational television was promising, but the promise has not been kept. The report alludes to "computer-aided instruction" but calls it the latest "rage of education" and insists that "the primary use of the computer is for drill" (p. 15). (Properly programmed instruction is *never* drill if that means gong over material again and again until it is learned.) The report also contains a timid allusion to "low-cost teaching stations that can be controlled by the learner" (p. 15), but evidently these stations are merely to give the student access to video material rather than to programs.

4. Program the subject matter. The heart of the teaching machine, call it what you will, is the programming of instruction—an advance not mentioned in any of the reports I have cited. Standard texts are designed to be read by the student, who will then discuss what they say with a teacher or take a test to see how much has been learned. Material prepared for individual study is different. It first induces students to say or do the things they are to learn to say or do. Their behavior is thus "primed" in the sense of being brought out for the first time. Until the behavior has acquired more strength, it may need to be prompted. Primes and prompts must then be carefully "vanished" until the behavior occurs without help. At that point the reinforcing consequences of being right are most effective in building and sustaining an enduring repertoire.

Working through a program is really a process of discovery, but not in the sense in which that word is currently used in education. We discover many things in the world around us, and that is usually better than being told about them, but as individuals we can discover only a very small part of the world. Mathematics has been discovered very slowly and painfully over thousands of years. Students discover it as they go through a program, but not in the sense of doing something for the first time in history.

Trying to teach mathematics or science as if the students themselves were discovering things for the first time is not an efficient way of teaching the very skills with which, in the long run, a student may, with luck, actually make a genuine discovery.

When students move through well-constructed programs at their own pace, the so-called problem of motivation is automatically solved. For thousands of years students have studied to avoid the consequences of not studying. Punitive sanctions still survive, disguised in various ways, but the world is changing, and they are no longer easily imposed. The great mistake of progressive education was to try to replace them with natural curiosity. Teachers were to bring the real world into the classroom to arouse the students' interest. The inevitable result was a neglect of subjects in which children were seldom naturally interested—in particular, the so-called basics. One solution is to make some of the natural reinforcers—goods or privileges—artificially contingent upon basic behavior, as in a token economy. Such contingencies can be justified if they correct a lethargic or disordered classroom, but there should be no lethargy or disorder. It is characteristic of the human species that successful action is automatically reinforced. The fascination of video games is adequate proof. What would industrialists not give to see their workers as absorbed in their work as young people in a video arcade? What would teachers not give to see their students applying themselves with the same eagerness? (For that matter, what would any of us not give to see ourselves as much in love with our work?) But there is no mystery; it is all a matter of the scheduling of reinforcements.

A good program of instruction guarantees a great deal of successful action. Students do not need to have a natural interest in what they are doing, and subject matters do not need to be dressed up to attract attention. No one really cares whether Pac-Man gobbles up all those little spots on the screen. Indeed, as soon as the screen is cleared, the player covers it again with little spots to be gobbled up. What is reinforcing is successful play, and in a well-designed instructional program students gobble up their assignments. I saw them doing that when I visited the project in Roanoke with its director, Allen Calvin. We entered a room in which 30 to 40 eighth-grade students were at their desks working on rather crude teaching machines. When I said I was surprised that they paid no attention to us, Calvin proposed a better demonstration. He asked me to keep my eye on the students and then went up on the teacher's platform. He jumped in the air and came down with a loud bang. Not a single student looked up. Students do not have to be made to study. Abundant reinforcement is enough, and good programming provides it.

The Teacher

Individually programmed instruction has much to offer teachers. It makes very few demands upon them. Paraprofessionals may take over some of their chores. That is not a reflection on teachers or a threat to their profession. There is much that only teachers can do, and they can do it as soon as they have been freed of unnecessary tasks.

Some things they can do are to talk to and listen to students and read what students write. A recent study (Goodlad, 1983) found that teachers are responding to things that students say during only 5% of the school day. If that is so, it is not surprising that one of the strongest complaints against our schools is that students do not learn to express themselves.

If given a chance, teachers can also be interesting and sympathetic companions. It is a difficult assignment in a classroom in which order is maintained by punitive sanctions. The word *discipline* has come a long way from its association with *disciple* as one who understands.

Success and progress are the very stuff on which programmed instruction feeds. They should also be the stuff that makes teaching worthwhile as a profession. Just as students must not only learn but know that they are learning, so teachers must not only teach but know that they are teaching. Burnout is usually regarded as the result of abusive treatment by students, but it can be as much the result of looking back upon a day in the classroom and wondering what one has accomplished. Along with a sense of satisfaction goes a place in the community. One proposed remedy for American education is to give teachers greater respect, but that is putting it the wrong way around. Let them teach twice as much in the same time and with the same effort, and they will be held in greater respect.

The Establishment

The effect on the education establishment may be much more disturbing. Almost 60 years ago Sidney Pressey invented a simple teaching machine and predicted the coming "industrial revolution" in education. In 1960 he wrote to me, "Before long the question will need to be faced as to what the student is to do with the time which automation will save him. More education in the same place or earlier completion of full-time education?" (Sidney Pressey, personal communication, 1960). Earlier completion is a problem. If what is now taught in the first and second grades can be taught in the first (and I am sure that it can), what will the second-grade teacher do? What is now done by the third- or fourth-grade teacher? At what age will the average student reach high school, and at what age will he or she graduate? Certainly a better solution is to teach what is now taught more effectively and to teach many other things as well. Even so, students will probably reach college younger in years, but they will be far more mature. That change will more than pay for the inconvenience of making sweeping administrative changes.

The report of the National Commission on Excellence in Education (1983) repeatedly mistakes causes for effects. It says that "the educational foundations of our society are being eroded by a rising tide of mediocrity," but is the mediocrity causing the erosion? Should we say that the foundations of our automobile industry are being eroded by a rising tide of mediocre cars? Mediocrity is an effect, not a cause.

Our educational foundations are being eroded by a commitment to laymanship and to theories of human behavior which simply do not lead to effective teaching. The report of the Convocation on Science and Mathematics in the Schools quotes President Reagan as saying that "this country was built on American respect for education. . . . Our challenge now is to create a resurgence of that thirst for education that typifies our nation's history" (Raizen, 1983, p. 1). But is education in trouble because it is no longer held in respect, or is it not held in respect because it is in trouble? Is it in trouble because people do not thirst for education, or do they not thirst for what is being offered?

Everyone is unhappy about education, but what is wrong? Let us look at a series of questions and answers rather like the series of propositions that logicians call a *sorites:*

1. Are students at fault when they do not learn? No, they have not been well taught.
2. Are teachers then at fault? No, they have not been properly taught to teach.
3. Are schools of education and teachers' colleges then at fault? No, they have not been given a theory of behavior that leads to effective teaching.
4. Are behavioral scientists then at fault? No, a culture too strongly committed to the view that a technology of behavior is a threat to freedom and dignity is not supporting the right behavioral science.
5. Is our culture then at fault? But what is the next step?

Let us review the sorites again and ask what can be done. Shall we:

1. Punish students who do not learn by flunking them?
2. Punish teachers who do not teach well by discharging them?
3. Punish schools of education which do not teach teaching well by disbanding them?
4. Punish behavioral science by refusing to support it?
5. Punish the culture that refuses to support behavioral science?

But you cannot punish a culture. A culture is punished by its failure or by other cultures which take its place in a continually evolving process. There could scarcely be a better example of the point of my book *Beyond Freedom and Dignity.* A culture that is not willing to accept scientific advances in the understanding of human behavior, together with the technology which emerges from these advances, will eventually be replaced by a culture that is.

When the National Commission on Excellence in Education (1983) said that "the essential raw materials needed to reform our educational system are waiting to be mobilized" it spoke more truly than it knew, but to mobilize them the commission called for "leadership." That is as vague a word as excellence. Who, indeed, will make the changes that must be made if education is to play its proper role in American life? It is reasonable to turn to those who suffer most from the present situation.

1. Those who pay for education—primarily taxpayers and the parents of children in private schools—can simply demand their money's worth.
2. Those who use the products of grade- and high-school education—colleges and universities on the one hand and business and industry on the other—cannot refuse to buy, but they can be more discriminating.
3. Those who teach may simply withdraw from the profession, and too many are already exercising their right to do so. The organized withdrawal of a strike is usually a demand for higher wages, but it could also be a demand for better instructional facilities and administrative changes that would improve classroom practices.

But why must we always speak of higher standards for students, merit pay for teachers, and other versions of punitive sanctions? These are the things one thinks of first, and they will no doubt make teachers and students work harder, but they will not necessarily have a better effect. They are more likely to lead to further defection. There is a better way: Give students and teachers better reasons for learning and teaching. That is where the behavioral sciences can make a contribution. They can develop instructional practices so effective and so attractive in other ways that no one—student, teacher, or administrator—will need to be coerced into using them.

Young people are by far the most important natural resource of a nation, and the development of that resource is assigned to education. Each of us is born needing to learn what others have learned before us, and much of it needs to be taught. We would all be better off if edu-cation played a far more important part in transmitting our culture. Not only would that make for a stronger America (remember Sputnik), but we might also look forward to the day when the same issues could be discussed about the world as a whole—when, for example, all peoples produce the goods they consume and behave well toward each other, not because they are forced to do so but because they have been taught something of the ultimate advantages of a rich and peaceful world.

REFERENCES

Botstein, L. (1983, June 5). Nine Proposals to Improve Our Schools. *New York Times Magazine.* p. 59.

Fisk, E. B. (Ed.). (1982, November 14). Fall Survey of Education [Supplement]. *New York Times.*

Fisk, E. B. (ed.). (1983a, January 9). Winter Survey of Education [Supplement]. *New York Times.*

Fisk, E. B. (Ed.). (1983b, April 24). Spring Survey of Education [Supplement]. *New York Times.*

Goodlad, J. L. (1983). *A Place Called School.* New York: McGraw-Hill.

Mosteller, F. (1981). Innovation and Evaluation. *Science, 211,* 881–886.

National Commission of Excellence in Education. (1983, April). *A Nation at Risk: The Imperative for Educational Reform.* Washington, DC: U.S. Department of Education.

National Institute of Education. (1980). Science and Technology and Education. In *The Five-Year Outlook: Problems, Opportunities and Constraints in Science and Technology* (Vol. 2, 391–399). Washington, DC: National Science Foundation.

National Research Council, Commission on Behavioral and Social Sciences and Education. (1984). Biennial program plan, May 1, 1983–April 30, 1985. Washington, DC: National Academy Press.

Raizen, S. (1983). *Science and Mathematics in the Schools: Report of a Convocation.* Washington, DC: National Academy Press.

Resnick, L. B. (1983). Mathematics and Science Learning: A New Conception. *Science, 220.* 477–478.

Rushton, E. W. (1965). *The Roanoke Experiment.* Chicago: Encyclopedia Britannica Press.

Siegler, R. S. (1983). Five Generalizations About Cognitive Development. *American Psychologist, 38,* 263–277.

Skinner, B. F. (1957). *Verbal Behavior.* New York: Appleton-Century-Crofts.

Skinner, B. F. (1971). *Beyond Freedom and Dignity.* New York: Alfred A. Knopf.

Skinner, B. F. (1981). Innovation in Science Teaching. *Science, 212,* 283.

Turkington, C. (1983, June). Cognitive Deficits Hold Promise for Prediction of Alcoholoism. APA *Monitor,* p. 16.

Mathematics and Science Learning: A New Conception

Lauren B. Resnick

In the last few years a new consensus on the nature of learning has begun to emerge, stimulated by research in the field that has come to be known as cognitive science. The emerging conception of learning has a direct bearing on how science and mathematics can be taught most effectively.

I will sketch here a few examples of recent findings in cognitive science, many of which support the intuition of our most thoughtful teachers. In physics and other sciences, according to these studies, even students who do well on textbook problems often cannot apply the laws and formulas they have been drilled on to interpreting actual physical events. This observation has been made on all kinds of students, including gifted middle-school children and students at some of our most prestigious universities (1, 2). The inability to apply routines learned in school is consistent with recent findings from the National Assessment of Educa-

From *Science* (April 1983):477–488. Reprinted with permission. Adapted from an address at the National Convocation on Precollege Education in Mathematics and Science. National Academy of Science and National Academy of Engineering, Washington, D.C., May 1982.

tional Progress showing that mathematical problem-solving skills of American children lag far behind their calculation abilities (3).

Another well-supported finding is that all students, the weak as well as the strong learners, come to their first science classes with surprisingly extensive theories about how the natural world works. They use these "naïve" theories to explain real world events before they have had any science instruction. Then, even after instruction in new concepts and scientifically supported theories, they still resort to their prior theories to solve any problems that vary from their textbook examples (4-6). Some studies have shown that students' prior theories can actually interfere with learning scientific concepts. The students' naive theories affect what they perceive to be happening in classroom demonstrations or laboratory experiments, and they continue to attach their naive meanings to technical terms (for example, the term acceleration).

Several studies show that successful problem-solving requires a substantial amount of qualitative reasoning (7-9). Good problem-solvers do not rush in to apply a formula or an equation. Instead, they try to understand the problem situation; they consider alternative representations and relations among the variables. Only when they are satisfied that they understand the situation and all the variables in it in a qualitative way do they start to apply the quantification that we often mistakenly identify as the essence of "real" science or mathematics.

These demonstrations of the potent role of naïve theories in science learning, and of the central role of qualitative understanding of a situation in problem-solving, contribute to a new conception of the learner and the learning process that is emerging from cognitive research in mathematics and science. This research has in just a few years produced a new consensus on the nature of learning that is not yet widely reflected in the way mathematics and science teaching is conducted in the schools.

There are many complexities, but the fundamental view of the learner that is emerging can be expressed quite simply.

First, learners construct understanding. They do not simply mirror what they are told or what they read (*10, 11*). Learners look for meaning and will try to find regularity and order in the events of the world, even in the absence of complete information. This means that naïve theories will always be constructed as part of the learning process.

Second, to understand something is to know relationships. Human knowledge is stored in clusters and organized into schemata that people use both to interpret familiar situations and to reason about new ones. Bits of information isolated from these structures are forgotten or become inaccessible to memory.

Third, all learning depends on prior knowledge. Learners try to link new information to what they already know in order to interpret the new material in terms of established schemata. This is why students interpret science demonstrations in terms of their naïve theories and why they hold onto their naïve theories for so long. The scientific theories that children are being taught in school often cannot compete as reference points for new learning because they are presented quickly and abstractly and so remain unorganized and unconnected to past experience.

What does this new understanding of the learner suggest about how we can improve mathematics and science education? First, it is never too soon to start. From their earliest years, children are developing theories about how the world works. There is reason to believe that naïve theories will not take hold so firmly if scientific theories become available to them early. Furthermore, it is becoming clear that it takes a long time, and many different examples, for understanding to develop. It is not reasonable to postpone the beginning of this process to a high school or college course.

Second, teaching has to focus on the qualitative aspects of scientific and mathematical problem situations. Too quick an advance to formulas and procedures will not help children acquire the kinds of analytical and representational skills they need. Extensive qualitative analysis is not common in science or mathematics teaching. It may seem to take too much classroom time, and many teachers are perhaps too inexperienced in these ways of thinking. But the new evidence about learning makes it clear that we cannot avoid taking on this task.

A focus on qualitative analysis and understanding of situations does not mean a retreat from the teaching of computational procedures or scientific formulas, or from the basic factual information in any discipline. There is definitely an important role for the traditional skills of mathematics and science and the facts that underlie them. But the procedures and formulas must be treated as matters that make sense, and children must be involved in the task of making sense of them. Research has not yet told us whether it is better to first become skillful at a procedure and then analyze it, or to allow procedures to grow out of understanding a situation. But research has made it clear that procedures must take on meaning and make sense or they are unlikely to be used in any situation that is at all different from the exact ones in which they were taught.

Finally, since naïve theories are inevitable, teachers will probably have to confront them directly. Students may have to be forced to pit their theories against the ones they are being asked to learn, to deal with conflict between theories in much the way that scientists do. This, too, is a new challenge, for only rarely today does teaching explicitly acknowledge children's prior theories (except to mark them wrong) or even recognize the difficult intellectual work entailed in giving them up or substantially revising them.

Research in cognitive science is not only changing our views of how people learn science and mathematics but is also shaping a theory of learning in which the content of what is learned plays a central role. In the past, it has often been difficult for mathematicians and scientists to find in the work done by psychologists and other behavioral scientists much that seemed directly relevant to the problems of teaching their disciplines. The general principles that psychologists produced seemed too far removed from the specific questions of curriculum content that concerned the scientists and mathematicians. That has changed.

A critical theme of the past several years of work in cognitive science has been that a person's intelligent performance is not a matter of disembodied "processes of thinking" but depends intimately on the kind of knowledge that the person has about the particular situation in question. This has led cognitive scientists to recognize that in order to understand complex learning they must study how people learn particular subject matters. As a result, there are now cognitive scientists actively engaged in studying mathematics learning in particular, physics learning in particular, and so forth. At the same time, mathematicians and physical and biological scientists have begun to study the cognitive processes involved in learning their disciplines, often in direct collaboration with psychologists.

This kind of collaboration has been significantly invigorated by grant programs of the National Institute of Education and the now disbanded Science Education Directorate of the National Science Foundation, but these collaborative links are still fragile. In times of retrenchment it is easy to return to traditional alliances and the familiarity of one's own discipline. To keep the collaboration alive, we must give careful attention to supporting vigorous programs of cognitive research in mathematics and science learning. If this is done, the educational payoffs are likely to be large and not unduly long in coming.

REFERENCES

1. A. B. Champagne, L. E. Klopfer, J. H. Anderson, *Am. J. Phys.* **48,** 174 (1980).
2. M. McCloskey, A. Caramazza, B. Green, *Science* **210,** 1139 (1980).
3. National Assessment of Educational Progress, *Changes in Mathematical Achievement, 1973–78* (ERIC Document Reproduction Service ED 177 011, Denver, Colo., 1979).
4. M. N. Brumby, *Sci. Educ.*, in press.
5. R. Gunstone and R. White, *ibid.* **65,** 291 (1981).
6. R. L. Selman, M. P. Krupa, C. R. Stone, D. S. Jacquette, *ibid.*, in press.
7. M. T. H. Chi, P. Feltovich, R. Glaser, *Cognitive Sci.* **5,** 121 (1981).
8. J. Larkin, J. McDermott, D. P. Simon, H. A. Simon, *Science* **208,** 1335 (1980).
9. M. S. Riley, J. G. Greeno, J. I. Heller, in *The Development of Mathematical Thinking*, H. P. Ginsburg, Ed. (Academic Press, New York, 1983), pp. 153–196.
10. J. S. Brown and K. VanLehn, in *Addition and Subtraction: A Cognitive Perspective*, T. P. Carpenter, J. Moser, T. A. Romberg, Eds. (Erlbaum, Hillsdale, N.J., 1982), pp. 117–135.
11. G. J. Groen and L. B. Resnick, *J. Educ. Psychol.* **69,** 645 (1977).

Should We Teach *for* Thinking, *about* Thinking, or *of* Thinking?

Among educators, interest in the teaching of thinking has never been higher. Articles on critical thinking appear regularly in such journals as *Educational Leadership, Educational Researcher,* and the *Phi Delta Kappan.* Programs to teach thinking are now available for children of all ages (for example: Covington et al., 1983; Feuerstein, 1980; Whimbey, 1975). A poll of professional educators found that 9 out of 10 said that instruction in thinking skills should be a major priority in educational planning (ASCD *Update,* 1983). Many leaders in government and business, as well as the general public, see the same need (National Commission on Excellence in Education, 1983; College Board, 1983; Maeroff, 1983). There is general support for improving instruction in thinking. But there is less agreement on the best way to do this.

Our articles on this issue represent three different approaches to improving thinking skills. These may be characterized as the direct teaching of thinking skills, teaching all subjects in a way that prepares students for thinking, and teaching what thinking is all about so that students will be conscious of their own mental processes.

Edward de Bono is a leading proponent of the direct teaching of thinking as a skill, the title of his article. He outlines the thinking behind the design of his widely used teaching program and then describes the program. He believes a specific place in the curriculum should be set aside for the program so that it is recognized as a subject in its own right. He suggests using part of another class, such as English, for this purpose.

Good teachers have always tried to teach *for* thinking, and Carl Bereiter's approach is to make thinking a necessary part of regular instruction. He believes that teaching thinking as enrichment or as a separate subject is not usually successful. Even if it is, he believes that in the competition for school time, the teaching of thinking separately will lose out to more standard subjects. He would make thinking activities part of the daily instruction in *all* subjects, and thinking skills necessary for achievement of *every possible* educational objective. He gives an example of this approach in mathematics.

Costa is one of an increasing number of psychologists and educators who advocate teaching thinking *about* thinking. Capable learners may be said to have the ability to think about their own thinking or "metacognitive skills." They know what they know and don't know, are able to develop a plan in their mind, and monitor their own thinking. According to Costa, instructional strategies to develop children's metacognitive abilities are necessary for the development of intelligent behavior or what he terms the "educated intellect." He describes strategies that can be used to make students more aware of their own thinking, and of more effective strategies of thinking that they can use. The success of these strategies can be judged as children are able to describe their thought processes.

Thought Questions

Creativity is the topic of another issue in this book. What is the relationship of creativity to thinking? Compare the suggestions of the present authors with respect to their provisions for teaching creativity.

Are you aware of your own thinking processes? Do you agree with Costa on the importance of self-monitoring and regulation in effective thinking? Why might Berliner think teaching students to do this is a fad? What do you think de Bono's position would be?

Think about your own educational experience. What did teachers do that may have discouraged or eliminated the need for thinking? What did they do that encouraged or improved your thinking skills? How are these positive and negative practices related to the recommendations of the authors for this issue?

What should be the balance between teaching for thinking in the context of particular subjects, and teaching for thinking in general? Would you agree that instruction in car repair or troubleshooting in electronics requires teaching in context? In what subjects would this not be true? What suggestions do the authors of the articles for this issue have for how to think about the unknown or about ill-defined problems of the future?

Should thinking skills be taught explicitly, or should they be discovered or constructed by the learner? Would the authors agree or disagree on this point? Which approach is likely to be more effective in teaching students to be more effective with specific kinds of problems? In teaching them to be able to solve problems that do not fit the problem types that have been taught? With young or inexperienced learners? With learners who have already made substantial progress in an area of study?

Should thinking skills be incorporated in all subjects, as Bereiter suggests, or taught separately, as de Bono proposes? Why shouldn't schools do both, just as they provide separate instruction in reading and writing and also expect it to be taught in work for other subjects?

Since Costa recommends teaching *about* thinking and de Bono the teaching of thinking, what would be wrong with teaching students to think about their use of de Bono's system? Or teaching them to use de Bono's system to think about their own thinking? Do you think the authors would agree? Why or why not?

The Direct Teaching of Thinking as a Skill

Edward de Bono

A major trend may be developing in education toward the direct teaching of thinking as a skill. I intend in this article to answer two basic questions related to this trend. First, what is thinking? And second, how can we teach thinking directly? My answers spring from 16 years of experience in the field. During this time I developed an instructional program on thinking skills that is now used by several million schoolchildren in many different countries and cultures.

Of course, some educators believe that thinking is simply a matter of innate intelligence. Two corollaries follow from this belief: 1) we do not have to do anything specific to help highly intelligent individuals learn how to think, and 2) there is little we can do to help less intelligent individuals learn how to think. Thus those who hold this belief rest content. Yet many highly intelligent individuals often seem to be rather ineffective thinkers. Such

people are often good at reactive thinking and puzzle solving—but less able to think about topics that require a broader view. They may show cleverness, but not wisdom.

I prefer to see the relationship between intelligence and thinking as similar to the relationship between a car and its driver. Engineering determines the innate potential of the car, but the skill with which the car is driven must be learned and practiced. Thus I would define thinking as "the operating skill with which intelligence acts upon experience."

What, then, is the relationship of information to thinking? It seems obvious to me that God can neither think nor have a sense of humor. Perfect knowledge precludes the need to move from one arrangement of knowledge to a better one. Thus perfect knowledge makes thinking unnecessary. Nonetheless, educators often seem to believe that we can attain such perfect knowledge. However, even if it were possible to absorb perfect knowledge about the past, we can only have very partial knowledge about the future. Yet, as soon as a youngster leaves school, he or she will be operating in the future. Every initiative, decision, or plan will be carried out in the future and thus will require thinking, not just the sorting and re-sorting of knowledge. I have coined the term "operacy" to stand alongside literacy and numeracy as a primary goal of education. Operacy is the skill of doing things, of making things happen. The type of thinking that my program (which I will describe later) teaches is very much concerned with operacy.

In short, information is no substitute for thinking, and thinking is no substitute for information. The dilemma is that there is never enough time to teach all the information that could usefully be taught. Yet we may have to reduce the time we spend teaching information, in order to focus instead on the direct teaching of thinking skills.

The relationship between logic and thinking is likewise not a linear one. The computer world has a saying, "Garbage in—garbage out." In other words, even if the computer is working flawlessly, this will not validate a given outcome. Bad logic makes for bad thinking, but good logic (like the flawless computer) does not insure good thinking. Every logician knows that a conclusion is only as good as the premises. Mathematics, logic (of various sorts), and—increasingly—data processing are excellent service tools. But the deeper we advance into the computer age, the greater the need to emphasize the perceptual side of thinking, which these tools serve.

Meanwhile, emotions, values, and feelings influence thinking at three stages. We may feel a strong emotion (e.g., fear, anger, hatred) even before we encounter a situation. That emotion channels our perceptions. More usually, there is a brief period of undirected perception, until we recognize the situation. This recognition triggers emotion, which thereafter channels perception. The trained thinker should be operating in the third mode: perception explores the situation as broadly as possible, and, in the end, emotions determine the decision. There is no contradiction at all between emotions and thinking. The purpose of thinking is to arrange the world so that our emotions can be applied in a valuable manner.

The relationship of perception to thinking is, to my mind, the crucial area. In the past, far too many of our approaches to thinking (e.g.,

mathematics, logic) have concerned themselves with the "processing" aspect. We are rather good at processing but poor in the perceptual area.

What do I mean by perception? Quite simply, the way our minds make sense of the world around us. Language is a reflection of our traditional perceptions (as distinct from the moment-to-moment ones). Understanding how perception works is not so easy. But this is a crucial point—one that has a direct effect on the way we teach thinking.

Imagine a man holding a small block of wood. He releases the wood, and it falls to the ground. When he releases it a second time, the wood moves upward. This is strange and mysterious behavior. The third time he releases the wood, it remains exactly where it is—suspended in space. This is also mysterious behavior. If I were now to reveal that, in the second instance, the man was standing at the bottom of a swimming pool, then it seems perfectly natural for the wood to float upward. In the third instance, the man is an astronaut in orbit; thus it is perfectly natural for the wood to remain suspended, since it is weightless. Behavior that seemed strange and unaccountable suddenly seems normal and logical—once we have defined the "universe" in which it is taking place.

The traditional universe of information handling is a "passive" one. We record information through marks on paper or marks on magnetic tape. We can handle and process that information. The marks on the surface of the paper or tape and the information itself do not alter, unless we alter them.

An "active" system is totally different; here, the information actually organizes itself into patterns. We human beings have self-organizing information systems. I first wrote about them in 1969 in my book, *The Mechanism of Mind*.[1] I showed then how such systems work, and I suggested how the structure of a nerve network would produce such pattern-making effects. My hypothesis has since been simulated by computer, and the nerve network functions substantially as I had suggested.[2] In the world of information handling, the concept of self-organizing information systems is now coming to the fore.[3] Such systems are quite different from our usual computers.

Once we enter the "universe" of active, self-organizing systems, then the behavior of such things as perception and creativity becomes quite clear. The processes are no longer mysterious. Just as happened with the block of wood, phenomena that seemed to be unaccountable are suddenly seen to be explicable—once we have identified the appropriate universe.

The function of a self-organizing system is to allow incoming experience to organize itself into patterns. We could loosely compare these patterns to the streets in a town. The self-organizing system is immensely efficient; it allows us to get up in the morning, cross a road, recognize friends, read and write. Without such a pattern-making and pattern-using system, we would spend about a month just in crossing a road.

However, the advantages of a patterning system are also its disadvantages. "Point-to-point thinking" is a good example. In this kind of thinking, we follow a pattern from one point to the next—and then follow the dominant pattern from that next point onward. In an experiment that I conducted jointly with the Inner London Education Authority,[4] I asked 24 groups of 11-year-olds to discuss the suggestion that "bread, fish, and milk should be free." Although many of the children came from deprived backgrounds, 23 of the 24 groups opposed the idea of free bread, fish, and milk. The point-to-point thinking that led to this stand went as follows: 1) the shops would be crowded; 2) the buses going to the shops would be crowded; 3) the bus drivers would demand more money; 4) the drivers would not get more money, and they would go on strike; 5) other people would go on strike as well; and 6) there would be chaos—so giving away bread, fish, and milk is a bad idea. Thus can point-to-point thinking lead us astray, as we miss the forest while fixating on the trees.

However, direct teaching of thinking can offset the disadvantages of a patterning system. At the end of a pilot project on the teaching of thinking in Venezuelan schools, for example, we held a press conference. A journalist attending that conference claimed that all attempts to teach thinking are really a form of brainwashing in western capitalist values. The journalist happened to be wearing spectacles. So I removed her spectacles and asked what she used them for. She told me that she used the spectacles in order to see things more clearly. I then explained that the perceptual tools we were teaching in the lessons on thinking served the same purpose. The tools enable youngsters to scan their experiences so that they can see things more clearly and more broadly. A better map of the world is the result. These thinkers can still retain their original values and choices, however. Giving spectacles to near-sighted individuals enables them to see three glasses on a table—containing wine, orange juice, and milk. The individuals still exercise choice as to which drink each prefers. In the same way, our instructional program cuts across cultures and ideologies. The program is used in industrialized nations, such as Canada and Great Britain, and in developing nations, such as Venezuela and Malaysia; it will soon be used in Cuba, China, and Bulgaria—as well as in Catholic Ireland.

My point is that, in terms of perception, we need to achieve two things: 1) the ability to see things more clearly and more broadly and 2) the ability to see things differently (i.e., creativity or "lateral thinking"[5]). As I have said, perception takes place in an "active" information system. Such systems allow experience to organize itself into immensely useful patterns, without which life would be impossible. But, as I said above, the very advantages of the patterning system are also its disadvantages. We must overcome these disadvantages and improve perception in two ways: in breadth and in creativity or lateral thinking (both of which fall under the heading of "change").

Let me turn now to the second question that I posed at the beginning of this article. How can we teach thinking as a skill? Such teaching is going on right now; it is not tomorrow's dream, but today's reality. Millions of children are involved. In Venezuela, for example, 106,000 teachers have been trained to use my program, and every schoolchild takes a course in thinking. By law, Venezuelan schoolchildren in every grade must have two hours of direct instruction per week in thinking skills. The contracts of some labor union members in Venezuela specify that their employers must make provisions to teach them thinking skills. My program is also in use in many other countries—including Australia, the U.S., and Israel, as well as those nations I have mentioned previously.

The program of which I speak is called CoRT. (The acronym stands for Cognitive Research Trust, located in Cambridge, England.) I have already outlined the theoretical foundation for the design of this program. The lessons themselves focus on the perceptual aspect of thinking. The design of the tools takes into account the behavior of self-organizing patterning systems.

The design criteria for a practical instructional program should include the following elements:

- The program should be usable by teachers who represent a wide range of teaching talents, not just by the highly gifted or the highly qualified. (The 106,000 Venezuelan teachers were not all geniuses.)

- The program should not require complicated teacher training, since it is difficult to generalize such programs. (The CoRT program can be used by teachers with no special training or with only simple training.)

- The program should be robust enough to resist damage as it is passed along from trainer to trainer—and thence from new trainer to teachers and, finally, to pupils.

- The program should employ parallel design so that, if some parts of the program are badly taught and other parts are skipped or later forgotten, what remains is usable and valuable in its own right. (This contrasts with hierarchical design, in which a student must

grasp a basic concept before moving on to the next concept layer; failure at any concept layer in a program of this type makes the whole system unworkable.)

- The program should be enjoyable for both teachers and youngsters.

- The program should focus on thinking skills that help a learner to function better in his or her life outside of school, not merely to become more proficient at solving puzzles or playing games.

Before considering ways of teaching thinking, we must confront a prior question: Should thinking be taught in its own right? Certain practical considerations affect the answer to this question. For example, there are no gaps in the school schedule as it now exists. Thus it seems to make more sense to insert thinking skills into an existing subject area. English makes a good home, because a natural synergy exists between thinking and the expression of thought in language. In addition, the teaching style is often more open-ended in English classes than in some other subject areas. However, the CoRT program has been used effectively by science teachers, by music teachers, and even by physical education teachers.

Despite these practical considerations, I believe that we should have a specific place in the curriculum that is set aside for the teaching of thinking skills. This formal recognition is essential so that pupils, teachers, and parents all recognize that thinking skills are being taught directly. In time, I would certainly hope that the skills taught in the "thinking lessons" would find their ways into such subject areas as geography, history, social studies, and science. However, the first step is to establish "thinking" as a subject in its own right.

Having dealt with this question, we can now look at some of the traditional approaches to the teaching of thinking:

- *Logic, mathematics, and data processing.* These are very important subjects, but they concern themselves with processing, not with the perceptual side of thinking. The better that students become at processing, the more they need to strengthen their perception.

- *Critical thinking.* This is a popular approach because it is traditional. It also employs a relatively easy teaching method (the spotting of faults). This approach has only limited value, however. The spotting of faults—regardless of its usefulness in debate or argument—is only one aspect of thinking. The approach includes no generative, constructive, or creative elements. The avoidance of faults does not improve one's ability to plan or to make decisions. The avoidance of faults is, to my mind, an aspect of thinking that has traditionally been overvalued.

- *Discussion.* Directly or indirectly, discussion must be the most widely used method of teaching thinking. Youngsters are asked to discuss (or write essays on) a subject. The aim is to provide practice in thinking. The teacher notes and comments on faults and inappropriate uses of evidence, hoping that students will extract from these clues some general principles of thinking, which they will then use in future, unrelated situations. In reality, relatively little transfer of thinking skills from one situation to another takes place.

- *Puzzles, games, and simulations.* I have used games and problems as motivators, to get people interested in thinking. However, because of the difficulty of transfer, I do not believe that such devices have much teaching value. A skillful chess player does not transfer to his or her everyday life the fine sense of strategy developed through playing this game. A youngster may develop a puzzle-solving method, but thinking does not seem to proceed in that same fashion in real life. I have grave reservations about the traditional information-processing model of thinking, which seems more a description than a system of operating.

This brings me to the central problem: transfer and content. Does a generalizable skill of thinking exist? Many theorists think not. They believe instead that there is thinking in mathematics, thinking in science, and thinking in history—but that in each case the rules are dif-

ferent, just as the rules for Monopoly differ from those for chess. I do not see this as a point of view with which I must either agree or disagree totally. Clearly, subject idioms exist. Nevertheless, it is possible to establish both habits of mind and specific thinking techniques that can be applied in any subject area. For example, the willingness to look for alternatives is a generalizable thinking habit. And deliberate provocation is a technique that can be applied to generate ideas in any situation.

Because we cannot succeed in teaching generalizable thinking skills through the use of specific content materials, some theorists believe that such skills cannot exist. But there is another way of looking at this situation: the view that generalizable thinking skills exist but cannot be taught using specific content. My experience has led me to the latter view. As I have already noted with regard to the "discussion method" of teaching thinking skills, little transfer of such skills seems to take place from one situation to another. Given the mechanics of perception and attention, this is hardly surprising. If the subject of a discussion is interesting, then—by definition—attention follows this interest. But this attention is not focused on the metacognitive level; that is, participants are not thinking about the *thinking* that they are using to discuss the subject. Moreover, it is very difficult to transfer a complex action sequence from one situation to another. That is why the CoRT program deliberately focuses on "tools" that can be transferred.

I have noticed among U.S. educators a tendency to try to teach thinking through content materials. This approach seems—to its proponents—to have two merits. First, this approach makes it easier to introduce thinking into the curriculum, because the material must be covered anyway (and it is already familiar to the teacher). Second, this approach seems to be killing two birds with one stone: teaching thinking *and* teaching content. But this approach is not effective. I am afraid that the nettle must be grasped. Either one wishes to teach thinking effectively or merely to make a token gesture. Attending to content distracts from attending to the thinking tools being used. Theory predicts this outcome: you cannot build meta-patterns on one level and experience patterns on another level at the same time. Experience backs up this expectation. Wherever there has been an attempt to teach thinking skills and content together, the training in thinking seems to be weaker than when those skills are taught in isolation.

So what is the CoRT method? It is best to illustrate this method with an example.

I was teaching a class of 30 boys, all 11 years of age, in Sydney, Australia. I asked if they would each like to be given $5 a week for coming to school. All 30 thought this was a fine idea, "We could buy sweets or chewing gum. . . . We could buy comics. . . . We could get toys without having to ask Mum or Dad."

I then introduced and explained a simple tool called the PMI (which I will describe later). The explanation took about four minutes. In groups of five, the boys applied the PMI tool to the suggestion that they should be given $5 a week for coming to school. For three to four minutes they talked and thought on their own. At no time did I interfere. I never discussed the $5 suggestion, other than to state it. I did not suggest that the youngsters consider this, think of that, and so forth. At the end of their thinking time, the groups reported back to me: "The bigger boys would beat us up and take the money. . . . The school would raise its charges for meals. . . . Our parents would not buy us presents. . . . Who would decide how much money different ages received? . . . There would be less money to pay teachers. . . . There would be less money for a school minibus."

When they had finished their reports, I again asked the boys to express their views on the suggestion of pay for attending school. This time, 29 of the 30 had completely reversed their opinion and thought it a bad idea. We subsequently learned that the one holdout received *no* pocket money at home. The important point is that my contribution was minimal. I did not interact with the boys. I simply explained the PMI tool, and the boys then used it on their own—as *their* tool. My "superior" in-

telligence and broader experiences were not influences. The boys did their own thinking.

The PMI is a simple scanning tool designed to avoid the point-to-point thinking that I mentioned earlier. The thinker looks first in the *P*lus direction (good points), and then in the *M*inus direction (bad points), and finally in the *I*nteresting direction (interesting things that might arise or are worth noting, even if they are neither good nor bad). Each direction is scanned formally, one after another. This formal scan produces a better and broader map. Thinking is used to explore, not merely to back up a snap judgment. The thinker then applies judgment to the better map. The PMI is the first of the 60 CoRT lessons.

For the rest of this particular lesson on thinking, I might have asked the boys to apply the PMI in various ways (e.g., one group doing only "Plus" or "Minus" or "Interesting") to a number of thinking items, such as: Should all cars be colored yellow? Would it be a good idea for everyone to wear a badge showing his or her mood at the moment? Is homework a good idea? Note that the items are not related. Moreover, the groups would be allowed to spend only two or three minutes on each. This is quite deliberate and essential to the method.

The items are switched rapidly so that attention stays on the PMI tool and *not on the content*. Once skill in the use of the tool is developed, students can apply the PMI to other situations in other settings. One girl told us how she used the PMI at home to decide whether or not to have her long hair cut. Some children report that they have used the PMI with their parents, in discussing such major decisions as moving to a new town or buying a car. This is the sort of transfer that the CoRT program aims to achieve.

The PMI is a scanning tool, not a judgment tool. If a thinker spots 10 "Plus" points and only two "Minus" points, this does not necessarily mean that the idea is a good one. Like all scanning, the PMI is subjective, depending on the thinker's perspective. One boy said, as a "Plus" point, that yellow cars would be kept cleaner. Another boy slated this as a "Minus" point—because he had to clean his dad's car and would therefore have to perform this chore more often. Both were right.

The PMI is designed to be artificial, memorable, and easy to pronounce. At first, some teachers rejected "PMI" as pointless jargon. They preferred to encourage or exhort the youngsters to look at the good points and the bad points in any situation. The youngsters probably did so—at that moment. However, without the artificial term "PMI" to crystallize the process and to create a meta-pattern, the exhortation does not stick. One teacher told me how he had used the term "PMI" and how his colleague, in a parallel lesson, had used exhortation. His colleague was soon convinced of the value of the term "PMI."

One girl said that she initially thought the PMI a rather silly device, since she knew how she felt about a subject. But she noted that, as she wrote things down under each letter (she was doing a written exercise instead of the usual oral approach), she became less certain. In the end, the points she had written down did cause her to change her mind. Yet *she* had written down the points. That is precisely the purpose of a scanning tool.

It is important to realize that the description of thinking and the design of tools are two totally different things. It is possible to describe the process of thinking and to break it into components. But then one is tempted to turn each component into a tool, on the premise that, if the components are taught, thinking skills must surely be enhanced. However, teaching someone how to describe a flower does not teach him or her how to grow a flower. The purpose of analysis and the purpose of an operating tool are separate and distinct.

The CoRT tools are designed specifically as operating tools. Such a design has two components: 1) the tool must be easy to use, and 2) it must have a useful effect. Abstract analyses and subdivisions of the thinking process may be intellectually neat, but this does not guarantee usability or effectiveness. My many years of experience, working with thousands of ex-

ecutives and organizations in different countries, have given me some insight into those aspects of thinking that have practical value. I have also worked with scientists, designers, lawyers, and many others who are involved in the "action world" of thinking, as distinct from the "contemplative world."

The CoRT program[6] has six sections, each consisting of 10 lessons: CoRT I (breadth), CoRT II (organization), CoRT III (interaction), CoRT IV (creativity), CoRT V (information and feeling), and CoRT VI (action). All teachers who use the program should teach CoRT I. (Some teachers use *only* the 10 lessons of CoRT I.) Thereafter, the sections can be used in any order. For example, a teacher might use CoRT I, CoRT IV, and CoRT V. The last section (CoRT VI) is somewhat different from the other sections, in that it provides a framework for a staged approach to thinking.

I believe that thinking is best taught to 9-, 10-, and 11-year olds. Youngsters in the middle grades really enjoy thinking, and motivation is very high. They have sufficient verbal fluency and experience to operate the thinking tools. The curriculum is more easily modified in the middle grades to include thinking as a basic subject. But the CoRT materials have also been used with children younger than 9 and with students ranging in age from 12 to adult.

So basic is thinking as a skill that the same CoRT lessons have been used by children in the jungles of South America and by top executives of the Ford Motor Company, United Kingdom. The lessons have been taught to students ranging in I.Q. from below 80 to above 140. The lessons have also been used with groups of mixed ability.

David Lane, at the Hungerford Guidance Centre in London, found that the teaching of thinking to delinquent and violent youngsters brought about an improvement in behavior, as measured by a sharp fall in the number of disciplinary encounters these youngsters had with supervisors.[7] William Copley and Edna Copley, in preliminary work at an institution for young offenders, found similar changes.[8] They recounted how one youth, on the verge of attacking an officer with a hammer, brought to mind a thinking lesson concerned with consequences—and quietly put the hammer down. I mention these changes in behavior for two reasons. First, I believe that the true test of teaching thinking is the effect of such teaching on behavior. Second, we do not really have any adequate way of measuring thinking performance. Standardized tests are largely irrelevant, because they do not allow us to observe the thinker's composite performance.

John Edwards taught the CoRT program in lieu of a portion of the science syllabus to a class in Australia. Using an analysis-of-discourse approach to measurement, he found that the trained students did significantly better at thinking than untrained peers; the trained students even seemed to do better in science, although they had had less instructional time devoted to that subject.[9] It is not difficult to show that pupils who have had training in thinking produce a wider scan when they are asked to consider some subject. In Ireland, Liam Staunton found that, before CoRT training, individuals produced an average of four sentences on a topic, whereas after CoRT training they produced an average of 47.[10] We are currently analyzing data from the experiment in Venezuela and data from the Schools Council project in England.

I prefer that CoRT users carry out their own tests and pilot projects. Tests carried out by the designers of a program are of limited value for two reasons: 1) the conditions of teaching are ideal (and often far removed from those prevailing in schools where the program will be used), and 2) such studies always contain an element of bias.

It is impossible, however, to measure the soft data: the confidence of those who have had training in thinking, the focus of their thinking, their willingness to think about things, the effectiveness of their thinking, their structured approach and breadth of consideration. Teachers often sum up these factors as "maturity," in commenting about those children who come to their classrooms after some training in thinking.

I would expect four levels of achievement in the acquisition of thinking skills through use of the CoRT program:

- *Level 1.* A general awareness of thinking as a skill. A willingness to "think" about something. A willingness to explore around a subject. A willingness to listen to others. No recollection of any specific thinking tool.
- *Level 2.* A more structured approach to thinking, including better balance, looking at the consequences of an action or choice (taking other people's views into account), and a search for alternatives. Perhaps a mention of a few of the CoRT tools.
- *Level 3.* Focused and deliberate use of some of the CoRT tools. The organization of thinking as a series of steps. A sense of purpose in thinking.
- *Level 4.* Fluent and appropriate use of many CoRT tools. Definite consciousness of the metacognitive level of thinking. Observation of and comment on the thinker's own thinking. The designing of thinking tasks and strategies, followed by the carrying out of these tasks.

In most situations, I would expect average attainment to fall somewhere between Levels 1 and 2. With a more definite emphasis on "thinking," this would rise to a point between Levels 2 and 3. Only in exceptional groups with thorough training would I expect to find average attainment at Level 4.

Perhaps the most important aspect of the direct teaching of thinking as a skill is the self-image of a youngster as a "thinker," however. This is an operational image. Thinking becomes a skill at which the youngster can improve. Such a self-image is different from the more usual "value" images: "I am intelligent" (I get on well at school) or "I am not intelligent" (I do not get on well at school, and school is a bore). Value images are self-reinforcing. So are operational images—but the reinforcement goes in opposite directions at the negative end. In other words, the less intelligent students find repeated evidence of their lack of intelligence, but they also notice those occasions when they do manage to come up with good ideas.

ENDNOTES

1. Edward de Bono, *The Mechanism of Mind* (New York: Simon & Schuster, 1969).

2. M. H. Lee and A. R. Maradurajan, "A Computer Package of the Evaluation of Neuron Models Involving Large Uniform Networks," *International Journal of Man-Machine Studies,* 1982, pp. 189–210.

3. John Hopfield, "Brain, Computer, and Memory," *Engineering and Science*, September 1982.

4. Unpublished material, Cognitive Research Trust.

5. Edward de Bono, *Lateral Thinking* (New York: Harper & Row, 1970).

6. CoRT Thinking Program, Pergamon, Inc., Maxwell House, Fairview Park, Elmsford, NY 10523.

7. Personal communication from David Lane.

8. William Copley and Edna Copley, *Practical Teaching of Thinking,* forthcoming.

9. Unpublished paper by John Edwards, James Cook University, Queensland, Australia.

10. Personal communication from Liam Staunton.

How to Keep Thinking Skills from Going the Way of All Frills

Carl Bereiter

Success in teaching thinking skills results when content objectives are contingent *on activities that also promote thinking and when thinking skills* permeate *the entire curriculum.*

Perhaps no one will be so indiscriminate as to call thinking skills instruction a frill, but it is often treated as one, just one more burden on an already heavily loaded curriculum, one more competitor with the things teachers are held accountable for. Consequently, no matter how readily teachers agree that more should be done to promote thinking skills, it is reasonable to predict that thinking skills instruction will tend to be passed over by more standard activities directed toward the three R's and subject-matter instruction.

This article's message is fairly simple but it is distilled from 15 occasionally frustrating years of school-based experiments on promoting thinking skills. As methods of teaching thinking skills, two approaches do not usually succeed: treating thinking skills (1) as enrichment or (2) as subject matter. Conversely, there are two main ways to guard against failure.

1. Make thinking skills activities an integral part of other, already-accepted instructional objectives (a *contingency strategy*).
2. Permeate the instructional program so thoroughly with thinking skills activities that they cannot be isolated and reduced to verbalized subject matter (a *permeation strategy*).

If It's Fun, This Must Be Friday

Games are a natural medium for teaching thinking skills. They provide motivation, feedback, and a structure within which it is easy to adjust the level and type of intellectual challenge. But because of their inevitable association with the lighter side of life, they are also especially susceptible to being regarded as nonessential. This fact was brought home to me during a three-year field test of the effects of thinking games. We had developed and tried out on a short-term basis about 60 games de-

From *Educational Leadership* (September 1984):75–77. Reprinted with permission.

signed to foster various kinds of thinking skills.[1] For the field test, 12 teachers volunteered to devote a minimum of two hours a week to these thinking games. In follow-up questioning they expressed enthusiasm for the games and pointed to a variety of cognitive benefits they claimed to have seen in their students. Yet by their own reports they had devoted an average of only 45 minutes per week to the games, and spot checks by our research staff suggested that 45 minutes was more the maximum than the average amount of time spent.

The fact was that thinking games were relegated to Friday afternoon doldrums and occasional odd moments when some group of children needed to be kept independently occupied. Not a bad use of the thinking games, certainly, but not a use that could be expected to produce much effect on developing thinking skills—and the test results showed this. There was not a trace of difference in reasoning and creativity test scores between classes that had used the games and those that had not. (On the other hand, questionnaires revealed that control group teachers had also made use of spare-time games and thinking activities.)

The Contingency Strategy Applied to Mathematical Games

The group I have been working with over the past 12 years in developing an elementary mathematics curriculum[2] decided at the outset that mathematical thinking activities should be part of the daily activities of all students from kindergarten up. Games represented only one of several channels for bringing thinking skills into the mathematics program, but a very important one.

To ensure that games were actually used, we determined that they should have a dual function. They should involve some kind of mathematical reasoning or problem solving, but at the same time they should play a significant role in reinforcing specific mathematical concepts of skills. We wanted to be able to insist

legitimately that if the games were omitted, students would be missing out not only on thinking skill activities but also on important work related to the more conventional mathematical objectives, such as computational skills.

A typical example of such a game is "Make a Problem," in which players roll dice to generate the digits to fill in, for instance, a multidigit addition problem. The object is to produce the problem that yields the largest sum. The game provides addition practice, obviously. However, since winning depends on getting the largest digits into the farthest-left columns, it is also a vehicle for promoting familiarity with the base 10 structure of our number system. Therefore, it is possible in good faith to tell teachers that if they skip the game, they will be shortchanging students on a crucial mathematical concept. Students who play the game not only exercise their base 10 and computational skills but also play a game of strategy involving considerations such as the probability of rolling a number higher or lower than the digit they are about to put in place. This example illustrates the essence of the *contingency strategy*—making already recognized instructional objectives contingent on activities that also promote thinking skills.

Experience with several hundred field test classes indicated that games of this dual-purpose kind were indeed treated differently. Teachers who approved of the mathematics games used them regularly as part of their instructional programs. A few teachers, usually in the upper grades, didn't think games were proper vehicles for instruction. But that is a difference of opinion one can respect and accept.

Teaching Thinking Versus Teaching About Thinking

An example from one of my colleagues illustrates another important point about the teaching of thinking skills. A teacher of educational psychology gave her students a long difficult article and told them they had ten minutes in which to learn as much from it as possible. Almost without exception they started with the first sentence and labored along as best they could until their time was up. Later, they all admitted they knew rules for handling that kind of task—skim for main ideas, consult section headings, and so forth. Somewhere along the line, all had apparently been taught high-level reading strategies. More precisely, they had been taught principles that, if translated into procedures, would constitute high-level reading strategies.

I am not suggesting that there is anything wrong with teaching verbalized principles of thinking. Such declarative knowledge can be an important first stage in acquiring cognitive skills.[3] But this step needs to be followed by a proceduralization stage in which that knowledge becomes manifested in the actual behavior of the learners. This is not a simple matter of reinforcing principles through practice. It means actually *constructing* the cognitive strategy that is referred to by the verbal rules.

The trouble is that, whereas cognitive strategies are hard to teach directly and take a long time to learn, verbalized rules are easily transferred to a textbook and can be thoroughly taught in a few lessons. Thus, we find textbooks purporting to teach mathematical problem-solving stategies and reading comprehension strategies when all they do is list a few rules, provide some examples, and then offer a few exercises in which students are urged to apply the rules (after having been carefully told which rules to apply where). This illustration shows what I mean by reducing thinking skills to subject matter. I fear we are going to see a lot more of that.

The Permeation Strategy

Condensing the teaching of cognitive strategies into a few pages and covering it in a week fits the conventions of instructional programming and the desire of textbook publishers to make their goods visible at a glance. Overcoming such tendencies is not easy. The permeation strategy probably cannot overcome this tendency but can possibly provide a counterforce. The essense of the permeation strategy is to apply a set of principles for promoting thinking skills in *every possible aspect* of the instructional program. Thus, thinking skills can never be wholly reduced to verbalized subject matter. For example:

> Don't let decisions that ought to require thought become automatic.

This principle has always been with us in developing the elementary mathematics program referred to previously. Don't group together word problems that all require the same operation, lest students stop thinking about what operation to use. Don't give consistent verbal clues (such as "more" always means "add"), lest students stop paying attention to what the problem means. Include problems that don't require computation at all (such as "If one greyhound can jump over a ditch two meters wide, about how wide a ditch can six greyhounds jump across?"). Include these with ordinary computational problems. Don't put them in a special section that warns students what to watch for.[4]

Both the contingency strategy and the permeation strategy spring from the same basic idea, which is that the promotion of thinking skills should be deeply embedded in the whole fabric of an instructional program. This means encouraging and challenging thinking. But it means something deeper as well. It means that some reasonably adequate cognitive theory ought to underlie all instruction. We are not likely to see that happening in published instructional materials until those responsible for selecting them start sharpening their demands. The question to ask textbook suppliers is not "Where do you teach such-and-such cognitive skills? Instead, open *any* page and say, "How is your approach to teaching thinking represented on this page?"[4]

ENDNOTES

1. Valerie Anderson and Carl Bereiter, *Thinking Games 1;* Carl Bereiter and Valerie Anderson, *Thinking Games 2* (Belmont, Calif.: Pitman Learning, 1980).

2. Stephen S. Willoughby, Carl Bereiter, Peter Hilton, and Joseph H. Rubenstein, *Real Math* (Le Salle, Ill.: Open Court, 1981).

3. John R. Anderson, "Acquisition of Cognitive Skills," *Psychological Review* 89 (1982): 369–406. For an example of the use of explicit principles accompanied by aids in translating these principles into cognitive behavior, see Marlene Scardamalia, Carl Bereiter, and Rosanne Steinbach, "Teachability of Reflective Processes in Written Composition," *Cognitive Science*, 8, 2 (1984): 173–190.

4. An even more penetrating question, of course, is "What evidence is there that your program does improve thinking skills?" In the case of *Real Math*, we were heartened by an independent study conducted by Robert P. Dilworth and Leonard M. Warren, "An Independent Investigation of Real Math: The Field Testing and Learner-Verification Studies" (La Salle, Ill.: Open Court, 1980). It showed through a time-lag study that mathematical problem solving was one of the skills that did improve significantly when our material was introduced. In many cases, however, it will be difficult to document effects; in those cases the best that can be demanded is a coherent approach to teaching thinking that goes beyond enrichment activities, drill, and the teaching of rules.

Mediating the Metacognitive

Arthur L. Costa

Students can learn to understand and articulate their mental processes if teachers specifically encourage thinking about thinking.

Try to solve this problem in your head:

How much is one half of two plus two?

Did you hear yourself talking to yourself? Did you have to decide if you should take one half of the first two or if you should sum the two's first?

If you caught yourself having an inner dialogue inside your brain, and if you had to evaluate your own decision-making/problem-solving processes, you were experiencing *metacognition*. Metacognition is our ability to know what we know and what we don't know. It occurs in the cerebral cortex and is thought by some neurologists to be uniquely human.

Metacognition is our ability to plan a strategy for producing what information is needed, to be conscious of our own steps and strategies during the act of problem solving, and to reflect on and evaluate the productivity of our own thinking. While inner language, thought to be a prerequisite, begins in most children around age five, metacognition—a key attribute of formal thought flowers at about age eleven. Interestingly, not all humans achieve the level of formal operations (Chiabetta, 1976). And, as Luria, the Russian psychologist found, not all adults metacogitate (Whimbey and Whimbey, 1976).

Students often follow instructions or tasks *without* wondering why they are doing what they are doing. They seldom question themselves about their own learning strategies or evaluate the efficiency of their own performance. Some children have virtually no idea of what they are doing when they perform a task and are often unable to explain their strategies for solving problems (Sternberg and Wagner, 1982). There is much evidence, however, to demonstrate that those who persevere in problem solving; who think critically, flexibly, and insightfully; and who can consciously apply their intellectual skills are those who possess well-developed metacognitive abilities (Bloom and Broder, 1950; Brown, 1978; Whimbey, 1980). Such people also effectively manage their intellectual resources. These resources include: (1) basic perceptual-motor skills; (2)

From *Educational Leadership* (November 1984): 57–62. Reprinted with permission.

language, beliefs, knowledge of content, and memory processes; and (3) purposeful and voluntary strategies intended to achieve a desired outcome (Aspen Systems, 1982).

If we wish to develop intelligent behavior as a significant outcome of education, instructional strategies purposefully intended to develop children's metacognitive abilities must be infused into our teaching methods, staff development, and supervisory processes (Costa, 1981). Interestingly, *direct* instruction in metacognition may *not* be beneficial. When strategies of problem solving are imposed rather than generated by the students themselves, their performance may be impaired. Conversely, when students experience the need for problem-solving strategies, induce their own, discuss them, and practice them to the degree that they become spontaneous and unconscious, their metacognition seems to improve (Sternberg and Wagner, 1982). The trick, therefore, is to teach metacognitive skills without creating an even greater burden on students' ability to attend.

Probably the major component of metacognition is developing a plan of action and then maintaining that plan in mind over time. Planning a strategy before embarking on a course of action assists us in keeping track of the steps in the sequence of planned behavior at the conscious awareness level for the duration of the activity. It facilitates making temporal and comparative judgments; assessing readiness for more or different activities; and monitoring our interpretations, perceptions, decisions, and behaviors. An example of this is what superior teachers do daily: develop a teaching strategy for a lesson, keep that strategy in mind throughout the instruction, then reflect upon the strategy to evaluate its effectiveness in producing the desired student outcomes.

Rigney (1980) identified the following self-monitoring skills as necessary for successful performance on intellectual tasks:

- Keeping one's place in a long sequence of operations.
- Knowing that a subgoal has been obtained.

- Detecting errors and recovering from those errors either by making a quick fix or by retreating to the last known correct operation.

Such monitoring involves both looking ahead and looking back. Looking ahead includes:

- Learning the structure of a sequence of operations.
- Identifying areas where errors are likely.
- Choosing a strategy that will reduce the possibility of error and will provide easy recovery.
- Identifying the kinds of feedback that will be available at various points and evaluating the usefulness of these kinds of feedback.

Looking back includes:

- Detecting errors previously made.
- Keeping a history of what has been done so far and therefore what should come next.
- Assessing the reasonableness of the present immediate outcome of task performance.

A simple example of this might be drawn from a reading task. It is a common experience while reading a passage to have our minds wander from the words. We see the words, but no meaning is being produced. Suddenly we realize that we are not concentrating and that we've lost contact with the meaning of the text. We recover by returning to the passage to find the place, matching it with the last thought we remember; once having found it, we read on with connectedness. This inner awareness and the strategy of recovery are components of metacognition.

Strategies for Enhancing Metacognition[1]

Teachers can use a variety of strategies to enhance metacognition, independent of grade level and subject area.

Planning strategy. Prior to any learning activity, teachers should point out strategies and steps for attacking problems, rules to remember, and directions to follow. Time constraints, purposes, and ground rules under which students must operate should be identified and internalized. Making these guidelines explicit helps students keep them in mind during the lesson and gives them a way to evaluate their performance afterwards.

During the activity, teachers can invite students to share their progress, thought processes, and perceptions of their own behavior. Asking students to indicate where they are in their strategy, to describe their trail of thinking up to that point, and to define alternative problem-solving pathways they intend to pursue next helps them become aware of their own behavior. It also provides teachers with a diagnostic cognitive map of students' thinking, which can be used to give more individualized assistance.

Then, *after* the learning activity, teachers can invite students to evaluate how well the rules were obeyed, how productive the strategies were, whether the instructions were followed correctly, and whether alternative, more efficient strategies could be used in the future.

I know a kindergarten teacher who begins and ends each day with a class meeting. During the morning, children make plans for the day. They decide upon what learning tasks to accomplish and how to accomplish them. They allocate classroom space, assign roles, and develop criteria for appropriate conduct. Throughout the day the teacher calls attention to the plans and ground rules made that morning and invites students to compare what they are doing with what was agreed. Then, before dismissal, another class meeting is held to reflect on, evaluate, and plan further strategies and criteria.

Generating questions. Regardless of the subject area, it is useful for students to pose study questions for themselves prior to and during their reading of textual material. This self-generation of questions facilitates comprehension and encourages students to pause frequently and think about whether, for instance, they know main characters or events, if they are grasping the concept, if they can relate it to what they already know, if they can give other examples, and whether they can use the main idea to explain other ideas or predict what may come next. They must then decide what strategic action to take to remove any obstacles to their comprehension. All of this helps students become more self-aware and to take conscious control of their own studying (Sanacore, 1984).

Choosing consciously. Teachers can promote metacognition by helping students explore the consequences of their choices and decisions prior to and during the act of deciding. Students will then be able to perceive causal relationships among their choice, their actions, and the results they achieved. Providing nonjudgmental feedback to students about the effects of their behaviors and decisions on others and on their environment helps them become aware of their own behaviors. For example, a teacher's statement, "I want you to know that the noise you're making with your pencil is disturbing me," will better contribute to metacognitive development than the command, "John, stop tapping your pencil!"

Evaluating with multiple criteria. Teachers can enhance metacognition by causing students to reflect upon and categorize their actions according to two or more sets of evaluative criteria. An example would be to invite students to distinguish what was done that was helpful and hindering; what they liked and didn't like; or what were pluses and minuses of the activity. Thus, students must keep the criteria in mind, apply them to multiple classification systems, and justify their reasons accordingly.

Taking credit. Teachers may cause students to identify what they have done well and invite them to seek feedback from their peers. The teacher might ask, "What have you done that you're proud of?" and "How would you like to be recognized for doing that?" (Name on the board, hug, pat on the back, handshake, applause from the group, and so on.) Students

will become more conscious of their own behavior and apply a set of internal criteria for
those behaviors that they consider good.

Outlawing "I can't." Teachers can inform
students that their excuses—"I can't"; "I don't
know how to . . . "; or "I'm too slow to . . . "—
are unacceptable behaviors in the classroom.
Instead, students should be asked to identify
what information is required, what materials
are needed, or what skills are lacking in their
ability to perform the desired behavior. This
helps students identify the boundaries between
what they know and what they need to know. It
develops a perseverant attitude and enhances
the student's ability to create strategies that will
produce needed data.

***Paraphrasing or reflecting back students'
ideas.*** Some examples of paraphrasing, building upon, extending, and using students' ideas
might be to say: "What you're telling me
is . . . "; "What I hear in your plan are the following steps . . . "; or "Let's work with Peter's
strategy for a moment." Inviting students to re-
state, translate, compare and paraphrase each
other's ideas causes them to become not only
better listeners to other's thinking, but better
listeners to their own thinking as well.

Labeling students' behaviors. When teachers place labels on students' cognitive processes, students become conscious of their own
actions: "What I see you doing is making out a
plan of action for . . . ": "What you are doing is
called an experiment"; "You're being very
helpful to Mark by sharing your paints. That's
an example of cooperation."

Clarifying students' terminology. Students
often use hollow, vague, and nonspecific terminology. For example, in making value judgments, students might say, "It's not fair," "He's
too strict," "It's no good." Teachers need to
clarify these values: What's too strict? What
would be more fair?

***Students sometimes use nominalisa-
tions.*** "They're mean to me." Who are *they*?

"We had to do that." Who is *we*? "Everybody
has one." Who is *Everybody*? Asking such clarifying questions causes students to define their
terminology operationally and to examine the
premise on which their thinking is based.

It is also helpful to clarify students' problem-solving processes. Causing students to describe their thinking while they are thinking
seems to beget more thinking. Teachers can invite students to talk aloud as they are solving a
problem; discuss what is going on in their
heads, for example, when they decode an unfamiliar word while reading; or ask what steps
they are going through in deciding whether to
buy something.

After a problem is solved, teachers can invite clarification of the processes used: "Sarah,
you figured out that the answer was 44; Shawn
says the answer is 33. Let's hear how you came
up with 44; retrace your steps for us." Clarifying helps students to reexamine their own
problem-solving processes, to identify their errors, and to self-correct. The teacher might ask,
"How much is three plus four?" The student
may replay "12." Rather than merely correcting the student, the teacher may choose to clarify: "Gina, how did you arrive at that answer?"
"Well, I multiplied four and three and got . . .
Oh, I see, I multiplied instead of added."

Role playing and simulations. Role playing
can promote metacognition because when students assume the roles of other persons, they
consciously maintain the attributes and characteristics of that person. Dramatization serves
as a hypothesis or prediction of how that person would react in a certain situation. Taking
on another role contributes to the reduction of
ego-centered perceptions.

Journal keeping. Writing and illustrating a
personal log or a diary throughout an experience causes students to synthesize thoughts
and actions and to translate them to symbolic
form. The record also provides an opportunity
to revisit initial perceptions, to compare
changes in those perceptions with the addition
of more data, to chart the processes of strategic

thinking and decision making, to identify the blind alleys and pathways taken, and to recall the successes and the tragedies of experimentation. (A variation on writing journals is making video and/or audio tape recordings of actions and performances.)

Modeling. Of all the instructional techniques suggested, the one with the probability of greatest influence on students is that of teacher modeling. Since students learn best by imitating the adults around them, the teacher who publicly demonstrates metacognition will probably produce students who metacogitate. Some indicators of teachers' public metacognitive behavior might be: sharing their planning—describing their goals and objectives and giving reasons for their actions; making human errors and then illustrating recovery from those errors by getting back on track; admitting they do not know an answer but designing ways to produce an answer; seeking feedback and evaluation of their actions from others; having a clearly stated value system and making decisions consistent with that system; being able to self-disclose—using adjectives that describe their own strengths and weaknesses; demonstrating understanding and emphathy by listening to and accurately describing the ideas and feelings of others.

Evaluating Growth in Metacognitive Abilities

We can determine if students are becoming more aware of their own thinking as they are able to describe what goes on in their heads when they are thinking. When asked, they can list the steps and tell where they are in the sequence of a problem-solving strategy. They can trace the pathways and dead ends they took on the road to a solution. They can describe what data are lacking and their plans for producing those data.

We should see students becoming more perseverant when the solution to a problem is not immediately apparent. This means that they have systematic methods of analyzing a problem, knowing ways to begin, knowing what steps must be performed and when they are accurate or are in error. We should see students taking more pride in their efforts; becoming self-correcting, striving for craftsmanship and accuracy in their products, and becoming more autonomous in their problem-solving abilities.

Teaching for thinking is becoming the great educational discovery for the 80s. Metacognition is an indicator of the "educated intellect" and must be included in the curriculum if thinking is to become a durable reality for the 90s and beyond.

ENDNOTE

For several of these techniques I am deeply indebted to Fred Newton, Superintendent of Schools, Multnomah County, Oregon; Juanita Sagan, a therapist in Oakland, California; and Ron Brandt, Executive Editor, ASCD.

REFERENCES

Aspen Systems. *Topics in Learning and Learning Disabilities* 2, 1 (April 1982).

Bloom, B. S., and Broder, L. J. *Problem-Solving Processes of College Students*. Chicago: University of Chicago Press, 1950.

Brown, A. L. "Knowing When, Where, and How to Remember: A Problem of Meta-Cognition." *Advances in Instructional Psychology*. Edited by Robert Glaser. Hillsdale, N.J.: Erlbaum, 1978.

Chiabetta, E. L. "A Review of Piagetian Studies Relevant to Science Instruction at the Secondary and College Level." *Science Education* 60 (1976): 253–261.

Costa, A. L. "Teaching for Intelligent Behavior." *Educational Leadership* 39, 1 (October 1981): 29–32.

Rigney, J. W. "Cognitive Learning Strategies and Qualities in Information Processing." Edited by R.

Snow, P. Federico, and W. Montague. In *Aptitudes, Learning, and Instruction,* Vol. 1. Hillsdale, N.J.: Erlbaum, 1980.

Sanacore, J. "Metacognition and the Improvement of Reading: Some Important Links." *Journal of Reading* (May 1984): 706–712.

Sternberg, R., and Wagner, R. "Understanding Intelligence: What's In It for Education." Paper submitted to the National Commission on Excellence in Education. 1982.

Whimbey, A. "Students Can Learn to Be Better Problem Solvers." *Educational Leadership* 37, 7 (April 1980): 560–565.

Whimbey, A., and Whimbey, L. S. *Intelligence Can be Taught.* New York: Bantam Books, 1976.

Is Direct Instruction More Effective than Methods that Give Students More Freedom?

For many years researchers have studied the relationship between teacher behavior and student achievement. Some reviewers have concluded that the most effective instruction is characterized by a pattern of teaching behavior which they call "direct instruction" (Rosenshine and Berliner, 1977).

With direct instruction (DI), the teacher is in control—interacting frequently with the students, showing them what to do, and assessing their progress. The focus of the instruction is academic—instructional groups tend to be large, students have little freedom of choice or movement, and the classroom is structured and orderly. This approach is said to increase students' "academic engaged time" (AET) which in turn leads to greater academic achievement.

Direct instruction may be contrasted with "experiential" approaches (Horowitz, 1979) in which there is less direct teacher control, more individual or small-group independent work, more student activity and movement, and flexibility in the use of materials and space. Proponents of experiential education believe their approach is more effective than direct instruction in preparing students to solve real problems independently.

In the first article for this issue, Rosenshine reviews studies in which teachers of regular classrooms have been trained in the use of direct instruction. When compared with students of teachers who were untrained, those in classrooms of trained teachers had more time on task and higher achievement. Basic skills were emphasized by these teachers, and results were generally best with younger, slower students, and those with poorer backgrounds. Rosenshine identifies the instructional "functions" which he finds are characteristic of successful direct instruction.

Janet Kierstead urges an end to the debate over direct instruction and experiential education. Her work with teachers has convinced her that the two approaches can complement each other. She agrees that direct instruction is of value for teaching basic skills, but finds that other approaches are needed for the attainment of some important objectives. She believes the exclusive use of direct instruction deprives students of opportunities to develop responsibility, independence, and higher-level thinking skills. The crucial issue separating advocates of direct instruction and experiential approaches may be seen as one of direct and indirect control by the teacher, and the problem for teachers may lie in learning when and how to share control with students.

Thought Questions

Do you think differences in student achievement are influenced more by teaching methods than by factors beyond the control of the school? How would you rank the relative influence of the teacher's method, peer relationships, home conditions, and the student's aptitude?

Compare your own experience with direct teaching and with more experiential approaches. What did you learn best with each? Which do you prefer? To what do you attribute your differing success and your present preferences?

Would you expect direct teaching to be more appropriate for children from homes that have emphasized order, discipline, and work? Would the experiential approaches better meet the needs of those from homes that value openness, feelings, creativity and spontaneity? Might the opposite be true? How might you use data from your fellow students to suggest an answer to these questions?

Do you agree with the logic of the following quote from Jerome Bruner (Bennett, 1976)?

> The more formal the teaching, the more time the pupils spend working on the subject matter at hand. And, in general, . . . the more time pupils spend working on a subject, the more they improve at it.
>
>   If you don't agree, why not? If you agree, why is the research reviewed by Rosenshine necessary?

Given the present emphasis on basic skills, some administrators may require that teachers use direct instruction. Do you think such a policy would be effective? Would you consider it a threat to the professionalism of teachers? Explain your answers.

Teaching Functions in Instructional Programs

Barak Rosenshine

In the past 5 years our knowledge of successful teaching has increased considerably. There have been numerous successful experimental studies in which teachers have been trained to increase the academic achievement of their students. In these studies, which have taken place in regular classrooms, one group of teachers received training in specific instructional procedures, and one group continued their regular teaching. In the successful studies the teachers implemented the training, and, as a result, their students had higher achievement and/or higher academic engaged time than did students in the classrooms of the untrained teachers. Particularly noteworthy studies include:

Texas First Grade Reading Group Study (Anderson, Evertson, & Brophy 1979, 1982),

Missouri Mathematics Effectiveness Study (Good & Grouws 1979) (for math in Grades 4–8),

From *The Elementry School Journal* (March 1983): 335–350. Copyright 1983 The University of Chicago. Reprinted with permission. This paper was prepared initially for a conference entitled Research on Teaching: Implications for Practice, sponsored by the National Institute of Education, at Airlie House in Warrenton, Va., February 25–27, 1982.

The Texas Elementary School Study (Evertson, Emmer, Sanford, & Clements 1982),

The Texas Junior High School Study (Emmer, Evertson, Sanford, & Clements 1982),

Organizing and Instructing High School Classes (Fitzpatrick 1981, 1982),

Exemplary Centers for Reading Instruction (ECRI) Reid 1978, 1979, 1980, 1981, 1982) (for reading in Grades 1–5),

Direct Instruction Follow Through Program (Distar) (Becker 1977).

For example, in the study by Good and Grouws (1979) 40 teachers (Grades 4–8) were divided into two groups. One group of 21 teachers received a 45-page manual which contained a system of sequential, instructional behaviors for teaching mathematics. The teachers read the manual, received two 90-minute training sessions, and proceeded to implement the key instructional behaviors in their teaching of mathematics. The control teachers did not receive the manual and were told to continue to instruct in their own styles. During the 4 months of the program all teachers were observed six times.

The results showed that the teachers in the treatment group implemented many of the key instructional behaviors and, in many areas, behaved significantly differently from the teachers in the control group. For example, the treatment teachers were much higher in conducting review, checking homework, actively engaging students in seatwork, and making homework assignments. The results also showed that the test scores in mathematics for students of the treatment teachers increased significantly more than did the scores for students of the control teachers.

Fitzpatrick (1982) conducted a similar study involving ninth-grade algebra and foreign language. Twenty teachers were divided into two groups, and the treatment group received a manual explaining and giving teaching suggestions on 13 instructional principles. The treatment group met twice to discuss the manual. All teachers were observed five times in one of their classrooms.

The results showed that the treatment teachers implemented many of the principles more frequently than did the control teachers. For example, the treatment teachers were higher in attending to inappropriate student behavior, commanding attention of all students, providing immediate feedback and evaluation, having fewer interruptions, setting clear expectations, and having a warm and supportive environment. In addition, overall student engagement was higher in the classrooms of the treatment teachers.

The other programs cited above were similar to these two. I would urge educators to use the manuals and training materials from these programs in preservice and in-service training. Four of the manuals are useful for general instruction (Emmer et al., 1982; Evertson et al., 1982; Fitzpatrick, 1982; Good & Grouws, 1979). The manual by Anderson et al. (1982) is oriented primarily toward instruction in elementary reading groups, and the programs by Reid (1978–1981) and by Englemann (Becker, 1977) include both general instructional methods and highly specific procedures for teaching reading.

The purpose of this paper is to study these successful teacher training and student achievement programs and identify the common functions which appear across these programs. These teaching functions form a general model of effective instruction, which will be discussed below. The model is also useful as a heuristic; it aids in thinking about teaching and suggests areas for future research.

An Overview of Effective Instruction

The studies cited above, as well as the correlational studies which preceded them, indicate that, in general, students taught with structured curricula do better than those taught with more individualized or discovery learning approaches. Furthermore, students who receive their instruction directly from the teacher achieve more than those expected to learn new material or skills on their own or from each other. In general, to the extent that students are younger, slower, and/or have little prior background, teachers are most effective when they:

structure the learning;

proceed in small steps but at a brisk pace;

give detailed and redundant instructions and explanations;

provide many examples;

ask a large number of questions and provide overt, active practice;

provide feedback and corrections, particularly in the initial stages of learning new material;

have a student success rate of 80% or higher in initial learning;

divide seatwork assignments into smaller assignments;

provide for continued student practice so that students have a success rate of 90%-100% and become rapid, confident, and firm.

It is most important that younger students master content to the point of over-learning. Basic skills (arithmetic and decoding) are taught hierarchically so that success at any level requires application of knowledge and skills mastered earlier. Typically, students are not able to retain and apply knowledge and skills unless they have been mastered to the point of overlearning—to the point where they are automatic. The high student success rates seen in classrooms of effective teachers and programs are obtained because initial instruction proceeds in small steps that are not too difficult and also because teachers see that students practice new knowledge and skills until they are overlearned (Brophy, 1982).

Overlearning basic skills is also necessary for higher cognitive processing. In a discussion of beginning reading, Beck (1978) noted that data support the position that the brain is a limited-capacity processor and that, if a reader has to spend energy decoding a word (whether through phonics or context), there is less energy available to comprehend the sentence in which the word appears. Similarly, Greeno (1978) noted that mathematical problem solving is enhanced when the basic skills are overlearned and become automatic. In simpler terms, successful learning requires a large amount of successful practice.

Surprisingly, these general procedures also work for older, skilled learners. As part of an introductory physics course at Berkeley for students with interests in biology and medicine, Larkin and Reif (1976) developed a program to teach the skills of studying scientific texts. The experimental students read the material, answered questions, and received ancillary instruction when they made errors so that ultimately all students mastered the material. Later in the course, all students read new material on marketing and new material on gravitational force and answered questions on each passage. Students who received direct instruction in studying scientific text performed better than the controls on each set of material. Larkin and Reif (1976, p. 439) concluded:

> Providing direct instruction in a general learning skill is a reliable way to help students become more independent learners. The results described here indicate that students do *not* automatically acquire a learning skill merely through experience in a subject matter. To enhance independent learning, learning skills should be taught directly.

The instructional procedures for teaching these physics students were quite similar to those described for young learners. The primary differences were that the size of steps was larger, and there were fewer questions.

Thus, across a number of studies we find (*a*) a general pattern of effective instruction; (*b*) an advantage to direct, explicit instruction—even explicit instruction in becoming independent learners; and (*c*) the importance of overlearning, particularly for hierarchically organized material.

Teaching Functions

Putting together ideas from all the studies cited in the first paragraph of this article, I developed the list of six instructional "functions" which appear in Table 1:

1. Review, checking previous day's work (and reteaching if necessary).
2. Presenting new content/skills.
3. Initial student practice (and checking for understanding).
4. Feedback and correctives (and re-teaching if necessary).
5. Student independent practice.
6. Weekly and monthly reviews.

These functions' are presented in more detail in Table 1 and will be discussed in the remainder of the paper. There is no hard, fast dogma here. It is quite possible to make a reasonable list of four or six or eight functions; however, these functions are meant to serve as a guide for discussing the general nature of effective instruction.

There is some difference in the time teachers spend on these functions in lower and upper grades. In the lower grades, particularly in reading and math, the amount of time spent presenting new material is relatively small, and much more time is spent in student practice (through teacher questions and student answers). In later grades, the time spent in presentation becomes longer, and the teacher-directed practice becomes shorter.

Table 1.
Instructional Functions

1. Daily review, checking previous day's work, and reteaching (if necessary):
   Checking homework
   Reteaching areas where there were student errors

2. Presenting new content/skills:
   Provide overview
   Proceed in small steps (if necessary), but at a rapid pace
   If necessary, give detailed or redundant instructions and explanations
   New skills are phased in while old skills are being mastered

3. Initial student practice:
   High frequency of questions and overt student practice (from teacher and materials)
   Prompts are provided during initial learning (when appropriate)
   All students have a chance to respond and receive feedback
   Teacher *checks for understanding* by evaluating student responses
   Continue practice until students are firm
   Success rate of 80% or higher during initial learning

4. Feedback and correctives (and recycling of instruction, if necessary):
   Feedback to students, particularly when they are correct but hesitant
   Student errors provide feedback to the teacher that corrections and/or reteaching is necessary
   Corrections by simplifying question, giving clues, explaining or reviewing steps, or reteaching last
      steps
   When necessary, reteach using smaller steps

5. Independent practice so that students are firm and automatic:
   Seatwork
   Unitization and automaticity (practice to over-learning)
   Need for procedure to ensure student engagement during seatwork (i.e., teacher or aide monitoring)
   95% correct or higher

6. Weekly and monthly reviews:
   reteaching, if necessary

NOTE: With older, more mature learners (*a*) the size of steps in the presentation is larger, (*b*) student practice is more covert, and (*c*) the practice involves covert rehearsal, restating, and reviewing (i.e., deep processing or "whirling").

Discussion

This paper has covered a number of teaching functions: review of previous learning, demonstration of new material, guided practice and checking for understanding, feedback and corrections, independent practice, and periodic review. As I wrote this paper I became impressed with the fact that different people, working alone, came up with fairly similar solutions to the problem of how to instruct effectively in classrooms. The major authors cited in the first paragraph of the article are more similar than they are different. The fact that these people, working alone, have reached similar conclusions and have student achievement data to support their positions helps validate each research study.

One advantage of this paper is that it provides a general view, an overview of the major functions in systematic teaching. What is missing, however, is the specific detail that is contained in the training manuals and materials developed by each of the investigators. I would hope that all teachers and trainers of teachers have a chance to study and discuss the individual training manuals.

These components are quite similar to those used by the most effective teachers. All teachers already perform some or all of the functions discussed above. However, the specific programs elaborate on how to perform these functions and provide more routines, procedures, and modifications than an individual teacher, working alone, could have thought of. These programs make teachers aware of the six instructional functions, bring this set of skills to a conscious level, and enable teachers to develop strategies for consistent, systematic implementation (Bennett 1982).

Now that we can describe the major teaching functions, we can ask whether there are a variety of ways in which individual functions can be fulfilled. We have already seen that the independent practice function can be met in three ways: students working alone, teacher leading practice, and students helping each other. (There are even a variety of ways for students to help each other.)

We have just begun to explore this issue of the variety of ways of meeting each function, and at present no conclusions can be drawn on this issue. It may be that each function can be met three ways: by the teacher, by a student working with other students, and by a student working alone—using written materials or a computer. Right now, however, not all functions can be met in all three ways—and we are limited in our choices by the constraints of working with 25 students in a classroom, the age and maturity of the students, the lack of efficient "courseware" for the student to use when working alone, and the lack of well-designed routines that will keep students on task and diminish the lost time when they move from activity to activity. For example, although the idea of students working together during independent practice always existed "in theory," such working together was also associated with students being off-task and socializing. We needed the routines such as those developed by Johnson and Johnson (1975), Reid (1981), and Slavin (1981) before we could be confident that students would work together during independent practice *and* be on task. Similarly, although "checking for understanding" could "theoretically" be accomplished by students working with materials or by students working with other students, we do not have effective routines for enabling this to happen— at present—in the elementary grades.

In sum, now that we can list the major functions or components which are necessary for systematic instruction, we can turn to exploring diffferent ways in which these functions can be effectively fulfilled.

REFERENCES

Anderson, L. M.: Evertson, C. M; & Brophy, J. E. An Experimental Study of Effective Teaching in First-Grade Reading Groups. *Elementary School Journal*, 1979, **79**, 193–222.

Anderson, L. M.; Evertson, C. M.; & Brophy, J. E., Principles of Small-Group Instruction in Elementary Reading. East Lansing: Institute for Research on Teaching, Michigan State University, 1982.

Beck, I. L. *Instructional Ingredients for the Development of Beginning Reading Competence*. Pittsburgh: Learning Research and Development Center, University of Pittsburgh, 1978.

Beck, I. L. & McCaslin, E. S. *An Analysis of Dimen-*

sions that Affect the Development of Code-Breaking Ability in Eight Beginning Reading Programs. Pittsburgh: Learning Research and Development Center, University of Pittsburgh, 1978.

Becker, W. C. Teaching Reading and Language to the Disadvantaged—What We Have Learned from Field Research. *Harvard Educational Review*, 1977, **47**, 518–543.

Bennett, D. Should Teachers be Expected to Learn and Use Direct Instruction? *Association for Supervision and Curriculum Development Update*, 4 June 1982, **24**, 5.

Brophy, J. Recent Research on Teaching. East Lansing: Institute for Research on Teaching, Michigan State University, 1980.

Brophy, J. Successful Teaching Strategies for the Inner-City Child. *Phi Delta Kappan.* 1982, **63**, 527–530.

Brophy, J. Classroom Organization and Management. *Elementary School Journal*, March, 1983.

Brophy, J. E., & Evertson, C. M. Process-Product Correlations in the Texas Teacher Effectiveness Study: Final Report. Austin: R & D Center for Teacher Education. University of Texas, 1974.

Brophy, J. E., & Evertson, C. M. *Learning from Teaching: A Developmental Perspective.* Boston: Allyn & Bacon, 1976.

Coker, H.; Lorentz, C. W.; & Coker, J. Teacher Behavior and Student Outcomes in the Georgia Study. Paper presented at the annual meeting of the American Educational Research Association, Boston, 1980.

Durkin, D. What Classroom Observation Reveals About Reading Comprehension Instruction. *Reading Research Quarterly*, 1978–1979, **14**, 481–533.

Durkin, D. Reading Comprehension Instruction in Five Basal Reading Series. *Reading Research Quarterly*, 1981, **4**, 515–544.

Emmer, E. T., & Evertson, C. M. *Teacher's Manual for the Junior High Classroom Management Improvement Study.* Austin: R & D Center for Teacher Education, University of Texas, 1981.

Emmer, E. T.; Evertson, C. M.; & Anderson, L. M. Effective Classroom Management. *Elementary School Journal*, 1980, **80**, 219–231.

Emmer, E. T.; Evertson, C. M.; Sanford, J.; & Clements, B. S. Improving Classroom Management: an Experimental Study in Junior High Classrooms. Austin: R & D Center for Teacher Education, University of Texas, 1982.

Evertson, C. M. Differences in Instructional Activities in Higher-and Lower-Achieving Junior High English and Mathematics Classrooms. *Elementary School Journal*, 1982, **82**, 329–351.

Evertson, C.; Anderson, C; Anderson, L.; & Brophy, J. E. Relationship Between Classroom Behaviors and Student Outcomes in Junior High Mathematics and English Classes. *American Educational Research Journal*, 1980, **17**, 43–60. (a)

Evertson C. M.; Emmer, E. T.; & Brophy, J. E. Predictors of Effective Teaching in Junior High Mathematics Classrooms. *Journal of Research in Mathematics Education*, 1980, **11**, 167–178. (b)

Evertson, C.; Emmer, E. T.; Sanford, J.; & Clements,

B. S. Improving Classroom Management: an Experimental Study in Elementary Classrooms. Austin: R & D Center for Teacher Education, University of Texas, 1982.

Fisher, C. W.; Berliner, D. C.; Filby, N. N.; Marliave, R.; Cahen L. S.; & Dishaw, M. M. Teaching Behaviors, Academic Learning Time, and Student Achievement: an Overview. In C. Denham & A. Lieberman (Eds.), *Time to Learn,* Washington, D.C.: Department of Education, 1980.

Fitzpatrick, K. A. An Investigation of Secondary Classroom Material Strategies for Increasing Student Academic Engaged Time. Unpublished doctoral dissertation, University of Illinois at Urbana-Champaign, 1981.

Fitzpatrick, K. A. The Effect of a Secondary Classroom Management Training Program on Teacher and Student Behavior. Paper presented at the annual meeting of the American Educational Research Association, New York, 1982.

Gersten, R. M.; Carnine, D. W.; & Williams, P. B. Measuring Implementation of a Structured Educational Model in an Urban School District. *Educational Evaluation and Policy Analysis*, 1981 **4**, 56–63.

Gibson, E. J.; Gibson, J. J.; Pick, A. D.; & Osser, H. A Developmental Study of the Discrimination of Letter-Like Forms. *Journal of Comparative and Physiological Psychology*, 1962, **55**, 897–906.

Good, T. L., & Grouws, D. A. *Process-Product Relationships in Fourth Grade Mathematics Classrooms.* Columbia: University of Missouri—Columbia, 1975.

Good, T. L., & Grouws, D. A. The Missouri Mathematics Effectiveness Project. *Journal of Educational Psychology*, 1979, **71**, 355–362.

Greeno, J. Understanding and Procedural Knowledge in Mathematics Instruction. *Educational Psychologist,* 1978, **12**, 262–283.

Hunter, M. Effective Practice. In *Increasing Your Teaching Effectiveness.* Palo Alto, Calif: Learning Institute, 1981.

Hunter, M., & Russell, D. Planning for Effective Instruction: Lesson Design. In *Increasing Your Teaching Effectiveness.* Palo Alto, Calif: Learning Institute, 1981.

Johnson, D., & Johnson, R. *Learning Together and Alone.* Englewood Cliffs, N.J.: Prentice-Hall, 1975.

Johnson, D., & Johnson, R. The Integration of Handicapped Students into Regular Classrooms: Effects on Cooperation and Instruction. *Contemporary Educational Psychology,* in press.

Kennedy, J. J.; Bush, A. J.; Cruickshank, D. R: & Haefele, D. Additional Investigations into the Nature of Teacher Clarity. Paper presented at the annual meeting of the American Educational Research Association, Toronto, March 1978.

Kulik, J. A., & Kulik, C. C. College Teaching. In P. L. Peterson & H. J. Walberg (Eds.), *Research on Teaching: Concepts, Findings, and Implications*. Berkeley, Calif.: McCutchan, 1979.

Larkin, J. H., & Reif, F. Analysis and Teaching of a General Skill for Studying Scientific Text. *Journal of Educational Psychology*, 1976, **68**, 431–440.

Reid, E. R. *The Reader Newsletter*. Salt Lake City: Exemplary Center for Reading Instruction, 1978, 1979, 1980, 1981, 1982.

Samuels, S. J. Some Essentials of Decoding, *Exceptional Education Quarterly*, 1982, **2**, 11–25.

Sharan, S. Cooperative Learning in Small Groups, *Review of Educational Research*, 1980, **50**, 241–271.

Slavin, R. E. Student Teams and Comparisons Among Equals: Effects on Academic Performance. *Journal of Educational Psychology*, 1978, **70**, 532–538.

Slavin, R. E. Cooperative Learning. *Review of Educational Research*, 1980, **50**, 317–343. (a)

Slavin, R. E. Effects of Student Teams and Peer Tutoring on Academic Achievement and Time on Task. *Journal of Experimental Education*, 1980, **48**, 252–257. (b)

Slavin, R. E. Student Team Learning: *Elementary School Journal*, 1981, **82**, 5–17.

Soar, R. S., & Soar, R. M. Classroom Behavior, Pupil Characteristics, and Pupil Growth for the School Year and the Summer. Gainesville: Institute for Development of Human Resources, University of Florida, 1973.

Stallings, J.; Gory, R.; Fairweather, J; & Needles, M. *Early Childhood Education Classroom Evaluation*. Menlo Park, Calif.: SRI International, 1977.

Stallings, J. A., & Kaskowitz, D. *Follow Through Classroom Observation Evaluation, 1972 -73*. Menlo Park, Calif.: Stanford Research Institute, 1974.

Stallings, J.; Needles, M.; & Stayrook, N. *How to Change the Process of Teaching Basic Reading Skills in Secondary Schools*. Menlo Park, Calif.: SRI International, 1979.

Zeigler, S. The Effectiveness of Classroom Learning Teams for Increasing Cross Ethnic Friendship: additional evidence. *Human Organization*, 1981, **40**, 264–268.

READING 17

Direct Instruction and Experiential Approaches: Are They Really Mutually Exclusive?

Janet Kierstead

The debate over classroom practices rages on. On one side stand proponents of direct instruction; on the other are those who argue for an experiential approach. Just when the challenge to education is the greatest, we are mired in this seemingly endless debate. Teachers are pulled in two directions, and students suffer from the confusion. Must we really aim for the mastery of basic skills *or* for the development of higher-level thinking processes along with the more affective outcomes? Or can we have both?

My experience suggests that direct instruction and experiential approaches are not mutually exclusive; that in the hands of teachers who have discovered how to synthesize them, they are actually complementary. We should be pooling our collective talents in search of ways to help teachers merge the two rather than debating which is more effective.

From *Educational Leadership* (May 1985): 25–30. Reprinted with permission.
AUTHOR'S NOTE: I wish to thank Georgea Mohlmann Sparks, who insisted that I write this article and so generously gave of her advice and support.

Definition of Terms

Direct instruction refers here to the approach Rosenshine (1979) describes as having an academic, teacher-centered focus with little student choice of activity and the use of large groups, factual questions, and controlled practice. With the intention of *directly transmitting* skills and concepts, the teacher presents what are commonly known as "directed lessons." Such lessons usually include an introduction, input, modeling, guided practice, check for understanding, and independent practice. The order of presentation may vary, but what remains constant is that *the teacher directly controls* the pace, sequence, and content of instruction.

An experiential approach, as described by Horowitz (1979), is characterized by flexible use of space, student choice of activity, richness of learning materials, integration of curriculum areas, and more individual or small-group than large-group instruction. Central to this approach are what Bossert (1977) has termed "multi-task activities": numerous individual or small-group projects in which students are encouraged to select and organize their own tasks. Here the teacher intends to *indirectly promote* skills and concepts through experience that captures students' interest and imagination. Such activities are purposeful in that they require students to go beyond the independent practice of skills (for the sake of skill acquisition alone) to create real-life products that could be used or shared with others (opinion surveys, recommendations, advertisements, scrapbooks, diaries, skits and plays, court trials, models, murals, sculptures, and so on). While carrying out such activities, *the student controls* most of the minute-by-minute decisions regarding the pace, sequence, and content of activities.

Background

I began to wrestle with the apparent conflict between direct instruction and experiential approaches three years ago when I co-authored a staff development program for the California State Department of Education (Mohlman, Kierstead, and Gundlack, 1982). This series of workshops for teachers and administrators—known as The Effective Classrooms Training—includes such topics as the quantitative use of class time, classroom management, teacher expectations and attitudes, direct instruction, and single- and multi-task instructional activities.

Originally, the training began with direct instruction and then added multi-task activities. During one session, participants learned how to design directed lessons and, in the next, how to have students apply their newly acquired skills to multi-task activities.

As I participated in training sessions throughout the state, however, I began to alter the original design. Influenced by the experiential approach I had taken with students as a classroom teacher, I found myself showing participants *first* how to design the framework of multi-task activites for an entire semester or year. Only after the experiential framework was in place did I have trainees design lessons to prepare students to carry out those activities. Beginning with the sequence of increasingly complex purposeful activities and using directed lessons to serve that sequence brought a critical change: the development of basic skills, rather than an end in itself, became a means to an end, specifically, the ability to *use* skills and concepts for real-life purposes. I have seen many teachers merge the two approaches in that fashion and think of such a synthesis as a "structured multi-task" approach.

Designing a Structured Multi-Task Approach

To highlight the planning process, let's consider an example from a sewing class, where the process is fairly straightforward, before looking at an example from an academic subject. Figure 1 outlines the initial steps in the process. Of course, the teacher may not actually write out much, if any, of the plan.

Having designed the broad-stroke plan of steps (or stages), the teacher proceeds through the year by taking each step in turn, first sequencing the skills in order of difficulty, and then *providing the directed lessons necessary to enable students to create the real-life product at that step.*

Teachers of academic subjects can use the same process. For example, suppose a teacher of a government class wants her students to understand the relationship between physical and cultural geography. The final product is a "perfect country" created and governed by students and illustrated through skits, maps, murals, models of transportation systems, written alliances, and so on—all related to the country's geography. At the first step, students produce maps showing how land forms affect climate and vegetation. (Several directed lessons precede the mapmaking session.) The second step is to create a visual display, including a time line, a collage depicting events, and so on, to illustrate how the mythical country's physical attributes affect population distribution and cultural history. (Again, creation of the visual display will follow several directed lessons.) Students proceed through several more steps until they acquire the skills and concepts needed to produce the final product—the "perfect country."

1. The teacher establishes the long-term goal and corresponding real-life product by answering the questions:

   "What do I want my students to be able to do/understand by the end of this semester?"

   "How will I know (other than by a paper/pencil test) that they have achieved this goal—what final product would serve as evidence?"

2. The teacher considers what skills and concepts will be needed to create the final product and begins to outline a series of increasingly complex "steps" by deciding:

   "What is the simplest product students could make, using a few of the basic skills I have listed here? And then, what would be something a bit more complex?"

Each step consists of one or several choices of multi-tasks (art or construction projects, experiments, investigations, and so forth) through which the students create the real-life products. These are the basis for multi-task work periods.

3. The teacher proceeds through the year by taking each step in turn, first sequencing the skills in order of difficulty, and then providing the direct instruction necessary to enable students to create the products as they work on them during multi-task work periods:

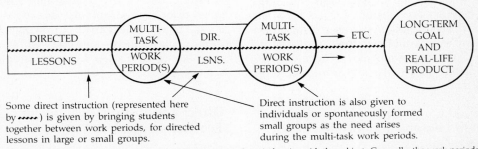

Some direct instruction (represented here by ∿∿∿) is given by bringing students together between work periods, for directed lessons in large or small groups.

Direct instruction is also given to individuals or spontaneously formed small groups as the need arises during the multi-task work periods.

Note: The time spent on directed lessons relative to the multi-task work period varies with the subject. Generally, the work periods increase as the steps become more complex. Also, during the multi-task periods, the teacher maintains indirect ("remote") control over students through rules, routines, and procedures established early in the school year.

Figure 1. Procedure for Designing a Structured Multi-Task Approach

A similar procedure guides young students through the developmental process of learning to write. For example, a primary teacher may have students author simple books to show that they have reached the long-term goal—the ability to communicate independently through writing. At the first step, students produce books of several one-sentence "stories." Each day they draw a picture, dictate a caption to an adult, and then trace over what the adult has written. At the next stage, they dictate and then copy the caption of their illustrations. Through repeated daily exposure, they learn to spell several words. This propels them into the next stage where they create their own sentences and receive help with spelling on request. From then on they simply expand their writing until they reach the long-term goal—a lengthy story, edited for spelling and punctuation. (After achieving independence, students begin another step-by-step process—first producing simple, then complex, research projects, integrating literacy skills with science and social studies.)

Directed lessons would be given throughout the lengthy process of learning to write. For instance, while recording a dictated story with the whole class, the teacher might take the time to explain, demonstrate, and give guided practice on using commas in a series. For some students this large-group directed lesson would suffice, but others would need a similar lesson when they first encounter the need to use commas in their work. Should several students reach that need at the same time, they would be called together to receive a second lesson. Or the teacher might give a directed lesson to one student individually. Since students readily share such new information as they work side by side, that one student could pass on to other class members what she or he learned. So, students *may* receive all or part of a directed lesson before they launch into their multi-task activities, and *will* continue to receive such lessons from the teacher and from each other as they work.

Directed Lessons and Group Size

In the examples just given, the teaching strategies commonly associated with the direct instruction and experiential approaches have been synthesized to create a structured multi-task approach. Directed lessons—the foundation of direct instruction—serve as a framework for connecting multi-tasks—the cornerstone of the experiential approach. The multi-tasks at each step require the students to apply and extend the skills they acquire through directed lessons.

Confusion over the issue of the group size clouds the question of how or even whether direct instruction and experiential approaches can be synthesized. Group size should not be used to define direct instruction. In a structured multi-task approach, directed lessons are given to the whole class, to small groups, and to individual students. Such lessons are given almost continuously during the multi-task work as the teacher circulates, pausing to assist individuals or "impromptu" small groups (formed on the spot as the need arises in the students' work and dissolved when the need is met).

Often, teachers who are concerned with "covering" the material decide to teach to groups to save time. Too often, however, such instruction is closely matched to the needs of only a few students. Instruction that is inappropriate for many of the students hardly saves time; it becomes, instead, a means of control.

The content of instruction—not the desire to maintain control over the students—should determine group size. Generally speaking, in the case of skills such as reading, writing, and sewing, most of the directed lessons should be given to individuals or to impromptu small groups. Conversely, large-group instruction given prior to the multi-task activity is probably the most efficient and time-saving means of introducing concepts and establishing a common set of terms, as in social studies and science.

Direct and Indirect Teacher Control

The issue of control lies at the heart of the difference between "pure" direct instruction and a structured multi-task approach. In the former, the teacher maintains *direct* control most of the time, allowing little student choice of activity; in the latter, the teacher shifts control to students for large portions of time, allowing them to make the minute-by-minute decisions regarding pace, sequence, and content of their work. It is critical to recognize that when that shift takes place, the teacher never completely relinquishes control, but maintains *indirect* control through strategies built into the environment. Those strategies create a system of remote control.

Maintaining indirect control over students so that they can assume some of the responsibility and control over their learning in the active setting is the critical issue—and the stumbling block—in practice. (See Kierstead, 1984, and in press for the features of such a management system.) Not only must the multi-task curriculum be in place, but it must be supported by strategies for ensuring student accountability, for monitoring and guiding growth, and for providing human and material resources for students.

Summary and Conclusion

Our charge as educators is to socialize our young—to guide them in a desired direction—so we *are* trying to control students. But when we exercise that control through the exclusive use of direct instruction, we prevent ourselves from getting the full range of desired student outcomes. *Sharing* control with students in a structured multi-task fashion gives us the best of both worlds, not only freeing students but also freeing the teacher to work with students individually. Thus, students are free to develop responsibility, independence, and the higher-level thinking skills. Teachers are free to assess student needs, strengths, and interests at close hand and to immediately respond accordingly,

often by giving immediate, personalized direct instruction.[1]

A great deal of valuable work has been done to describe how to directly convey information to students and help them practice skills—how to conduct effective direct lessons. Now the challenge is to understand how to *indirectly* promote skills and concepts in active settings. We need to know how to share control with students so that they are free to apply their skills and concepts to real-life purposes.

Because so few teachers have worked out a means for sharing control, we tend to assume that only few *can* do so. As I work with teachers, I am increasingly convinced that their greatest obstacle comes from outside the classroom. We send mixed messages: we say that we value student enthusiasm, responsibility, independence, and the willingness and ability to use skills for real-life purposes, but we measure student (and thus teacher) success by scores on standardized tests. By overemphasizing test scores and continuing to suggest that good scores result only from large-group direct instruction, we paralyze teachers so that they are afraid to move toward a more experiential approach.

The teachers I know who have worked out a structured multi-task approach have done so with little outside support, and often in the face of tremendous outside pressure. We must begin to support and assist such teachers. Or, at the very least, we must not stand in the way of teachers who are struggling to do so on their own.

REFERENCES

Bossert. S. "Tasks, Group Management and Teacher Control Behavior: A Study of Classroom Organization and Teacher Style." *School Review* (August 1977): 552–565.

Horowitz, R. "Effects of the Open Classroom." In *Educational Environments and Effects: Evaluation, Policy, and Productivity.* Edited by Herbert J. Walberg. Berkeley, Calif.: McCutchan Publishing Corp., 1979. Chapter 14.

Kierstead, J. *Outstanding Effective Classrooms: A Study of the Interdependence of Compositional, Psy-*

---

[1] I suspect the percentage of teachers who know how to share control with students is presently so small that such teachers are outliers in the effective teaching studies. Thus, from that research it *appears* that large-group, direct teacher control is the more effective approach.

chological, Behavioral, and Organizational Properties in Four Primary Classrooms. 1984 doctoral dissertation. Claremount Graduate School, available through University Microfilms.

Kierstead, J. "Outstanding Effective Classroom." In *The Claremont Reading Conference Forty-Eighth Yearbook.* Edited by Malcolm Douglass. Claremont, Calif.: The Claremont Reading Conference Center for Developmental Studies, in press.

Mohlman, G.; Kierstead, J.; and Gundlack, M. "A Research-Based Inservice Model for Secondary Teachers." *Educational Leadership* (October 1981): 16–19.

Rosenshine, B. "Content, Time, and Direct Instruction." In *Research on Teaching Concepts, Findings, and Implications.* Edited by Penelope L. Peterson and Herbert J. Walberg. Berkeley, Calif.: McCutchan Publishing Corp., 1979.

Mastery Learning: Effective for Whom?

Equality in education has traditionally meant equality of *opportunity*, not equal *outcomes* for all, regardless of aptitude or prior learning. The reality of individual differences was expected to hold for the achievement of students; some would surely achieve more than others.

Since the early 1970s, Benjamin S. Bloom and James Block have been the leading spokesmen for an instructional strategy challenging the assumption that individual differences in school achievement are inevitable. This strategy, termed *mastery learning*, is designed to ensure that all, or nearly all, students reach the same level of achievement. It is based on repetitive applications of the simple formula *plan, teach, and test*. The plan itself is not that different. The difference lies in the definition of specific objectives in terms of performance, in tests that reveal the causes of learner failure, and in the systematic individualized approaches adopted to eliminate these causes.

Block's previous reviews of mastery learning research (Block, 1974: Block & Burns, 1976) lend support to the claim that mastery learning can bring the achievement levels of approximately 80% of students up to the levels usually achieved by only the upper 20%. But won't the more able students achieve mastery quickly and waste their time waiting for the less able "slower" students to catch up? Mastery learning may be effective for less able students, but is it effective for the more able?

Critics of mastery learning (Cronbach, 1972; Mueller, 1976; Resnick, 1977) argue that when achievement is held constant, as it is in mastery learning, individual differences in students will be reflected in the time needed to learn. They claim that "fast" learners will be unfairly penalized.

In the first article for this issue one critic, Marshall Arlin, describes a model of how teachers allocate instructional time, and how the use of time may be affected by mastery learning approaches. He then reports a time management study of teachers who used the mastery learning approach. The teachers were questioned and observed. Arlin found that mastery learning teachers were aware of time differences; however, they tended to adjust the instruction to slower students. As predicted by critics of mastery learning (Mueller, 1976; Resnick, 1977), they appeared to be more successful in keeping faster students occupied after they had achieved mastery than they were in providing "enrichment" activities.

In Block's article, he states that his own findings concerning learning rates are contrary to those reported by the mastery learning critics. He has not found that "fast" students are slowed to the pace of "slow" students—he has found just the opposite: with mastery learning, the learning rates of "slow" students are said to increase to match those of students who are usually "faster."

Block criticizes Arlin's "speculations" about the effects mastery learning has on learning rates, and the way his investigation of teacher responses was conducted. Block recommends that the study be repeated with changes that will correct what he identifies as faults or shortcomings.

Block suggests that when mastery learning programs have problems with individual differences in learning rates, it is because they are *remedial*, for students with chronic learning problems. He urges the design of mastery learning programs that are *preventative* in that they will avoid the development of learning problems. He predicts that such preventative programs, together with remedial programs, will "cut learning rate problems down to size."

Block's article appeared in a publication for mastery learning users and others interested in equality of the *outcomes* of instruction. They are the "network" to which he refers.

Thought Questions

After reading both articles do you agree with critics of mastery learning who claim it discriminates against more able students because teachers will accept lower levels of achievement from students who could do much better? How can mastery learning be combined with other teaching approaches to counter this criticism?

Who should determine the objectives for mastery? How should they go about it? How can we obtain evidence of the wisdom of their choice?

Block argues that using mastery learning before learning differences develop will prevent them from developing. Do you believe this would happen? Why, or why not?

The goals of mastery learning are based on minimal evidence of students' ability to perform in the present. Some have argued that, in this case, the goals of student motivation, retention, and application will suffer. What reasons are there to believe this to be any more true of mastery learning than of conventional methods?

What relationship do you see between approaches to individualized learning, such as programmed instruction or computer assisted instruction, and mastery learning? What relationship do you see between criterion-referenced testing and mastery learning? To what extent do the criticisms of these innovations apply to mastery learning also?

To what extent is mastery learning an adequate answer to the demand that schools give us evidence of their value? To what extent does it answer the demands of the poor for more equal education?

Teacher Responses to Student Time Differences in Mastery Learning

Marshall Arlin

A model to assist in the analysis of teachers' time allocation procedures is presented. An instructional technique, mastery learning, is analyzed within the context of this model. A qualitative analysis of 10 elementary school teachers who implemented short sequences of mastery learning is presented to illustrate possible ways teachers adjust various conditions that are formulated in the model. A major concern of teachers was the differential time students need to achieve mastery. Teachers appear to adjust instructional timing to slower students.

In this paper, a model will be presented for analyzing teachers' time allocation procedures in collective instruction. It will be suggested that teachers adjust various conditions that are formulated in this model to achieve a workable classroom environment. It will also be suggested that mastery learning shifts some of these conditions, and consequently a workable environment might take a different form than

From *American Journal of Education* (August 1982):334–352. Copyright 1982 The University of Chicago. Reprinted with permission.

that found with nonmastery instruction. Finally, a qualitative analysis of a study in which teachers attempted to implement mastery learning will be presented in order to illustrate features of the model.

A Model of Teacher Time Allocation

In the model of teachers' timing decisions, it is proposed that teachers take as their starting point student aptitudes and allocate time in order to achieve depth and breadth of learning as well as student cooperation. These are obviously not the only considerations bearing on teachers' timing decisions, but they are sufficiently important to justify an investigation of this topic.

Aptitude is construed similarly to Carroll's (1963) usage; it represents an individual's time needed to learn. It is assumed to be related to more traditional measures of aptitude or intellectual potential. For example, a student with high mathematical aptitude is assumed to need less time to learn new mathematical skills than one with low mathematical aptitude. "Depth" is used in much the same way that Abrahamson (1974), Westbury (1973), and Hauwiller

(1976) have used the terms "mastery" and "coverage." "Depth" refers to the degree, level, or intensity of learning. This term is preferred to the term "mastery" because it conveys the notion of a continuum better than "mastery," which to some people connotes an all-or-none state. "Breadth" refers to the amount or extent of learning and is very similar in meaning to "coverage". One of the main reasons for using "breadth" rather than "coverage" is simply to maintain the parallel with "depth." As an example of the two terms, consider two teachers of ninth-grade algebra. One teacher covers only six chapters of the book but attempts to ensure that students learn the material very well. A second teacher "gets through the book," exposing students to all 13 chapters, even though students might have had only a superficial grasp of some of the material. The first teacher has a primary concern for depth; the second is primarily concerned with breadth. "Cooperation" is a term used by Doyle (1979) to reflect the degree to which students participate in learning in a manner congruent with the teacher's intentions. This is similar to what Westbury (1973) and Abrahamson (1974) refer to as "affect," or what is sometimes referred to as "good classroom management." The five components of the model are shown in Figure 1.

The components of the model are seen as closely interrelated; an alteration in one is likely to result in alteration of most or all of the others. If students are not provided with sufficient time to learn, they will experience decreased depth, breadth, or both. As a consequence, they may become frustrated, and cooperation with the teacher may suffer. Breadth and depth are seen as competing goals,

particularly within the constraint of limited time. Given limited time in relation to student aptitudes, a teacher may increase depth of learning by sacrificing breadth. The teacher can present a smaller amount of material but attempt to insure that students learn it very well. Conversely, the teacher may feel it is necessary to cover a certain amount of material in a school year and may be willing to sacrifice some depth in order to expose students to more material.

Given the variability of student aptitudes in collective instruction, the interrelations among the components of the model place considerable managerial demands on teachers. If they allocate sufficient time to allow slower students to achieve a high degree of depth, faster students may become bored or restless, and their cooperation may decrease. But if the teacher paces rapidly, providing only enough time for the faster students, slower students may become frustrated and their cooperation may decrease.

Arlin (1980) found that teachers were more likely to allocate time to achieve depth than to achieve coverage, as did Webster (1982). In addition, Webster (1982) found teachers pacing students more in accord with the needs of students with slower ability than those who were faster. This was achieved in collective instruction by decreasing coverage so that the class as a whole could achieve greater depth on a limited number of objectives. Arlin and Westbury (1976) and the Swedish researchers Dahloff (1971) and Lundgren (1972) have also presented evidence suggesting that teachers direct their pacing toward the slower students. Timing decisions may be influenced by the gains and losses resulting from moving in one direction or another on the depth-breadth continuum. For example, perhaps frustration of slower students disrupts cooperation more than does boredom and wasted time of faster students. Consequently, teachers may be more willing to hold back faster students than to leave behind slower students.

Generally, teachers can spend more or less time to achieve greater or less depth and greater or less breadth. Although time may ap-

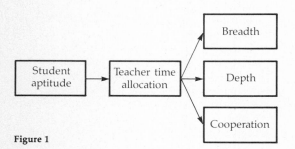

Figure 1

pear fixed, as by a 50-minute class period, and breadth may seem fixed through a recommended curriculum or text, teachers have latitude on these dimensions. They can adjust the pace and allocate time within the 50-minute constraints. They can neglect the coverage of topics considered peripheral or of an enrichment nature. Moreover, at the lower grade levels, teachers often have control over total time allocation to a subject area. Within the same school district, one third-grade teacher might spend 25 minutes per day on arithmetic, and another third-grade teacher might spend 50 minutes. At the lower grade levels, it might be easier to delete or add 10 or 15 minutes to a lesson in response to how difficult it is for students to understand.

Teachers can adjust breadth or depth in relation to students of varying aptitude. A common procedure, particularly at upper grade levels, is to provide instructional time and breadth uniformly to all students, with a resultant differentiation in depth as reflected by student achievement or grades. At the lower grade levels, greater adaptation to differential aptitudes appears more common. For example, through grouping procedures in elementary reading, the depth and breadth requirements can be different for a high aptitude group. Slower students may achieve at less depth by reading less challenging material. Or they may achieve less breadth by being introduced to fewer stories.

Prior to discussing the implications of this model for mastery learning, it should be noted that the model is heuristic, and it is developed for analytical purposes. It does not purport to represent the conscious decision processes of teachers. In fact, teachers may not be explicitly aware of their timing considerations. For example, the teachers with whom I have spoken about timing and pacing do not deliberate systematically about reducing a specified amount of breadth to achieve a specified increase of depth. Nor is the model meant to be exhaustive. It excludes, for example, a wide variety of affective considerations, such as student interests and motivations (except as reflected in cooperation). It is intentionally bounded to sug-

gest avenues for investigating certain aspects of time allocation or pacing. The components of aptitude, time, depth, breadth, and cooperation can be seen as topics or commonplaces, which may serve to generate thought about timing procedures.

The Time Allocation Model and Mastery Learning

It may be helpful to begin the discussion with a brief description of mastery learning. Mastery learning is a procedure in which students learn sequences of hierarchically ordered material. They are not permitted to begin subsequent units of material until they have mastered each previous unit. Mastery is typically determined by end-of-unit formative evaluation. A criterion score such as 85 percent is used to indicate that a unit has been mastered and thus when students can proceed to the next unit. A group version of mastery learning will be the focus of this study. Mastery learning proponents have recommended a group version in addition to the more commonly used individualized approach (e. g., Anderson 1980; Block 1979; Block and Anderson 1975; Block and Burns 1976; Bloom 1976).

Mastery learning alters the constraints on the time allocation model, and consequently the workable classroom environment achieved by teachers may have a different form than for nonmastery teaching. Within the mastery procedure, breadth or time must be traded off to attain mastery. But unlike nonmastery instruction, depth cannot be traded off to attain breadth. Adaptation to differential aptitudes is achieved most conspicuously through differential time allocation and perhaps through coverage reduction.

Mastery teaching should result in different time needs among students of differing abilities, becoming more of an explicit concern of the teacher. Slower students will need more time on review and remediation before they are ready to proceed to the next unit. Teachers who are accustomed to viewing students with lower aptitude as low achievers may begin to see them as students requiring more time to achieve mastery. Their managerial concerns for engendering cooperation may focus increasingly on the different learning rates of students. The most obvious indicator of learning rate variability may be what Webster (1982) calls "finishing rate"—namely, when a student has completed the assignment given by the teacher.

The relation of aptitudes to learning time is more problematic in collective instruction than in tutorial instruction. In tutorial instruction, time and breadth can be adapted to the needs of a particular student, who can proceed at his or her own pace. But in the group model of mastery learning, virtually all students must master a unit before the group as a whole proceeds to the subsequent unit. Students cannot progress to subsequent units at their own pace. Rather, faster students may have to wait for slower students, as Resnick (1977) and Mueller (1976) suggest. Barr and Dreeben (1977) suggest that students with time on their hands are a perennial problem of classroom instruction and that this and similar topics relevant to collective instruction are not addressed adequately in the mastery learning literature. They argue that this is because mastery learning is based on a tutorial model and that most of its conceptual statements are defined in individual, not aggregate, terms. As an example, they mention that there are constraints on time within a school day, but the tutorial model of mastery assumes no constraints on time. Teachers implementing mastery learning may be faced with the problem of obtaining extra time to bring slower students to mastery levels.

Mastery theorists suggest several techniques for accommodating students with differential time needs or learning rates, but these techniques may not be entirely satisfactory. Two common ones are using faster students to tutor the slower students and providing enrichment activities for the faster ones. But the tutors themselves might finish at different rates, thus making it difficult to match them with slower students learning at different rates. The enrichment activities would have to be sufficient to engage students, from the fastest to almost the slowest in the class. As faster students would have the most time available for enrichment and could progress the most rapidly, a considerable amount of enrichment might be necessary for them. But some enrichment would also be necessary for students finishing just prior to the last students. Since it is likely that the teacher's attention during review/enrichment activities would be directed toward helping the slower students, the enrichment activities might be relatively less supervised. Toward the end of a unit, when the majority of the class is engaged in less supervised enrichment, the varied aptitudes of learners may require different levels and amounts of enrichment adapted to individual needs. Under such conditions, obtaining the cooperation of all students might place considerable demands on the managerial skills of the teacher.

Many of these time-related issues are not as fully discussed as one might wish in the mastery learning literature. Most of the emphasis there is placed on discussion of achievement, an area in which mastery learning researchers have been able to demonstrate impressive results. Perhaps the relative neglect of time issues is because some mastery theorists believe that the differential time needs of students become progressively homogeneous over the course of mastery learning, even to the extent of reaching a vanishing point of individual differences in learning time (Block 1974; Bloom 1971, 1976). If eventual time homogeneity were probable, then the problem of differential learning or finishing rates would only be short-term, at the beginning of mastery procedures. I have argued elsewhere (Arlin 1973, 1982, 1983; Arlin and Webster 1983) that individual differences in time do not decrease across the course of mastery learning, and in this paper I will proceed on the assumption that differential learning rates continually remain a condition requiring the teacher's managerial consideration. In fact, I suggest that a concern for differential learning rates may be the most important one considered by teachers in trying to achieve workable combinations of depth, breadth, and cooperation.

In the remainder of the paper, qualitative

descriptions of teachers implementing mastery learning will be presented. This description is not intended as an empirical confirmation, in the sense of rigorous hypothesis testing, of the model of teacher time allocation described. Rather, the description should serve to illustrate some of the inter-relationships among the components of the model described above.

The observations are organized around four topics that bear on the model. The first is the degree to which teachers in mastery learning experience an awareness of time considerations and their consequent reflection on this. The second is how teachers allocate time to help slower students achieve mastery. A third, and related, topic is where teachers obtain the extra time needed for slower learners. The fourth is how teachers allocate time to faster learners and, in particular, how they keep faster learners productively occupied.

Method

Sample

The participants were 10 elementary school teachers and their students in 10 classrooms located in seven schools. There were three first-grade classrooms, one fourth-grade classroom, one fourth-fifth combination, two fifth-sixth combinations, one sixth-grade classroom, one sixth-seventh combination, and one seventh-grade classroom. The classrooms were located in two semirural school districts of British Columbia within a 200-mile radius of one another. The teachers were all experienced, with an average of more than 10 years teaching.

Preparation

Prior to the beginning of the school year, most teachers in both districts attended a professional development day on mastery learning initiated by the administrative staff of the two districts. Volunteer teachers were solicited by the central administration to attempt mastery learning pilot projects in their classrooms. Twenty-eight elementary teachers responded.

The volunteers were provided with Block and Anderson's (1975) book on classroom implementation of mastery learning, as well as other articles on the same topic. I then worked for one day with the superintendent and the principals in both districts on administrative aspects of mastery learning and for two days with the teachers in each of the two districts. During this period, teachers worked both individually and in teams formulating mastery units, objectives, and quizzes. Teachers were provided released time both to attend the training sessions and to develop a mastery learning module. They were given six weeks to develop the mastery unit, which would then be taught during three weeks in January. On completion, the mastery units were read by a district administrator with training in mastery learning and by me; feedback was supplied to the teachers. The units were subsequently revised. After initial attempts to develop mastery units, 11 teachers felt the task was too time consuming and terminated the project, leaving 17 teachers in the sample.

Mastery Unit Materials

Teachers were asked to plan for a three-week mastery learning phase in January. They selected a hierarchical unit involving new material that could be brought to an intermediate conclusion over a period of approximately 10 teaching days. A pretest was developed to assess the entry behaviors that the teachers considered immediately necessary to begin the unit. Eight daily formative quizzes for days 1–4 and days 6–9 were also completed. Alternate forms of the quizzes and tests were developed. Lesson plans, including objectives, teaching procedures for entire-group instruction, and review procedures, were developed for each of the 10 days. A second test was constructed for the fifth day, and a third test was made for the tenth day. All the materials were sequential and were materials typically covered by the teachers. In order to have a sequential unit during January, some teachers saved a unit that normally would have been taught earlier, and others introduced a unit that would have been taught later. (The units introduced earlier did not depend on material that would have been covered at a later date.) All lesson plans were developed to accommodate total-class instruction (rather than individualized instruction) followed by group or individualized remediation.

Procedure

One week prior to the initial lesson, all students were given the pretest. Those students who were not able to achieve at a level of 90 percent were given special reteaching over the period of a week by the teacher and were allowed extra time to attain mastery of the pretest entry behaviors. Some students spent less than one hour in remediation, while others spent as much as 10 hours during classes, lunchtime, and after school. Approximately 92 percent of all students were able to reach mastery of the prerequisite entry behaviors prior to beginning the mastery units.

Each day the teacher taught a lesson to the whole class for a period of 15–30 minutes. The lessons included lecture-recitation, demonstration, and (less frequently) group activity. Following the lesson, a short quiz of approximately 2–3 minutes' length was given and corrected immediately, most often by the students themselves (correcting in ink the original pencil responses). Immediately following the formative quiz, those who had not reached a mastery level were assigned to a remediation strategy such as peer tutoring, individualized rereading, or small-group instruction by the teacher. Because of the brevity of the quizzes, 100 percent correct achievement (all questions correct) was typically used as the mastery criterion. The exception to the above procedure was on days 5 and 10. The lesson was a review of the previous days' work, followed by a longer test of all previous material. Following this test, students participated in remedial activities, as on the other days, then took alternative forms of the test until they achieved mastery. Because the tests were longer, a criterion of 85–90 percent could be used. Teachers used the closest criterion, depending on the

number of items they used (e.g., one item missed on a 10-item test [90 percent], two items missed on a 14-item test [86 percent]).

It should be noted that the mastery teaching units of the 10 teachers were not intended as typical mastery learning procedures but as short-term simulations of longer-term implementations. They were similar in length and procedures to the "micro studies" cited by Bloom (1976) in support of mastery learning theory. For example, the frequent test procedures typical of the micro studies and this study would be spread out over a longer period of time in long-term implementations. Nevertheless, the 10-day units can be used to illustrate the time allocation model and to illuminate time issues that need to be addressed by mastery learning theory.

Observation

All teachers were observed initially to determine the degree to which they implemented the mastery learning procedures. In four classes, the teachers adhered to the mastery procedures so that student times could be observed and recorded in a precise manner. (The students in these classes provided data for a related study of individual differences in time needs; see Arlin 1983). On the basis of an initial observation and follow-up discussion with the teachers, I judged that 10 of the 17 participants (including the four described above) adhered sufficiently closely to mastery procedures to warrant further observation. The primary criterion was a systematic teach-test-review procedure until mastery (at least 80 percent) was achieved by most students (typically at least 90 percent) prior to beginning the next lesson.

Seven research assistants observed all 10 teachers for all 10 lesson days of the study and kept a record of time usage during the 100 lessons. The assistants recorded the topic and the remedial procedure used. In addition to the observations of the research assistants, I personally observed two lessons of each teacher and after the lessons discussed the lesson with each teacher. I took unstructured notes during the classroom observations and kept notes of our discussions. Additionally, I noted the number of students off-task at various parts of the lesson in a manner described in Arlin (1979).

Results

Awareness of Time Differences

One of the benefits of the mastery learning procedure experienced by most of the teachers in the study was an increased awareness not only of the differences between the fast and slow learners in their classes but also the actual learning time needed by their fast and slow learners. In another study (Arlin 1979) and in many conversations with teachers, I have found that teachers are not used to articulating their notions of time allocation or pacing. Many of the teachers in this study seemed to become aware of timing and pacing considerations. Their comments included: "You know, I never used to know if the kids had it or not, so I'd go over and over again to be sure, but now I know when I can stop"; "Well, I always knew ———— was faster than the rest, but I didn't know ————, ————, and———— could get through the stuff so fast"; "If you don't use something like this mastery learning, how are you going to give the right time for everybody? It's impossible, isn't it? I guess I just shoot at the middle some place and hope it's OK for the rest"; "I'm probably not going to use mastery learning again, but now I'm going to be worried that [the faster students] are bored to hell or else I'll feel more guilty about not giving enough time to [the slower students]." Some teachers indicated an increased awareness of the needs of the slower learners. "The thing is there's a whole bunch of kids who just don't get it the first time. I usually don't use tests much, and when I look at them they seem to get it; but when you give them these tests right after you've taught it to them, they don't know it. That was a real shock the first couple of quizzes."

Many of the comments compared the teachers' usual method of teaching with mastery teaching. The mastery approach seemed to cause these teachers to reflect on a possible "leveling" procedure (Arlin and Westbury 1976) that they used in their ordinary (nonmastery) teaching. This possible awareness of a leveling approach seemed to be heightened by reflection on the problem of absentee children. In all classrooms there were children absent for two or more days. It was more difficult to deal with them in mastery learning than during their usual teaching because they had missed a definite segment of material. Teachers felt the need to reteach the lesson to them, although obtaining the time was a problem. (This problem is discussed further in the section on extra time.) But this need was less apparent during their usual teaching. "Usually when they come back [from an absence] they just fit right in. Except when they've been out for a long time. But now you have to do something to make sure they get the lesson they missed." I suggest that comments made about their usual teaching, such as easily "fitting in," indicate that there is probably a considerable redundancy in most lessons, a possibility in keeping with leveling (Arlin and Westbury 1976) or pacing based on slower students, such as the twenty-fifth percentile "steering criterion group" suggested by Dahloff (1971) and Lundgren (1972). This type of pacing indicates that teachers may allocate time to increase depth for students at or below the steering criterion and decrease breadth for students above it.

Remarks such as "shooting at the middle" and "going over it again and again" in reference to their usual teaching indicate an awareness of timing to accommodate a lower common denominator, which may not be appropriate for faster students. But an awareness of leveling or of differential needs of fast and slow learners may be dysfunctional in typical (nonmastery) group-based classrooms. Perhaps one of the reasons teachers with whom I have spoken have not reflected to a great degree on their timing and pacing procedures is that not much could be done in the face of heightened awareness. (". . . to give the right time for everybody. It's impossible.") A teacher might feel uneasy about inability to accommodate faster and slower students. ("[I'm] going to be worried. . . . I'll feel more guilty.").

In contrast to their usual procedures, the mastery strategy gave teachers a feeling of being able to accommodate the time needs of particular learners to an extent they usually had not been able to achieve before. This seemed to give many a sense of satisfaction and a feeling that they were "doing their job." Teachers appeared to derive satisfaction primarily from the increased depth of lower-aptitude learners.

Teachers appeared to use the number of students needing remediation as feedback for the subsequent day's pacing. In several cases, teachers had more than 50 percent of students needing remediation after the original lesson. These teachers seemed either to simplify their subsequent lesson or to teach the subsequent lesson for a longer time so that almost 100 percent of students mastered the lesson. But when close to 100 percent of students mastered the lesson, many teachers felt that the lesson must have been too easy or they spent too long at it, and the subsequent lesson was made more difficult or was taught for a shorter period of time.

After experiencing this type of feedback and modifying lessons accordingly, most teachers seemed comfortable when about eight students needed remediation. (An exception was one teacher who would ask questions and continue teaching until sure the whole class had achieved mastery before giving the mastery quiz.) Teachers may have felt comfortable with eight students in part because they could deal with them as a small remedial group. More than this number began to be a "class" situation and did not permit as much give and take between teacher and individual students. One or two students needing remediation seemed too few to justify holding up the rest of the class, so teachers would often continue with another subject after all but one or two had reached mastery on the original lesson. Helping the one or two students individually would occur later in the day. It seemed as if teachers were seeking a balance between too many students needing help and too few.

The fact that teachers were comfortable

with eight students in classes of about 25 also provides indirect support for the steering criterion group of Dahloff (1971), Lundgren (1972), and Arlin and Westbury (1976). They have suggested that teachers might pace their lessons according to the time needs of students in the twenty-fifth percentile. The teachers in the present experiment seemed to feel comfortable pacing for mastery in accordance with the time needs of students near the thirty to thirty-fifth percentile. Perhaps the steering group and the present results suggest that there are equilibria toward which teachers tend when accommodating individual differences in collective instruction. These equilibria would seem to be considerably less than a mathematically balanced point at the fiftieth percentile.

Time Allocation for Slower Learners

How do teachers provide the extra time and help to slower learners? Teachers were conscious of the mastery theory recommendation that remedial procedures should be distinct from original teaching procedures. This idea is no doubt based on the assumption that, if students have difficulty with original learning, they will also have difficulty with "more of the same." Teachers tried alternative methods, such as cassettes, games, flash cards, diagrams, and alternate books. Inevitably, these alternative procedures were the least successful and least satisfying attempts for the teachers. Prepackaged materials such as cassettes were often not keyed precisely to the lesson taught by the teacher and, frequently, students were unable to profit from the games.

Teachers seemed to become particularly frustrated in using these alternate materials when explanation of the procedures was necessary to individuals and small groups. Arlin (1979) found that transition times, when one activity was terminated and another was begun, were potentially the most disruptive to a smooth "time flow" of classrooms. The alternative procedures of the present study could be seen as a set of simultaneous, interruptive transitions following the main lessons. Teachers seemed to find it difficult to explain how to complete the enrichment puzzles or how to fix the tape recorder while six students were impatiently waiting for their reteaching. The teaching strategy that was required seemed similar to the "ringmastership" described by Smith and Geoffrey (1968). The more teachers tried to use a multiplicity of remedial procedures, the more harried they seemed to become. This is not to imply that alternative methods are necessarily inappropriate for mastery learning; but they seemed particularly difficult to structure so as to be directly relevant to the lesson and capable of eliciting self-sustaining involvement (Westbury 1973).

The remedial techniques most preferred by the teachers were reteaching of small groups and peer tutoring. Some teachers attempted to group students by the items missed so they could review only those pertinent aspects. But since many students missed more than one item and it was difficult to deal with the others waiting for help, specific group sessions became a managerial nightmare. Most teachers who used group remediation eventually retaught the entire lesson, in a simpler, longer manner, to everyone who needed remediation. The reteaching to small groups worked more effectively at the primary level, perhaps because children not directly supervised by the teacher were accustomed to working quietly during small-group reading periods. At the upper grade levels, off-task behavior increased from approximately 10 to 40 percent during all-group lecturing to approximately 10–80 percent during reteaching. This latter percentage refers only to those students who were not in the remedial session. The on-task levels of the small remediation group remained high and often exceeded levels during large-group teaching.

The least preferred remedial technique was peer tutoring. Students seemed capable of peer tutoring only at the upper elementary levels. Initial attempts to match students needing tutoring with students who initially achieved mastery on a particular lesson resulted in managerial difficulties. Assignment "on the spot" was difficult. Many teachers resolved this problem by preassigning their faster students as tutors because "I can count on them to get it the first time. Then I don't have to waste time figuring out who's going to be a tutor." Three or four tutors were preassigned, and each day they divided students needing tutoring among themselves.

It seemed that teachers derived more satisfaction from small-group reteaching and felt that they were much more capable of explaining the lesson than tutors. My observations of the tutoring led me to believe that tutors were reasonably effective and could explain the material in simple language to their peers. Perhaps the reason teachers preferred to conduct the reteaching themselves was that they then felt personally responsible for the increased depth of slower learners.

Obtaining Extra Time

The question of where teachers obtain the extra time and help for students raises a persistent problem experienced by the teachers in this study. Teachers were not sure where they were going to get the extra time to accommodate slower learners. "Sure you can do it with these short lessons when you have a lot of time in the rest of the lesson. But what if I want to go back to my usual [i.e., longer] lessons? What am I supposed to do? Let [slower students] do it during art or socials?" The solution most teachers adopted was to make the lessons shorter than originally planned so that they could have considerable time left in the class period to include at least one remedial session and retest. (Consequences of this will be discussed below.) Usually students who needed additional remedial sessions were seen by the teacher during recess or lunch, a practice that was not likely to be received favorably over a long period of time. "I don't mind [helping at recess], but you can't do it all the time. But when else can I do it? If I help him during seatwork, then he's going to miss out on the seatwork."

An additional problem was posed by students who were absent. Sometimes, if a faster student was absent for one day only, the teacher included the student in the class and merely omitted the lesson and the quiz of the previous day. But for a slower student or a student who missed two or more lessons, there was no simple solution. Extra time from other classes and recess, lunch time, or after-school time was often used. This problem was even more pressing than that for students needing extra sessions of remedial help, because the teacher was usually needed to teach the original lesson to the absent student. Furthermore, most teachers taught their mastery units in the morning, so the absent student had to be retaught prior to the day's mastery class or the student would not be able to profit from the day's class. But most other academic subjects were also in the the morning, and the teachers were unwilling to take themselves away from the teaching of these other "important" subjects to help the student. They were also unwilling to have students taken away from one of these subjects (usually math or reading) to work with a tutor. None of the teachers in the experiment was able to resolve this dilemma satisfactorily. Teachers would only sacrifice small amounts of time in one "important" subject for increased depth to another. Therefore, time for increased depth had to be obtained primarily within the subject itself, typically taken from time that would otherwise have been allocated to increase breadth.

Time Allocation for Faster Learners

What do mastery teachers do with their faster learners? It has already been mentioned that teachers made their lessons short and discrete in order to have time to provide remediation for slower learners in a typical 50-minute class period. Many teachers originally planned enrichment work for the faster students, such as more advanced work on the topic under consideration. However, it became difficult for teachers to plan advanced work that did not foreshadow or duplicate subsequent lessons. In order to avoid this, some of them assigned advanced work in tangentially related areas, such as difficult math puzzles in an arithmetic class. Much of the "enrichment" could be labeled as such only by using very generous criteria. As

one teacher put it, "To tell you the truth, it's really just high-powered busywork so they don't bug me while I'm working with [the slower children]." Many teachers eventually gave up assigning enrichment and allowed activities such as free reading, work in other subjects, trips to the library, or quiet socializing at the back of the room. Cooperation of faster students took precedence over further depth, and particularly over further breadth, for them.

The major concern with faster students did not seem to be with enrichment but with the managerial requirement to keep them occupied. In order to do this, the enrichment task needed to be relatively bounded, able to be started or stopped at interim points, and capable of self-sustained interest and independent use. The tasks had to be able to serve as "fillers" that could involve the student for 10 minutes or 40 minutes. Few of the enrichment tasks were able to satisfy this criterion. Westbury (1973) has described the difficulty of obtaining such self-sustaining curricular materials and suggested that a technology such as open education could not be implemented successfully without such materials. Perhaps a similar argument could be made for the technology of mastery learning. In the present experiment, carefully prepared enrichment tasks developed by the teachers to deepen understanding of a lesson typically involved a specific activity with a specific termination of that activity. Students would often finish either too soon or continue beyond the end of the period trying to finish one. "You can't just leave them hanging with these things. You've got to give them time to finish. But then there are going to be others who'll finish too fast. You can't give them enrichment of the enrichment." During the course of the mastery units it became clear to most teachers thay they had to hold back the faster students from going ahead too swiftly. "You can call it enrichment if you want, but when it gets down to it, I guess you have to say I'm keeping [the faster students] back, aren't I?"

Other teachers used their faster students as tutors. This solved a problem of what to do with the faster students, until the students they were tutoring were finished. Then there were two problems—the tutors and their charges. Moreover, as explained above, most tutors were assigned in advance and were the fastest students. Each day an unpredictable number of average students reached mastery on the first quiz, and teachers had difficulty assigning them as tutors.

While many teachers felt that faster students were held back to wait for slower students, they also felt that this was no worse than their normal teaching because they perceived students were now learning more. Even though many of the classes were shortened to allow time for remediation of slower students, teachers were impressed by the amount that students did learn. "Even though it's short, they all seem to learn as much as in a regular long lesson, even the fast ones." These comments indicate that teachers felt mastery learning resulted in both greater breadth and depth than nonmastery learning. Nevertheless, their comments about holding back faster learners indicate an awareness that time was allocated toward increasing depth of slower learners at the expense of even greater depth and breadth of faster ones.

Perhaps a side benefit of mastery learning is the task focus it provides for students, as Anderson (1976) has suggested. I observed several classes prior to commencement of the mastery lesson. In one, the lesson seemed aimless, and 92 percent of students were off-task at one point. As soon as the mastery lesson started, the number of students off-task declined to 24 percent. Students seemed to have a clearer conception of what was expected from them and what they were supposed to do, and they paid attention to be able to pass the daily quiz on the first try. As several students told me, "It's neat, because if you get them all right the first time, you don't have to do any more work." While the "reward" of no more work is probably not what mastery theorists intended, they would undoubtedly be pleased with how many students in the present experiment attended to the original lesson. They would be less pleased with the subsequent activities by which the faster student appeared to "waste time."

Conclusion

Generalization of the present results must be limited to teachers' initial responses as they attempted to implement mastery learning procedures. It is possible that, with additional experience and over a longer period of time, the procedures and responses might be different. With this caution in mind, the following conclusions can be drawn.

First, mastery procedures appeared to heighten the teachers' awareness about time considerations, particularly student differences in time needed to learn. This was a mixed blessing for some, however, for it made them more aware of the dilemma of providing appropriate learning time for a wide variety of students.

Second, providing differential review and time to slower students proved unfeasible in this experiment. Most teachers eventually provided the same time and reinstruction to everyone who had not achieved mastery on the formative quiz.

Third, as suggested by Barr and Dreeben (1977) and Torshen (1977), time is not an unlimited resource, and obtaining extra time for slower learners is problematic. It becomes particularly problematic when the teacher is faced with the choice of taking time away from one subject to ensure mastery in another. Since teachers in the present study placed considerable importance on achieving mastery over the 10 lessons, they were willing to take time from other subjects as well as spend time during lunch and recess to ensure mastery for slower learners. But this would not be possible if the other subjects as well were to be learned to a mastery level. Moreover, some of the teachers felt that taking time from other subjects was defensible for their short pilot experiment, but they could not accept it on a longer-term basis.

Fourth, the problem of faster learners finishing earlier, which was noted by Barr and Dreeben (1977), was felt by many teachers in the study. Many teachers approached this problem by providing alternative activities for faster learners, such as enrichment or tutoring. However, some teachers had misgivings about the true function of these activities. In a sociological framework, the manifest function of these activities was to "challenge" or "enrich" faster students, but the latent function appeared to be that of holding them back, as predicted by Mueller (1976) and Resnick (1977).

It is hoped that the observations of teachers implementing mastery learning have helped to illustrate some of the features of the model for analyzing teachers' timing procedures. Under mastery learning, depth is constrained at mastery levels, so there are fewer variables that can be adjusted to accommodate individual differences in aptitude. Individual differences in aptitude are reflected primarily in differences in learning time or finishing rates. The primary focus of the teachers' managerial concerns was directed toward keeping the faster students meaningfully occupied while assisting slower students in their review toward mastery. Student cooperation may have been achieved because slower students felt that instruction and the teacher's attention were directed toward them. Faster students did not seem to object to missed learning opportunities. Even when teachers abandoned their "enrichment activities," the basis of the cooperation of the faster learners seemed to be an implicit arrangement by the teacher—"If you're quiet and don't bother me or the rest of the class, you can do what you want with your free time." Although the workable environment may be different in the mastery case than in the nonmastery case, it may be achieved in both cases at the expense of faster students. A workable environment seemed to be achieved by timing instruction to the needs of students with lower aptitude.

NOTE

Thanks are extended to William Baldry, superintendent of Grand Forks and Kettle River Districts, and to the teachers in these districts whose cooperation made this study possible. Thanks are also given to the Social Sciences and Humanities Research Council of Canada for partial funding of this study.

REFERENCES

Abrahamson, J. H. "Classroom Constraints and Teacher Coping Strategies." Ph. D. dissertation, University of Chicago, 1974.

Anderson, L. W. "An Empirical Investigation of Individual Differences in Time to Learn." *Journal of Educational Psychology* 68 (1976): 226–233.

Anderson, L. W. "Mastery Learning Confusion." *Educational Leadership* 38 (1980): 372.

Arlin, M. "Learning Rate and Learning Rate Variance under Mastery Learning Conditions." Ph. D. dissertation, University of Chicago, 1973.

Arlin, M. "Teacher Transitions Can Disrupt Classroom Time Flow." *American Educational Research Journal* 16 (1979): 42–56.

Arlin, M. "An Instrument for Assessing Teacher Preferences for Depth and Breadth." Unpublished test, Department of Educational Psychology and Special Education, University of British Columbia, 1980.

Arlin, M. "Time, Equality, and Mastery Learning." Unpublished manuscript, Department of Educational Psychology and Special Education, University of British Columbia, 1982.

Arlin, M. "Time Variability in Mastery Learning." *American Educational Research Journal* 20 (1983), in press.

Arlin, M., and J. Webster. "Time Costs of Mastery Learning." *Journal of Educational Psychology* (1983), in press.

Arlin, M., and I. Westbury. "The Leveling Effect of Teacher Pacing on Science Content Mastery." *Journal of Research in Science Teaching* 13 (1976): 213–219.

Barr, R. C., and R. Dreeben. "Instruction in Classrooms," In *Review of Research in Education* 5, edited by L. S. Shulman, Itasca, Ill.: Peacock, 1977.

Block, J. H. "Mastery Learning in the Classroom: An Overview of Recent Research." In *Schools, Society, and Mastery Learning*, edited by J. H. Block. New York: Holt, Rinehart & Winston, 1974.

Block, J. H. "Mastery Learning—Current State of the Craft." *Educational Leadership* 37 (1979): 114–117.

Block, J. H., and J. H. Anderson. *Mastery Learning and Classroom Instruction.* New York: Macmillan. 1975.

Block, J. H., and R. B. Burns. "Mastery Learning." In *Review of Research in Education,* vol. 4, edited by L. S. Shulman, Itaska, Ill.: Peacock, 1976.

Bloom, B. S. "Individual Differences in School Achievement: A Vanishing Point? *Education at Chicago* 4 (1971): 14.

Bloom, B. S. *Human Characteristics and School Learning.* New York: McGraw-Hill, 1976.

Carroll, J. B. "A Model of School Learning." *Teachers College Record* 64 (1963): 723–733.

Dahloff, U. *Ability Grouping, Content Validity, and Curriculum Process Analysis.* New York: Teachers College Press, 1971.

Doyle, W. "Making Managerial Decisions in Classrooms." In *Classroom Management,* 78th Yearbook of the National Society for the Study of Education, edited by D. Duke. Chicago: University of Chicago Press, 1979.

Hauwiller, J. G. "A Naturalistic Study of Professional Education Instructors' Handling of the Mastery/ Coverage Dilemma." Ph. D. dissertation, University of Illinois at Urbana-Champaign, 1976.

Lundgren, U. P. *Frame Factors and the Teaching Process.* Stockholm: Almqvist & Wiksell, 1972.

Mueller, D. J. "Mastery Learning: Partly Boon, Partly Boondoggle." *Teachers College Record* 78 (1976): 41–52.

Resnick, L. D. "Assuming That Everyone Can Learn Everything, Will Some Learn Less?" *School Review* 85 (1977): 445–452.

Smith, L. M., and W. Geoffrey. *The Complexities of an Urban Classroom.* New York: Holt, Rinehart & Winston, 1968.

Torshen, K. P. *The Mastery Approach to Competency-based Education.* New York: Academic Press, 1977.

Webster, J. B. "Individual Differences in Time Needed to Learn: Teacher Coping Strategies." Ed. D. dissertation, University of British Columbia, 1982.

Westbury, I. "Conventional Classrooms, 'Open' Classrooms, and the Technology of Teaching." *Journal of Curriculum Studies* 5 (1973): 99–121.

READING 19

Learning Rates and Mastery Learning

James H. Block

One of the most ancient criticisms of mastery learning has been a variant of the "Robbing Peter To Pay Paul" argument. By making time—not learning—the variable in school teaching, critics contend that mastery learning simply exchanges the normal curve in student learning for the normal curve in student learning rates. Over the long-haul, therefore, mastery learning programs must either extend the education of "slow" learners until they are oldsters (Cronbach, 1972) or "hold back" "fast" learners until the "slow" catch up (Mueller, 1976; Resnick, 1977).

I had hoped that this hoary criticism had been laid to rest in writings such as Block (1974), Block and Anderson (1975), Bloom (1976) and Block and Burns (1977). These writings addressed the two critical assumptions upon which the criticism rests and found them wanting. One assumption was that there are wide natural individual differences in students' learning rate. Our work suggested that most individual differences in students' learning rate are unnatural and artifacts of their in-

struction. The other assumption was that mastery learning approaches cannot do much to eradicate these differences. Our research indicated that mastery instruction could press individual differences in students' learning rate to a vanishing point, i.e., to help the "slow" learners learn as fast as the "fast" ones. Moreover, this vanishing point seemed to be reached not by dragging-down "fast" students to the rate of the "slow" but by dragging-up "slow" students to the rate of the "fast."

Apparently, though, my hope was misplaced. Not only have thoughtful advocates of individually-based/student-paced approaches to mastery learning breathed new life into the corpse, now a previous advocate of group-based/teacher-paced approaches has darn near made the corpse sit-up and talk. I am speaking of Marshall Arlin of the University of British Columbia in a series of provocative studies of student and teacher time issues in mastery learning (Arlin, 1982, 1983; Arlin and Webster, 1983).

I wish to comment on one of these studies here: "Teacher Responses to Student Time Differences In Mastery Learning." I shall summarize the study and then react to its content, findings, and conclusions.

From *Outcomes* (Winter 1983):18–25. Reprinted with permission.

Study Content

Arlin begins this study by schematizing a model of how teachers allocate classroom time to accommodate students' "aptitudes." These aptitudes are conceived a la Carroll (1963) as determining student learning rates, so the model boils down to a heuristic analysis of how teachers allocate classroom time to adjust for variability in these rates.

According to the model, classroom time is allocated according to concerns of learning and control. On the learning side, teachers are supposed to allocate time depending on desired *depth*—the"degree, level, or intensity of learning"—or *breadth*—the "amount or extent of learning" (p. 335). Depth and breadth are viewed as competing teacher concerns: more depth implies less breadth and vice-versa. On the control side, teachers are believed to allocate time depending on student *cooperation,* i. e., "the degree to which students participate in learning in a manner congruent with the teacher's intentions" (idem). Arlin's graphics suggest that learning and control matters are equally important to the teacher. His prose suggests, however, that learning matters might be more salient.

Arlin illustrates the applicability of the model by attempting to understand the peculiar classroom time-allocation constraints of mastery learning approaches to teaching. He begins his illustration by speculating that:

1. Mastery approaches should trade-off breadth and time since depth is fixed.
2. Mastery approaches should evince more explicit teacher concerns regarding the different learning time needs of students with different abilities.
3. Group-based mastery approaches should be more problematic to manage than individually-based approaches since it may be more difficult to obtain the extra time "slow" students will require in a collective learning situation.

Then, Arlin criticizes typical group-based mastery learning techniques for handling learning rate issues. Peer tutoring, he contends, poses real management problems of matching tutors to tutees because of the various rates at which both parties complete their learning. Enrichment techniques, he argues, pose real curricular problems of developing materials that are sufficiently engrossing to engage students no matter when they complete their learning.

Next, Arlin chastises primarily Bloom and me for what he perceives as our relative neglect of time issues in mastery learning. He is concerned that we have ignored these issues because we believe that the differential learning rates of students should become progressively more similar when learning for mastery. Whereas he believes "that differential learning rates continually remain a condition requiring the teacher's managerial consideration" (p. 339).

Finally, Arlin reports the qualitative results of a micro-study designed to put his speculations, criticisms, and chastisements to the test. This study was executed in two semirural districts in south central British Columbia and involved seven schools and ten classrooms of about twenty-five students each. Veteran teachers with limited mastery teaching experience taught a ten-day learning unit using group-based mastery learning procedures. Students were taught, formatively tested and corrected or enriched each day while trained observers watched over the proceedings and tracked selected students' learning rates.

Study Results

The study under review here gives only Arlin's teacher observation data; his learning rate data will appear elsewhere (Arlin, 1983; Arlin and Webster, 1983). Let us summarize these data using Arlin's own report subheadings.

Awareness of Time Differences

Mastery learning teachers were more aware than others of differences in student learning and learning rate, and of the timing and pacing considerations required to adjust to these differences. And they seemed satisfied with mastery learning because it gave them a tool to accommodate these differences—a tool not readily available in their ordinary instruction. But even mastery learning could not stop the teachers from trying to level these individual differences in learning rate by targeting their instruction to a particular group of students. All that mastery learning could do was to encourage the teachers to target their instruction higher than usual. Their instruction was calibrated for students of about the 30 to 35th percentile whereas ordinarily it might have been calibrated for students of about the 25th percentile.

Time Allocation for Slower Learners

The teachers tried a variety of alternative correctives like cassettes, games, flash cards, diagrams, and alternative books, but they found prepackaged materials like cassettes and games not well-suited to their lesson plans, a pain to explain how to use, and a definite interruption in class time "flow." They preferred reteaching small-groups and peer tutoring as correctives. The teachers seemed to derive more satisfaction from small-group reteaching and felt more capable of explaining the lesson than their tutors. Besides, real problems cropped up in assigning tutors as they finished; teachers had to preassign their "faster" students as tutors from the start.

Obtaining Extra Time

Teachers were not sure where to get extra learning time to accommodate their "slower" students, so they tended to shorten their lessons to leave time for correction. They even provided additional remedial sessions at recess and lunch, a situation which Arlin doubts might be feasible over the long haul. But the teachers seemed unwilling to sacrifice small amounts of time from other important subjects to increase the depth in the mastery taught subject. So, depth had to come out of the mastery taught subject's breadth.

Time Allocation for Faster Learners

Some teachers used "fast" students as tutors. But this procedure only solved the problem of "fast" learners until they were done tutoring. Other teachers planned enrichments for the "faster" students, but eventually they abandoned them and allowed these students to engage in other activities—free reading, work in other subjects, trips to the library, and quiet socializing. Arlin contends that these teachers seemed preoccupied with maintaining "faster" students' cooperation rather than increasing their depth or breadth. And he suggests they seemed aware they were holding these learners back. The teachers felt, however, that mastery learning was no worse for "fast" students than their normal teaching methods since students were now learning more. And outside observers noted that they appeared to attend to their lessons very well.

Study Conclusions

On the basis of these findings Arlin draws the following conclusion. I quote *in extenso:*

> Under mastery learning depth is constrained at mastery levels, so there are fewer variables that can be adjusted to accommodate individual differences in aptitude. Individual differences . . . are reflected primarily in differences in learning time or finishing rates. The primary focus of the teachers' managerial concerns was directed toward keeping the faster students meaningfully occupied while assisting slower students in their review toward mastery. Student cooperation may have been achieved because slower students felt that instruction and the teacher's attention were directed toward them. Faster students did not seem to object to missed learning opportunities. Even when teachers abandoned their "enrichment activities," the basis of the cooperation of the faster learners seemed to be an implicit arrangement by the teacher—"If you're quiet and don't bother me or the rest of the class, you can

do what you want with your free time." Although the workable environment may be different in the mastery case, it may be achieved in both cases at the expense of faster students. A workable environment seemed to be achieved by timing instruction to the needs of students with lower aptitude. (pp. 351–352)

Study Reactions

What is my reaction to this study, its findings, and its conclusions? I have three.

The cynic in me says that Arlin's study demands no reaction. After all, the research contains several possible flaws. Some of the flaws are conceptual: for example, the notion that time for mastery learning can only be drawn from inside the classroom. Other flaws are practical; for example, the unnaturally compressed nature of his mastery treatment. And, even with these conceptual and technical flaws, his results are still generally encouraging. Teachers seemed to find mastery learning to be effective: it did seem to help students of "lower" aptitude and was no worse than normal for students of "higher" aptitude. And teachers found mastery learning to be self-satisfying and to generate a feeling they were "doing their job."

The scholar in me cries, however, for a less ostrich-like response. I would recommend that Arlin's study be replicated under a wider range of ordinary mastery learning conditions. While Arlin may be right that time issues have been relatively ignored in mastery learning theory and research, I cannot believe they have been ignored in mastery learning practice. Surely there are enough sites already in the Network to execute a series of more naturally occurring classroom time allocation studies.

I would also recommend that the research be replicated with a view to repairing some of the study's most notable conceptual and technical flaws. Arlin's own comments and some of mine suggest, for example, that Network time allocation studies might use teachers better "grooved" in the use of mastery learning ideas; spread out the length of the treatment and cut

the number of feedback/correction points; ensure that the correctives are better tailored to the teachers' original lesson plans; take steps to teach students how to use each corrective before the teaching begins; design the enrichments in a more systematic less busy work fashion; and make greater use of a combination of time in class, in school outside of class, and out of school. Then we could be more sure which of Arlin's findings really deserve our attention.

I know Arlin personally and respect his sincerity and research skills. I also know that a good deal of mastery learning theory, research and practice has been based on compressed micro-studies such as Arlin reports here. Indeed, my initial work on mastery learning in the late 60's has served as the genotype for most of these micro-studies. So, while the scholar in me leans strongly to the research reaction just stated, the leader in me opts for still a third reaction. This reaction pivots on the assumption that Arlin is essentially right; that current group-based approaches to mastery learning cannot handle the learning rate issue without holding back "faster" learners. But whereas Arlin and my colleagues in the individually-based wing of the mastery learning movement might abandon group-based mastery learning strategies for this reason, I do not. My third reaction to Arlin's study is that the resolution of the learning rate issue resides less in *how* we teach for mastery—group based or individually based—and more in *when*.

I am convinced on the basis of my fifteen years of experience with the evolution of mastery learning ideas and practices that the reason that group-based mastery advocates now face so many problems with individual difference in students learning rates stems directly from the fact that we have allowed these programs to be used almost exclusively as remedial programs. More and more these programs are being used at later or intermediate stages in students' learning careers and only when their collective learning problems are viewed as being acute and infectious and in need of a quick fix. By this time, not only have a host of small teaching errors multiplied and accumulated in time into large individual differences in student learning and learning rate, but they have multiplied and accumulated into differences that are difficult if not impossible to resolve. Sure, group-based techniques can be gerrymandered to respond to these differences, but eventually so much time, effort, and money must be spent on such gerrymandering that it becomes prohibitively costly and fundamental renovations are in order.

Accordingly, I believe it is time for a fundamental change of course in the design of group-based mastery learning programs. Rather than designing these programs to be solely remedial in nature, I propose that we also begin to design them to be more *preventative* in nature too. As I have written in a relatively recent "State of the Craft" article:

> Although from the outset mastery learning theorists have been concerned with the development of talent rather than its selection, we have tended to attack only part of the talent development issue. Specifically, we have formulated our theory in terms that tell the practitioner or researcher what to do only *after* misdevelopments in learning occur. Remediation of misdevelopments, however, is only one way to develop talent. Prevention of misdevelopments in talent in the first place is another way. It is time, I believe, that we add to our present remedial formulations of mastery learning theory some new preventative ones. These new formulations would tell the practitioner and researcher what to do *before* misdevelopments in learning occur.
>
> Note that I said we must add to our present theoretical formulations. I am not saying that our current formulations are passe. Clearly, schools throughout the world have many students, especially older ones, who have already failed to learn excellently, and we must find ways to *discontinue* their failure. However, schools throughout the world also have many students, especially younger ones, who have not yet failed to learn excellently. Mastery theorists must also find ways to *continue* these students' success. (Block, 1979, p. 117).

I view preventative group-based mastery learning strategies as treating all students' learning problems as if they were potentially chronic and degenerative. Such strategies would, therefore, get to students earlier in their careers and would stay with them throughout. They would have as their goal learning maintenance and promotion, much as preventative strategies in public health have as their goals health maintenance and promotion.

I am not yet sure of all the technical characteristics of preventative group-based mastery strategies. I am sure of some of their defining conceptual properties however. One is that the strategies teach students to care more for themselves in learning matters. *Self-care* seems to be a prerequisite for *self-responsibility* in learning and in students who *want* to master swiftly. Two is that the strategies teach students to treat themselves more in learning matters; to self-orient, self-plan, and self-manage their learning to a greater extent. *Self-treatment* seems to be a prerequisite for *self-responsibility* in learning and in students who *can* master swiftly. Third is that the strategies teach students to assess themselves more in learning matters; to judge how they are progressing as learners as well as to judge how their learning is progressing. *Self-assessment* seems to be a prerequisite for *self-respondability* in learning and in students who *do* master swiftly.

My hunch is that the preventative use of mastery learning ideas when coupled with our current remedial uses will cut the learning rate problem down to size. Past micro-studies have suggested, in fact, that differences between faster and slower learners might be cut from about 6 to 1 to about 1.25 to 1. Clearly even individual differences of 1.25 to 1 pose some managerial problems for the teacher. These differences should be so slight, however, that they can be reasonably accommodated within a group-based mastery learning framework.

These, then, are my suggested reactions to the Arlin research: Network members need do nothing, do some naturally occurring replications, or add to our current remedial formulations some new preventative formulations for group-based, classroom use. I encourage interested Network members to think especially hard about my second and third reactions. Some follow-through on my second reaction holds great promise of pushing Network members' data to the front pages of professional and scholarly forums that of late have been dominated by critics' data. Serious follow-through on Reaction Three might even get some of you on the cover of *Newsweek* or *Time!*

REFERENCES

Arlin, M. Teacher Responses to Student Time Differences in Mastery Learning, *American Journal of Education, 90* (1982), 334–352.

Arlin, M. Time Variability in Mastery Learning, *American Educational Research Journal, 20* (1983), in press.

Arlin, M. and Webster, J. Time Costs of Mastery Learning, *Journal of Educational Psychology,* (1983), in press.

Block, J. Mastery Learning in the Classroom: An Overview of Recent Research. In *Schools, Society, and Mastery Learning,* edited by J. Block. New York: Holt, Rinehart, and Winston, 1974.

Block, J. Mastery Learning—the Current State of the Craft, *Educational Leadership, 37* (1979). 114–117,

Block, J. and Anderson, L. *Mastery Learning and Classroom Instruction.* New York: Macmillan, 1975.

Block, J. and Burns, R. Mastery Learning. In *Review of Research in Education, 4,* edited by L. Shulman. Itasca, Illinois: Peacock, 1976.

Bloom, B. *Human Characteristics and School Learning.* New York: McGraw-Hill, 1976.

Carroll, J. A Model of School Learning. *Teachers College Record, 64* (1963), 723–733.

Cronbach, L. Book Review of Block, J. (ed.) *Mastery Learning: Theory and Practice, International Review of Education, 18* (1972), 250–252.

Mueller, D. Mastery Learning: Partly Boon, Partly Boondoggle. *Teachers College Record, 78* (1976), 41–52.

Resnick, L. Assuming That Everyone Can Learn Everything. Will Some Learn Less?, *School Review, 85* (1977), 445–452.

Alternative Strategies
for Modifying Social
and Emotional Behavior

The readings presented here illustrate three different approaches to changing the social and emotional behavior of students. They have been derived from three different models of the learning process. These models, and the psychologists with whom they are associated, are: (1) operant conditioning—B. F. Skinner; (2) modeling or social theory—Albert Bandura; (3) cognitive behavior modification—Donald Meichenbaum, building on the work of the Soviet psychologists, Luria and Vygotsky. Our concern here is with the application of these three approaches to social and emotional learning, although their use to promote traditional academic learning is also well established.

Becker's operant conditioning (Skinnerian) strategy has been derived from ways in which behavior is influenced by its consequences. He focuses attention on the selection and modification of learner behavior by control of the "contingencies of reinforcement." *Reinforcement* refers to the after-effects or consequences of behavior which brings pleasure or a relief from pain, and *contingencies* refers to what is reinforced when reinforcement occurs, and what the reinforcement is.

Becker describes the experimental use of an operant conditioning strategy in elementary classrooms. Similar operant techniques have been effective with a broad age range from preschool to adolescence, and with a variety of clinical populations, including the mentally retarded, emotionally disturbed, hearing-impaired, and learning disabled (See Gresham, 1981, 1985 for reviews).

Becker reports that teachers trained in this strategy have used commonly available reinforcers to increase the frequency of appropriate classroom behaviors, such as studying quietly or paying attention. These reinforcers are also successful in decreasing disruptive behaviors, such as whistling, shouting, and running.

Various terms have been used to describe learning by observation. Familiar examples include *imitation, copying,* and *identification.* Bandura's term *modeling* is intended to encompass them all. Our excerpt from his book, *Psychological Modeling: Conflicting Theories,* makes it clear that Bandura believes this method of learning to be more common and more practical than conditioning.

In other writing, Bandura (1969) theorizes that a learner does not have to respond overtly. An observed response is learned when it is represented in memory by images or words. Later, if the circumstances are right, the learner behaves in a manner similar to the model observed. Of course, we must witness behavior to know that it has been learned.

Modeling can be used to encourage new patterns of student behavior or to inhibit unwanted patterns of behavior. Two questions of central importance in teaching strategies based on modeling theory are: (1) What are the characteristics of effective models? and (2) What factors in the observed situation affect a model's influence? Bandura gives major attention to both these questions in our selection from his book.

An interesting, currently popular extension of the use of models is self-modeling (Dowrick, 1983). Dowrick defines self-modeling as the behavior change that results from observing oneself on videotapes that show only desired behaviors. The inspiration for this use of modeling came from findings that show observational learning is enhanced by models of similar age, sex, appearance, etc. What other model could be more similar to one than one's self? The videotapes to be observed are planned and edited to insure that the self one sees is behaving in the desired way. The result is not only a demonstration of how to behave, it is convincing evidence that the learner has done it once and can do it again.

After years of relative neglect by behavioral psychologists, the learner's mental or thought processes are again receiving major attention. There is a growing belief among psychologists that knowledge of the learner's cognitive or thought processes will be more productive and useful than merely knowing how instruction affects behavior, without regard to the learner's capacity for information-processing and self-direction. Resnick's article on another issue in this book suggests how the cognitive approach can improve instruction in science and mathematics; and a special issue of the *Journal of Abnormal Child Psychology* (September, 1985) is devoted to reviews of the use of cognitive behavioral modification (CBM) to treat a variety of adjustment problems in children and adults. Although CBM is most often used with individuals, there is some evidence that it can be used successfully with groups. Harris and Brown (1982) used a CBM procedure that combined teacher demonstrations, self-instructions, and relaxation tapes with small groups of shy children to reduce their fear of social and public speaking situations.

Meichenbaum and Burland's report tells us how one CBM approach is used to teach problem children to control their own behavior. Although the procedure emphasizes thought processes, it includes elements of modeling and operant strategies as well. First, learners are taught to control their behavior by "thinking aloud." Modeling is an important part of the procedure. Principles of operant conditioning are then used to modify this verbal behavior until the self-directions are no longer audible, but silent—not speech, but thought. CBM aims to bring about cognitive changes such as understanding and self-control, that will in turn lead to desirable social and academic behavior. According to these psychologists, these are outcomes to be more highly prized than behavior change alone.

Thought Questions

Interpret the statement, "Operant conditioning influences performance, but not learning." What is the difference? What evidence on this point can you find in the experiment reported by Becker?

After reading Bandura, outline the conditions under which he would expect violence on television to influence the behavior of viewers. Is this possibility a cause for social concern? Why or why not?

Can modeling be used as reinforcement? Can it be used as a means of prompting behavior to be reinforced? Can operant conditioning be used to prompt behavior that is "model" or speech that influences thought? Give examples of these and other possible interactions between different types of learning or strategies of instruction.

Conditioning has been criticized as a denial of the value of reasoning with children about their behavior, and as a totalitarian approach to manipulating them. What basis is there for such criticism? Do you believe these criticisms are justified? Why or why not?

Meichenbaum and Burland's article emphasizes studies and programs for children with behavior or learning problems. Would you expect their approach to be equally useful with more typical children and youth? What modifications might be necessary or desirable?

Videotapes of the self as a model have often been used by psychologists working with individual students, clients, or patients. What possibilities do you see for the use of this technique with classroom groups? How might the teacher go about arranging for a group to demonstrate desirable social behaviors, such as cooperation, fair play, and group problem solving, so that "model" behaviors might be videotaped?

Compare the role and responsibility of the learner in the approaches described in these three readings. Is there a difference in the respect shown the learner as a person? What are the social implications of the differences in approach?

What should the teacher do about diverse theoretical emphases or models for behavior modification? Should priority be given to one strategy regularly, or as difficulties arise in the classroom? Describe a possible synthesis of strategies that assigns a definite role to each.

Technical Note

Becker's report summarizes the results that were achieved by the application of operant conditioning graphically. Refer to Figure 3 in his article for an example.

The percentage of student behavior, which is of the type being counted, study behavior, is shown by the distance of the points above the bottom line of the graph. The percentage corresponding to any point is read from the vertical scale to the left. The points were plotted during several different periods of observation in which students were treated differently.

These several time periods are indicated by the names along the bottom of the graph. The first such period is labeled "baseline," and it lasts for about seven sessions. The points plotted during this period show the percentage of student responses of the type being counted under typical classroom conditions. No experimental conditions have yet been introduced.

As we move to the right from the baseline period, the next period is one in which students were reinforced for study behavior by operant conditioning principles. The percentages plotted during the "reinforcement" period show what happened to the student behavior. A comparison of these percentages with those recorded during the baseline period show that more desirable behaviors occurred during the reinforcement period. This is shown by the plotted points being higher in this period than they were initially. For the third period, when reinforcement was discontinued, the plotted points are lower than in the reinforcement period, but still higher than during the baseline period, indicating that some effect of reinforcement persisted after it was discontinued. The other figures in the Becker article are similar to Figure 3, except that several have data for more than one student plotted on the same graph to enable the teacher to judge how the effects of the conditions may vary for different students.

Applications of Behavior Principles in Typical Classrooms

Wesley C. Becker

Use of Commonly Available Consequences

The behavioral technologist entering the typical classroom can be at once both overwhelmed by the range and variety of potential reinforcers available to teachers and dismayed by the infrequency with which potential reinforcers are used. In the author's experience with all kinds of classroom behavior problems, it seems that 80 to 90 percent of such problems can be handled by little more than a change in the teacher's verbal behavior, e.g., when she says what to whom. There are three classes of consequences typically available to teachers (without introducing food, prizes, or token systems) which will be investigated in detail in this section. Our objective is to make clear to the reader the research basis underlying the conclusions to be drawn.

The research strategies used in the majority of studies covered by this report share the following three features: First, individuals are studied under specified experimental conditions, with the same individuals going through the various phases of the experiment. This approach leads more directly to knowledge of procedures which will work with individual children. Second, the experimental procedure is often withdrawn after being introduced to show its effect more clearly. For example, when teacher praises *more*, task behavior *increases;* when teacher praises *less,* task behavior *decreases.* Third, the behaviors to be changed are defined in terms of observables—events which the teacher can see and do something about. Reliability of observations is established before the experiment starts by checking the agreement between several observers. A review of field experimental research procedures may be found in Bijou, Peterson, and Ault (1968).

Elementary Classroom Studies

Studies by Becker and by Hall and their students have been conducted to assess the possibility of extending the findings on preschool children to the elementary school setting.

From W. C. Becker, "Applications of Behavior Principles in Typical Classrooms." In *Behavior Modification in Education,* C. A. Thoreson, ed. Chicago: Seventy-second Yearbook of the National Society for the Study of Education, Part 1, 1973, pp. 79–80, 83–89. Reproduced by permission of the publisher and author.

***Combined effects of rules, ignoring, and
praise.*** Becker, Madsen, Arnold, and Thomas
chose two problem children from each of five
elementary school classes. Categories of child
behaviors were defined which disrupted learning or violated the teacher's rules. For example, gross motor behavior was defined as getting out of seat, standing, running, skipping,
jumping, and the like. Other disruptive behaviors included making noise with objects,
aggression, orienting away from work, blurting
out, talking to peers, and other off-task behavior. Observers were trained to rate reliably the
frequency of occurrence of these behaviors.
Deviant behavior was defined as any twenty-
second interval in which one or more disruptive behaviors occurred. The children were
rated for three twenty-minute sessions each
week. Observations of teacher behaviors were

made to determine if the experimental program was being carried out effectively.

After a five-week base line, the teachers
began the experimental program which had
three components. The teacher's *rules* for
classroom behavior were made explicit and repeated frequently. Teachers were also to *show
approval* for appropriate behaviors (conducive
to learning) and to *ignore* disruptive behaviors.
If a child was hurting someone, the teacher
could intervene as she saw fit. This rarely happened. The teachers were instructed to give
praise for achievement, prosocial behavior,
and following the rules of the group. They were
to praise students for such behaviors as concentrating on individual work, raising hand
when appropriate, responding to questions,
paying attention to directions, following directions, sitting at desk, studying, and sitting qui-

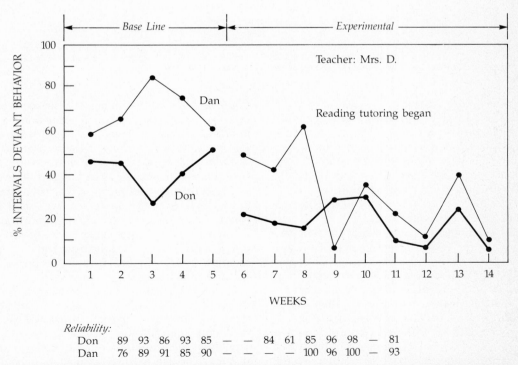

Reliability:

Don	89	93	86	93	85	—	—	84	61	85	96	98	—	81
Dan	76	89	91	85	90	—	—	—	—	100	96	100	—	93

Figure 1. Percentages of deviant behavior for two children in Class D. (Becker, W. C.; Madsen, C. H., Jr.; Arnold,
C. R.; and Thomas, D. R. "The contingent use of teacher praise and attention in reducing classroom behavior problems." *Journal of Special Education* 1, no. 3 (1967): 302.)

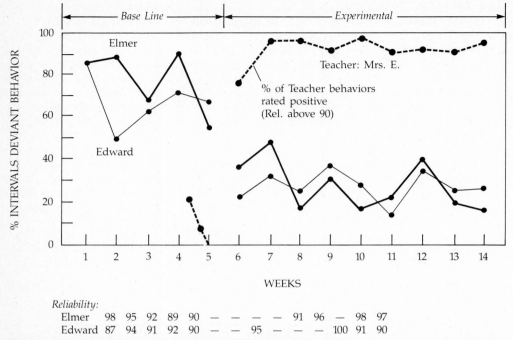

Reliability:

Elmer	98	95	92	89	90	—	—	—	—	91	96	—	98	97
Edward	87	94	91	92	90	—	—	95	—	—	—	100	91	90

Figure 2.   Percentages of deviant behavior for two children in Class E, and change in Teacher E's behavior. (Becker, W. C.; Madsen, C. H. Jr.; Arnold, C. R.; and Thomas, D. R. "The contingent use of teacher praise and attention in reducing classroom behavior problems." *Journal of Special Education* **1, no. 3 (1967): 305.)**

etly. They were instructed to use variety and expression in their comments and to smile when delivering praise. Teachers were to walk around the room during study time and give a pat on the back to children doing good job. The teachers were given daily feedback regarding their effectiveness in showing approval contingent on appropriate behavior and in ignoring inappropriate behavior.

The percentage of intervals of deviant behavior for the ten children dropped from 6.1 percent of the time during base line to 29.2 percent of the time during the experimental program when approval, ignoring deviant behavior, and rules were introduced. Detailed results for only two of the five classes are presented here. The data for Don and Dan are found in Figure 1. Don is a boy of average IQ who earlier as a fourth-grader had been recommended for placement as an educable retarded. He had a

high frequency of moving about the room and talking during study time. He responded well to approval and his level of deviant behavior fell from 40 percent to 20 percent. Dan, who was more than two years behind in reading, responded well to teacher attention only after tutoring in reading was begun. It was not enough to reinforce him for staying in his seat if he could get no measure of success from his academic work. Dan was considered by the school psychologist to be a severely disturbed boy who required psychotherapy if he was going to be able to function in school.

Teacher E (Figure 2) had relied mainly on shouting to maintain order in an "unruly" class. The children engaged in much whistling, running about the room, yelling at other children, loud incessant talk, hitting, pushing, and shoving. The average level of deviant behavior for the two boys fell from about 70 percent to

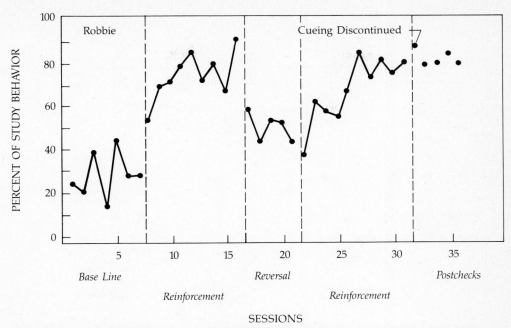

Figure 3.   A record of study behavior for Robbie. Postcheck observations were made during the fourth, sixth, seventh, twelfth, and fourteenth weeks after the completion of Reinforcement conditions. (Hall, R. V.; Lund, D.; and Jackson, D. "Effects of teacher attention on study behavior." *Journal of Applied Behavior Analysis* 1 (1968).)

about 25 percent, a drastic reduction. The teacher also reported many changes in other members of her class.

Hall, Lund, and Jackson reported a series of experiments further demonstrating the effects of teacher social reinforcement for study behavior and withdrawal of attention (ignoring) for disruptive behaviors. For example, Robbie (see Figure 3) was a very disruptive boy who spent much of his time snapping rubber bands, talking and laughing with peers, and playing with toys from his pocket. He spent less than 25 percent of work time actually working. During the base-line period, 55 percent of the attention Robbie received followed nonstudy behavior. When off-task behavior was ignored and good work behavior praised, Robbie improved dramatically. In this classroom the teacher was signaled by the experimenter when to praise or otherwise give attention to study behavior. This was done to help her learn

to manage her own behavior more effectively. The reversal condition demonstrated the critical importance of the teacher's behavior in maintaining Robbie's on-task behavior. Reinstatement of the reinforcement condition once again established good study behavior. Follow-up checks made during the fourteen weeks following the experimental conditions showed that the teacher was able to maintain good study behavior without continued assistance. Similar positive findings were reported with other children and with other teachers.

In as subsequent report, Hall et al. showed again (with a variety of problem children) the continuing importance of teacher attention in changing problem behaviors. Furthermore, he showed that teachers can reliably take data themselves on the children they are helping. By using a second person to check the reliability of observations, Hall found the percent of agreements ranging from 84 to 100 percent.

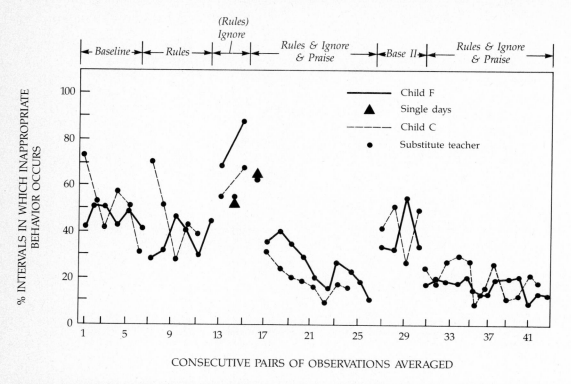

Figure 4.   Inappropriate behavior of two problem children in Classroom A as a function of experimental conditions. (Madsen, C. H., Jr.; Becker, W. C.; and Thomas, D. R. "Rules, praise, and ignoring: Elements of elementary classroom control." *Journal of Applied Behavior Analysis* 1 (1968).)

The implication is that teachers can be trained to monitor their own plans for helping children with behavior problems. Other studies on the training of teachers are also to be noted.

Separate effects of rules, ignoring disruptive behavior, and praise. Madsen, Becker and Thomas attempted to determine the relative effectiveness of the three components of the experimental program used in their first study. After base line, each of the three components of the experimental program (rules, ignoring, and praise) were introduced separately. The general experimental design can be discerned from Figure 4.

The *rules* phase of the experiment consisted of the teacher forming four or five rules (or in-

structions) for classroom behavior and repeating them four to six times a day, e.g., "Sit quietly while working," "Walk," "Raise hand," and so forth.

The *ignore* phase of the experiment consisted of the teacher attempting not to respond to disruptive behaviors with scolding or reprimands. She was to act as if such behavior had not happened. This part of the program was very difficult for the teacher to follow.

Finally, *praise* was added to rules and ignoring inappropriate behavior. Appropriate behaviors incompatible with deviant inappropriate behaviors were to be given social approval. The teacher was to show approval of as many good behaviors as possible during the first few days. A prime rule was "Catch the children being good." Moreover, she was to give approval to improvements in behavior in order to shape the child's behavior. For example, a problem child who frequently wandered around the room would be given approval when found in his seat even if he was not working on a task. As the time spent in his seat increased, the teacher would begin to praise him only when he was both seated and working on a task. In each case, the teacher would explicitly state the behaviors she approved, e.g., "Tommy is sitting nicely and working hard on his assignment."

The results indicate that the introduction of rules alone was not effective in modifying behavior (Figure 4). The procedure of ignoring inappropriate behavior was difficult for the teacher to maintain. She would ignore for a while and then scold as the children got out of hand. When praise for appropriate behavior was added in conjunction with the ignoring of inappropriate behavior, the latter behavior fell from about a 70 percent level (during base line) to 30 percent. Inappropriate behavior returned to the base-line level when the teacher approximated her behavior of the base-line period. Finally, when the experimental procedures were reinstated, the level of inappropriate behavior again fell. This correspondence between the experimental changes in teacher's behavior and the level of inappropriate child behavior points to the marked influence a teacher can have over classroom behavior.

These findings indicate that simply instructing children what to do is not enough. Reinforcement for following instructions is also necessary. A study by Schutte and Hopkins with five kindergarten children helps to show more clearly the contribution of instructions to classroom management. A list of ten instructions related to classroom routines was formed, such as "Pick up the toys," "Sit down," "Write your name on the paper," "Get out your mat," "Be quiet." These instructions were repeated daily for twenty days. The data recorded were the number of instructions followed each day. When instructions only were given (without praise for following the instructions), 60 percent of the instructions were followed by the five children. When praise was added, following instructions increased to 78 percent. A return to the instructions without praise led to a drop in following instructions to 69 percent and the addition of praise led to an increase to 84 percent.

These findings are in keeping with laboratory-based findings on the discriminative control of behavior. Signals or instructions as discriminative stimuli become important because certain behavior has been followed by reinforcers in their presence, but not in their absence. Such signals cannot stand alone and remain effective. They must at least periodically be supported by reinforcing consequences.

READING 21

Analysis of Modeling Processes

Albert Bandura

Among the numerous topics that have attracted the interest of psychologists over the years, the phenomenon of learning has occupied a central position. Most of the research in this area examines the process of learning as a consequence of direct experience: This volume is principally concerned with learning by example.

It is evident from informal observation that human behavior is transmitted, whether deliberately or inadvertently, largely through exposure to social models. Indeed, as Reichard (1938) noted some years ago, in many languages "the word for 'teach' is the same as the word for 'show'." It is difficult to imagine a culture in which language, mores, vocational activities, familial customs, and educational, religious, and political practices, are gradually shaped in each new member by direct consequences of their trial-and-error performances without benefit of models who display the cultural patterns in their behavior.

Although much social learning is fostered through observation of real-life models, advances in communication have increased reliance upon symbolic models. In many instances people pattern their behavior after models presented in verbal or pictorial form. Without the guidance of handbooks that describe in detail how to behave in particular situations, members of technologically advanced societies would spend much of their time groping for effective ways of handling situations that arise repeatedly. Pictorially presented models, provided in television and other filmed displays, also serve as influential sources of social behavior.

Considering the prevailing influence of example in the development and regulation of human behavior, it is surprising that traditional accounts of learning contain little or no mention of modeling processes. If the peripatetic Martian were to scrutinize earth man's authoritative texts on learning, he would be left with the belief that there are two basic modes of learning: People are either conditioned through reward and punishment to adopt the desired patterns, or emotional responsiveness

From A. Bandura, ed., *Psychological Modeling, Conflicting Theories*. Reprinted by permission of the publishers, Lieber-Atherton and the author. Copyright © 1971 Aldine-Atherton. All rights reserved. The preparation of this paper and research by the author which is reported here was facilitated by grants M-5162 and 1F03MH42658 from the National Institute of Mental Health, United States Public Health Service. The author also gratefully acknowledges the generous assistance of the staff of the Center for Advanced Study in the Behavioral Sciences.

is established by close association of neutral and evocative stimuli. If these methods alone were applied on the distant planet, the life span of Martians would not only be drastically shortened, but their brief period of survival would be expended in prolonged and laborious efforts to master simple skills.

The marked discrepancy between textbooks and social reality is largely attributable to the fact that certain critical conditions present in natural situations are rarely, if ever, reproduced in laboratory studies of learning. In laboratory investigations experimenters arrange comparatively benign environments in which errors do not create fatal consequences for the organism. By contrast, natural environments are loaded with potentially lethal consequences for those unfortunate enough to perform hazardous errors. For this reason it would be exceedingly injudicious to rely on differential reinforcement of trial-and-error performances in teaching children to swim, adolescents to drive automobiles, medical students to conduct surgical operations, or adults to develop complex occupational and social competencies. Had experimental situations been made more realistic so that animals toiling in Skinner boxes and various mazes were drowned, electrocuted, dismembered, or extensively bruised for the errors that invariably occur during early phases of unguided learning, the limitations of instrumental conditioning would have been forcefully revealed.

There are several reasons why modeling influences are heavily favored in promoting everyday learning. Under circumstances in which mistakes are costly or dangerous, skillful performances can be established without needless errors by providing competent models who demonstrate the required activities. Some complex behaviors can be produced solely through the influence of models. If children had no opportunity to hear speech it would be virtually impossible to teach them the linguistic skills that constitute a language. It is doubtful whether one could ever shape individual words by selective reinforcement of random vocalizations, let alone grammatical utterances. Where desired forms of behavior can be

conveyed only by social cues, modeling is an indispensable aspect of learning. Even in instances where it is possible to establish new response patterns through other means, the process of acquisition can be considerably shortened by providing appropriate models (Bandura and McDonald, 1963; John, Chesler, Bartlett, and Victor, 1968; Luchins and Luchins, 1966).

In social learning theory (Bandura, 1969a) the phenomena ordinarily subsumed under the labels imitation and identification are designated as *modeling*. The latter term was adopted because modeling influences have much broader psychological effect than the simple response mimicry implied by the term imitation, and the distinguishing properties of identification are too diffuse, arbitrary, and empirically questionable either to clarify issues or to aid scientific inquiry. Research conducted within this frame-work has shown that modeling influences can produce three separable types of effects depending on the different processes involved. First, observers can acquire new patterns of behavior by watching the performances of others. This *observational learning effect* is demonstrated most clearly when models exhibit novel responses which observers have not yet learned to make and which they later reproduce in substantially identical form.

A second major function of modeling influences is to strengthen or to weaken inhibition of previously learned responses. The effects that modeled activities have on behavioral restraints are largely determined by observation of rewarding and punishing consequences accompanying the actions. *Inhibitory effects* are indicated when observers show either decrements in the modeled class of behavior or a general reduction of responsiveness as a result of seeing the model's behavior produce punishing consequences. Observed punishment has been shown to reduce exploratory behavior (Crooks, 1967), aggression (Bandura, 1965b; Wheeler, 1966), and transgressive behavior (Walters and Parke, 1964; Walters, Parke, and Cane, 1965). Comparable reductions in performance are obtained in observers when models respond self-punitively to their own behavior (Bandura, 1971a; Benton, 1967).

Disinhibitory effects are evident when observers increase performance of formerly inhibited behavior after observing models engage in threatening or prohibited activities without adverse consequences. This type of change is most strikingly illustrated in the treatment of phobic conditions through modeling procedures (Bandura, 1971b). People who strongly inhibit even attenuated approach responses toward objects they fear are able to interact closely with them after observing bold performers engaging in threatening activities without experiencing any untoward consequences.

The behavior of others can also serve as cues in facilitating performance of existing responses in the same general class. People applaud when others clap; they look up when they see others gazing skyward; they adopt fads that others display; and in countless other situations their behavior is prompted and channeled by the actions of others. *Response facilitation effects* are distinguished from observational learning and disinhibition because no new responses are acquired, and disinhibitory processes are not involved because the behavior in question is socially sanctioned and hence is unencumbered by restraints.

Correlates of Modeling

In discussions of imitation the question often arises as to the types of people who are most responsive to modeling influences, and the kinds of models most likely to evoke imitative behavior from others. A great deal of research has been published on this topic (Bandura and Walters, 1963; Campbell, 1961; Flanders, 1968), but the generality of the findings is open to question because of the limited conditions under which observer and model correlates of imitative behavior have been measured.

It is often reported that persons who lack self-esteem, feel incompetent, are highly dependent, of low intelligence, or who have been frequently rewarded for imitative responses, are especially prone to adopt the behavior of successful models. These prosaic correlates are based mainly on results from ambiguous experimental situations in which unfamiliar models perform inconsequential responses that have little or no functional value for subjects. In such situations the main rewards for brighter and bolder subjects are derived from outwitting the experimenter by disregarding the modeling influences.

Unfortunately, there is a paucity of research studying the degree to which people differing in intelligence, perceptiveness, and confidence emulate idealized models and those whose behavior has high utilitarian value. It is exceedingly unlikely that dull, dependent, and self-devaluative students would profit more from observing skillful performances by ski instructors, brain surgeons, airline pilots, or ingenious researchers than understudies who are bright, attentive and self-assured. When modeling influences are explicitly employed to teach people how to communicate effectively, how to conduct themselves in given interpersonal situations, and how to perform occupational activities competently, the more venturesome and talented are apt to derive the greater benefits from observation of exemplary models.

The traditional model correlates of imitation should also be accepted with reservation for similar reasons. It has been abundantly documented in social-psychological research (Bandura, 1969b; Blake, 1958; Campbell, 1961) that models who are high in prestige, power, intelligence, and competence are emulated to a considerably greater degree than models of subordinate standing. The influence of model status on matching behavior is generally explained in terms of differential reinforcement and generalization processes (Miller and Dollard, 1941). According to this interpretation, the behavior of high status models is more likely to be successful in achieving desired outcomes, and hence have greater value for observers, than the behavior of models who possess relatively low vocational, intellectual and social competencies. As a result of experiencing different outcomes for imitating models who possess diverse attributes, the identifying characteristics and status-confering symbols assume informative value in signifying the probable consequences associated with behavior exemplified by different models. The effect of a model's prestige tends to generalize from one area of behavior to another and even to unfamiliar models who share characteristics with known reward-producers.

Model characteristics exert the greatest influence on imitation under conditions in which individuals can observe the model's behavior but not its consequences. When the value of modeled behavior is not revealed, observers must rely on such cues as clothing, linguistic style, general appearance, age, sex, likeableness, and various competence and status symbols as the basis for judging the probable efficacy of the modeled modes of response. Since the informative value of these cues is mainly derived from their correlation with reinforcement in the observer's past experience, they may not always be reliable predictors of how

useful the behavior of new models, who happen to resemble former persons in some way, might be.

Ordinarily, modeled performances produce evident outcomes both for the model and the imitator. Response consequences generally outweigh model characteristics in promoting imitative behavior. One would not expect matching behavior that is primarily sustained by anticipatory consequences arising from model attributes to survive for long in the face of actual adverse outcomes. A prestigious or attractive model may induce a person to try a given course of action, but if the behavior should prove unsatisfactory, it will be discarded and the model's future influence diminished. For these reasons, studies conducted under conditions in which response consequences are not displayed may exaggerate the role played by model characteristics in the long-term control of imitative behavior.

REFERENCES

Bandura, A. "Behavioral Modifications Through Modeling Procedures." In L. Krasner and L. P. Ullmann (eds.), *Research in Behavior Modification.* New York: Holt, Rinehart, and Winston, 1956b, pp. 310–340.

Bandura, A. *Principles of Behavior Modification.* New York: Holt, Rinehart, and Winston, 1969a.

Bandura, A. "Social-learning Theory of Identificatory Processes." In D. A. Goslin (ed.), *Handbook of Socialization Theory and Research.* Chicago: Rand McNally, 1969b, pp. 213–262.

Bandura, A. "Vicarious and Self-reinforcement Processes." In R. Glaser (ed.), *The Nature of Reinforcement.* Columbus: Merrill, 1971a.

Bandura, A. "Psychotherapy Based upon Modeling Principles." In A. E. Bergin and S. L. Garfield (eds.), *Handbook of Psychotherapy and Behavior Change.* New York: Wiley, 1971b, pp. 653–708.

Bandura, A., and McDonald, F. J. "The Influence of Social Reinforcement and the Behavior of Models in Shaping Children's Moral Judgments." *Journal of Abnormal and Social Psychology,* 1963, 67: 274–281.

Bandura, A., and Walters, R. H. *Social Learning and Personality Development.* New York: Holt, Rinehart, and Winston, 1963.

Benton, A. A. "Effect of the Timing of Negative Response Consequences on the Observational Learning of Resistance to Temptation in Children." *Dissertation Abstracts,* 1967, 27: 2153–2154.

Blake, R. R. "The Other Person in the Situation." In R. Tagiuri and L. Petrullo (eds.), *Person Perception and Interpersonal Behavior.* Stanford, Calif.: Stanford University Press, 1958, pp. 229–242.

Campbell, D. T. "Conformity in Psychology's Theories of Acquired Behavioral Dispositions." In I. A. Berg and B. M. Bass (eds.), *Conformity and Deviation.* New York: Harper, 1961, pp. 101–142.

Crooks, J. L. "Observational Learning of Fear in Monkeys." Unpublished manuscript, University of Pennsylvania, 1967.

Flanders, J. P. "A Review of Research on Imitative Behavior." *Psychological Bulletin,* 1968, 69: 316–337.

John, E. R.; Chesler, P.; Bartlett, F.; and Victor, I. "Observation Learning in Cats." *Science,* 1968, 159: 1489–1491.

Luchins, A. S., and Luchins, E. H. "Learning a Complex Ritualized Social Role." *Psychological Record,* 1966, 16: 177–187.

Miller, N. E., and Dollard, J. *Social Learning and Imitation.* New Haven: Yale University Press, 1941.

Reichard, G. A. "Social Life." In F. Boas (ed.), *General Anthropology.* Boston: Heath, 1938, pp. 409–486.

Walters, R. H., and Parke, R. D. "Influence of Response Consequences to a Social Model on Resistance to Deviation." *Journal of Experimental Child Psychology,* 1964, 1:269–280.

Walters, R. H.; Parke, R. D.; and Cane, V. A. "Timing of Punishment and the Observation of Consequences to Others as Determinants of Response Inhibition." *Journal of Experimental Child Psychology,* 1965, 2: 10–30.

Wheeler, L. "Toward a Theory of Behavioral Contagion." *Psychological Review* 73 (1966): 179–192.

READING 22

Cognitive Behavior Modification with Children

Donald Meichenbaum and Susan Burland

Abstract

This paper reviews the recent shift in behavior therapy towards the use of more cognitively oriented interventions in the treatment of behavior disorders in school children. The cognitive behavioral paradigm has now been used successfully to teach self-control skills to a wide variety of disruptive children. Whereas past efforts have been directed towards social behaviors, recent applications of cognitive behavior modification have dealt with traditional academic concerns.

Cognitive behavior modification (CBM) appears to be a contradiction in terms. A brief historical perspective will prove helpful in understanding both the emergence of this approach and its likely future directions.

Whereas the CBM work with adults had its impetus in the alteration of "standard" behavior therapy procedures in order to make them more cognitive in orientation, the CBM work with children had a somewhat different origin. One impetus for the CBM procedure with children was the theoretical work of the Soviet psy-

chologists Luria (1961) and Vygotsky (1962). On the basis of his work with children, Luria (1959) proposed three stages by which the initiation and inhibition of voluntary motor behaviors come under verbal control. During the first stage, the speech of others, usually adults, controls and directs a child's behavior. The second stage is characterized by the child's overt speech becoming an effective mediator or regulator of his behavior. Finally, the child's covert or inner speech comes to assume a self-governing role. From this hypothetical developmental sequence, a treatment paradigm was developed and successfully used to train impulsive children to talk to themselves as a means of developing self-control (Meichenbaum and Goodman, 1971).

A General CBM Training Strategy

The training regimen was designed to teach the child to engage in mediating responses that exemplify a general strategy for controlling behavior under various circumstances. The following procedural steps were included:

1. An adult model performed a task while talking to himself out loud (cognitive modeling);
2. The child performed the same task under

From *School Psychology Digest* 8 (1979): 426–433. Reprinted with permission.

the direction of the model's instructions (overt, external guidance);

3. The child performed the task while instructing himself aloud (overt self-guidance);

4. The child whispered the instructions to himself as he went through the task (faded, overt self-guidance); and finally

5. The child performed the task while guiding his performance via inaudible or private speech or nonverbal self-direction (covert self-instruction).

Over a number of training sessions the package of self-statements modeled by the experimenter and rehearsed by the child (initially aloud and then covertly) was enlarged by means of response chaining and successive approximation procedures. For example, in a task that required the copying of line patterns, the examiner performed the task while cognitively modeling as follows:

> Okay, what is it I have to do? You want me to copy the picture with the different lines. I have to go slowly and carefully. Okay, draw the line down, down, good; and then to the right, that's it; now down some more and to the left. Good, I'm doing fine so far. Remember, go slowly. Now back up again. Just erase the line carefully . . . Good. Even if I make an error I can go on slowly and carefully. I have to go down now. Finished. I did it! (Meichenbaum and Goodman, 1971, p. 117)

In this thinking-out-loud phase, the model displayed several performance-relevant skills: (1) problem definition ("What is it I have to do?"); (2) focusing attention and response guidance ("Carefully . . . Draw the line down"); (3) self-reinforcement ("Good, I'm doing fine"); and (4) self-evaluative coping skills and error correcting options ("That's okay . . . Even if I make an error I can go on slowly").

A variety of tasks was employed to train the child to use self-instructions to control his nonverbal behavior. The tasks varied from simple sensorimotor abilities to more complex problem-solving abilities. The sensorimotor tasks, (such as copying line patterns and coloring figures within boundaries) provided first the model, then the child, with the opportunity to produce a narrative description of the behavior, both preceding and accompanying performance. Over the course of a training session the child's overt self-statements about a particular task were faded to the covert level. The difficulty of the training tasks was increased over the training sessions, using more cognitively demanding activities. Hence, there was a progression from tasks such as reproducing designs and following sequential instructions, taken from the Stanford-Binet intelligence test, to completing such pictorial series as those in the Primary Mental Abilities test, to solving conceptual tasks such as Raven's Matrices. The experimenter modeled appropriate self-verbalizations for each of these tasks and then had the child follow the fading procedure.

In the initial Meichenbaum and Goodman (1971) study, the self-instructional training procedure, relative to placebo and assessment control groups, resulted in significantly improved performance on Porteus Mazes, performance IQ on the WISC, and increased cognitive reflectivity on the Matching Familiar Figures Test (MFF). The improved performance was evident in a one-month follow up. Moreover, it was observed that 60 percent of the self-instructionally trained impulsive children were talking to themselves spontaneously in the posttest and follow-up sessions.

The cognitive behavioral paradigm has now been used successfully to establish inner speech control over the disruptive behavior hyperactive children (Douglas, Parry, Marton, and Garson, 1976), aggressive children (Camp, Blom, Hebert, and Van Doorninck, 1977), disruptive preschoolers (Bornstein and Quevillon, 1976), cheating behavior of kindergarten and first graders (Monahan and O'Leary, 1971), Porteus maze performance of hyperactive boys (Palkes, Stewart, and Freedman, 1972; Palkes, Stewart, and Kahana, 1968), and the conceptual tempo of emotionally-disturbed boys (Finch, Wilkinson, Nelson, and Montgomery, 1975), as well as that of normal children (Bender, 1976; Meichenbaum and Goodman, 1971).

The Douglas et al. study nicely illustrates the general treatment approach. The hyperactive children were initially exposed to a model who verbalized the following cognitive strategies, which the child could in turn rehearse, initially aloud and then covertly. These strategies included stopping to define a problem and the various steps within it, considering and evaluating several possible solutions before acting on any one, checking one's work throughout and calmly correcting any errors, sticking with a problem until everything possible has been tried to solve it correctly, and giving oneself a pat on the back for work well done. Verbalizations modeled by the trainer to illustrate these strategies included:

> "I must stop and think before I begin." "What plans can I try?" "How would it work out if I did that?" "What shall I try next?" "Have I got it right so far?" "See, I made a mistake there—I'll just erase it." "Now let's see, have I tried everything I can think of" "I've done a pretty good job!" (Douglas et al., 1976, p. 408)

The cognitive behavioral training was applied across tasks in order to ensure that the children did *not* just develop task-specific response sets, but instead developed generalizable cognitive representations. This latter point needs to be underscored. The process by which socialized (or external) speech develops into egocentric (or internal) speech and then into inner speech requires much consideration. As Vygotsky (1962) noted in *Thought and Language,* this process of internalization and abbreviation should *not* be viewed merely as a process of faded speech; instead the transformation from interpersonal speech to thought represents qualitative differences in structure. How interpersonal instructions modeled by a therapist, teacher, or parent change into the child's own private speech and thought is a major theoretical and practical question. The answer to this question will have major implications for the potential of cognitive behavioral training with children (see Meichenbaum, 1977, and Toulmin, 1978, for a discussion of these issues).

Elsewhere (Meichenbaum, 1977), the senior author has described a host of clinical suggestions for conducting CBM self-instructional training with children. These included (1) using the child's own medium of play to initiate and model self-talk; (2) using tasks that have a high "pull" for the use of sequential cognitive strategies; (3) using peer teaching by having children cognitively model while performing for another child; (4) moving through the program at the child's own rate, and building up the package of self-statements to include self-talk of a problem-solving variety as well as coping and self-reinforcing elements; (5) guarding against the child's use of self-statements in a mechanical noninvolved fashion; (6) including a therapist who is animated and responsive to the child; (7) learning to use the self-instructional training with low intensity responses; (8) supplementing the training with imagery practice such as the "turtle technique" (Schneider and Robin, 1976); (9) supplementing the self-instructional training with correspondence training between saying and doing (Rogers-Warren and Baer, 1976); and, (10) supplementing the self-instructional training with operant procedures such as a response cost system (Kendall and Finch, 1976, 1978; Nelson and Birkimer, 1978; Robertson and Keeley, 1974). A host of CBM treatment manuals with children are now available as discussed in the Meichenbaum CBM newsletters (e.g., Bash and Camp, 1977; Hinshaw, Alkus, Whalen, and Henker, 1979; Kendall, 1978; and Wilson, Watson, and Hall, 1978). It is important to recognize that these CBM manuals are experimental in nature and further critical evaluation is now under way. A number of major review papers on CBM with children have been written recently (Craighead, Craighead-Wilcoxon, and Meyers, 1978; Karoly, 1977; Kendall, 1977; Mash and Dalby, 1978; Meichenbaum and Asarnow, 1979; and Rosenthal (in press).

Problem-Solving Training

Closely aligned with the CBM self-instructional approach is a CBM problem-solving approach as exemplified by the work of Shure and Spivack (1978) and Spivack and Shure (1974). Shure and Spivack have developed a CBM program to provide children with training in two types of social reasoning. One type of reasoning involved the child's thinking of alternative solutions to simple conflict situations with peers. A related ability was the child's anticipation of likely consequences should his solution be put into effect. The focus of the training, which takes the form of a variety of games, was *not what* to think, but rather, *how* to think about interpersonal problems. The initial games dealt with developing specific language and attentive skill, identifying emotions, thinking about how people have different likes and dislikes, and learning to gather information about other people. Final games posed the problem of finding several alternative solutions to interpersonal problems and evaluating cause and effect in human relationships. The training resulted in significant increases in social reasoning abilities, and most importantly—and rather uniquely for a training study—the children showed significant and enduring positive effects in social behaviors with peers, changes which were maintained at a one-year follow-up kindergarten. A most important aspect of the training program is that positive results were obtained when teachers trained children and when mothers trained their own children. In a personal communication, Spivack described his training as follows:

> Training reduces socially maladaptive behavior by enhancing certain mediating interpersonal cognitive skills of direct relevance to social adjustment . . . These skills involve the capacity to generate alternative solutions and consequences, and in older individuals the ability to generate means-ends thought.

Recently a number of programs tailored after Spivack and Shure have been developed to teach children a variety of skills, including self-control. These programs have been conducted by Allen, Chinsky, Larcen, Lochman, and Selinger (1976), Gesten et al. (1978), Elardo (1974), McClure et al. (1978), Meijers (1978), Poitras-Martin and Stone (1977), Russell and Thoresen (1976), and Stone, Hinds, and Schmidt (1975). In order to teach such skills several teaching modes are used, including verbal, behavioral, videotape, cartoon-workbook, poster-pictorial and flash-card activities.

CBM Treatment of Academic Problems

Recently there has been increasing research on the possible application of cognitive behavior procedures to traditional academic concerns, such as reading comprehension, arithmetic, and creativity. At this point we can share the general training strategy that is being employed and make a call for more research to assess the pedagogical potential of such CBM training procedures.

In the same way that the CBM procedures with hyperactive children found impetus in the work of Soviet psychologists, the CBM training approach with academic problems got its start in the work of the American psychologist Gagne. Gagne (1966) uses a task-analysis approach by beginning with a behavioral statement of the instructional objective. He then pursues the prerequisite behaviors the child must possess in order to perform the desired terminal behaviors. For each of the identified behaviors the same question is asked, thereby generating a hierarchy of objectives. Gagne is proposing that an individual's learning of a complex behavior is contingent on his prior acquisition of a succession of simpler behaviors. Thus, the instruction can be based on the cumulative learning process.

The cognitive behavioral training approach follows a similar strategy, except that each step in the hierarchy is translated into self-statements and images or cognitive strategies that can be modeled and rehearsed. Practically, this means that in performing a task analysis, a teacher must be sensitive not only to the behaviors, but also the cognitions, strategies, and rules required to do a task. The teacher can discover the hierarchy of cognitive abilities required by such means as observing his or her own thinking process while performing the task, in addition to observing and interviewing children who do poorly or well on the task. The teacher can then translate these cognitive strategies into sets of self-statements that can be modeled and then rehearsed by a student.

Moreover, the teacher can model not only task-relevant, problem-solving self-statements, but also coping self-statements. Teachers at all levels very infrequently, if at all, model how they cope with frustrations and failures while doing a particular task (i.e., they have tended to be mastery, not coping models). They rarely share with their students the thinking processes and other events that are involved in how they performed the task.

The student is told to perform a task, but rarely is shown (a) how to break the task down into manageable units, (b) how to determine the hierarchy of skills required to do the task, or (c) how to translate these skills into self-statements and images that can be rehearsed.

CBM is designed to teach children to use executive processes or cognitive strategems. Such executive processes have been described as metacognitive processes or cognitions about cognitions (see Brown and Campione, 1978; Flavell, 1976; Meichenbaum and Asarnow, 1979). The goal of metacognitive training is to provide the child with a generalizable, content free cognitive framework or blueprint that he or she can bring to bear in handling more adaptively a host of self-control, interpersonal and academic problem situations. Subsumed under the heading of metacognition is the individual's ability to both carry out cognitive operations and oversee his or her own progress. Several requirements of such a cognitive control system include an ability to identify and characterize the problem at hand, to assess one's capacity to meet the particular task demands, to plan and schedule appropriate problem-solving routines, and to monitor the effectiveness of the routines tried. The cumulative impact of such training is to sensitize the child's anticipation of his own capacity limitations more generally, and his awareness of his own repertoire of problem-solving strategies. What makes these executive processes particularly pertinent for the school psychologist is that several recent studies have suggested that particular child populations are deficient in just such metacognitive skills. For example, Torgesen (1977) has recently suggested that many of the failures of learning disability children may be due to defective meta-processes. Similar observations have been noted by Meyers and Paris (1978) and Ryan (in press) for children who have problems in reading comprehension, Douglas (in press) for hyperactive children and Borkowski and Cavanaugh (1978) and Brown, Campione, and Murphy (1977) for retarded children.

In short, the CBM technology that has emerged for the alleviation of self-control problems in children may also be of value in helping children who have academic problems. Elsewhere, Meichenbaum and Asarnow (1979) have discussed how CBM and metacognition can be combined in the classroom.

The "shotgun" marriage of the technology of behavior therapy and the clinical concerns of cognitive-semantic therapy and cognitive developmental psychology have resulted in some productive offspring, and like most offspring they will in turn likely change their parents.

REFERENCES

Allen, G.; Chinsky, J.; Larcen, S.; Lochman, J.; and Selinger, W. *Community psychology and the school: A behaviorally oriented multi-level preventive approach.* Hillsdale, N.J.: Lawernce Erlbaum Associates, 1976.

Bash, M., and Camp, B. Think aloud program. An unpublished CBM treatment manual. University of Colorado Medical School, Denver, Colorado, 1977.

Beck, A.; Rush, J.; Hollon, S.; and Shaw, B. *Cognitive therapy with depressions.* New York: Guilford Press, 1979.

Bender, N. Self-verbalization versus teacher verbalization in modifying impulsivity. *Journal of Educational Psychology*, 1976, 68: 34, 54, 347–354.

Borkowski, J., and Cavanaugh, J. Maintenance and generalization of skills and strategies by the retarded. In N. Ellis (Ed.), *Handbook of mental deficiency: Psychological theory and research.* Second Edition. Hillsdale, N.J.: Lawrence Erlbaum, 1978.

Bornstein, P., and Quevillon, R. The effects of a self-instructional package on overactive preschool boys. *Journal of Applied Behavior Analysis,* 1976, 9: 176–188.

Brown, A., and Campione, J. Permissible inference from the outcome of training studies in cognitive development research. *Quarterly Newsletter of the Institute for Comparative Human Development,* 1978, 2: 46–53.

Brown, A.; Campione, J.; and Murphy, M. Maintenance and generalization of trained metamnemonic awareness of educable retarded children. *Journal of Experimental Child Psychology,* 1977, 24: 191–211.

Camp, B.; Blom, G.; Hebert, F.; and Van Doorninck, W. "Think aloud": A program for developing self-control in young aggressive boys. *Journal of Abnormal Child Psychology,* 1977, 8: 157–169.

Craighead, E.; Craighead-Wilcoxon, L.; and Meyers, A. New directions in behavior modification with children. In M. Hessen, R. Eisler, and P. Miller (Eds.), *Progress in behavior modification.* (Vol. 6) New York: Academic Press, 1978.

Douglas, V. Treatment and training approaches to hyperactivity: Establishing internal or external control? In C. Whalen and B. Henker (Eds.), *Hyperactive children: The social ecology of identification and treatment.* New York: Academic Press, in press.

Douglas, V.; Parry, P.; Martin, P.; and Garson, C. Assessment of a cognitive training program for hyperactive children. *Journal of Abnormal Child Psychology, 1976,* 4: 389–410.

D'Zurilla, T., and Goldfried, M. Problem-solving and behavior modification. *Journal of Abnormal Psychology,* 1971, 78: 107–126.

Elardo, P. Project AWARE: A school program to facilitate social development of children. Paper presented at the Fourth Annual Blumberg Symposium, Chapel Hill, North Carolina, 1974.

Ellis, A., and Greiger, R. *Handbook of rational-emotive therapy.* New York: Springer, 1978.

Finch, A.; Wilkinson, M.; Nelson, W.; and Montgomery, L. Modification of an impulsive cognitive tempo in emotionally disturbed boys. *Journal of Abnormal Child Psychology,* 1975, 3: 49–52.

Flavell, J. Metacognitive aspects of problem-solving. In L. Resnick (Ed.), *The nature of intelligence.* Hillsdale, N.J.: Lawrence Erlbaum, 1976.

Gagne, R. Problem solving. In A. Melton (Ed.), *Categories of human learning.* New York: Academic Press, 1964.

Gesten, E.; Flores de Apadaca, R.; Rains, M.; Weissberg, R.; and Cowen, E. Promoting peer-related social competence in school. In M. Kent and J. Rolf (Eds.), *The primary prevention of psychopathology,* Vol. 3. Hanover, N.H. University Press of New England, 1978.

Hinshaw, S.; Alkus, S.; Whalen, C.; and Henker, B. STAR training program. Unpublished cognitive behavior modification training manual, UCLA, 1979.

Karoly, P. Behavioral self-management in children: Concepts, methods, issues and directions. In M. Hersen, R. Eisler, and P. Miller (Eds.), *Progress in Behavior Modification,* Vol. 5. New York: Academic Press, 1977.

Kendall, P. On the efficacious use of verbal self-instructional procedures with children. *Cognitive Therapy and Research,* 1977, 1: 331–341.

Kendall, P. Developing self-control in children: A manual of cognitive-behavioral strategies. Unpublished manuscript, University of Minnesota, 1979.

Kendall, P., and Finch, A. A cognitive-behavioral treatment for impulse control: A case study. *Journal of Consulting and Clinical Psychology,* 1976, 44: 852–859.

Kendall, P., and Finch, A. A cognitive-behavioral treatment for impulsivity: a group comparison study. *Journal of Consulting and Clinical Psychology,* 1978, 46: 110–118.

Luria, A. The directive function of speech in development. *Word,* 1959, 15: 341–352.

Luria, A. *The role of speech in the regulation of normal and abnormal behaviors.* New York: Liveright, 1961.

Mahoney, M. *Cognition and behavior modification.* Cambridge, Mass.: Bullinger, 1974.

Mahoney, M., and Arnkoff, D. Cognitive and self-control therapies. In S. Garfield and A. Bergin (Eds.), *Handbook of psychotherapy and behavior change.* Second edition. New York: John Wiley, 1979.

Mash, E., and Dalby, J. Behavioral interventions for hyperactivity. In R. Trites (Ed.), *Hyperactivity in children: Etiology, measurement and treatment im-*

plications. Baltimore, Md.: Universtiy Park Press, 1978.

McClure, L.; Chinsky, J.; and Larcen, S. Enhancing social problem-solving performance in an elementary school setting. *Journal of Educational Psychology*, 1978, 70: 504–513.

Meichenbaum, D. *Cognitive-behavior modification: An integrative approach*. New York: Plenum Press, 1977.

Meichenbaum, D. Cognitive behavior modification newsletter. Volumes 1, 2, and 4. Unpublished manuscripts, University of Waterloo, 1975–1979.

Meichenbaum, D. Teaching children self-control. In B. Lahey and A. Kazdin (Eds.), *Advances in child clinical psychology*. Vol. 2. New York: Plenum Press, 1978.

Meichenbaum, D., and Asarnow, J. Cognitive-behavior modification and metacognitive development: Implications for the classroom. In P. Kendall and S. Hollon (Eds.), *Cognitive behavioral interventions: Theory research and procedures*. New York: Academic Press, 1979.

Meichenbaum, D., and Goodman, J. Training impulsive children to talk to themselves: A means of developing self-control. *Journal of Abnormal Psychology*, 1971, 77: 115–126.

Meijers, J. *Problem-solving therapy with socially anxious children*. Amsterdam, The Netherlands: Alblasserdam-Kanters, B. V., 1978.

Meyers, M., and Paris, S. Children's metacognitive knowledge about reading. *Journal of Educational Psychology*, 1978, 70: 680–690.

Monahan, J., and O'Leary, D. Effects of self-instruction on rule-breaking behavior. *Psychological Reports*, 1971, 29: 1059–1066.

Nelson, W., and Birkimer, J. Role of self-instruction and self-reinforcement in the modification of impulsivity. *Journal of Consulting and Clinical Psychology*, 1978, 46: 183.

Palkes, H,; Stewart, M.; and Freedman, J. Improvement in maze performance on hyperactive boys as a function of verbal training procedures. *Journal of Special Education*, 1972, 5: 237–342.

Palkes, H.; Stewart, M.; and Kahana, B. Porteus maze performance after training in self-directed verbal commands, *Child Development*, 1968, 39: 817–826.

Poitras-Martin, D., and Stone, G. Psychological education: A skill-oriented approach. *Journal of Counseling Psychology*, 1977, 24: 153–157.

Robertson, D., and Keeley, S. Evaluation of a mediational training program for impulsive children by a multiple case study design. Paper presented at American Psychological Association, 1974.

Rogers-Warren, A., and Baer, D. Correspondence between saying and doing: Teaching children to share and praise. *Journal of Applied Behavior Analysis*, 1976, 9: 335–354.

Rosenthal, T. Applying a cognitive behavioral view to clinical and social problems. In G. Whitehurst and B. Zimmerman (Eds.), *The functions of language and cognition*. New York: Academic Press, in press.

Russell, M., and Thoresen, C. Teaching decision making skills to children. In J. Krumboltz and C. Thoresen (Eds.), *Counseling methods*. New York: Holt, Rinehart, and Winston, 1976.

Ryan, E. Identifying and remediating factors in reading comprehension: Toward an instructional approach for poor comprehenders. In T. Waller and E. Mackinnon (Eds.), *Advances in reading research*. Vol. 2. New York: Academic Press, in press.

Schneider, M.; and Robin, A. The turtle technique: A method for the self-control of impulsive behavior. In J. Krumboltz and C. Thoresen (Eds.), *Counseling methods*. New York: Holt, Rinehart, and Winston, 1976.

Shure, M., and Spivack, G. *Problem solving techniques in childrearing*. San Francisco: Jossey-Bass, 1978.

Spivack, G., and Shure, M. *Social adjustment of young children: A cognitive approach to solving real-life problems*. San Francisco: Jossey Boss, 1974.

Stone, G.; Hinds, W.; and Schmidt, G. Teaching mental health behaviors to elementary school children. *Professional Psychology*, 1975, 6: 34–40.

Suinn, R., and Richardson, F. Anxiety management training: A nonspecific behavior therapy program for anxiety control. *Behavior Therapy*, 1971, 2: 498–510.

Torgesen, J. The role of nonspecific factors in the task performance of learning disabled children: A theoretical assessment. *Journal of Learning Disabilities*, 1977, 10: 27–34.

Toulmin, S. The Mozart of Psychology. *New York Review of Books*, 1978, 25: 50–56.

Turk, D. Coping with pain. A review of cognitive control techniques. In M. Feuerstein, L. Sachs and I. Turkat (Eds.), *Psychological approaches to pain control*; in press.

Ullmann, L., and Krasner, L. *Case Studies in Behavior Modification*. New York: Holt, Rinehart, and Winston, 1965.

Varni, J., and Henker, B. A self-regulation approach to the treatment of the hyperactive child. *Behavior Therapy*, in press.

Vygotsky, L. *Thought and Language*. New York: Wiley, 1962.

Watson, D.; and Hall, D. Self-control of hyperactivity. Unpublished manuscript, LaMesa School District, 1977.

Wilson, C.; Hall, D.; and Watson, D. Teaching educationally handicapped children self-control: Three teacher's manuals grades 1 to 9. Unpublished manuscripts, San Diego County School Boards, 1978.

Matching Teaching and Learning Styles

Psychologists and educators have always recognized that students have best or preferred ways of learning. Some learn best through reading; others by listening; and still others by actually doing things. Some do their best work in a group; others when they work alone. Some do well under the pressure of tests and deadlines; others do not. Another issue in this volume explores individual differences that some believe to be related to which hemisphere of the brain is dominant, the left or the right.

In recent years, there have been attempts to define students' learning styles more precisely. Several that have attracted widespread attention are described in a publication of the National Association of Secondary School Principals edited by J. W. Keefe (1979). All the contributors to that volume believe in the concept of learning styles, but they do *not* agree on their nature or assessment. One team of researchers (Rita Dunn, Kenneth Dunn, and Gary Price) defines and seeks to measure learning style in terms of students' opinions about how they learn. These authors use a questionnaire to identify learners' styles. Another researcher, David E. Hunt, says "Learning style describes a student in terms of those educational conditions under which he is most likely to learn." Hunt recommends that teachers assess learning styles informally, vary their instruction accordingly, and evaluate the results.

Messick's more recent review (1984) of what he terms "cognitive styles" notes that some definitions of learning style imply that they are *preferences;* and some suggest *habits of information processing.* Messick does not see them as *simple* habits or preferences. He cites the work of psychologist Herman Witkin (1978,1981) as support for the view that styles are linked to basic personality differences, not merely modes of thinking. Witkin, for example, distinguishes between persons who are "field dependent" and "field independent."

Garger and Guild, in our first article dealing with this issue, describe the implications of Witkin's distinction for both learners and teachers. They recommend use of a short test to classify individuals on this characteristic, and suggest that serious consideration be given to the implications of style differences among learners and teachers for both "matching" and "mismatching."

Hyman and Rosoff identify three issues related to "learning style based education" (LSBE): (1) lack of clarity in the concepts, (2) the appropriateness of letting style determine teachers' actions, and (3) undesirable and unintended consequences. Then, they present their recommendations for reorientating thinking about matching learning and teaching styles. One recommendation is that teachers and students share responsibility for LSBE leadership. They suggest that students help teachers to diagnose learning styles and choose teaching styles. They refer to a University of Wisconsin program that prepares future teachers for this change.

Thought Questions

After reading both selections, would you recommend grouping students by learning style? If so, which do you think better: grouping within a class, or different classes for different styles?

Would you classify yourself as a field-dependent or a field-independent person? Do you think this affects the way you learn and the teachers you prefer? Would this affect the way you would prefer to teach?

What do you think is the better way to identify learning styles: self-reports, tests, or observation? Explain.

Evaluate the argument that students should experience teachers with different teaching styles so that they may gain experience using different learning styles.

Do you think it probable that some style differences are inherent and some learned? If so, give examples.

Who do you think should make the decisions about which students should work with which teachers? Why?

Does equality of opportunity imply equal opportunity to work with any teacher or all teachers?

Can a person's philosophy be opposed to ability grouping but in favor of style grouping?

Learning Styles: The Crucial Differences

Stephen Garger and Pat Guild

Can you find this isolated figure

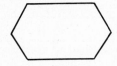

in this more complex figure?

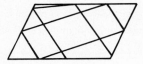

It takes some people as little as three seconds to perform this task, while others with similar intelligence search for several minutes and cannot locate it. What about you?

People vary in their ability to differentiate an object from its background or "field." This difference in perception can be extreme: a highly "field-independent" person will succeed at this task quickly, no matter how difficult the problem, while an extremely "field-dependent" person often needs to have the figure pointed out. Although few people are at either extreme, most people exhibit tendencies toward one mode of perception or the other; the difference lies in the time it takes them to complete the task and the complexity of problems they are able to solve.

This perceptual characteristic of field-dependency, originally studied in the area of "cognitive style," has been linked to learning, teaching, and many other behavioral characteristics. How people respond on a test such as the one above clearly indicates how they generally perceive things and make sense of the world. This difference among people is critical for educators to understand in order to address individual learning styles.

Do You See What I See?

The above figure and others like it are contained in the Group Embedded Figures Test[1] which is derived from the work of the late Herman A. Witkin. In the latter half of the 1940s, Witkin and his associates began exploring distinctive perceptual characteristics among peo-

From *Curriculum Review* (February 1984): 9–12. Reprinted with permission.

Learning Styles

FIELD-DEPENDENT	FIELD-INDEPENDENT
perceives globally	perceives analytically
experiences in a global fashion, adheres to structures as given	experiences in an articulated fashion, imposes structure or restrictions
makes broad general distinctions among concepts, sees relationships	makes specific concept distinctions, little overlap
social orientation	impersonal orientation
learns material with social content best	learns social material only as an intentional task
attends best to material relevant to own experience	interested in new concepts for their own sake
requires externally defined goals and reinforcements	has self-defined goals and reinforcements
needs organization provided	can self-structure situations
more affected by criticism	less affected by criticism
uses spectator approach for concept attainment	uses hypothesis-testing approach to attain concepts

Teaching Styles

FIELD-DEPENDENT	FIELD-INDEPENDENT
prefers teaching situations that allow interaction and discussion with students	prefers impersonal teaching situations such as lectures. Emphasizes cognitive aspect of instruction.
uses questions to check on student learning following instruction	uses questions to introduce topics and following student answers
uses student-centered activities	uses a teacher-organized learning situation
viewed by students as teaching facts	viewed by students as encouraging to apply principles
provides less feedback, avoids negative evaluation	gives corrective feedback, uses negative evaluation
strong in establishing a warm and personal learning environment	strong in organizing and guiding student learning

How to Motivate Students

FIELD-DEPENDENT	FIELD-INDEPENDENT
through verbal praise	through grades
through helping the teacher	through competition
through external rewards (stars, stickers, prizes)	through choice of activities, personal goal chart
through showing the task's value to other people	through showing how the task is useful to them
through providing outlines and structure	through freedom to design their own structure

What Teachers Expect From an Administrator

FIELD-DEPENDENT	FIELD-INDEPENDENT
to give warmth, personal interest, support	to focus on task
to provide guidance, modeling	to allow independence and flexibility in teaching approach
to seek teachers' opinions in making decisions	to make decisions based on analysis of the problem
to "practice what they preach"	to be knowledgeable about curriculum and administration
to have an "open door"	to maintain professional distance

ple. The researchers were interested in knowing to what extent a person's perception of an item is influenced by the context in which it appears. In other words, do some people see the tree, while others more readily see the forest?

In an early aspect of his work, Witkin sought to determine why certain pilots who lost sight of the ground mistakenly flew their planes upside down. In one experiment designed to assess people's perceptions of their own orientation in space, subjects were seated in a moving chair which they had to bring to an "upright" position, regardless of the slant of a small "room" surrounding the chair. In similar experiments, subjects had to turn a rod upright in the space of a frame, when both rod and frame could be tilted independently.

These and other experiments led Witkin and his associates to define two extreme indicators of the extent to which the surrounding organized field influences a person's perception of an item within it. A person leaning toward a field-dependent (FD) mode of perception is strongly dominated by the prevailing field, while the field-independent (FI) person perceives items as more or less separate from the surrounding field.

Thus, field-independent persons are more successful in attaining a correct upright placement of the chair and the rod in the above experiments by their ability to ignore the surrounding "room" or frame.

Witkin began expanding his studies into different aspects of these polar characteristics of perception. What do the people tending toward each side of the continuum have in common?

Do people with FD or FI modes of perception have certain consistent personality characteristics? Witkin and his associates became convinced that whether one is field-dependent or field-independent influences a person's perceptual and intellectual domains as well as personality traits such as social behavior, body concept, and defenses.

The results of over 35 years of research provide a rich and useful fount of information.[2] This information becomes especially important in the field of education in light of increasing interest in student learning styles.

Style Makes a Difference

Learning styles are stable and pervasive characteristics of an individual, expressed through the interaction of one's behaviors and personality as one approaches a learning task. In light of this definition, the implications of Witkin's research for educators are extensive, including the effect field-dependence/independence has on behaviors in teaching, administering, and learning. The effect extends not only to how and what students learn, but also to the style demands made by teachers, curriculum materials, methods, and evaluation techniques.

Despite a solid research base for field-dependent/independent concepts, a wider knowledge of and application of Witkin's work within educational circles is needed. Witkin recognized the importance of his research for educators and prepared an extensive article on this aspect of his work.[3] However, since Witkin's concern was primarily psychological research, educators must devise their own methods for properly applying this knowledge in the educational setting. The following lists of field-dependent/independent characteristics are extracted from Witkin's research and adapted for educational applications.

The actual diagnosis of student's styles has been made more accessible to educators through the development of fully-validated paper-and-pencil instrumentation.[4] One of these instruments, the Embedded Figures Test, is administered individually to the student and takes about 30 minutes. In testing this form of the instrument on the high school level, the authors found that the information, which was later verified through a verbal interview with the student, was very useful for academic counseling.

For example, students testing as relatively field-dependent usually enjoy courses in the humanities. Sometimes such a student will state that he or she "hates history." After some discussion, the FD student, being more alert to social cues, discovers that it is not the *subject* that is creating the problem, but rather a conflict with the instructor's teaching style. The student may then be counseled on learning/teaching style differences and begin to work on coping with these conflicts. The understanding of personality differences among people should enable the student to allow for these differences and to do better in history, a subject one would expect the student to enjoy.

Another similar instrument that teachers can use is the Group Embedded Figures Test. This instrument can be administered to a large group (up to 30 people) and takes only 20 minutes. It also yields good results.[5]

Accepting Diversity

In applying his concepts to teaching and learning experiences, educators can derive several messages from Witkin's work. His studies have consistently demonstrated cognitive styles to be independent of intelligence and thus "field-dependence/independence appears to be more related to the 'how' than to the 'how much' of cognitive functioning." Since cognitive style is neutral in terms of one or the other being "better," both field-dependent and field-independent people make equally good students and teachers. Therefore an important goal is for teachers and students to accept and value the diversity of styles. But since styles affect the success people have with specific kinds of situations, educators must also be sensitive to these cognitive style differences.

In offering advice to respond to these differences, Witkin urges us to consider the advantages of both matching and mismatching. He points out that the "development of greater diversity in behaviors within individuals seems as important an objective as the recognition and the utilization of diversity among individuals." Knowledge of field-dependence/independence among people should contribute to the teachers' and students' ability to utilize their own style strengths, appreciate the style differences of others, and develop diverse strategies to facilitate success in learning.

In summary, the cognitive style characteristics defined by Witkin's work should be seriously considered and studied by educators. The research available has been carried out by many people with diverse subjects. In addition, many longitudinal studies have been done on the concept of field-dependence/independence. The instrumentation, especially the Embedded Figures Test and the Group Embedded Figures Test, are well validated, available, and accessible to educators. The implications for all aspects of the teaching/learning process are extensive.[6]

Perhaps the most precious gift each person brings to the learning situation is that person's individuality. Learning styles represent a systematic way to define some of those individual differences among educators and students. When we begin to understand and apply the concepts of learning styles we owe it to students and our profession to be as well versed in the theories and instrumentation as possible. Herman A. Witkin's work offers a firm foundation for this understanding.

NOTES

1. Philip K. Oltman, Evelyn Raskin, and Herman A. Witkin, *Group Embedded Figures Test*. (California: Counsulting Psychologists Press, 1971).

2. In 1973, Witkin published a bibliography of 1508 items appearing in research from 1948 to 1972. A supplement of 392 entries was published in 1974, a second supplement of over 400 entries was published in 1976, and a third supplement of entries was published in 1978. All are available from Consulting Psychologists Press, 577 College Avenue, Palo Alto, California, 94306.

3. Herman A. Witkin, C. A. Moore, D. R. Goodenough, and P. W. Cox. "Field-Dependent and Field-Independent Cognitive Styles and Their Educational Implications," *Review of Educational Research*, Vol. 47 (Winter, 1977), pp. 1–64.

4. The instruments described in this section are available from Consulting Psychologists Press.

5. There is also a children's version of the instrument for youngsters between the ages of 5 and 9, a pre-school version for children 3 to 5 years, an auditory version, and a tactile version. For information, contact Consulting Psychologists Press or Educational Testing Service in New Jersey.

6. Useful discussions of these concepts can be found in:

Garger, Stephen Joseph. *Learning Styles: A State of the Art and A Curriculum Design for Application*. Ann Arbor: University Microfilm International, 1982.

Guild, Patricia O'Rourke Burke. *Learning Styles: Knowledge, Issues and Applications for Classroom Teachers*. Ann Arbor: University Microfilm International, 1980.

Messick, Samuel and Associates. *Individuality in Learning*. San Francisco: Jossey-Bass, 1976. The first five chapters (one of which was authored by Witkin) are concerned primarily with field-dependence/independence.

Witkin, Herman A. and Donald R. Goodenough. *Cognitive Styles: Essence and Origins*. New York: International Universities Press, Psychological Issues, Monograph 51, 1981. Available from Consulting Psychologists Press.

Witkin, Herman A. "Cognitive Styles in the Educational Setting," *New York University Education Quarterly*, Vol. 3 (1977–78), pp. 14–20.

Witkin, Herman A. et al. *Psychological Differentiation*. Hillsdale, N. J.: Erlbaum, 1974.

Matching Learning and Teaching Styles: The Jug and What's in It

Ronald Hyman and Barbara Rosoff

The educational literature today often contains the term *learning style* along with the recommendation that learning style be matched with teaching style so as to augment achievement. It is also possible to read about "learning style based education," or simply LSBE. What is meant by these new terms and the recommendations associated with them? The answer to this question depends, of course, on one's perspective. We shall provide an answer via an analysis of three major LSBE issues and a further set of recommendations from our perspective as educators concerned with teacher-student interaction. First, we remind the reader encountering new terms and recommendations of the old adage about the jug: Do not look at the jug but at what's in it. There can be an old jug filled with wine, and there can be a new jug without much wine in it at all.

The advocates of the learning style proposal employ a fairly simple, straightforward model. It is a four-step paradigm which is not new. Indeed, it is a variation of the familiar paradigm used in years past by personality psychologists:

(1) examine the student's individual learning style, (2) understand it and classify it according to several large categories, (3) match it with a teaching style of an available teacher or, if no available teacher has the appropriate style, then request that a teacher adjust his/her teaching style to match the student's learning style; and (4) teach teachers to do steps 1, 2, and 3 in their preservice and inservice training programs.

The requirements for implementing this four-step paradigm are clear. First we need a clear concept of learning style so that we can communicate effectively with each other and know what we are searching for when we work with the student. Second, once we have a clear concept, we need to develop an operational approach to determining what a student's learning style is. We need some practical instrument that will easily and accurately indicate a student's learning style. Third, we need to figure out what a teacher can and should do with each type of learning style so as to maximize learning. That is, we need to know which teaching styles go well with which learning styles and then what teachers working within each teaching style need to emphasize. In short, we need to know the effects of the interaction between specified learning styles and specified teaching

From *Theory into Practice* (Winter 1984):35–43. Reprinted with permission.

styles. Fourth, since most teachers do not have the necessary teaching styles to match their students' range of learning styles, we need to be able to train teachers to adjust their current teaching styles so that they will match their students' learning styles.

Definitions of Learning Style: The Need for Clarity and Specificity

Naturally, with the learning style paradigm and its requirements before us some issues quickly arise. We are concerned here only with three of them. The first, of course, centers on the concept of learning style itself. If the concept of learning style is not clear, then it is impossible to perform even step one of the paradigm. Therefore, let us begin by looking at the definition of learning style proposed by a well-known team of LSBE advocates. For Rita Dunn, Kenneth Dunn, and Gary Price (hereafter referred to as Dunn) learning style is "the manner in which at least 18 different elements from four basic stimuli affect a person's ability to absorb and retain." (Dunn, Dunn, & Price, 1979, p. 41). These 18 elements from four types of stimuli are: sound, light, temperature, design (environmental); motivation, persistence, responsibility, need for structure (emotional); working alone, working with another student, working with many students, working with a team of students, working with an adult, working with some combination of adults and peers (sociological); perceptual strengths, intake, time of day, need for mobility (physical). (Also see Dunn, 1983; Dunn & Dunn, 1979).

Such a definition is not at all clear, perhaps raising more questions about learning style than are answered. How did these educators decide on these 18 elements and 4 types of stimuli? How do these 18 elements interact? Is there a synergistic effect that any one element has when it interacts with two or three others, analogous to the way certain drugs react differently in combination than when alone? (Note that the 12 elements from the environmental, emotional, and physical stimuli appear to be present at all times in one degree or another.

However, only one of the six sociological elements can be present at any given moment. Thus 13 elements are interacting at any given time while five are not present. Hence, the question about synergism.) And perhaps most significantly, where is the element of intelligence?

Intelligence, however defined, is not listed in Dunn's definition. Is it possible that Dunn is claiming that intelligence (good, old-fashioned brain power) is not an element helping to determine learning style? Indeed, intelligence does not appear to fit easily into the four types of stimuli—environmental, emotional, sociological, and physical. If intelligence is not one of the 18 elements or does not become the 19th, then Dunn's definition suffers because it flies in the face of what we all know—a brilliant person with a superior capacity to learn, remember, and create new knowledge has a different learning style from an average person or a brain-damaged person. It simply goes counter to common sense and linguistic logic to exclude intelligence as an element of learning style since intelligence is related to the concepts of brain and learning.

Furthermore, Dunn's definition is unclear because of the suggested limitations it puts on learning. It adopts—probably unwittingly—a particular learning theory through the metaphor it uses. The words *absorb* and *retain* suggest the sponge metaphor in which one physical object sucks up in its pores (absorb) a liquid material (information) and keeps it inside (retain) without changing or using that material substantially. Surely, this is a limited concept of school learning, for it does not clarify at all how the 18 elements affect anything beyond absorption and retention (of information). Hopefully, a concept of learning style would account for processes other than absorbing and retaining. In what ways, for example, does learning style deal with valuing and skills-performing? How does learning style deal with explaining and analyzing, two processes related to information?

However, no matter which responses we receive to the above questions, one major problem remains. Dunn's definition does not tell us what the student does as he/she learns but only how certain elements affect a person's ability to absorb and retain. It would seem that learning style would deal with behavior and not ability. By analogy, when we speak of teaching style we speak of the characteristics of the ways a teacher acts. We do not refer to what the teacher *is* but rather to what is characteristic of how the teacher *acts* with students when teaching. For example, we speak of how the teacher questions, uses voice tone, organizes the lesson and students, calls on students, tests students, moves around the classroom, and introduces new ideas. That is, we speak about observable actions, not characteristics of being. We do not talk about the teacher's inherent characteristics (for example, high IQ) when we talk about teaching style. The term *style* leads us to refer to the actions of the teacher.

Similarly, a definition of learning style would be helpful and meaningful if it referred to or indicated actions which a student performs. We want and need to know the actions that constitute learning style so as to help us explicate the unobservable act called *learning*. But Dunn's definition does not refer to actions; it refers only to the ability to absorb and retain. Ability is a characteristic, not an action. This flaw in Dunn's definition is serious and leads us to seek clarity about the entire concept of learning style. (See also Davidman's 1981 *Phi Delta Kappan* article for a critique of Dunn's approach to learning style). There is a way to resolve the problem raised by Dunn's definition—use a different definition of learning style. Fortunately, other learning style advocates offer alternative definitions to Dunn's.

Hunt, also a leading LSBE advocate, describes learning style as the educational conditions under which a student "is most likely to learn" (Hunt, 1979, p. 27). He then narrows his definition by dealing with "how much *structure* the student needs in order to learn best." He focuses on the student's conceptual level as the way to characterize learning style. "Conceptual level is a characteristic based on developmental personality theory that describes persons on a developmental hierarchy of increasing conceptual complexity, self-re-

sponsibility, and independence" (Hunt, 1977–1978, p. 78). In short, in defining learning style as those educational conditions under which a student is most likely to learn, Hunt deals with the degree of conceptual complexity with which a student processes information about people, things, and events.

This definition of learning style certainly is more manageable, but it, too, is not relieved of problems. While conceptual level includes elements of conceptual complexity (which is related to intelligence, that missing important element in Dunn's definition) and the two personality traits of responsibility and independence, Hunt's definition also is not helpful. We are not clear how we are to measure conceptual level nor do we have any idea how or who is to determine the degree of structure which the student requires in order to learn best. We learn from Hunt later that through a paper and pencil test we can determine the conceptual level of the student which indicates the degree of structure the student needs. Based on the results of this test Hunt classifies all students into essentially two groups—high and low conceptual level. There is also a third group (very low) which is a modified low conceptual level. Thus, there are three types of learning style according to the need for structure: needs less structure (high conceptual level), needs some structure (low conceptual level), and needs much structure (very low conceptual level).

It is not clear how Hunt's paper and pencil test measures conceptual level. The Paragraph Completion Method is a writing test which takes about 20 minutes. The student, in writing two or three sentences to describe his feelings on each of six to eight topics, indicates how he/she learns best. The content of the writing is not critical. Nevertheless, based on the results of 20 minutes of writing the scorers determine the student's conceptual level. It is not clear how from such a small amount of writing Hunt can describe a student on the three dimensions of conceptual complexity, self-responsibility, and independence. Is it possible on the basis of two or three sentences about six or eight topics to measure three such major dimensions? Or, is conceptual level rather a euphemism for "the degree of order I think I need in order to learn best?" Indeed, one would imagine that conceptual level would deal with thinking and concepts rather than with structure needed in order to learn.

Another major problem is that Hunt's definition does not indicate student actions either. Instead of a definition referring to action we have one referring to a personality-based characteristic which describes a student in terms of being on a high or low conceptual level. We promptly note that to his credit Hunt does not claim to have offered a comprehensive concept of learning style. Rather, he has limited himself to conceptual level and does not make claims beyond the reach of his term. Nevertheless, Hunt's conceptual level does not describe how a student learns. It only indicates how much structure a student requires.

Briefly, let us look at two more definitions which will indicate still further need for clarity. Gregorc writes, "Learning style, from a phenomenological viewpoint, consists of distinctive and observable behaviors that provide clues about the mediation abilities of individuals" (Gregorc, 1979, p. 19). Keefe, in his overview essay in a book to which Dunn, Hunt, and Gregorc contribute, writes, "Learning styles are characteristic cognitive, affective, and physiological behaviors that serve as relatively stable indicators of how learners perceive, interact with, and respond to the learning environment" (Keefe, 1979, p. 4). Both of these definitions refer to behavior and in this sense are acceptable. Gregorc limits the behaviors to giving clues about the ability to mediate, which is a cognitive ability. He leaves us in need of clarification of the term *mediation abilities*. He goes on to indicate four learning styles based on observation and interviews: concrete sequential, concrete random, abstract sequential, and abstract random.

A problem with Gregorc's definition, as well as with Dunn's and Hunt's, is raised by Keefe in points made when clarifying his own definition above. Keefe specifically and strongly notes that learning style and cognitive style are not equivalent: "Learning style and cognitive style have often been used synonymously in

the literature although they decidedly are not the same. Learning style, in fact, is the broader term and includes cognitive along with affective and physiological styles" (Keefe, 1979, p. 4). Even Hunt in his article in the same book distinguishes learning style from ability or intelligence. He writes, "A student's conceptual level (the degree of structure required) is relatively distinct from his ability or intelligence, and thus for students in grade 6 and above, learning style (CL) and ability can be distinguished from one another" (Hunt, 1979, p. 30). Yet Gregorc appears to restrict his learning style behaviors to the realm of the cognitive. In this sense, Gregorc's definition of learning style is too limited since it does not take into consideration the affective and physiological realms.

Keefe's definition, while concerning itself with the three dimensions of behavior, has a flaw. Keefe offers us a broad definition which does include the cognitive, affective, and the physiological aspects of learning. However, Keefe offers us no specificity about the behaviors. We have types of behaviors but no specific behaviors. Nor do we have any operational way to determine these behaviors. Thus, we are left without a clear and readily usable concept of learning style.

Additional Problems with the Paradigm: Focus and Unilateralism

The second major issue which arises from the paradigm employed by LSBE advocates deserves our attention at this point. The LSBE paradigm calls for the teacher to focus on the student's learning style when deciding how to teach. This call is misleading just as is the call for the teacher to focus on the student's personality factors when deciding how to teach. It is misleading in that the teacher is subtly led to conceive of teaching as a dyadic relationship between the teacher and the student's learning style. Such a conception is flawed on two counts.

Teaching is not a dyadic relationship between teacher and student. To teach, the teacher must relate to the student in terms of subject matter. This subject matter may be knowledge, and/or skills, and/or values. It is what the teacher wants to teach, what the teacher wants the student to learn. When the teacher considers subject matter, he/she does so in light of the particular students involved. Similarly, when the teacher considers the characteristics of and potential actions by the student, he/she does so in light of an understanding of what subject matter is involved. There is always a connection between teacher, student, and subject matter. Teaching is thus a triadic relationship made up of three critical and constant elements: teacher, student, and subject matter.

The learning style paradigm suffers because it omits consideration of subject matter. If the teacher wishes to teach a student how to divide a three-digit number by a two-digit number, then the nature of mathematics must come into the picture. Sure, the teacher must look at the student. But such a look is inadequate. The teacher must also consider what the field of mathematics is and what it demands of teacher and student. In an important article on the theory of teaching, Smith points out the need to consider the demands subject matter makes on the teacher in determining how to teach (that is, in adjusting teaching style). "What distinguishes instruction from other forms of social behavior is that instructional behavior is controlled by the requirements of a body of knowledge and by the commitment to develop cognitive structures coordinate with that knowledge" (Smith, 1963, p. 296). Smith reminds us that the act of teaching demands more than a focus on the student. Teaching requires us to look at our subject matter when we decide on what actions to perform for and with the student.

The determining factor for the teacher in the teaching triad is not the "whom" but the "what," which is the subject matter. This is what Smith means when he says that teaching is "controlled" by the subject matter. Teachers think of themselves as teachers of history, or mathematics, or art, or gymnastics, or literature, or writing, or whatever. "While the teacher's behavior is influenced by his understanding of the student—by his perception and diagnosis of the student's behavior—still the determining factor in the teacher's behavior is not his understanding of the student but his comprehension of the subject matter and the demands which clear instruction in the subject matter make upon him" (Smith, 1963, p. 296). The LSBE advocates err in asking us to consider the student's learning style first and foremost. In teaching, the teacher considers what he/she must do in order to teach the facts, concepts, principles, skills, and values which we commonly associate with such subjects as social studies, language arts, science, mathematics, fine arts, and physical education.

The third major issue arising from the LSBE paradigm centers on unilateral decision making and its consequences. The paradigm calls for the teacher to examine the student's learning style and then to decide, based on that diagnosis, what kind of teaching style will maximize the student's learning. This is a classical example of unilateral means-end action. The paradigm calls for the teacher to decide what is best for the student and then to provide what is best. The teacher is the decision maker and then the actor acting on the student who may be unaware of the deliberate action being taken.

Argyris has labeled such teacher behavior as Model I (Argyris, 1974; Argyris & Schön, 1974). Model I behavior is common in our society and prevalent in teaching. In Model I, according to Argyris, there are four action strategies which describe how people act: (1) "Design and manage the environment unilaterally"; (2) "own and control the task"; (3) "unilaterally protect yourself"; and (4) "unilaterally protect others" (Argyris & Schön, 1974, p. 68–69). These four action strategies apply to teaching in the learning style paradigm. The teacher unilaterally designs the teaching environment and controls it by acting upon a diagnosis of the student's learning style. The student, other than responding to items on a test or survey, does not determine or even contribute to the action of the teacher. The teacher "owns" the task and acts upon the student.

The consequences of such behavior are important for us to keep in mind as we assess LSBE. Argyris identifies four consequences for the behavioral world which correspond to the four action strategies above: (1) "Actor seen as defensive, inconsistent, incongruent, competitive, controlling, fearful of being vulnerable, manipulative, withholding of feelings, overly concerned about self and others or underconcerned about others"; (2) "defensive interpersonal and group relationship (dependence upon actor, little additivity, little helping others"; (3) "defensive norms (mistrust, lack of risk-taking, conformity, external commitment, emphasis on diplomacy, power-centered competition, and rivalry)"; and (4) "low freedom of choice, internal commitment, and risk taking" (Argyris & Schön, 1974, pp. 68–69). These four items, too, apply to the LSBE situation and are similar to student criticisms of our schools. Students and critics, in the establishment and outside it, generally use the same terms to describe their feelings, emphasizing, for example, lack of trust, low freedom of choice, manipulation, and dependency. Such are the terms which generally appear in any analysis of the school and bureaucracy (Haubrich, 1971).

We feel confident that the LSBE advocates do not intend such consequences when they suggest how teachers should act. Nevertheless, the consequences of what they advocate are real. For the student who has low freedom of choice and who lacks commitment it makes little difference if the consequences are intended or unintended. The consequences of Model I behavior are strong and undesirable, and it is not comforting to recognize them as being unintended when they appear.

In summary, we have shown that three major issues arise from the learning style paradigm and present serious difficulties: (1) the concept of learning style is unclear, even among the advocates of LSBE; (2) the focus on learning style in determining teaching action is inappropriate theoretically and realistically; and (3) the action strategies and unintended consequences (Model I) of following the learning style paradigm are undesirable. Furthermore, since we recognize that it is insufficient

only to offer a critique of the learning style paradigm and its advocates, we now must shift to the last part of our task in this article—the presenting of our recommendations for teachers.

Recommendations

Our set of recommendations regarding learning styles and teaching styles contains six parts. These six are not sequential steps but together consititute a reorientation of thinking about the matching of learning styles and teaching styles. First, we recommend that educators who aim to help teachers improve accept a more inclusive perspective on teaching. That is, teaching is an act which has three elements, the *teacher*, the *student*, and the *subject matter* (these three are the triad mentioned earlier), which interrelate in an *environment* (that is, the "place" context) and in a particular *time* period. When there is teaching going on, all five items are present. We can conceive of teaching either as a pentadic relationship or as a triadic relationship within a context of environment and time. Either way the same five items appear.

With this broader perspective on teaching, it is improper to focus on learning style as the sole or even main element which influences the teacher's actions. With such a perspective, the teacher must always keep in mind the nature of the subject matter under study and also his/her own interests, knowledge, skill, and personality because all of these are involved. The teacher must give weight to the influence of the particular subject matter even if he/she does not accept Smith's view totally. That is, even if the teacher does not believe that the *determining* factor is the subject matter, as Smith claims it is (see above), the teacher must recognize and consider what is being taught as a significant influence in deciding how to teach.

Second, we recommend that the teacher realize the teaching relationship is constantly changing. Teaching is dynamic, not static. Even if a teacher can assess a student's learning style (whatever definition we subsequently agree upon), the teacher ought not to believe that the student's learning style of today is the learning style of next week. Granted that students are not in total flux but have some degree of stability from day to day, it still is wrong to accept learning style as a static phenomenon. Thus, all educators, but especially current LSBE advocates, must be careful not to view scores on learning style preference or description tests as being final and unchangeable. Indeed, learning style, which is part of the student element in the teaching relationship, is not an enduring intractable trait but a malleable trait (Davidman, 1981). The student's learning is always changing and always adapting to the four other elements of the teaching relationship.

Third, we recommend that when the teacher looks at the student to diagnose personal characteristics such as "learning style" and personality type, the teacher should conceive of learning style as referring to *actions* of the student rather than ability of the student. We also recommend a multidimensional perspective (cognitive, affective, and physiological) on student action. Therefore, we recommend that teachers tentatively accept Keefe's comprehensive definition (see above) and that they use an informal approach to determining a student's learning style. The informal diagnostic approach, which gets its information from student feedback and keen observation, will permit teachers to operationalize the definition of learning style with ease and without waiting for a perfect formal diagnostic instrument.

Two educators, Hunter and Hunt, offer guidance here. Hunter makes a strong case for diagnostic teaching and advocates informal diagnosis, in contrast to formal and inferential diagnosis, as the "heart and core of diagnostic teaching" (Hunter, 1979). Informal diagnosis promotes the idea that learning style is changing although it might superficially appear to be static. Informal diagnosis yields a readily available description or classification of the student's learning style and allows the teacher to consider the student as he/she is at the present time rather than at some specified earlier testing time. Hunt shows that classroom teachers

can and do diagnose their students' learning styles as they teach, informally using concepts and psychological theories which are similar to those utilized in formal diagnostic methods. Teachers informally "read" the teaching situation's elements. In reaction, they adapt and "flex" in order to create conditions which maximize learning (Hunt, 1980, 1981).

Fourth, we recommend that teachers accept a concept of learning which is broader than cognitive achievement as determined by a numerical score on a paper and pencil test. The teacher's aim is to teach knowledge in terms of information (for example, Copenhagen is the capital and main city of Denmark), concepts (for example, momentum, scarcity of resources, and harmony), generalizations (for example, hot water dissolves salt faster than cold water), and laws, principles, and theories (for example, Boyle's law that the volume of a gas kept at a constant temperature varies inversely with the pressure; Darwin's theory of evolution). Teachers also aim to teach skills such as writing, drawing one-point perspective, measuring liquid in a test tube, reading, harmonizing, playing a musical instrument (e.g., a recorder), and somersaulting. Teachers aim to teach values such as justice, cooperation, equality, respect, humility, loyalty, and compassion.

The task of teachers is complex and diverse. What the student learns from a teacher goes far beyond our present ability to measure. The student learns humanness as he/she blends the knowledge, skills, and values taught by teachers, explicitly or implicitly. What the student learns does not remain separated into neat cubbyholes but becomes an integrated whole. The student learns as he/she experiences, reflects individually and with the aid of teachers, and reconstructs experience, so it is impossible to identify one bit of learning from the other (Dewey, 1897/1959; 1938). This broader concept of learning is not presently (will it ever be?) compatible with precise measurement. Yet teachers—and the learning psychologist—are in peril if they neglect this broader concept in favor of a restricted cognitive concept of learning which can be quantified.

Fifth, we recommend that teachers recognize and attend to the only actions which they can control—their own. No matter what the student's learning style and no matter what the subject matter, teachers can only control their own actions. They can suggest, guide, and direct students, but they cannot make students learn and act in specific ways. No one can do so. Everyone is in the same boat with teachers—parent, doctor, minister, neighbor, psychotherapist. Teaching requires action by the teacher, and the teacher is responsible for that action whether it is considered initiating action toward the student or reactive action based on the student's initiative. (Perhaps this dichotomy between initiative and reactive action is unrealistic because when two people have a series of reciprocal interactions over a period of time it may be impossible to distinguish what is initiation from what is reaction. Is not what is often called initiation nothing more than a delayed reaction to a previous action?)

By attending to their own actions teachers will focus on what they can control. Teachers will come to accept that there are a variety of teaching models—or strategies—which they can learn and employ in forms adapted to their particular combination of the five teaching elements. The learning, practicing, and utilizing of a variety of teaching strategies will give teachers a sense of efficacy in the classroom. Being knowledgeable and skillful regarding their own actions—what they do, control, and are responsible for—is a requisite for teachers being able to match learning styles with teaching styles. Or, to use Hunt's words, to "read" and to "flex" regarding the teaching situation it is necessary to know intensively various teaching strategies and also a host of facilitative teaching tactics.

In this regard we recommend that teachers attend to the literature on teaching and become students of teaching. They can study the strategies and tactics of teaching set forth by such people as Socrates, Dewey, Herbart, Smith, Ausubel, Bruner, Taba, and a host of others (Joyce & Weil, 1980; Hyman, 1974; 1979; 1980; 1982a; 1982b). They can read journals such as this one which feature articles on teaching. They can attend workshops which encourage and facilitate the improvement of their own knowledge and skills, as well as the re-examination of their own values. They can form mutual aid clusters to provide on-the-job feedback when they match/adapt teaching styles to learning styles and to the time and environmental contexts.

Sixth, we recommend that teachers drop their unilateral approach to influencing student action and accept an approach which rests on mutuality, jointness of purpose, and bilateralism. We oppose the unilateral diagnostic procedure which is now utilized in attempts to match learning style with teaching style. As discussed earlier, the current learning style/ teaching style paradigm is a specific instance of Model I behavior described by Argyris. It is one that we recommend avoiding because it serves only to accomplish the exact opposite of the desired aims of our schools. Instead of Model I's negative consequences which include lack of trust, low freedom of choice, manipulation, and dependency, the consequences we want to develop include trust and trustworthiness, high freedom of choice, collaboration, and independence, along with the capacity to make intelligent decisions (See Hyman, 1974, Chapter 1; Scheffler, 1958).

Teachers need not continue their unilateral approach. With a bilateral approach the determination of learning styles and matching teaching styles can be a learning experience for both student and teacher. It can be positive and yield growth without ending up with the negative consequences of Model I. The key lies in striving toward utilizing four Model II action strategies: (1) "design situations or environments where participants can be origins and can experience high personal causation (psychological success, confirmation, essentiality)"; (2) "tasks is [sic] controlled jointly"; (3) "protection of self is a joint enterprise and oriented toward growth (speak in directly observable categories, seek to reduce blindness about own inconsistency and incongruity)"; and (4) "bilateral protection of others" (Argyris & Schön, 1974, p. 87).

The consequences of Model II behavior are quite different from Model I's. These Model II consequences are the ones we teachers desire.

When people act according to the four Model II action strategies,

> . . . others will tend to see them as minimally defensive and open to learning, as facilitators, collaborators, and people who hold their theories-in-use firmly (because they are internally committed to them but are equally committed to having them confronted and tested). Defensiveness in interpersonal and group relationships will tend to decrease, and people will tend to help others, have more open discussions, exhibit reciprocity, and feel free to explore different views and express risky ideas. Moreover, group norms will tend away from defensiveness and toward growth and double-loop learning; for example, trust, individuality, power-sharing, and cooperation will tend to become norms, with competition being confronted when it becomes dysfunctional. As these norms are emphasized, authenticity, autonomy, and internal commitment will tend to increase. (Argyris & Schön, 1974, p. 91)

This picture is desirable but most difficult to put into practice. Argyris admits that we currently know "pitifully little" about designing learning environments based on Model II (Argyris & Schön, 1974, p. 181). Indeed, often teachers believe they are creating an alternative to their current Model I school programs only to realize all too late that they are merely perpetuating their Model I failures (Argyris, 1974). Model II with its governing variables and action strategies is desirable but perhaps beyond our reach today in our society.

However, we believe there is a middle ground between the unacceptable Model I and the apparently utopian Model II. This middle ground, the Transition Model, is within our reach. It allows and encourages us to strive toward the ideal Model II. It guides us in creating environments conducive to developing "individual awareness and growth that lead to the development of new behavioral competence" (Argyris, 1974, p. 96). Such an approach and striving are very different from the unilaterial LSBE paradigm which employs a familiar medical metaphor: teacher administers the learning style test, diagnoses the test results, prescribes the current teaching style for the "patient," and renders a prognosis for the parents and school officials.

In the bilateral transition Model the teacher is a person who shares leadership, encourages the students to speak out, and feels successful as teacher once the students express themselves as individuals. The students help diagnose their own learning style, help determine the appropriate teaching style, and at times even confront the teacher regarding the teaching situation's five essential elements. The teacher does not act unilaterally, does not define goals unilaterally, and does not impose ideas and values unilaterally.

We recognize that the six recommendations require a different type of preservice and inservice program. For an illustration of change we will not refer to the vast literature calling for the ideal reform of teacher education. Rather, we will refer only to what is already in place in one preservice program as one possible step in the implementation of the Transition Model. In the student teaching seminars at the University of Wisconsin five themes form the essential core of the discussions:

1. helping students to take a critical approach in the examination of educational issues or classroom problems;
2. helping students to see beyond conventional thought about classroom practice;
3. helping students to develop a sense of the history of their own particular classroom and to examine the rationales underlying classroom and school regularities;
4. helping students to examine their own assumptions and biases and how these affect their classroom practice; and
5. helping students to examine critically the processes of their own socialization as teachers (Zeichner, 1981–1982, p. 12).

We believe that treatment of these five themes sensitizes the students to the problems of unilateral decision making in our schools, to the issues surrounding currently used paradigms, and to the need for alternative assumptions, strategies, and consequences. Such a seminar can lead to a solution, at least in part, because it guides the students toward a solid examination of the problems teachers face. We believe it is a step in the right direction.

In summary, the issue of matching teaching styles with learning styles is not as simple as some LSBE advocates would have us believe. However, the LSBE advocates are correct in that the learning style issue is important for all teachers concerned with the proper education of their students. For this reason the current learning style "jug" demands that we look into it to see what is there. We have looked, found the "wine" in the "jug" inadequate, and made six recommendations which we believe will yield an acceptable way to match learning styles with teaching styles.

REFERENCES

Argyris, C. (1974). Alternative schools: A behavioral analysis, *Teachers College Record, 75,* 429–452.

Argyris, C., & Schön, D. A. (1974). *Theory in practice: Increasing professional effectiveness.* San Francisco: Jossey-Bass.

Davidman, L. (1981). Learning style: The myth, the panacea, the wisdom. *Phi Delta Kappan, 62,* 641–645.

Dewey, J. (1938). *Experience and education.* New York: Macmillan.

Dewey, J. (1959). My pedagogic creed, reprinted in M. S. Dworkin (Ed.), *Dewey on education.* New York: Teachers College Press, 19–32. (Original work published 1897).

Dunn, R. (1983). Can students identify their own learning styles? *Educational Leadership, 40,* 60–62.

Dunn, R. S., & Dunn, K. J. (1979). Learning styles: Should they, can they, be matched? *Educational Leadership, 36,* 238–244.

Dunn, R., Dunn, K., & Price, G. E. (1979). Identifying individual learning styles. In *Student learning styles: Diagnosing and prescribing programs.* Reston, VA: National Association of Secondary School Principals, 39–54.

Gregorc, A. F. (1979). Learning/teaching styles: Their nature and effects. In *Student learning styles: Diagnosing and prescribing programs.* Reston, VA: National Association of Secondary School Principals. 19–26.

Haubrich, V. F. (ed.). (1971). *Freedom, bureaucracy, and schooling.* 1971 Yearbook. Washington, D.C.: Association for Supervision and Curriculum Development.

Hunt, D. E. (1977–1978). Conceptual level theory and research as guides to educational practice. *Interchange, 8,* 78–90.

Hunt, D. E. (1979). Learning style and student needs: An introduction to conceptual level. In *Student learning styles: Diagnosing and prescribing programs.* Reston, VA: National Association of Secondary School Principals. 27–38.

Hunt, D. E. (1980). How to be your own best theorist. *Theory into Practice, 19,* 287–293.

Hunt, D. E. (1981). Teacher's adaptation: "Reading" and "flexing" to students. In B. R. Joyce, C. C. Brown, & L. Peck (Eds.), *Flexibility in teaching.* New York: Longman, 59–71.

Hunter, M. (1979). Diagnostic teaching. *The Elementary School Journal, 80,* 41–46.

Hyman, R. T. (1974). *Ways of teaching.* Philadelphia: J. B. Lippincott.

Hyman, R. T. (1979). *Strategic questioning.* Englewood Cliffs, N.J.: Prentice-Hall.

Hyman, R. T. (1980). Fielding student questions. *Theory into Practice, 19,* 38–44.

Hyman, R. T. (1982a). Questioning for improved reading. *Educational Leadership, 39,* 307–309.

Hyman, R. T. (1982b). *Questioning in the college classroom,* Idea Paper No. 8. Center for Faculty Evaluation and Development, Kansas State University.

Joyce, B. & Weil, M. (1980). *Models of teaching.* Englewood Cliffs, N.J.: Prentice-Hall.

Keefe, J. W. (1979). Learning style: An overview. In *Student learning styles: Diagnosing and prescribing programs.* Reston, VA: National Association of Secondary School Principals. 1–17.

Scheffler, I. (1958). Justifying curriculum decisions. *The School Review, 66,* 461–472.

Smith, B. O. (1963). A conceptual analysis of instructional behavior. *The Journal of Teacher Education, 14,* 294–298.

Zeichner, K. M. (1981–1982). Reflective teaching and field-based experience in teacher education. *Interchange, 12,* 1–22.

REFERENCES AND ADDITIONAL READINGS FOR UNIT 2

Do Learning Theories Aid Classroom Practice?

Ausubel, D. P. *Learning Theory and Classroom Practice*. Toronto, Ont.: Ontario Institute for Studies in Education, 1967.

Bandura, A. "Behavior Theory and the Models of Man." *American Psychologist*, 29 (1974): 859–869.

Bruner, J. "Models of the Learner," *Educational Researcher*," 14, No. 6 (June/July 1985): 5–8.

Gagné, E. D. *The Cognitive Psychology of School Learning*. Boston: Little, Brown, in press.

Gagné, R. M. *Conditions of Learning*, 3rd ed. New York: Holt, Rinehart and Winston, 1977.

Hebron, C. d. W. "Can We Make Sense of Learning Theory?" *Higher Education*, 12, No. 4 (August 1983): 443–462.

Hilgard, E. R. and Bower, G. H. *Theories of Learning*, 5th ed. Englewood Cliffs, N. J.: Prentice–Hall, 1981.

Hilgard, E. R., ed. *Theories of Learning and Instruction*. Sixty-third Yearbook of the National Society for the Study of Education, Part 1. Chicago: University of Chicago Press, 1964.

Joyce, B. R., & Weil, M. *Models of Teaching*, 2nd ed. Englewood Cliffs, N. J.: Prentice–Hall, 1981.

Skinner, B. F. "The Science of Learning and the Art of Teaching." *Harvard Educational Review* 24 (1954): 86–97.

Wittrock, M. C. "Learning as a Generative Process." *Educational Psychologist* 11 (1974): 87–95.

The Improvement of Instruction: Suggestions from Behavioral and Cognitive Science

Anderson, J. R. *Cognitive Psychology and Its Implications*. San Francisco: W. H. Freeman, 1980.

Breuning, S. Precision Teaching in the High School Classroom: A Necessary Step Towards Maximizing Teacher Effectiveness and Student Performance. *American Educational Research Journal* 25 (1978): 125–140.

Brophy, J. E. "Precision Teaching in High School Classroom: A Commentary. *American Educational Research Journal* 15, No. 1 (1978): 141–144.

Brophy, J. E. "If Only It Were True: A Response to

Greer." *Educational Researcher* 12, No. 1 (January 1983): 10–12.

Bruner, J. "Models of the Learner." *Educational Researcher* 14, No. 6 (June/July 1985): 5–8.

Gage, N. L. *The Scientific Bases of the Art of Teaching*. New York: Teachers College Press, 1978.

Gagné, E. D. *The Cognitive Psychology of School Learning*. Boston: Little, Brown, in press.

Greeno, J. G. "Understanding and Procedural Knowledge in Mathematics Instruction." *Educational Psychologist* 12 (1978): 262–283,.

Greer, R. D. "Contingencies of the Science and Technology of Teaching and Prebehavioristic Research Practices in Education." *Educational Researcher* 12, No. 1 (January 1983): 3–9.

National Commission on Excellence in Education. *A Nation at Risk: The Imperative for Educational Reform*. Washington, D.C.: U.S. Department of Education, 1983.

Skinner, B. F. *The Technology of Instruction*. New York: Appleton-Century-Crofts, 1968.

Winne, P. H. "Steps Toward Promoting Cognitive Achievements." *Elementary School Journal* 85, No. 5 (May 1985): 673–693.

Should We Teach for Thinking, about Thinking, or of Thinking?

Beyer, B. K. "Improving Thinking Skills—Defining the Problem." *Phi Delta Kappan* 65, N. 7 (March 1984): 486–490.

Beyer, B. K. "Improving Thinking Skills—Practical Approaches." *Phi Delta Kappan* 65, No. 8 (April 1984): 556–560.

Bondy, E. "Thinking about Thinking." *Childhood Education* 60 (March/April 1984): 234–238.

deBono, E. "Critical Thinking Is Not Enough." *Educational Leadership* 42, No. 1 (September 1984): 16–17.

Getzels, J. W. "Problem-Finding and the Inventiveness of Solutions." *Journal of Creative Behavior* 9, No. 1 (October 1975): 12–18.

Lipman, M. "The Cultivation of Reasoning Through

Philosophy." *Educational Leadership* 42, No. 1 (September 1984): 51–56.

Nickerson, R. S. "Kinds of Thinking Taught in Current Programs." *Educational Leadership* 42, No. 1 (September 1984): 26–36.

Sadler, W. A., Jr. and Whimbey, A. "A Holistic Approach to Improving Teaching Skills." *Phi Delta Kappan* 67, No. 3 (November 1985): 199–203.

Sigel, I. E. "A Constructivist Perspective for Teaching Thinking." *Educational Leadership* 42, No. 3 (November 1984): 18–21.

Sternberg, R. J. "Teaching Critical Thinking, Part 1: Are We Making Critical Mistakes? *Phi Delta Kappan* 67, No. 3 (November 1983): 194–198.

Sternberg, R. J. "Teaching Critical Thinking, Part 2: Possible Solutions." *Phi Delta Kappan* 67. No. 4 (December 1985): 277–280.

Weinstein, C. E. and Mayer, R. E. "The Teaching of Learning Strategies." In M. C. Wittrock, ed. *Handbook of Research on Teaching*. 3rd ed. New York: Macmillan, in press.

Is Direct Instruction More Effective Than Methods That Give Students More Freedom?

Anderson, Linda, and Scott, C. "The Relationship Among Teaching Methods, Student Characteristics, and Student Involvement in Learning." *Journal of Teacher Education* 29 (1978): 52–57.

Bennett, N. with Jordan, J.; Long, G.; and Wade, B. *Teaching Styles and Pupil Progress*. Cambridge, Mass.: Harvard University Press, 1976.

Brophy, J. E. "Advances in Teacher Research." *The Journal of Classroom Interaction* 15 (1979): 1–7.

Clark, C. M. "Five Faces of Research on Teaching." *Educational Leadership* 37 (October 1979): 29–32.

Good, T. L. "Teacher Effectiveness in the Elementary School." *Journal of Teacher Education* 30 (March–April 1979) 52–64.

Horowitz, R. "Effects of the Open Classroom." In *Educational Environments and Effects: Evaluation, Policy, and Productivity*, ed. by H. J. Walberg. Berkeley, Cal.: McCutchan, 1979, Ch. 14.

McCabe, J. and Crozier, J. "The Open Classroom is Alive and Well." *Principal* 64 (November 84): 48–49.

McFaul, S. A. "An Examination of Direct Instruction." *Educational Leadership* 40, 7 (April 1983): 67–69.

Peterson, P. L. "Direct Instruction: Effective for What

and for Whom?" *Educational Leadership* 37 (October 1979): 46–48.

Peterson, P. L. and Swing, S. R. "Beyond Time on Task: Students' Reports of Their Thought Processes During Classroom Instruction." *The Elementary School Journal* 82, No. 5 (1982): 481–491.

Mastery Learning: Effective for Whom?

Arlin, M. "Time, Equality and Mastery Learning." *Review of Educational Research*, 54 (1984): 65–87.

Arlin, M. and Webster, J. "Time Costs of Mastery Learning." *Journal of Educational Psychology* 75 (1983): 187–195.

Block, J. H. "Belief Systems and Mastery Learning." *Outcomes* 4, No. 2 (Winter 1985): 3–13.

Block, J. H. "Promoting Excellence Through Mastery Learning." *Theory into Practice* XIX, No. 1 (1980): 66–74.

Block, J. H. "Making School Learning Activities More Playlike: Flow and Mastery Learning." *Elementary School Journal* 85, No. 1 (September, 1984): 65–75.

Block, J. H. and Anderson, L. *Mastery Learning and Classroom Instruction*. New York: Macmillan, 1975.

Block, J. H. and Burns, R. "Mastery Learning." In *Review of Research in Education*. L. Shulman ed. Vol. 4. Itasca, Ill.: Peacock, 1976.

Bloom, B. S. "Recent Developments in Mastery Learning." *Educational Psychologist* 10 (Spring 1973): 53–57.

Carroll, J. B. "A Model of School Learning." *Teachers College Record* 64 (1963): 723–733.

Cronbach, L. J. "Comments on Mastery Learning and its Implications for Curriculum Development." In *Confronting Curriculum Reform*, ed. E. W. Eisner. Boston: Little, Brown and Company, 1971.

Gettinger, M. G. "Individual Differences in Time Needed for Learning: A Review of the Literature." *Educational Psychologist* 19, No. 1 (Winter 1984): 15–29.

Laska, J. A. "Mastery Learning, The Basic Principles." *Clearinghouse* 58 (1985): 307–309.

Mueller, D. "Mastery Learning: Partly Boon, Partly Boondoggle." *Teachers College Record* 78 (September 1978): 41–52.

Resnick, L. "Assuming That Everyone Can Learn Everything. Will Some Learn Less?" *School Review* 85 (1977): 445–452.

Alternative Strategies for Modifying Social and Emotional Behavior

Bandura, A. *Principles of Behavior Modification.* New York: Holt, Rinehart, and Winston, 1969, pp. 118–216.

Bandura, A. *Social Learning Theory.* Englewood Cliffs, N. J.: Prentice-Hall, Inc., 1977.

Becker, W.: Thomas, D.: and Carnine, D. *Reducing Behavior Problems: An Operant Conditioning Guide for Teachers.* Urbana, Ill.: ERIC Clearinghouse on Early Childhood Education, National Laboratory on Early Childhood Education, 1969 (ERIC No. D2300).

Christian, B. T. "A Practical Reinforcement Hierarchy for Classroom Behavior Modification." *Psychology in the Schools,* 20, No. 1 (January, 1983): 83–84.

Dowrick, P. W. "Self-Modelling." ed. P. W. Dowrick, and S. J. Biggs. *Using Video: Psychological and Social Applications.* New York: John Wiley, 1983, pp. 105–124.

Gresham, F. M. "Social Skills Training with Handicapped Children: A Review." *Review of Educational Research,* 51, 139–176.

Gresham, F. M. "Utility of Cognitive-Behavioral Procedures for Social Skills Training with Children: A Critical Review." *Journal of Abnormal Child Psychology,* 13, No. 3 (September 1985): 411–423.

Harris, K. R. and Brown, R. D. "Cognitive Behavior Modification and Informed Teacher Treatments for Shy Children." *Journal of Experimental Education,* 50, No. 3 (Spring, 1982): 137–143.

Klein, R. D.; Hapkiewicz, W. G.; and Roden, A. H., eds. *Behavior Modification in Educational Settings.* Springfield, Ill.: Charles C. Thomas, 1973.

Krumboltz, John D., and Deckham-Schoor, Laurie. "Reward Direction, Not Perfection." *Learning* 8 (August/September 1979): 154–159.

Martin, G. and Pear, J. *Behavior Modification: What It Is and How To Do It,* 2nd ed. Englewood Cliffs, N. J.: Prentice-Hall, 1983.

Scriven, M. "The Philosophy of Behavioral Modification." In *Behavioral Modification in Education,* ed. C. E. Thorson. Seventy-second Yearbook of the National Society for the Study of Education, Part 1. Chicago: National Society for the Study of Education, 1973, pp. 442–445.

Shepp, M. S. and Jensen, B. F. "A Comparison of the Treatment Effects of an Operant Strategy, A Cognitive Strategy, and a Combined Approach with a Hyperactive Boy," *School Psychology Review,* 12, No. 2 (Spring 1983): 199–204.

Spivak, G., and Shure, M. *Social Adjustment of Young Children: Cognitive Approach to Solving Real-Life Problems.* San Francisco, Cal.: Jossey-Bass, 1974.

Matching Teaching and Learning Styles

Andrews. J. D. W. "Teaching Format and Student Style: Their Interactive Effects on Learning." *Research in Higher Education* 14 (1981): 161–178.

Davidman, L. "Learning Style: The Myth, The Panacea, The Wisdom," *Phi Delta Kappan* 62, No. 9 (May 1981): 641–645.

Dunn, R. "Learning—A Matter of Style," *Educational Leadership* 36, No. 6 (March 1979): 430–432.

Dunn, R. "Learning Style: State of the Science." *Theory into Practice* XXIII, 1 (Winter 1984): 10–19.

Hunt, D. E. "Learning Style and the Interdependence of Practice and Theory." *Phi Delta Kappan* 62, No. 9 (May 1981): 647.

Friedman, P. and Alley, R. "Learning/Teaching Styles: Applying The Principles." *Theory into Practice* XXIII, 1 (Winter 1984): 77–81.

Guild, P. D. and Garber, S. *Marching to Different Drummers.* Association for Curriculum Development and Supervision, 1986.

Keefe, J. W., ed. *Student Learning Styles: Diagnosing and Prescribing Programs.* Reston: VA: National Association of Secondary School Principals. 1979.

Lindfors, J. W. "How Children Learn or How Teachers Teach? A Professional Confusion." *Language Arts* 61 (October 1984): 600–606.

Messick, S. "The Nature of Cognitive Styles: Problems and Promise for Educational Practice," *Educational Psychologist* 19, No. 2 (Spring 1984): 59–74.

UNIT 3

Measurement and Evaluation of Individual Differences

Stricter Standards for the Nation's Schools

Competency (Certification) Testing for Teachers

Minimum Competency Testing

Norm-Referenced Versus Criterion-Referenced Measurements

The Computer Revolution

Stricter Standards for the Nation's Schools

"Our Nation is at risk. . . . If an unfriendly foreign power had attempted to impose on America the mediocre educational performance that exists today, we might well have viewed it as an act of war." So stated The National Commission on Excellence in Education in *The Nation at Risk* (1983, p. 5). That report was one of the first and most prestigious of a whole series of local, state, and national reports on excellence. Cross has stated that "There were, at last count, about 30 national reports on educational reform, most of which concluded that excellence must be found and returned to the schools. In addition, the 50 states have appointed nearly 300 task forces and have sent them forth in search of excellence" (1984, p. 168).

The first article reprinted below was written by two staff members of the National Commission on Excellence. As they suggest, "excellence costs. But in the long run mediocrity costs far more." The recommendations of the report, briefly summarized in the article, included strengthening the high school graduation requirements; raising college requirements for admission; and devoting significantly more time to learning the "New Basics," through more effective use of the existing school day, a longer school day, or a lengthened school year. The Commission suggested that students in high school should be assigned far more homework, and that schools should strongly consider 7-hour school days, as well as a 200- to 220-day school year. Finally, they made seven recommendations on teaching, each intended to improve the preparation of teachers or to make teaching a more rewarding and respected profession. These included recommending an effective evaluation system of teachers, so there could be differential financial rewards, and development of career ladders for teachers.

Few people object to the abstract notion that we should offer excellence in our educational institutions. However, there are differences of opinion on how to define and achieve excellence. Further, some individuals worry about what the stress on excellence will do to our commitment to equity. Much has been written about these issues. Hacker, in the second article in this section, takes a careful look at four of the many reports by task forces and commissions. He raises the question of whether we really want to try to teach everyone subjects that only some need to know. He suggests that "we have no evidence that factory workers who have taken high school physics are more effective at their jobs or show more concern for the quality of their product." He laments that fantasies many of the critics of education hold which are underpinned by the belief that education "is a subject in which anyone can be an expert."

Our final article in this section is a parady of the recommendations non-teachers make to teachers. Schimmels makes some analogous recommendations to the American automobile industry.

Other educators have also taken issue with the recommendations in *A Nation at Risk* and other similar reports. Ohanian, a third-grade teacher and senior editor of *Learning: The Magazine for Creative Teaching* caustically states that

> The good gray managers of the U.S., the fellows who gave us Wonder Bread, the Pinto, hormone-laden beef wrapped in Styrofoam, and *People* magazine—not to mention acid rain, the Kansas City Hyatt, $495 hammers, and political campaigns—are now loudly screaming that we teachers should mend our slothful ways and get back to excellence. . . . All of this education commission razzle-dazzle is nothing new: it constitutes just one more in a long, histrionic string of repudiations of teacher savvy and sensitivity. When national leaders decide that it's time to find out what's going on in the schools, they convene a panel of auto dealers and their fellow Rotarians. Individually, these folks are undoubtedly witty, astute, and kind to cats. Collectively, they produce a lot of bluster and blunder; their notions of reform are, at best, spongy. They say, in effect, 'I'll huff and I'll puff and I'll blow your schoolhouse excellent.' . . . We are ill-served by cheap shots from the corporate and political remittance men and their consulting mercenaries whose words are akin to a nasty swarm of blood-sucking mosquitoes. Their bites may not kill, but they sure don't help us do our job" (1985, pp. 316 & 319).

Albrecht, a professor of school administration, suggests that *A Nation at Risk* "contains within it the seeds of immense mischief" (1984, p. 684). He quotes a principal who suggested that "We have now found a way to legitimize chasing kids out of school." Others worry that the reforms will either increase dropouts or dilute the curriculum. A task force of The Association for Supervision and Curriculum Development reports that

> As low-achieving students enroll in academic classes they would have preferred to avoid, teachers will be faced with two unattractive options—they can either simplify courses so that a fairly large percentage of students have a reasonable chance to earn credit, or they can maintain standards and hand out discouraging grades to more students (as quoted by Currence, 1985, p. 5).

Obviously the various task force and commissions' reports have been a mixed blessing. On the one hand, they have increased the public's awareness of the importance of education and of some of the problems that come with it. On the other hand, the reports have not always made recommendations that have won the support of professional educators—the group that will eventually need to implement any changes thrust upon them.

Thought Questions

Do *you* believe that our education is so mediocre that the nation is at risk? Support your answer.

Do *you* believe that recommendations for reform, as summarized by Goldberg and Harvey, would result in better education?

Think back to your high school days. If *all* students had been required to take second year algebra, do you think it would have been a watered down course? What if everyone had been required to take physics? Would such requirements be apt to promote excellence in the schools?

Hacker suggests that while the reports "criticize students and teachers, at no point do they hold parents responsible for their children's poor performance. . . ." Goldberg and Harvey state that *A Nation at Risk* "bluntly reminds parents of their responsibility to launch their children into the world with the soundest possible education, coupled with respect for first-rate work." Are these statements factually contradictory?

A Nation at Risk: The Report of the National Commission On Excellence in Education

Milton Goldberg and James Harvey

Two hundred leaders of U.S. education, industry, and government gathered in the White House on April 26 to watch the ceremonial presentation to President Reagan of the report of the National Commission on Excellence in Education. Nearly five months later, the tumultuous reception of the report by the press and the public has yet to subside.

Such magazines as *Time, Newsweek,* and *U.S. News & World Report* have provided detailed coverage of the report, which has also been the focus of extensive discussions on several network television programs, among them "The McNeil-Lehrer Report," "Good Morning America," and "Nightline." Prompted by this publicity, the public demand for the Commission's report has been astonishing. The Government Printing Office, besieged by requests for the report, is now into the fourth printing; at least 200,000 copies of the text have been printed separately by various education publications, and an estimated three million readers have had access to shortened versions of the report in such newspapers as the *Portland Orego-*nian, the *Washington Post,* and the *New York Times.*

The public's response suggests that Secretary of Education Terrel Bell, who created the Commission in 1981, is correct in hailing the report as a possible "turning point" in an era when U.S. schools face "the challenge of the postindustrial age." Bell also vowed not to allow the report "to be remembered as the warning our Nation failed to heed."

If the public response to the report has been remarkable, so are the activities already under way in response to it. The Pennsylvania State Board of Education recently announced its intention to adopt new high school graduation requirements that will triple the amount of science and mathematics required for graduation and that will add computer science as a diploma requirement. Within weeks of the release of the report, the school board in Ypsilanti, Michigan, announced its intention to lengthen the school day for elementary students and to increase high school graduation requirements. The Tulsa, Oklahoma, superintendent published an extensive "Open Letter to the People of Tulsa," outlining the standing of schools in that city with respect to the National Commission's recommendations.

Not since the heady days following the

From *Phi Delta Kappan, 65,* No. 1 (1983): 14–18. Reproduced with permission.

launching of Sputnik I has U.S. education been accorded so much attention. Although the Commission released its report almost five months ago, major U.S. newspapers and network television programs continue to focus on the problems of education. President Reagan has already discussed the report at several regional forums, with other such forums scheduled for early fall. Individual members of the Commission and of the Commission staff continue to be deluged with requests to address meetings and convocations across the nation. Meanwhile, other prestigious individuals and panels have added their voices to the rising chorus of concern about the quality of U.S. schools; these include the Twentieth Century Fund, the College Board, and the Task Force on Education and Economic Growth (chaired by Gov. James Hunt of North Carolina).

The unprecedented attention now being paid to education is evidence of public concern. But this attention also provides—as the president of the American Federation of Teachers, Albert Shanker, pointed out to his constitutents in early July—"unprecedented opportunities" for education in the coming months.

The Imperative for Reform

What has generated all this fuss? The answer is: a deceptively short report to the nation, in which a panel of distinguished Americans warns that the "educational foundations of our society are presently being eroded by a rising tide of mediocrity that threatens our very future as a Nation and a people." Titled *A Nation at Risk: The Imperative for Educational Reform*, this report has sparked a national debate on education that could prove to be seminal to the development of an ethic of excellence in education and in American life.

Commission Aims and Process

That debate was quite consciously sought by members of the Commission, under the lead-

ership of David Gardner, then president of the University of Utah, who has recently assumed the presidency of the University of California. It was Gardner's idea that the report be in the form of an open letter that would, in the words of Commission member Gerald Holton, serve as a "clarion call" to the American public. The call was intended to remind Americans of the importance of education as the foundation of U.S. leadership in change and technical invention and as the source of U.S. prosperity, security, and civility.

The National Commission conducted its work and collected its information in an extraordinarily open manner, which also helped to encourage public response to *A Nation at Risk*. Practically everywhere one turned in the last two years, there was evidence of the Commission at work. Six public hearings and three symposia were held across the U.S., so that administrators, teachers, parents, and others could discuss their perceptions of the problems and accomplishments of American education. Forty papers were commissioned from a variety of experts and presented to the full Commission.

In virtually every city in which the Commission held a meeting or a hearing, the Commission members also visited local schools and corporate training facilities. It has been estimated that, during the 18 months between the first Commission meeting and the release of *A Nation at Risk*, Commission members were involved in a public event somewhere in the U.S. every three weeks. All of this highly visible activity created a national audience for the Commission's work; indeed, we knew several months before the report was issued that the response to it was likely to be unprecedented in education.

The Commission also examined the methods that other distinguished national panels had used to generate public and governmental reactions to their findings. The commissioners learned that the effective reports concentrated on essential messages, described them in clear and unmistakable prose, and drew the public's attention to the national consequences of continuing on with business as usual.

Essential Messages

The first essential message from the National Commission on Excellence in Education is found in the title of the report: the nation is at risk. It is at risk because competitors throughout the world are overtaking our once unchallenged lead in commerce, industry, science, and technological innovation. As the Commission observed, the problem has many causes and dimensions; education is only one of them. But education is the primary factor undergirding our "prosperity, security, and civility."

The Commission is not the first national body to draw attention to the central importance of education to our national well-being. Indeed, in 1980 the President's Commission for a National Agenda for the Eighties reported that "the continued failure of the schools to perform their traditional role adequately . . . may have disastrous consequences for this Nation."

Just as assuredly, the Commission is not the last national body to draw attention to the central importance of education. One week after the release of *A Nation at Risk*, the Twentieth Century Fund Task Force called U.S. schools "the Nation's most important institution for the shaping of future citizens" and warned that "threatened disaster can be averted only if there is a national commitment to excellence in our public schools."

But the Commission may be the first national body to insist—as the essential first premise, not simply as an afterthought— that inattention to the schools puts the very well-being of the Nation at risk.

The second essential message from the Commission is that mediocrity, not excellence, is the norm in American education. *A Nation at Risk* paid tribute to "heroic" examples of educational excellence, but it made clear the fact that, on balance, "a rising tide of mediocrity" threatens to overwhelm the educational foundations of American society. And the consequences of that tide are staggering.

- On 19 international assessments of student achievement, U.S. students never ranked first or second; in fact, when compared only with students from other industrialized nations, U.S. students ranked in last place seven times.
- Some 23 million American adults are functionally illiterate.
- About 13% of U.S. teenagers (and up to 40% of minority adolescents) are functionally illiterate.
- From 1963 to 1980 a virtually unbroken decline took place in average scores on the Scholastic Aptitude Test (SAT).
- Similarly, a dramatic decline took place in the number of students who demonstrate superior achievement on the SAT.
- Between 1975 and 1980 the number of remedial mathematics courses offered in four-year public colleges increased by 72%.
- Only about one-fourth of the recent recruits to the Armed Services were able to read at the ninth-grade level, the minimum necessary to follow safety instructions.

The third essential message from the Commission is that we don't have to put up with this situation. We *can* do better, we *should* do better, and we *must* do better.

That message is found most clearly in a section of the report titled "America Can Do It." This section cites the remarkable successes of the American educational system in responding to past challenges as justification for the Commission's optimism that we can meet the current challenges. The past successes of U.S. education have included:

- the research and training provided by land-grant colleges and universities in the 19th century, which helped us develop our natural resources and the rich agricultural bounty of the American farm;
- the educated workforce that U.S. schools provided from the late 1880s through the mid-20th century, which sealed the success of the Industrial Revolution and provided the margin of victory in two world wars; and
- the schools' role to this very day in transforming vast waves of immigrants into productive citizens.

The message that "America Can Do It" also appears in the letter from Gardner that accompanied the formal submission of the Commission report to Bell. Said Gardner: "The Commission deeply believes that the problems we have discerned in American education can be both understood and corrected if the people of our country, together with those who have public responsibility in the matter, care enough and are courageous enough to do what is required."

The message can be found as well in the first paragraph of the report, which notes that Americans can take "justifiable pride in what our schools and colleges have historically accomplished and contributed to the United States and the well-being of its people." But the Commission's optimism is perhaps most apparent in the recommendations it sets forth in *A Nation at Risk*. These recommendations provide more than a prescription for improving American schooling; they also provide a framework within which parents and educators across the U.S. can consider their own unique situations and then determine for themselves how best to proceed. The elements of this framework—the amount of time devoted to learning, the content to which students are exposed, the expectations we hold for ourselves and our children, the teaching, and the leadership—constitute, in the final analysis, the tools that local districts can use to improve the processes of education.

Recommendations

The Commission made five broad recommendations, each with several implementing recommendations.

Content

The recommendations regarding content were grounded in the Commission's conclusion that secondary school curricula have been homogenized, diluted, and diffused to such an extent that they no longer have a central purpose. According to *A Nation at Risk*, today's U.S. high

schools offer "a cafeteria-style curriculum in which the appetizers and the desserts can easily be mistaken for the main courses."

The Commission recommended that all students seeking a high school diploma be required to lay a foundation in "five new basics" by taking four years of English, three years of mathematics, three years of science, three years of social studies, and one-half year of computer science. Several implementing recommendations suggested the kinds of skills that high school graduates should possess in each of these areas. The implementing recommendations also stressed the desirability of proficiency in a foreign language and stated that the teaching of foreign languages should begin in the elementary grades. In addition, the Commission recommended that the schools offer rigorous coursework in the fine and performing arts and in vocational education; that the elementary curriculum be improved and upgraded; and that such groups as the American Chemical Society and the Modern Language Association continue their efforts to revise, update, improve, and make available new and more diverse curricular materials.

Standards and Expectations

The Commission concluded that we expect far too little of our students and that we get, by and large, exactly what we expect. Evidence of our low expectations is widespread. For example:

- the schools are requiring less and less homework of students;
- two-thirds of the states require only one year of mathematics and one year of science for a high school diploma;
- one-fifth of the four-year public colleges and universities offer open admissions to all graduates of high schools in the state, regardless of the courses they have taken or the grades they have earned; and
- many U.S. colleges and universities reported lowering their admissions requirements during the 1970s.

The Commission recommended that high schools, colleges, and universities adopt more rigorous and measurable standards and higher expectations, both for academic performance and for student conduct, and that four-year colleges and universities raise their requirements for admission. The implementing recommendations focused on improving the reliability of high school grades as indicators of academic achievement, on raising college and university admissions requirements (including the scores required on standardized achievement tests in the five basics), on establishing a nationwide—but not federal—program of achievement testing for students who are passing from one level of schooling to another, on upgrading textbooks, and on the need for new instructional materials that reflect the most current applications of technology.

Time

The members of the National Commission were struck by the fact that many other industrialized nations have much longer school days and far longer school years than does the United States. Because the level of mastery of curriculum content is directly related to the amount of time that students devote to learning, the Commission made a number of recommendations designed to use available time more effectively and to prompt consideration of extending the amount of time available for learning.

The Commission recommended that significantly more time be devoted to learning the "five new basics." This will require more effective use of the existing school day, a longer school day, or a lengthened school year. The implementing recommendations included more homework, the provision of instruction in study and work skills, consideration of a seven-hour school day and of a 200- to 220-day school year, the reduction of disruption, the improvement of classroom management, and stronger policies on school attendance.

Teaching

The Commission concluded that too few academically able students are attracted to teach-

ing; that teacher preparation programs need substantial improvement; that the professional working life of teachers is, on the whole, unacceptable; and that a serious shortage of teachers exists in key fields. The recommendation on teaching has seven parts, quoted here in full:

1. Persons preparing to teach should be required to meet high educational standards, to demonstrate an aptitude for teaching, and to demonstrate competence in an academic discipline. Colleges and universities offering teacher preparation programs should be judged by how well their graduates meet these criteria.

2. Salaries for the teaching profession should be increased and should be professionally competitive, market-sensitive, and performance-based. Salary, promotion, tenure, and retention decisions should be tied to an effective evaluation system that includes peer review so that superior teachers can be rewarded, average ones encouraged, and poor ones either improved or terminated.

3. School boards should adopt an 11-month contract for teachers. This would ensure time for curriculum and professional development, programs for students with special needs, and a more adequate level of teacher compensation.

4. School boards, administrators, and teachers should cooperate to develop career ladders for teachers that distinguish among the beginning instructor, the experienced teacher, and the master teacher.

5. Substantial nonschool personnel resources should be employed to help solve the immediate problem of the shortage of mathematics and science teachers. Qualified individuals, including recent graduates with mathematics and science degrees, graduate students, and industrial and retired scientists, could, with appropriate preparation, immediately begin teaching in these fields. A number of our leading science centers have the capacity to begin educating and retraining teachers immediately. Other areas of critical teacher need, such as English, must also be addressed.

6. Incentives, such as grants and loans, should be made available to attract outstanding stu-

dents to the teaching profession, particularly in those areas of critical shortage.

7. Master teachers should be involved in designing teacher preparation programs and in supervising teachers during their probationary years.

Leadership and Fiscal Support

Finally, the Commission recommended that citizens across the U.S. hold educators and elected officials responsible for providing the leadership necessary to achieve these reforms—and that citizens provide the fiscal support and stability required to bring about the reforms. The implementing recommendations in this area concentrated on the leadership roles of principals and superintendents; on the roles of local, state, and federal governments; and on the need for educators, parents, and public officials to assist in implementing the reforms proposed by the Commission. This section of *A Nation at Risk* concluded with these words: "Excellence costs. But in the long run mediocrity costs far more."

Other Issues

Although the overall response to the Commission's report is gratifying, several of us associated with the report have been disappointed at the scant attention paid to several major themes.

Learning Society

For example, the press has frequently misinterpreted *A Nation at Risk* as an attack on education and educators. Far from it. The report stands instead as an eloquent reaffirmation of education as a key element undergirding our society. Indeed, in light of new developments in computers, miniaturization, robotics, lasers, and other technologies, the report calls for the development of a learning society. The Commission states that:

At the heart of such a society is the commitment to a set of values and to a system of education that affords all members the opportunity to stretch their minds to full capacity, from early childhood through adulthood, learning more as the world itself changes. . . . In our view, formal schooling in youth is the essential foundation for learning throughout one's life. But without life-long learning, one's skills will become rapidly dated.

Excellence

In similar fashion, little comment has been forthcoming about the Commission's careful definition of "excellence" in education, particularly the Commission's view of excellent individual performance. For the individual, the Commission defined excellence as performing on the boundary of individual ability in ways that test and stretch personal limits, both in school and in the workplace.

Implicit in this definition is the notion that each of us can attain individual excellence—although the boundaries that each of us tests and extends will clearly differ. This concept of excellence prompted the Commission to state that "our goal must be to develop the talents of all to their fullest." It also led the Commission to insist that the pursuit of excellence and the pursuit of equity are not incompatible educational goals and that we cannot permit one to yield to the other "either in principle or in practice."

Public Commitment

There has also been little attention given to the Commission's stand that, of all the tools at hand for improving education, "the public's support . . . is the most powerful." On the contrary, when informed of the report's findings and its recommendations, many educators and legislators have asked how these suggested reforms can possibly be funded. In the eyes of many of the commissioners, this response puts the cart before the horse. As one of them said, "If education demonstrates that it is willing to put its house in order, then the public will respond with increased support." As justification for this belief, the Commission cites results of national polls that indicate the public's steadfast regard for education as a major foundation of the nation's strength, the public's conviction that education is important to individual success, and the public's support for rigorous curricular offerings.

But it was toward another facet of the public's support for education that the Commission turned in seeking constructive reform:

> The best term to characterize [this facet] may simply be the honorable word "patriotism." Citizens know intuitively what some of the best economists have shown in their research: that education is one of the chief engines of a society's material well-being. They know, too, that education is the common bond of a pluralistic society and helps tie us to other cultures around the globe. Citizens also know in their bones that the safety of the United States depends principally on the wit, skill, and spirit of a self-confident people, today and tomorrow. . . .
>
> And perhaps more important, citizens know and believe that the meaning of America to the rest of the world must be something better than it seems to many today. Americans like to think of this Nation as the preeminent country for generating the great ideas and material benefits for all mankind. The citizen is dismayed at a steady 15-year decline in industrial productivity, as one great American industry after another falls to world competition. The citizen wants the country to act on the belief, expressed in our hearings and by a large majority in the Gallup Poll, that education should be at the top of the Nation's agenda.

Parents and Students

Finally, although our correspondence provides ample evidence that educators understand the importance of the Commission's message to parents and students, the message has received too little attention. Because the roles of parents and students in the improvement of educational quality are even more important than the responsibilities of teachers, administrators, or legislators, the Commission took the unusual step of addressing these groups directly in its report.

A Nation at Risk bluntly reminds parents of their responsibility to launch their children into the world with the soundest possible edu-

cation, coupled with respect for first-rate work. It also reminds them of their right to demand the best that our schools and colleges can provide and of their obligation to serve as living examples of the kind of excellence the U.S. requires.

Students receive equally forthright advice: "You forfeit your chance for life at its fullest when you withhold your best effort in learning. When you give only the minimum to learning, you receive only the minimum in return. . . . [I]n the end it is *your* work that determines how much and how well you learn."

From Risk to Confidence

Americans have not only lived with change in the past but also welcomed and encouraged it. Faced with the dangers of an uncharted continent, they spanned and mastered it; awed by the vastness of space, they investigated and explored it; perplexed by the mystery of the atom, they plumbed and solved it. Now a new challenge beckons: how to use our enormous educational system to turn to advantage the current risk to our values, our standard of living, and our international security.

The evidence that we can do so successfully is all around us. It can be found in the past successes of American education, from the development of the one-room schoolhouse to the development of our great research universities. It can be found in the attention paid to the Commission's report by the President and the secretary of education, as well as in the high visibility of education as a major issue on the national agenda. It can be found in the spirited debate we are witnessing on the issue of merit pay for teachers, for this issue touches on many of the elements we must address in seeking excellence—merit, reward for performance, evaluation, and the role and status of teaching.

The evidence can be found in the letters that the National Commission has received from students. Predictably, some students have complained about increased homework or a longer school day. One letter writer suggested that

President Reagan contact his junior high school and cancel the book reports that teachers had assigned for the summer vacation. Other letters have been less amusing.

One seventh-grader wrote a six-page letter of despair. Teaching study skills during study hall would be fine, she wrote, "if there was anything to study, and if anybody did any studying. There isn't and they don't." She said she would opt instead for six demanding hours of history, math, composition, foreign languages, geography, literature, and science. "Then my school days would be worth getting up for. To lengthen our existing days would be merely to extend the monotony, boredom, frustration, and agony. . . ."

The evidence that we are up to the challenge is perhaps most apparent in the many schools, districts, and states that have already responded to the Commission's report or have appointed task forces and commissions of their own to chart their next steps. But it is also apparent in corporate and foundation boardrooms, in legislative cloakrooms, in meetings of the Cabinet, and in meetings of learned societies, where discussions of the report, of its implications for the nation, and of what the discussants should do about it are the order of the day.

All of this is as it should be, for it was precisely this kind of discussion, debate, and excitement about education that the Commission set out to provoke. If the level of interest remains high and leads to the kind of positive responses anticipated by the Commission, then we may eventually look back on the release of *A Nation at Risk* as a turning point in American education.

Clearly, the Commission's report has touched that chord in the American consciousness which governs the hopes, aspirations, and apprehensions of Americans about the future well-being of their children, their schools, and their society. The task for all of us now is to take this renewed commitment and dedicate it to the creation of a learning society. That responsibility does not belong solely to any one group. As *A Nation at Risk* concludes:

It is . . . the America of all of us that is at risk; it is to each of us that this imperative is addressed. It is by our willingness to take up the challenge, and our resolve to see it through, that America's place in the world will be either secured or forfeited. Americans have succeeded before, and so we shall again.

Have the Schools Flunked Out?

Andrew Hacker

The past year or so has been one for sounding alarms about schools, mainly by a number of task forces and commissions, titles taken by committees to suggest vital issues are at stake: *A Nation at Risk,* by the National Commission on Excellence in Education; *Action for Excellence,* by the Education Commission of the States; *Making the Grade,* by the Twentieth Century Fund; and *Educating Americans for the 21st Century,* by the National Science Board. Something must be in the air, when four independent panels dealing with education choose "excellence" as their common denominator.

All four reports concentrate on public education, from kindergarten through high school, and call for a more rigorous approach to learning, beginning as early as possible. The reports also share a singleness of purpose. Nowhere is it avowed that learning may be pursued for its own sake, or that there may be reason to esteem a cultivated mind. The stakes are economic, with our living standards in the balance. Yet there remains the question of whether reorganizing the schools will improve our competitive position in the world. And even if such a connection can be shown, we must ask how far we want to recast our assumptions about the aims of education.

The reports also profess a broader goal: excellence for everyone. Of course, this is the American way of discourse. The panelists omit saying that what they are proposing is both unprecedented and radical: As a practical matter, we have never sought to close the gaps between different classes of schools. High-quality schooling, as defined by the educators themselves, at best reaches about a third of young Americans. Nor is this solely a matter of spending money: Expanding the number of people with comparable qualifications can threaten those in comfortable positions.

The reports are highly critical of teachers, especially on grounds of competence, but, curiously, the commissions show no more than passing interest in who our teachers are or why we end up with the ones we do. All the panels say they support across-the-board raises to attract better teachers. At the same time, they do not pursue the matter, doubtless because they realize that raises of $5,000 to $10,000 multiplied would be very costly. So they settle instead for keeping the stars in the system. All the panels favor differentials in pay, presumably based on merit, although none hints at how quality would be rated. Furthermore, there are few signs that the commission members made an effort to find out what goes on in some actual classrooms, though three of the four groups thought to include a teacher.

If the commission members couldn't manage to sit in on some typical classes, the next best thing would have been to examine some of the research done by John Goodlad, whose *A Place Called School* officially appeared at the same time as the task force and commission reports. According to Goodlad's disquieting picture, education, in its essentials, has not changed since it moved indoors. Students sit at desks for five or more hours every day, listening to an adult. The trouble with all that sitting is that most young people don't see the purpose in what they have to learn, or at least in the way it is presented; consequently, the teachers face a form of passive resistance.

As Theodore Sizer's *Horace's Compromise*, also published in the past year, makes clear, the first attribute of a good teacher is to be able to evoke the respect of an assorted group of students. Unfortunately, too many people who take up teaching lack this capacity. None of the commissions confronted this issue, preferring to believe that pupils will learn a lot more if demanding standards are set. They have it the wrong way around. Teachers who are first admired for their personal qualities end up getting better performances, because their students make extra effort.

One sour note runs through all the commission reports. So far as I can ascertain, almost all of the members are in their 40s or older, and they take pains to differentiate themselves from the generation currently in school and recent graduates—in their eyes, largely a lost generation, indulged by their parents and spoon-fed by the schools. Let us assume, however, that many of today's middle-aged Americans—say, those between 45 and 60—went through a more rigorous academic regimen. Has this been an especially able generation? If the United States has "fallen behind" in various fields, they were in or very close to presiding positions. Moreover, except for those who entered technical professions, there are few signs that adults who studied calculus or physics at school can claim the "scientific literacy" they now wish instilled in youngsters.

Still, Scholastic Aptitude Test scores have been declining ever since the baby-boom generation began taking the tests. Equally disturbing, high school graduation rates are actually declining. None of the panels made a serious effort to ascertain why this has been happening. Today's youngsters, however, differ markedly, in character and constitution, from their counterparts in earlier generations. More students in the past tended to acquiesce to authority, and dutifully did their assignments. By and large, they were anxious to become adults, and looked for cues offered by that world. Through the 1950s, students who stuck it out at school performed pretty much as expected. Young people nowadays are less members of their own families than citizens in a nation of their own—that of "youth," a span that runs from about age 12 often into one's 30s. This youthful nation has a language and sensibilities of its own, holding a skeptical view toward adult authority. In a curious way, the reports acknowledge this. While they criticize students and teachers, at no point do they hold parents responsible for their children's poor performance, in what amounts to an admission that parents have little influence over their own offspring. Another dimension of the dropout problem, also ignored by the reports, is that the rate for boys is considerably higher than for girls, with society about to feel the side effects as more women move ahead of men in educational attainment.

Despite the dropout statistics, all four commissions call for mandatory courses considerably more demanding than those required now. Interestingly, none of the reports alludes to an earlier effort of this sort—New Math. Teaching mathematical theory, as New Math required, may have been a fine theory, but in the classrooms it didn't work. Not only could most students not follow what was going on, but the New Math also obstructed learning ordinary arithmetic. Eventually, it was dropped.

Specialized Subjects

Do we really want to try to teach everyone subjects that only some need to know? At this point, we have no evidence that factory workers who have taken high school physics are more effective at their jobs or show more concern for the quality of their product. The supply-side conservative writer George Gilder has pointed out that, for most jobs, "What education is required can be given selectively to motivated workers, who learn rapidly for some clear purpose. Most skills in the United States economy are learned on the job and well under half require the knowledge entailed in a high school diploma." In Gilder's view, a Korean immigrant working by his wits contributes more to the economy than a dozen MBAs. To this it may be added that scientific training is not the only factor in becoming number one. The Japanese turn out well-engineered products, but part of their appeal is that they are also pleasing to behold. The Japanese, moreover, are superb at sales. This does not mean that schools should teach international sales and industrial design. Clever management and the widespread desire to make good are the critical factors in Japanese success. Stressing deficiencies in our schools can deflect attention from shortcomings in areas occupied entirely by adults.

Despite their professions of egalitarianism, all the reports end up hedging their bets. Thus, while *A Nation at Risk* asks that we "demand the best effort and performance from all students, whether they are gifted or less able, affluent or disadvantaged," it does not assume that all will rise to the challenge. Accordingly, the National Commission on Excellence in Education goes on to propose that "placement and grouping . . . should be guided by the academic progress of students." In other words, tracking. And, as a contingency plan, it also suggests "alternative classrooms, programs, and schools" for "continually disruptive students." The only problem is that once pupils are grouped by performance or progress, or segregated in special schools, few in the slow lanes ever manage to catch up.

We also frequently hear of exceptional youngsters who need—and deserve—special educational treatment. But in trying to identify the meritorious at an early age, we too often end up with the precocious, and they are quite a different group—there is no evidence that precocious children as a group go on to contribute more to society than those whose talents emerge later.

Ernest Boyer disputes the view that the schools should be skewed to the supposed needs of the work force. In *High School*, another book of the past year, he asks that we make liberal education a universal goal, and his most emphatic recommendation is that the schools should show students how to write. My own experience has been that writing is often self-taught; if frequent papers are assigned and criticized, however, students become more coherent and emerge with styles of their own. Insofar as this is so, the need is less for brilliant teachers than for reasonably competent ones with time to read those stacks of themes.

Stratified Society

Boyer also holds that "the school program should offer a single track for all students"; he does not, however, tell us how single-track instruction will succeed in schools with youngsters at different levels of preparation. Class segregation is evident in our schools, a fact Boyer does not directly confront. Nevertheless, Boyer's book stands out by trying to define how education can contribute to a more interesting and thoughtful life—and not just a more competitive one.

Apart from a portion of Sizer's *Horace's Compromise,* the books and reports already mentioned avoid discussing private schools. This could be construed as a commitment to public education, or—more likely—an admission that the private schools as a subject are too hot to handle. For example, honesty might require evaluating some religious schools as mediocre. Also, the issue of public aid is one few people wish to raise. But the findings of James Coleman and his associates, in *High School Achievement: Public, Catholic, and Private Schools Compared*, indicate that the low-income parents who apply to Catholic schools have a notably strong desire for something better for their children. Of course, most poor families can hardly afford to send their children to private schools. Indeed, few send their children to "magnet" schools in the public system, or take advantage of voluntary busing programs. None of the books or reports discussed here proposes what might be done for youngsters from low-income homes where adult determination is lacking.

Financial and Moral Support

Taken together, these books and reports devote surprisingly little space to financing their proposals or to potential sources of support—at a time when school-age children and their parents are at an all-time low as a proportion of the total population. Most calls on public funds in the United States today involve adult wants and needs; public education lacks the kind of constituency it had when birthrates were high and schools were linked to social mobility. The last infusion of funds involved special programs for handicapped children. While this was a cause no one could object to, such classes have proved very costly. Another problem is that public enrollments are becoming increasingly nonwhite, with the consequence that some citizens cease identifying with the schools. As matters now stand, I can detect no visible sen-

timent for raising education's share of federal or local outlays. Nor does it seem likely that fears of economic decline will spur support for increasing teachers' salaries in any serious way, or reducing the size of classes or work loads.

The current debate over education, like so many before it, illuminates the symbolic uses of our schools. We project onto them nostalgia for a past that only partially existed, plus blueprints for a future we may not entirely want; and our fantasies about them are underpinned by the belief that here is a subject in which anyone can be an expert. At this point, all we can say with certainty is that no one really knows how far classroom education contributes to the kind of people we ultimately become. But if the schools leave a lot to be desired, the quality of educational commentary has declined even further. We no longer have commanding figures like John Dewey and Robert Hutchins, who, in their different ways tried to create a vision of an educated citizenry whose members would have some chance at something that could be called the good life. That this goal, however nebulous, is all but absent from current books and reports is far more disconcerting than our lag in teaching algorithms to restless teenagers.

An Open Letter to American Industry

Cliff Schimmels

I have an American automobile made in 1979 that has been recalled by the manufacturer five times. Obviously, this machine was engineered, designed, and built by people who are either incompetent, indifferent, or lazy.

Based on this solid evidence, I must assume that the quality of contemporary American industrial workmanship is inferior to that of other nations and poses a serious threat to our national security. In 1955 I bought a new American-made automobile that was never recalled by the manufacturer for any reason. Thus I can only conclude that the quality of workmanship in this country has declined significantly in the last 24 years. In fact, if a foreign power had corrupted any American institution as severely, we would call it an act of war.

The American automobile industry is clearly in need of reform. To assist the corporations in carrying out an effective reform effort, I offer the following list of suggestions.

1. *Longer working hours.* If they can't build a decent car in an eight-hour day, they should work 10 hours.

2. *Shorter vacations.* When workers go on vacation, they forget all about their work. They forget how to run their machines, and they forget which bolt goes where. The first few weeks after vacation are spent in unproductive review.

3. *More homework.* Although workers can't take a whole automobile home every night, they can take minor parts to polish or minute piecework to do. This homework will actually be valuable on several levels. Not only will we get more work done for the same cost (which will lower the price of the automobile), but that homework will also give workers something constructive to do with their time rather than spend it drinking beer and watching television.

4. *Raise standards for salary increases.* In recent years, salary increases have come too easily. We must get back to a system that rewards those workers who work hard and punishes those who don't.

5. *Eliminate frills.* There are absolutely too many frills in the modern factory. Such distractions as coffee breaks, rest breaks, smoke breaks, recreational breaks, parties, and picnics should be eliminated completely. These do not contribute to automobile production. I suspect that some workers come to work only for these frills.

6. *Limit the assignment of special tasks to the best workers only.* Every office and shop has

From *Phi Delta Kappan* 67, No. 2, (1985): 150. Reprinted with permission.

a number of these special jobs. Someone takes care of the flower fund; someone runs the football pool; someone is a union officer. Although I am not opposed to making these little jobs a part of corporate life, we must realize that such activities are extraneous to the company's overall objectives. Consequently, these special tasks should be assigned exclusively to those workers who have earned the right to hold such positions by performing their jobs better than their fellows.

To administer this last suggestion fairly, each company should issue a rating sheet to each employee. This sheet would be signed weekly by the employee's immediate supervisor. If, on any given week, an employee's performance falls below average, he or she will be ineligible to perform special tasks for the next week.

Although by trade I am a schoolteacher who has never had any direct experience in industry, I am a consumer of industrial products. This qualifies me, I believe, to offer these suggestions. I am also available for corporate consulting.

Competency (Certification) Testing for Teachers

Teacher certification tests are not new. They were administered as early as the 18th Century. However, they are currently enjoying a revival. By October of 1983, 28 states had decided to make passing a test one of the requirements for an initial professional teaching certificate. Twelve additional states were contemplating such a teacher competency examination (Lehmann and Phillips, 1985).

The motivating factor behind teacher competency tests is that the public believes that some of our teacher-training institutions have admitted low quality candidates and then have granted diplomas to prospective teachers who are not minimally competent. States have then certified these graduates. The public believes that our colleges and our state certification boards both have failed as gatekeepers. Thus, the very rapid spread of teacher testing programs is politically based and supported by the public. Gallup polls (1984) indicate that 89 percent of the public (and 63 percent of the teachers) believe that teachers "should be required to pass a state board examination to prove their knowledge in the subjects they will teach." About 75% of both teachers and principals also believe new teachers should be tested on their knowledge of teaching methods (Newsnotes, 1984).

The American Federation of Teachers (AFT) has long favored such examinations prior to initial certification:

> "We think it is perfectly appropriate and desirable to test new entrants in the teaching field to ensure that they meet minimum standards" (Shanker & Ward, 1982, p. 8).

Early in the movement to test teachers, The National Education Association (NEA) was opposed to such tests. Writing on behalf of NEA, Hodgkins and McKenna stated that: "We believe that tests . . . are the wrong criteria, at the wrong time, and for the wrong purposes" (1982, p. 11). Recently the NEA has changed its position and currently supports teacher competency tests. At the 1985 convention the NEA delegates called "for 'rigorous' standards for new teachers, including 'valid and unbiased' tests" (A.P., 1985). Thus, although specific tests have been challenged in the courts by those who fail, the wisdom of giving tests to teachers prior to initial certification has come to be generally accepted.

A more current debate is the issue of giving tests to *currently* certified teachers. By the time this book is published there are likely to be at least three states (Arkansas, Georgia, and Texas) that will require currently employed teachers to be tested for recertification. In the first article that follows professors from two states that require such testing describe the rationale behind such testing, and discuss some policy implications for such testing. They suggest that the professionalization of education is at issue.

Although both teacher unions currently favor testing for initial certification, they are opposed to testing currently certified teachers. In the second article Cameron, writing for the NEA, argues that such testing will make "*all* teachers suffer the ignominy of having doubt cast on them and their profession." In the third article Shanker, President of the AFT, supports testing for initial certification but suggests that such testing should be limited to new entrants into the teaching profession.

Thought Questions

In any certification decision, there is a possibility of making two kinds of errors: (1) certifying someone who is incompetent or (2) not certifying someone who is competent. In teacher certification decisions, which of the two errors is more costly?

Data show that a smaller percentage of minority candidates pass teacher certification tests than majority candidates. This may result in fewer minority teachers. Should we lower the standards for minorities? Which would have the more negative impact on children: the lack of minority teachers as role models, or teachers who do not meet minimum qualifications?

Would it be fair to ask a teacher who had been teaching biology for five years to pass a science test that included questions on physics and chemistry in order to be recertified as a "science" teacher? Would it be fair to recertify someone as a "science" teacher if the person had forgotten important subject matter content in physics and chemistry?

Do you believe that certification examinations will increase the public confidence in, and the status of, the teaching profession?

READING 28

Why We Are Testing Teachers: Some Policy Issues

Richard S. Podemski and Cherie K. Lohr

Although the majority of states require some form of testing prospective teachers for the initial teaching certificate, only Arkansas and Texas have required that currently employed teachers be tested for recertification. The Arkansas law was passed as part of a comprehensive educational reform package proposed by Governor Bill Clinton in 1983 that substantially improved educational standards and resulted in the passage of a referendum to dedicate to education revenues from a one percent increase in the state sales tax. HB 72 in Texas also mandates the testing of teachers for recertification, but the state has yet to begin full implementation of the testing provision.

The Arkansas law specifies that all currently certified teachers (including administrators) in the state must pass a basic skills (literacy) test that measures reading, math, and writing competence. In addition, all teachers must pass the NTE specialty area test in their area of certification or successfully complete 6 hours of approved university course work. As a penalty,

the teaching certificates of teachers who do not successfully complete these requirements by 1987, when all of the new education standards become effective, will not be renewed when their certificates would regularly expire. This recertification testing is a "one time only" procedure for currently certified teachers. Newly trained teachers seeking an initial teaching certificate have been required for some time to pass the NTE professional knowledge and specialty area test in their area of certification, but are not required to take the recertification literacy test.

The specially developed literacy test was first administered in March, 1985, to all currently employed teachers in the state. Approximately 25,000 of the more than 29,500 teachers in the state took the literacy test. An estimated 3,000 were officially excused from this administration of the test with the remaining teachers either boycotting the test or deciding not to take it for other reasons. A second administration of the test was given in May, 1985. State Department of Education officials have indicated that teachers who fail the basic skills test will be given opportunities for remediation and may retake the test. Additional administrations of the test will be scheduled until 1987.

Results from the first two administrations

From *Educational Measurement: Issues and Practice* 4 (1985), No. 3, 20–23. Reprinted with permission of the authors and publisher.

indicated that state-wide, approximately 10% of those taking the test failed one or more sections. County-wide percentages of those failing ranged from 2.6% to 34.5% with 20 of the 75 counties in Arkansas having failure rates of 12% or more ("90 pct. pass," 1985).

Without a doubt teacher testing was the most volatile issue before the 1985 session of the Arkansas General Assembly where numerous bills were introduced to eliminate the test, expand the population of educators who must take the test, or substitute in place of the test other forms of district-based personnel evaluation. The Arkansas Educational Association lobbied heavily against the test. On one occasion 3,000 teachers across the state took personal leave to attend a rally in front of the capitol steps, causing several districts near the state capitol to close because insufficient numbers of substitutes could be found. The governor countered this political pressure by indicating that he would veto any attempt to eliminate the test, appealing to citizens to phone their legislators and voice approval for the test. A bill to eliminate the test handily passed the State House of Representatives but was finally defeated in the Senate after several postponements during which the AEA and the governor lobbied heavily to win votes. At test time a projected boycott of over 8,000 teachers did not materialize. However, prior to administration of the test several copies of the test were stolen by individuals who apparently wished to discredit the process.

The purpose of this article is to describe the rationale employed by advocates of teacher testing and discuss some of the policy implications of that position. Most of the examples used are from the Arkansas experience; to date, this is the only state that has fully implemented this form of teacher testing.

Why Are We Testing Teachers?

We believe that at issue here is the professionalization of education. Although teachers are dedicated, relatively well educated individuals who provide a unique social service by most

formal definitions of the term, teaching has not achieved true professional status. Lieberman (1956) discusses several reasons why education has not achieved professional status. First, the teacher's ability to exercise decision-making autonomy is hampered by the external control exerted by boards of education, administrators, and the state. Second, teachers neither individually nor collectively govern and police themselves. Further, he believes that teachers are less willing to accept total responsibility for their decisions—another key characteristic of a profession—because they do not have control over factors affecting those decisions. For similar reasons a report of the American Association of Colleges for Teacher Education (Howsam, Corrigan, Denemark, & Nash, 1976) describes education as a semi-profession.

Forsyth and Danisiewicz (1985) describe the important role played by the public's perception of the abilities and performance of members of an occupation in the professionalization of that occupation. In their view, professionalism is not a status that the members of an occupation can ascribe to themselves, but is an achieved status granted by the public as an indication of respect and trust. Many citizens believe that past trust placed in the educational system has been violated when administrators and teachers have condoned poor teaching performance and refused to fire incompetent teachers. Since marked public dissatisfaction with education and the quality of teaching continues (Gallup Poll, 1984), any attempt to improve the professional status of teachers, as well as aspects of that status such as salary and benefits, must address the issue of public confidence. Regarding testing of prospective teachers Hyman (1984) states:

> The testing of teachers will serve the positive social function of indicating to the public that elected officials, professional educators. . . . and our teacher education departments are responsive to the public will. People will be gratified to know that their voices are heard. Even if it is but a first step toward improvement of our public schools, it is always necessary to take that step (p. 16).

In an address before the 1983 Special Legislative Assembly, Governor Clinton (1983) clearly emphasized this relationship, stating,

> To those who feel insulted by the test, I can only reply that I think it is a small price to pay in exchange for the biggest tax increase for education in Arkansas history and for the contribution the testing process would make in our efforts to restore the teaching profession to the position of public trust and esteem that it deserves (p. 11).

For Clinton, teacher testing is the *quid pro quo* for public support of his educational reform package and more specifically the one percent sales tax increase that was needed to fund those reforms. Citing an opinion poll indicating that 80% of the public favored teacher testing, he threatened to veto attempts to abolish the test and seek repeal of the sales tax increase should the legislature override his veto.

Testing is clearly unpopular with many educators and their professional associations that question the propriety and validity of testing practicing teachers. Their many arguments are dealt with in detail elsewhere in this issue of *EM*. Proponents of testing, however, also have much at stake as the very issue of testing currently practicing teachers raises important professional, ethical, and political issues.

Professional Issues

There has been much confusion about the character and purpose of the Arkansas "teacher test." The basic skills test has been described frequently as a competence test when, if anything, it should be viewed as a *literacy* test in that it assesses basic skills in reading, grammar, mathematics, and composition. Teachers have complained that such a test is not a valid measure of their competence to teach subject matter. The validity of testing teachers in the basic skills is discussed in Popham's article in this issue.

However, the fact that literacy is an important component of general pedagogical competence has not been adequately stressed. The actual failure rate in some counties is substantial enough to indicate a need to be concerned about the literacy of some of Arkansas' teachers.

Current educational reforms as well as a projected increase in the school-age population will soon result in a major shortage of teachers. Texas, for example, projects a shortage of 20,000 teachers within the next 2 years. In addition, state officials project that 5% of the state's teachers will leave teaching rather than take a recertification test and another 5% will fail the test (Bynum, 1984). Testing may help to remove incompetent teachers and/or discourage individuals of lesser ability from becoming teachers, but it may also serve to drive out large numbers of dedicated, competent teachers. The psychological effects of the testing movement on currently employed teachers should not be underestimated. Although many teachers are insulted by the test, others view the test as a necessary rite of passage for the profession. No advantage will be gained if the impending teacher shortage catches policymakers unprepared, forcing districts to use ill prepared, emergency certified teachers to cover classes.

It is possible that school administrators may have more at stake in the testing movement than the teachers themselves. Those who have been responsible for the yearly evaluations of teachers may find their credibility questioned when certain teachers fail the test. The lack of rigorous, comprehensive personnel evaluation systems in schools and the poor training of administrators in curriculum supervision and personnel evaluation have contributed to the current crisis. It is interesting to note that in spite of the fact that personnel evaluation systems in most schools in Arkansas are not sophisticated, the Arkansas Educational Association sponsored legislation that would substitute periodic on-the-job evaluations for the test. Efforts at improving education cannot stop with the testing and remediation of teachers. Improvements in the training, selection, and performance of administrators as well as in the procedures by which they manage the school and judge the performance of others must become a top priority in any reform effort.

Ethical Issues

It is important that competence tests be valid. Most competence tests use knowledge taught in teacher preparation programs as the criteria for validation and hence do not necessarily predict on-the-job success, a fact clearly acknowledged by the Educational Testing Service, which does not recommend that their subject matter tests be used for recertification purposes ("Compentency Tests," 1984). At issue here is the appropriateness of labeling a teacher as incompetent by seemingly invalid means. Few would question the need to get rid of poor teachers; no one is yet completely sure that the test results will identify the teachers who need to be terminated. Follow-up, on-site evaluations may also be needed.

Testing in the basic skills may have a disproportionate effect on minorities. Competence tests when used for initial certification have resulted in few blacks entering the teaching profession. For example, since 1978 only 15% of 1,394 black students attending public institutions in Louisiana who took the NTE achieved a passing score (Kauchak, 1984). Because many states have begun to implement competence tests, it is projected that by 1990 less than 5% of the national teaching force will be represented by blacks and Hispanics (Smith, 1984). Results from the first two administrations of the Arkansas test indicated that failure rates were highest in predominantly black counties ("Blacks' Apparent Higher Rate," 1985). Minorities may claim that the test is discriminatory or that they are victims of past discrimination resulting from poor teacher preparation programs and the lack of improvement opportunities on the job.

Political Issues

Much is at stake politically in the current testing debate. Teachers and their professional associations risk the potential wrath of citizens who view the test as a means of educational reform. Although many teachers throughout Arkansas had threatened to boycott the test ("Test Law Slaps Teachers," 1985), no substantial boycott materialized. Such acts of civil disobedience coupled with indications that some teachers may have reviewed stolen copies of the test in advance may incite public scorn rather than sympathy ("Teacher Testing Troubles," 1985). Further, political attention on the testing issue has so overshadowed other educational reform measures that the image of the entire reform effort may suffer. Clinton has stated that, "It was a 'terrible tragedy' that the focus on teacher testing has detracted from other steps the state has taken to improve education." ("Clash Won," 1985).

Governors such as Clinton also stand to lose political capital should the test prove to be an ineffective means of identifying incompetent teachers or should general educational measures fail to validate the success of the state's reform effort. For example, what gain will have been accomplished if the test fails to identify the teachers that local citizens and educators believe to be incompetent? What will be the effect on public opinion if test scores and other educational indices of student success fail to improve even after supposedly weak teachers have been eliminated? Advocates of the test no doubt believe that the higher instructional standards mandated by the reform measures will themselves bring about academic success and thus also serve to vindicate the role of teacher testing. Yet these reforms are still in progress and hence the "jury is still out" as to their effectiveness.

Probably the most sensitive political issue is the establishment of cut scores for the test. Pugach and Raths (1983) believe that in order for public opinion to be assuaged teacher tests must be perceived as difficult to pass. Public citizens and professional educators were quick to express their indignation when the Arkansas advisory committee on teacher testing recommended passing scores of only 50% for the reading and 60% for the math tests ("Governor On Scores," 1985). Although the State Board of Education finally decided to establish a 70% cut score for both tests, the procedure used was one of political deliberation rather than some other "competence-based" method. It is clear that no one will win if teachers are forced to take a test that is perceived as lacking rigor or too easy to pass.

Ultimately the courts will decide the fate of the testing movement. Clearly the testing of teachers is an educational experiment, the effects and implications of which are not fully known. Individuals who fail the test may claim injury and seek a legal remedy. Teacher professional associations may already be planning test cases to challenge controversial elements of the test ("Won't Suggest Scores," 1985). Because legal remedies can occur only after the fact, any damage done to teachers or the credibility of the profession may be difficult to repair.

We believe that critics of testing have done a disservice to the professionalization of education by focusing on the testing of teachers at the expense of the large issue of educational reform, especially as testing has become a condition for the public's acceptance of educational reform. However, as this article has indicated, the recertification testing of teachers also raises issues with which advocates must deal. Teachers, administrators, and state-level officials must be willing to put the test behind them and get on with the business of reforming education, for that is ultimately what the public will demand.

REFERENCES

Bynum, R. (1984). *Address to the Texas Association of School Administrators and School Boards Meeting.* San Antonio.

Clash won by Clinton on testing. (1985, March 1). *Arkansas Gazette*, p. 9A.

Clinton, B. (1983). *Address Before the Special Session of the Arkansas General Assembly.* Little Rock.

Competency tests raise a storm down south. (1984, April 20). *The New York Times Educational Supplement.* pp. 3538–3539.

Despite blacks' apparent higher rate of test failure, Clinton sees no bias. (1985, July 8). *Arkansas Gazette.* p. 1A.

Forsyth, P. B., & Danisiewicz, T. J. (1985). Toward a theory of professionalization. *Work and Occupations*, 12(1), 59–75.

Gallup, G. H. The 16th annual Gallup poll of the public's attitudes toward the public schools. *Phi Delta Kappan.* 66(1), 23–38.

Governor on scores: Too low. (1985, March 5). *Arkansas Gazette.* pp. 1A, 3A.

Howsam, R. B., Corrigan, D.C., Denemark, G. W., & Nash, R. J. (1976). *Educating a profession.* Wash-

ington, DC: American Association of Colleges for Teacher Education.

Hyman, R. T. (1984). Testing for teacher competence: The logic, the law, and the implications. *Journal of Teacher Education*, 35(20), 14–18.

Kauchak, D. (1984). Testing teachers in Louisiana: A closer look. *Phi Delta Kappan*, 65(9), 626–628.

Lieberman, M. (1956). *Education as a profession.* Englewood Cliffs, NJ: Prentice-Hall.

90 pct. pass basic skills test. (1985, June 27). *Arkansas Gazette*, p. 1A.

Pugach, M. C., & Raths, J. D. (1983). Testing teachers: Analysis and recommendations. *Journal of Teacher Education*, 34(1), 37–43.

Smith, G. P. (1984). The critical issue of excellence and equity in competence testing. *Journal of Teacher Education*, 35(2), 6–9.

Teacher testing troubles legislators. (1985, January 27). *Arkansas Gazette*, p. 17B.

Test law slaps teachers in the face. (1985, January 27). *Arkansas Gazette*, p. 17B.

Won't suggest scores, test faulty. Eilers says (1985, March 7). *Arkansas Gazette*, p. 1A.

The NEA Position on Testing In-Service Teachers

Don Cameron

Until recently, debates over whether or not to test *practicing* teachers were purely intellectual exercises. But testing practicing teachers is no longer a theoretical issue; it has become a reality.

The first mandated testing of in-service teachers took place in Arkansas on March 23, 1985. The Arkansas test represents the first time that a state's practicing teachers have been forced to put their existing jobs on the line over their performance on a single written test. I believe that all of us in education need to look closely at the Arkansas experience. What has happened there is, in a very real sense, a test of whether or not practicing teachers should be tested. Does such testing actually measure competency or improve education? That should be the ultimate question.

It is significant to note that in Arkansas school administrators did not demand a competency test for practicing teachers. Neither did the Arkansas Department of Education. Neither did Arkansas parents. The idea—and

From *Educational Measurement: Issues and Practice* 4 (1985), No. 3, 26–27. Reprinted with permission of the author and publisher.

the impetus—for the teacher-testing program came solely from the state's governor. Only by instituting such a testing program, Arkansas Governor Bill Clinton maintained, could the state rid itself of "incompetent teachers."

Experts testified that the literacy test proposed for Arkansas would not fairly achieve this goal. They pointed out that putting an experienced teacher's professional career in jeopardy on the basis of a one-time test would be an injustice to the teacher and a misuse of a test. Their warnings went unheeded.

The NEA's Arkansas affiliate, the Arkansas Education Association (AEA), fought the literacy test requirement—largely because its members felt insulted by it and considered it a political placebo.

Despite such opposition, the literacy test requirement became law in 1983. In 1984, the Arkansas Department of Education implemented the law by contracting the IOX Assessment Associates in California to develop the test, which came to be known as the Arkansas Educational Skills Assessment, or AESA. This contract was made after Educational Testing Service (ETS), the nation's largest and most respected testing agency, refused to allow the Core Battery of its NTE Programs (formerly National Teacher Examinations) to be used as a make-or-break competency test for Arkansas teachers. ETS believes that veteran teachers seeking recertification should have an alternative to a written test to prove their continuing competence.

Last spring, some 28,000 teachers took the AESA, and 90 percent of them "passed" it. That means that 90 percent met or exceeded the cut scores for each subtest set by the Arkansas State Board of Education: 70% in math and reading and *pass* (on a pass/fail basis) in writing. The remaining educators must pass all three subtests by June 1, 1987, or they will be ineligible for recertification when their current certificates expire.

By test day last March, Arkansas teachers were upset and angry. Staff morale had never been lower. Parents and the public were confused. Students were making wisecracks about teachers. The school environment was not conducive to learning. In that atmosphere, the test became a failure even before the test scores were tabulated. Weeks before the literacy exam actually took place, it was clear the test would exact a negative toll on education in Arkansas.

Some people in Arkansas did not—and do not now—accept that contention. They maintain that by identifying people in the teaching profession who don't pass the test the examination program improves education in Arkansas, no matter how many or how few incompetents are actually identified.

Let me underscore a central point: Many "incompetent" teachers can pass any written exam. Making teachers pass an exam may satisfy a political need, but it is illusory and is no substitute for a comprehensive evaluation procedure that truly identifies incompetent teachers. Further, making *all* teachers suffer the ignominy of having doubt cast on them and their profession because of a misguided effort to identify a few "incompetent" teachers is just plain wrong. Every good teacher knows that you don't punish everyone to get at an unknown culprit in the classroom.

I want to make the NEA's position on this point as plain as it can be. NEA wants a competent teacher in every classroom, without exception, and I wish there were a quality teacher in every American classroom right now.

Professional competence is a vital concern both to the public and today's practicing teachers. NEA believes that the best way to ensure the professional competence of teachers is to make certain that those entering the profession have the knowledge and skills needed to excel. We believe that teachers already in the profession should be evaluated regularly and given opportunities to improve and develop their skills. NEA believes our nation must insist on the highest standards for teacher preparation and practice. These standards should reflect the following five basic preconditions for excellence in teaching:

- Teaching education programs should maintain rigorous admission and graduation requirements.
- Prospective teachers should complete a strong liberal arts curriculum and master an academic major before entering a teacher preparation program.
- Teacher candidates should successfully master the professional knowledge and skills taught in teacher education and apply what they learn in progressively more demanding student teaching experiences.
- Newly credentialed teachers should successfully complete a teaching internship with the support of experienced teachers.
- All practicing teachers should be evaluated at least annually and provided with professional development opportunities.

We in NEA believe that students interested in entering the teaching profession must be prepared for challenging careers. Only the most qualified candidates should be allowed to become teachers. Each prospective teacher should complete a rigorous two-part examination at the end of teacher education. The first part, a written test, would examine students' mastery of the professional knowledge and skills taught in teacher education. All paper-and-pencil tests, of course, have their limitations. Such tests cannot measure a prospective teacher's dedication, integrity, motivation, caring, or sensitivity. For this reason, a written test should be only one criterion for determining a student's readiness to practice the profession. The second part of the examination would measure the knowledge and skills of prospective teachers as demonstrated by their ability to perform effectively in the classroom.

Newly credentialed teachers who have been successful on both parts of the exam should then begin an internship program with the help of experienced classroom teachers. During this period, the prospective teachers' academic preparation, subject matter expertise, and professional skills and knowledge would be evaluated on a continuous basis.

As professionals, teachers have a continuing responsibility to keep up to date in their teaching specialties and to sharpen and improve their skills. NEA believes that all teachers should be evaluated by trained evaluators at least annually throughout their teaching careers. If the evaluation process uncovers weaknesses in a teacher's performance, the teacher should be given an opportunity to make improvements. If, after receiving help, there are still serious deficiencies, that person's employment as a teacher should be terminated with due process.

If our politicians were serious about improving the quality of teaching, they would insist that every school district possess and utilize a real and meaningful system of evaluation. They would insist that school districts stop hiring and coddling incompetent teachers.

As professionals in measurement, many of you who read this article may be asked to design or give advice about systems for testing pre-practitioners or evaluating practicing teachers. I encourage you to develop systems and instruments that give teachers—and administrators, too—useful feedback on how they can do their work more effectively. Let me also encourage you to let legislators and the public know when the testing process is being abused—at the expense of teachers and students who must live with the upheaval that ill advised and simplistic testing procedures inevitably produce.

A National Teacher Examination

Albert Shanker

American education is at a critical crossroads. The direction it takes now will determine its future—and in no small measure the future productivity, competitive edge, and quality of life of our country, as well as our national security. We have had 2 years of national reports on how to improve our schools. While the federal government now seems to march to a different drummer, the states have enacted important measures to require more of students and teachers alike and to provide better funding for elementary and secondary education. Overwhelmingly these actions move in the right direction.

Yet something is missing. We have tiptoed around that something in a "second wave" of education reform that focuses on the central role of teachers in the education of students. We have talked about paying teachers more; about providing scholarships to bright high school students if they promise to teach after college; about the content and quality of teacher education; about career ladders and merit pay schemes; about improving supervi-

sion and creating a more collegial atmosphere in which teachers are empowered to make most of the educational decisions; about how to address the single most frequent teacher complaint—that, like Rodney Dangerfield, they "don't get no respect."

These things are being talked about because knowledgeable people are worried. In the last decade of this century—a short 5 years from now—we will have had to replace half of our existing teachers, those bright young people who came into our schools less because of the attractions of teaching than because of the disincentives of war or discrimination elsewhere, and who are now ready to retire. There are not enough people in the pipeline to replace them, and those who are there are not of the same quality.

We have been thrashing about in the search for "solutions," nagged by the real fear that in the coming time of massive teacher shortage, school districts will do what they have always done with the complicity of states: they will hire uncertified, not fully qualified, perhaps unqualified "temporary" teachers, warm bodies to stand in the front of a classroom only a chapter ahead of the students. Once in, the "temporaries" will become "permanents." And a couple of generations of American kids will grow up without a full understanding or

From *Educational Measurement: Issues and Practice* 4 (1985), No. 3, 28–31. Reprinted with permission of the author and publisher.

appreciation of math or science or a foreign langauge or the English language or a good book or how to think critically. Some kids will slip through the cracks altogether; the dropout problem won't be solved—it will increase. The highly skilled workers our country needs won't be there. Nor will highly skilled teachers for the succeeding generations. We will have another round of education reform reports—and the next set won't be as generous in spreading the blame for the poor quality of our schools; the reform reports of 2003 will focus, with perfect justification, on the poor quality of our teachers.

Disaster looms. It can only be averted if we act now. Many of the items we've been talking about are indeed necessary and overdue. Teacher salaries, for example, are a disgrace from bottom to top, and must be moved up immediately by thousands of dollars at every level if we intend to keep the good teachers we already have in mid-career and attract even average newcomers. But I don't believe we will get what we really want, what our schools really need, and what our kids and our country really deserve unless we in education take a major leap forward to professionalize teaching.

We are not going to get the teachers we need unless we give teachers adequate respect, autonomy, and compensation—unless we treat them as fullfledged professionals. Yet this will not happen unless we are far more selective than we have been about whom we admit to teaching and whom we retain in teaching.

Can we really expect the public to react with outrage every time an uncertified "teacher" is hired to meet a shortage—as it would if license requirements were similarly suspended for "temporary" surgeons or lawyers—if school boards and superintendents and principals say it's perfectly okay? Can we expect taxpayers to pay teachers what they're really worth if every day we in education confirm the insulting adage that "those who can, do—those who can't, teach"? Yet that is the signal we send when we lower standards in every crunch, when the feather-under-the-nose test is the main standard for teacher selection (if it moves, you're hired).

An Exam That Will Challenge the Best and the Brightest

There must be a grueling national (but not governmental) teacher examination devised by a commission of excellent practitioners, leading college presidents, those with experience in the licensure of other genuine professions, and the best research experts we can find, that will inspire fear and loathing among those about to be examined—exactly the way the bar and medical examinations do—and that will, by the very degree of its difficulty, challenge the best and the brightest among us to take it, to pass it, and to teach in our schools. Once they pass such an examination, they may also have sufficient incentive to stay in teaching. The world isn't populated with former doctors and former lawyers as it is with former teachers, partly because teaching up to now has been "easy come, easy go."

There ought to be a national pass/fail cutoff point that is not lowered to accommodate periods of shortage or any other consideration. Vast amounts of pressure must be put on states not to permit school districts to hire anyone who has not met this qualification. To put further pressure on noncomplying districts and states, within a short time after the widespread institution of this examination throughout our country, we in the American Federation of Teachers will not admit to membership any teacher who has not passed the test. We challenge the National Education Association to do likewise.

There is no other way to make teaching a genuine profession, to convince the public to pay teachers what they're worth, to empower teachers to make the educational decisions, to attract the best and the brightest to our ranks, or to ensure high-quality education for the country's children.

Why a National Examination?

Why a *national* examination at a very high level? After all, education is mostly a state responsibility, and states delegate substantial

222 COMPETENCY (CERTIFICATION) TESTING FOR TEACHERS

portions of that responsibility to local school districts.

What's required of prospective teachers varies among the 50 states and 15,000 local school districts, but it's clear that they haven't done the job of assuring teacher quality. Only 29 of the states now require or will require that teachers-to-be pass any kind of examination, and most of these requirements are fairly new. Even in a state with a high level of educational expenditure and achievement like New York, an examination for all new teachers in the state was not required until September 1984. Until then only prospective teachers in the cities of Buffalo and New York took examinations; the remainder of the state's teachers were certified on the basis of their colleges' testimony that they had satisfactorily completed the prescribed coursework.

Second, the examinations have tested not the knowledge and understanding of subject matter or pedagogical skills required to apply different approaches to different learners but the most rudimentary information. When Florida instituted a new teacher examination a couple of years ago, sixth grade students passed with flying colors (the lowest grade was 70, the highest 100), while about 15% of the teacher applicants actually failed. Would we admit doctors to medical practice by testing them at the level of a junior high school biology class? Of course, in a number of states it took great political courage to institute tests for teachers at all. These efforts represent a necessary first step. But stopping there won't professionalize teaching or inspire public confidence in teachers. A much stronger signal is needed.

Third, there is the dismal history of lowering even these minimal requirements when a shortage looms, or when some useful social purpose such as racial balance is to be served. Schools have always been used partly for custodial purposes, and when there are not enough qualified teachers, far better that almost any adult be hired than that students be turned away. (And far better to keep costs down than to raise salaries enough to attract skilled people from other disciplines! Unlike businesses, schools have lacked the external pressure to be market sensitive.) Some of this probably stems from the thinking—widespread among the public—that just about anyone can teach; that public notion is represented a great deal on school boards.

Moreover, the worthwhile effort to recruit more minorities into teaching has resulted in some dilution of testing standards, some lowering of score requirements, because minority candidates—themselves the victims of poorer education in segregated and/or poorly funded schools—do not pass teacher tests at the same rate or level as non-minority candidates. Of course, no one has explained how current generations of minority children are going to get a first-rate education without first-rate teachers, of whatever race or ethnic background, or why it isn't a cruel hoax to inflict less than the best teachers on children who most need the best.

Thus there is no historical reason to trust states or local districts to establish appropriate standards or to maintain them when push comes to shove. We need something that states will first be encouraged and then forced to use, as parents, taxpayers, and businesses indicate their willingness to relocate to places where teachers are acknowledged professionals and schools are doing a great job. We live in a highly mobile society in which the word gets around quickly about preferred places to live, work, and do business. I have few doubts that once an instrument is established and an "American Board of Professional Education" is put in place, with attendant widespread publicity, states will eventually fall into line.

What Should Be Tested?

A tough national teacher examination should consist of at least three parts. The first is the subject matter that a teacher needs, which will vary with the level at which the teacher intends to teach. A person teaching mathematics at the high school level should probably be as steeped in mathematics and as able to demonstrate it as a college professor of the subject. But even in the earliest grades, the motivation of a teacher to teach a child to read is not likely to be very great if that teacher has not experienced the joy of reading great books; motivation of teaching elementary arithmetic is not likely to be very high if at some point the teacher has not experienced the power of that language. Hence a national examination has to measure subject matter knowledge far in excess of what students are expected to learn from the teacher.

Second, the examination should assess what no teacher exam that I know of now tests—the ability to make judgments that would justify instructional decisions. There is a knowledge base in education. It is right to do certain things and wrong to do others. It is even important for prospective teachers to know what is not yet known, just as it is important for a doctor to know about diseases for which we as yet have no cure. According to Linda Darling-Hammond (1984),

> . . . Appropriate teaching techniques must be determined by diagnosing student needs and matching those diverse needs to appropriate methods of instruction. In this context, professional judgment is a pre-requisite for good teaching, because unless students are treated according to their *particular* learning needs, they will be mistreated. Standardized practice is, in essence, malpractice. The need for diagnosis of individual situations and for judgments about appropriate strategies and tactics is what defines a profession.

So the new examination, in addition to testing subject matter knowledge, should measure the ability to apply general principles and research knowledge to specific situations.

Third, the examination should not be considered passed, nor full certification awarded, without successful completion of an internship program. Teaching is the only profession in which a person begins the first day with the same responsibilities he or she will have on the last day, a profession in which, although practice and performance are certainly as important as intellectual knowledge, it is just assumed that someone who has been to college for 4 or 5 years can be thrown into a classroom to sink or swim. An internship of at least one year—perhaps as long as 3 years—should be required for certification.

Who Should Be Tested?

All new teachers should be tested, and as a national examination becomes a barometer of the quality of the people coming into the profession, the pressures will be strong on states and local districts to adhere to the new standard. The question arises, of course, about those already in place, some of whom have gone through some examination process before being hired (the 60,000 teachers in New York City, for example, and all their predecessors for more than half a century have had to pass examinations) and the vast majority to date who have had to meet no such requirements.

Ultimately there is no reason for teachers not to confront the same requirements as other professions. To the extent that we eventually require the relicensing, by examination, of doctors or lawyers (fields where the knowledge base expands and changes far more rapidly than in education as a result of medical advances or court rulings), so should we require the recertification, by examination, of teachers. But it would be wrong to single out teachers for this process.

There is, of course, another consideration. Whereas medical and bar exams are generally accepted by potential and actual practitioners, the result of long institutionalization in our society, many teachers and many communities will need some time to accept what is a fairly revolutionary idea in teaching, especially where the immediate rewards of this rite of passage will be nowhere near, yet, the compensation or prestige of the medical or legal professions. The way to reduce opposition to such an examination, especially given that over the next decade half the teachers in this country will be new teachers, is to limit it to new entrants.

There are one or two states where zealous legislatures already have imposed a testing requirement on existing practitioners. In such instances, common decency requires that they do more than just administer an examination. After all, if the local education agency, with state approval, employed someone 5, 10, or 20 years ago and has rated that person satisfactory over all the years and continued to employ the teacher, the hiring and evaluating hands are not exactly clean. The employee is owed, at minimum, a number of opportunities to pass the examination and some special help in doing so.

Testing existing teachers without the caveats indicated here would send exactly the wrong message to prospective teachers. It would tell them that no matter what entry requirements they meet now, sometime in the future there may be some new requirements imposed that could cost them their jobs. Job security is important to most people; undermining it would surely create another barrier to recruiting good teachers.

Problems and Prospects

For the short haul, a tough national teacher examination might serve to further exacerbate the coming shortage of teachers. But that is precisely why it is being proposed. The lowering of standards, the traditional method of dealing with shortage, cannot be allowed to happen at a time of universal recognition that American public education must be reformed and improved. Indeed, the need to replace the existing crop as teachers retire gives us the opportunity to bring in, over a relatively short period of time, new recruits who will be better than might otherwise be expected. There are other, more sensible ways to deal with shortages.

The most obvious, of course, is to improve pay and working conditions sufficiently to attract those who are not now planning on becoming teachers—the high school seniors and college freshmen who might gravitate toward other careers. The Talented Teacher Act and similar state undertakings to provide scholarship incentives to those promising to teach for some years after graduation are useful moves along these lines.

What else might be done? There are recently retired teachers who might return for a period of time if conditions improved and if there were no pension, tax, or Social Security penal-

ties involved in their doing so. Executives from business and industry with vast experience might be lured into teaching after early retirement—or just as a change of pace—with sufficient incentives. The Harvard Graduate School of Education offers a master's degree program in teaching to just such people in current areas of shortage—math and science, for example. There are other university programs along similar lines that could be expanded over the next few years. The redesign of schools to take advantage of large-group instruction where appropriate, seminar-type study where required, and even independent work by students is another possibility.

The shortage can be dealt with for the near future if imagination and will exist among those in charge of our schools. What will not be capable of solution is the admission to our schools of inadequate, unqualified people who will then remain with us well into the next century.

Another major problem is one raised earlier: What about an even greater underrepresentation of minorities in teaching ranks than now exists? If minority candidates do not pass current examinations at the same rate as nonminorities, won't an even tougher examination exclude even more from teaching? Can we ignore this factor?

No, we can't ignore it, but if we are committed to not lowering standards to meet "the coming crisis in teaching," how can we justify lowering them to meet even a worthwhile social purpose like better integration of the teaching ranks? Don't subaverage minority teachers have the same potentially damaging effect on the education of young people—including minority youngsters—as subaverage nonminority teachers?

The solutions here must be along the same line as those put in place to meet the imminent shortage: better pay and conditions that will lure bright minority students now seeking other professions, just as women are gravitating toward other professions, into teaching; intensive outreach to minority teenagers to identify and attract promising ones to teaching via special help, college scholarships, and the like;

and, most important, making sure the minority young people now in our elementary and secondary schools get the kind of education that will qualify them for good colleges and universities and any work they aspire to afterward. We wouldn't put any child, or ourselves on an airplane with a less than fully qualified, fully trained pilot; why would we put that child into a classroom with a less than excellent teacher?

In teaching, as in everything else, you get what you pay for. I believe the American public will be ready to pay a premium price for good teachers as soon as it can be assured of that quality, for it knows that the future of American education is at stake.

REFERENCES

Darling-Hammond, L. (1984). *Beyond the commission reports/the coming crisis in teaching.* Santa Monica: The Rand Corporation.

Minimum Competency Testing

Minimum competency testing (MCT) is certainly one of the most controversial topics in measurement, and perhaps in all of education, at this time. What is minimum competency testing and why has it caused so much turmoil?

Many definitions of MCT exist. Perkins presents nine in the first article reprinted here, and suggests that there are two distinctive features: (1) the presence of an explicit performance standard; and (2) use of the results to make decisions about individual students. The decisions can be divided into two major classes: (1) Using the outcome to control grade-to-grade promotions; and (2) using the outcome to determine high school graduation (or type of diploma).

By 1984, forty states were actively pursuing some form of minimum competency testing (Anderson & Pipho, 1984). Why the big push for such mandated programs? Basically, because many believe the evidence suggests that (1) the quality of our children's education is deteriorating, and that (2) minimum competency testing will improve educational quality (or reverse the deteriorating process if the first point is true). Both points are debatable.

There is currently much controversy around the nation about whether such state-mandated programs will have positive or negative effects. Perkins summarizes and discusses both the perceived benefits and perceived costs of minimum competency testing.

These are some of the questions which have been discussed:

1. What competencies should be measured?
2. How should they be measured?
3. When should they be measured?
4. How should one set the minimum cutting score?
5. What should be done with those who do not pass?

There is also some debate regarding the legality of witholding diplomas from students who do not pass minimum competency examinations. Citron discusses this briefly in our second article, and a brief update is in order. At the time the article was written, the Fifth Circuit Court of Appeals had remanded the case back to the original trial court. In order to make passing the test a requirement for high school graduation, the state had to show that the MCT that was used accurately reflected what was taught in classrooms in the state. Further, the state was required to show that there were no lingering effects of previous school desegregation. The Federal district court upheld the Florida testing program on both issues (Debra P. v. Turlington, 1983). Thus, in May of 1983, about 1300 high school seniors in Florida did not receive diplomas because they failed the state's minimum competency test (Citron, 1983).

Thought Questions

Do you think the perceived benefits or the perceived costs as listed by Perkins present the more convincing points? Why?

Some people have argued that to deny a high school diploma to a nonreader is like "blaming the victim." Others assert that learning by its very nature cannot be imposed but must be the ultimate responsibility of the student. State and defend your position on this issue.

Setting the minimum cutting score on a minimum competency test is, in the final analysis, an arbitrary decision. What considerations and/or data gathering should precede this decision?

Discuss what you think would be a good procedure for reaching a statewide decision on what content should be placed in a minimum competency test.

What would be some consequences of allowing students unlimited attempts at passing a minimum competency test?

Minimum Competency Testing: What? Why? Why Not?

Marcy R. Perkins

What is Minimum Competency Testing?

"When I use a word," Humpty Dumpty said, in rather a scornful tone, "it means just what I choose it to mean—neither more nor less."

"The question is," said Alice, "whether you can make words mean so many different things."

"The question is," said Humpty Dumpty, "which is to be master—that's all." Lewis Carroll, Through the Looking Glass

If there is one point upon which all testing specialists, program administrators, and educational policymakers agree, it is that there is no consistent terminology for minimum competency testing (MCT) in use in the testing field. "Standards" in some programs can mean "competencies" in others; "competencies" can be synonymous with "competency areas," "objectives," "skill statements," and "performance indicators," to cite only a few terms. With this wealth of terminology, some of which is specific to only a few programs, how then, is minimum competency testing defined?

From *Educational Measurement: Issues and Practice*, 1 (1982), No. 4, 5–9, 26. Reprinted with permission of the author and publisher.

Are there components that are common to all programs?

Table 1 presents the nine definitions of MCT found in the literature. In the first five, there is a clear emphasis on student acquisition of certain minimum skills, and on assessment of that achievement. In the sixth and seventh definitions, potential effects of minimum competency testing, rather than its strict defining characteristics, are delineated. In the last two, the specific components and procedures of MCT programs are presented. Even in these, however, the concept of some kind of a standard is evident.

At least two features appear to be distinctive, and these formed the selection criteria for programs to be included in a nationwide study of MCT programs (Gorth & Perkins, 1979). They are (1) the presence of an explicit standard for determining acceptable performance; and (2) the use of test results to make decisions about individual students.

No other features such as the reasons for initiating a program (e.g., certification of students for graduation, grade promotion decisions, indentification of students in need of remediation), or the grade levels set for testing (e.g., high school grades only, a mix of elementary, junior high and high school grades, ele-

Table 1
Definitions of Minimum Competency Testing Employed in the Field

- Minimum competency testing programs are "organized efforts to make sure public school students are able to demonstrate their mastery of certain *minimum* skills needed to perform tasks they will routinely confront in adult life." (AFSC, 1978).

- Minimum competency tests are constructed to measure the acquisition of competence or skills to or beyond a certain defined standard. (Miller, 1978)

- Minimum competency testing programs are "testing programs which attempt to learn whether each student is at least 'minimally competent' by the time the student graduates from public school." (NSBA, 1978)

- Minimum competency testing is "a certification mechanism whereby a pupil must demonstrate that he/she has mastered certain minimal [sic] skills in order to receive a high school diploma." (Airasian et al., 1978)

- Minimum competency testing is "a device to increase emphasis on the three R's or basics." (Airasian et al., 1978)

- Minimum competency testing is "a mechanism for tightening up promotion requirements; certifying early exit from the school system; holding educators responsible for poor student achievement; increasing the cost-effectiveness of education; identifying and remediating pupils who have learning difficulties; or increasing the public's confidence in the schools and their graduates." (Airasian et al., 1978)

- Nearly all minimum competency testing programs seek "to define minimum learning outcomes for students in a variety of academic areas" and "to insure that these standards are satisfied." (Cohen & Haney, 1978)

- Minimum competency testing involves:

  (1) the use of objective, criterion-referenced competency tests;

  (2) the assessment of reading and computation using "real life" or "life skill" items;

  (3) the requirement of a specified mastery level for high school graduation;

  (4) the early introduction of such testing for purposes of identification and remediation. (Elford, 1977)

- Competency-based education (used in this paper nearly synonymously with minimum competency testing) is "a data-based, adaptive, performance-oriented set of integrated processes that facilitate, measure, record, and certify within the context of flexible time parameters the demonstration of known, explicitly stated, and agreed upon learning outcomes that reflect functioning in life roles." (Spady, 1977)

mentary grades only), were taken into account for selection.

The presence of a standard gives meaning to the concept of pass/fail, and so distinguishes MCT from statewide assessments. In the latter, student achievement may be monitored individually (although many assessments use sampling rather than census testing), but not with respect to any specific standard; that is, a student does not pass or fail the tests. Student results are generally reported according to groups if sampling is used, rather than by individuals. If individual results are reported, they are usually interpreted at the discretion of individual teachers. In minimum competency testing, by contrast, students are required to achieve certain minimum standards of performance; that there are specific consequences to students for meeting or not meeting the standards is the second distinctive feature of MCT.

In existing programs, consequences to students who achieve the minimum standards may range from the receipt of a high school diploma, or certificate of special recognition, to promotion from grade to grade. Consequences for not meeting the standards can include compulsory enrollment in remedial classes, grade retention, or the receipt of a certificate of school attendance instead of a high school diploma. Regardless of the importance of the consequences or whether they are applied for passing versus failing the tests, the fact remains that some kind of consequences are present in programs accepted as minimum competency testing programs.

Minimum competency testing is, without question, one of the most hotly debated subjects in testing today. Proponents make strong claims about its potential benefits, and opponents argue just as strongly about its potentially harmful effects. This article presents major issues for policymakers to consider as they make decisions about whether MCT will serve the particular goals and purposes established for their testing programs. For Policymakers on the point of making a decision about minimum competency testing, weighing its advantages and disadvantages, especially as they relate to a particular program, will help them to reach decisions that are well-informed and reasoned. One of the chief criticisms of MCT programs today concerns the speed with which implementation has been required, a speed which has not always allowed program developers the time to plan as carefully as they would like to plan.

Perceived Benefits of Minimum Competency Testing

Listed in Table 2 are perceived benefits of MCT that have been culled from various sources. Each of these has been cited as a benefit, poten-

tial purpose, or useful effect of minimum competency testing by at least one author in the field. Most have been cited as reasons for implementing MCT either locally or statewide. The benefits appear to fall into a set of types: MCT may (1) restore confidence in the high school diploma, (2) involve the public in education, (3) improve teaching and learning, (4) serve a diagnostic, remedial function, and (5) provide a mechanism of accountability.

Let us consider first the view that minimum competency testing can restore confidence in the high school diploma. It has been apparent for some time that there is widespread public disillusion and dissatisfaction with the quality of American education. Employers complain that applicants with high school diplomas are unable to complete job applications correctly. Colleges and universities complain that they must institute remedial reading classes in order to raise the reading ability of incoming students to levels high enough for college work. The public points to declining test scores as an indication of the inadequate skills that students possess at graduation. In light of this evidence, all segments of the public want to know what a high school diploma actually certifies about the student. And MCT is seen as a way of clearly and precisely demonstrating what students can do and of ensuring that they have those "minimum" skills necessary to function in society (e.g., AFSC, 1978; NSBA, 1978). An auxiliary benefit is that along with a precise definition of skills and a demonstration that students indeed have those skills, will come a greater public confidence in the educational system (e.g., AFSC, 1978: Nickse, 1978).

According to Walker (1978), the main support for MCT has come from the public, and the second category of perceived benefits relates to the involvement of the public in educational goal setting. Proponents of MCT cite as one of its benefits the fact that responsibility for defining the goals and intended outcomes of a high school education is shared by educators and the public (e.g., NSBA, 1978; Nickse, 1978). It is certainly the case that, in most MCT programs, administrators have considered it

Table 2
Perceived Benefits of Minimum Competency Testing

- restores meaning to a high school diploma
- reestablishes public confidence in the schools
- impels us to face squarely the question of "what is a high school education?"
- sets meaningful standards for diploma award and grade promotion
- challenges the validity of using seat time and course credits as basis for certifying student accomplishments
- certifies that students have specific minimum competencies
- involves the public and local educators in defining educational standards and goals
- focuses the resources of a school district on a clear set of goals
- defines more precisely what skills must be taught and learned for students, parents, and teachers
- promotes carefully organized teaching and carefully designed sequential learning
- reemphasizes basic skills instruction
- helps promote competencies of life after school
- broadens educational alternatives and options
- motivates students to master basic reading, mathematics, and writing skills
- stimulates teachers and students to put forth their best efforts
- identifies students lacking basic skills at an early stage
- encourages revision of courses to correct identified skill deficiencies
- ensures that schools help those students who have the greatest educational need
- can bring about cohesiveness in teacher training
- can truly individualize instruction
- shifts priorities from process to product
- holds schools accountable for educational products
- furnishes information to the public about performance of educational institutions
- provides students with an opportunity to remedy the effects of discrimination
- provides greater holding power for students in the senior year
- provides for easier allocation of resources

important to involve representatives from such constituencies as parents, the business community, and outside educational organizations. Frequently, surveys of these groups have also been conducted for the purpose of providing input to the processes of defining and/or validating competencies and setting standards.

The realms of teaching and learning comprise a third area in which its proponents consider that minimum competency testing will have a beneficial impact. Because a legal question may arise as to whether one may test a skill that has not been directly taught, many supporters see MCT as an impetus to a careful examination of the curriculum in light of the goals of the MCT program (e.g., AFSC, 1978). Other MCT advocates believe that a reemphasis of the basic skills is in order and can be accomplished through minimum competency testing (e.g., NSBA, 1978). Still others, who advocate a systems or competency-based approach to education, consider MCT to be the means for restructuring curricula to reflect such an approach. Finally, there are those who feel that MCT will increase the motivational levels of both students and teachers (e.g., NSBA, 1978).

Related to the hope that MCT will help to improve teaching and the curricula is the expectation that it will stimulate the establishment of remedial programs for students shown to be deficient in the basic skills (e.g., NSBA, 1978; Wilson, 1976). In many MCT programs, the major goal of testing is to identify those students who need additional instruction; the intended remedy for deficiency is most often remediation.

Finally, although some MCT programs specifically forbid the use of test results for accountability purposes, accountability is still a live issue in the education field, and MCT is seen as one way of establishing accountability. Students, teachers, and administrators alike can be held accountable for their respective educational responsibilities (e.g., Scott, 1978).

Perceived Costs of Minimum Competency Testing

Enumerated in Table 3 are the perceived disadvantages of MCT commonly cited by opponents of minimum competency testing. Like the perceived benefits, the perceived costs center on MCT's potential effects on a variety of elements, and these effects are seen to be harmful in some way. Once again, the discussion can be facilitated by grouping the points according to the element affected. Therefore, perceived disadvantages may be seen in terms of the potential harmful effects of MCT on (1) various populations of students, (2) the curriculum, (3) teachers and administrators, and (4) control of education.

With respect to its effects on various student populations, there are several criticisms of minimum competency testing. Opponents of MCT believe that underachievers, diagnosed as being "below competency standards," will suffer from further labeling, especially if receiving a standard high school diploma is contingent upon passing a competency test. On the other hand, it is claimed that average students are unrecognized and gifted students go unchallenged in MCT programs (e.g., AFSC, 1978; AASA, 1978). Advocates of racial, ethnic, or special education students assert that competency testing may promote bias against these groups, especially if school systems are believed to be already segregated or discriminatory against these student populations in some other way (Airasian, Pedulla, & Madaus, 1978; Scott, 1978). Finally, minimum competency testing may unfairly place the burden of failure squarely on the student, rather than making failure a shared responsibility of student, teacher, and school system (AFSC, 1978).

"Minimums will become maximums!" is a commonly expressed fear about the effect of minimum competency testing on curriculum. Most educators admit that it is difficult to define "minimum competency," and therefore, critics raise questions about what a diploma can really mean if different definitions of competency are derived by individual local districts (NSBA, 1978). There are also fears that MCT may lead to a narrow and overly limited curriculum because of the emphasis that such programs seem to place on a certain few basic skills and on those skills that lend themselves to definition in measurable terms.

Issues of teacher and school accountability seen by some as beneficial are seen by others as harmful effects of minimum competency testing. Opponents of MCT assert that educators are often held unfairly accountable and that minimum competency testing only intensifies the conflict between "humaneness" and "accountability" in the role of the educator (NSBA, 1978). Furthermore, the initiation of MCT may unfairly place additional burdens on school teachers and administrators in the form of extra record keeping and, in some cases, mandatory curriculum reform

Table 3
Perceived Costs of Minimum Competency Testing

- emphasis on the practical will lead to an erosion of liberal education
- causes less attention to be paid to difficult-to-measure learning outcomes
- promotes teaching to the test
- will be the "deathknell for the inquiry approach to education"
- oversimplifies issues of defining competencies and standards and of granting credentials to students
- promotes confusion as to the meaning of the high school diploma when competency definition is left to local districts
- fails to adequately consider community disagreement over the nature and difficulty of competencies
- will exclude more children from schools and further stigmatize underachievers
- will cause "minimums" to become "maximums," thus failing to provide enough instructional challenge in school
- may unfairly label students and cause more of the "less able" to be retained
- may cause an increase in dropouts, depending on the minimum that is set
- provides no recognition of the "average" student
- fails to provide alternatives that can "inspire" average students to excel in some areas
- ignores the special needs of gifted students, giving them less opportunity to be challenged and to expand their horizons
- may have adverse impact on a student's future career as a result of a withheld diploma
- may promote bias against racial, ethnic, and/or special needs groups
- places the burden of "failure" on the student
- causes educators to be held unfairly accountable
- intensifies the conflict for educators between humaneness and accountability
- increases the record-keeping burden for administrators
- does not assure that students will receive effective remediation
- does not assure that all the perceived needs and benefits will be met and realized
- promotes the power of the state at the expense of local district autonomy
- can be costly, especially where implementation and remediation are concerned

(NSBA, 1978). Already busy school personnel, in other words, will be expected to assume additional roles and tasks with the effect, perhaps, of decreasing their time to produce enriched curricula.

Finally, MCT's effect on control of education is seen to be a disadvantage (Nickse, 1978). In many states, local autonomy is a valued prerogative, and MCT mandated on the state level is seen as an infringement of that prerogative. Local school districts also complain that the states often impose certain requirements and yet give little or no financial or technical support to help the local districts comply. This same argument also can apply at the state level, since in some cases the legislature may enact certain requirements and yet fail to appropriate funds to support compliance.

Criticism of a Different Nature

In addition to the perceived advantages and disadvantages of minimum competency testing enumerated above, writers in the field have offered other criticisms of a somewhat different nature. Those costs and benefits already discussed generally are predicated on the assumptions (1) that the identification and definition of competencies is a straightforward process, and (2) that principles and techniques exist for the construction of reliable and valid test instruments. The other criticisms, by contrast, tend to focus on these two assumptions and also on the actual implementation procedures for minimum competency testing.

With respect to the first assumption, some critics have taken issue with the "seductive nature" of the vocabulary used in minimum competency testing programs. "Undefined, perhaps undefinable terms are used without consideration in discussing MCT programs, and it is only when one thinks through the meaning and application of such terms that the apparent simplicity of MCT is stripped away revealing its true complexity" (Airasian et al., 1978, p. 21). In conferences held for the purpose of aiding participants in the identification of competencies, "some participants were surprised and at times disappointed at the lack of consensus regarding answers to such questions as 'what are the definable skills which adults cannot live without?'" (Miller, 1978, p. 11). Airasian also raises a concern about the particular selection of competencies by suggesting that schools may have promised too much. It is possible, for instance, that schools may have attempted to identify and measure competencies that cannot be achieved by a majority of students, and Airasian asserts that, if this is so, it would be unfair for the schools to expect mastery, and then to penalize students for not achieving it.

Those challenging the second assumption—that adequate technology exists for measuring competency achievement—point to the problems inherent in validating tests of life skills achievement. A danger already mentioned is that of making competencies trivial in order to render them measurable.

Finally, implementation issues that are raised typically revolve around the methods chosen to solve such problems as what grades to assess, when to apply sanctions for passing or failing the tests, what standards to establish, who should be involved in planning the program and how to promote their involvement, how to deal with students whose native language is not English, and how to integrate competency testing with the curriculum and with other forms of testing (Greene, 1979; see also NAESP, 1979).

Conclusion

Beyond, or even with respect to, the considerations for and against minimum competency testing discussed above, "school leaders recognize a diverse and contradictory set of motivations: to cut spending and to raise it, to prove schools good and to prove them bad, to cause curriculum change, to help minorities and to legitimize discrimination" (NSBA, 1973, p. 31). There is an old proverb that says "Where there are two people, there are at least three opinions." That is certainly the case in the controversy over minimum competency testing, and it is also the case that what appears to be an advantage of MCT according to one person is a disadvantage according to another. What can be learned from any discussion then? "The decision of whether or not to implement a minimum competency testing program should involve a weighing of the positive and negative consequences of either decision" (NSBA, 1978, p. 19). Furthermore, it has been urged "that the primary needs people perceive being met by minimal [sic] competency programs be articulated and that these needs be examined in the light of whether such programs, as currently conceived, actually respond to those needs" (Airasian et al., 1978, p. 2).

A number of authors suggest, then, that program developers analyze their own needs, consider both sides of the MCT issue in relation to those needs, and also look into possible alternatives to competency testing for meeting those needs. While many advocate using MCT to diagnose students for remediation, for example, it has been suggested that "teachers have probably already identified these students and their problems" (Elford, 1977, p. 10). In addition, "the effective use of test data already collected would seem the most logical approach to early identification and remediation at this level. Local studies could demonstrate the degree to which the elementary achievement tests predict later success in the high school competency test" (Elford, 1977, pp. 10–11). MCT, in other words, may not be the best method by which to collect diagnostic information about students who need remedial aid.

Finally, some authors have suggested that, in making a decision as to whether to implement minimum competency testing, program developers would do well to consider the lead-in time available. The answers to these questions could determine how feasible minimum competency testing is at a particular time, given that it suits all other needs of the developer.

REFERENCES

Airasian, P., Pedulla, J., & Madaus, G. *Policy issues in minimal competency testing and a comparison of implementation models.* Boston: Heuristics, 1978.

American Association of School Administrators (AASA). *The competency movement: Problems and solutions.* Sacramento, Calif.: Education News Service, 1978.

American Friends Service Committee (AFSC). *A citizen's introduction to minimum competency programs for students.* Columbia, S.C.: Southeastern Public Education Program, 1978.

Cohen, D., & Haney, W. *Minimums, competency testing, and social policy.* Cambridge, Mass.: The Huron Institute, 1978.

Elford, G. *A review of policy issues related to competency testing for high school graduation.* Paper presented at the meeting of the New England Educational Research Organization. Manchester, N.H., May 1977.

Gorth, W. P., & Perkins, M. R. *A study of minimum competency testing programs.* Amherst, Mass.: National Evaluation Systems, 1979.

Greene, L. F. What can minimum competency testing accomplish? *National Elementary Principal,* 1979, *58* (2), 23–24.

Miller, B. S. (Ed.). *Minimum competency testing: A report of four regional conferences.* St. Louis, Mo.: CEMREL, 1978.

National Association of Elementary School Principals (NAESP). Down and out in the classroom: Surviving minimum competency. *National Elementary Principal,* 1979, *58* (2, whole issue).

National School Board Association (NSBA). *Minimum competency. A research report.* (Denver: Author, 1978).

Nickse, R. S. Comments on MCT. *Proceedings of the National Conference on Minimum Competency Testing.* Portland, Ore.: Northwest Regional Educational Laboratory, October 1978.

Spady, W. Competency-based education: A bandwagon in search of a definition. *Educational Researcher,* 1977, *6* (1), 9–14.

Scott, L. *Summary of the Fall 1978 Conference of the National Consortium on Testing.* Cambridge, Mass.: The Huron Institute, November 1978.

Walker, D. F. The impact of MCT on school curricula, teaching, and students' learning. *Proceedings of the National Conference on Minimum Competency Testing.* Portland, Ore.: Northwest Regional Educational Laboratory, October 1978.

Wilson, H. A. *Two sides to test: Positive, negative.* Denver: National Assessment of Educational Progress, June 1976.

Competency Testing: Emerging Principles

Christiane Hyde Citron

The 1970s saw a significant trend toward use of competency testing by schools to help in placement of children or to determine qualifications for graduation. The few cases that have generated court decisions continue to be litigated in the 1980s. Some are on appeal to higher courts, while others are back in trial court for a second round following an appellate court decision. Despite the formative stage of this area of law, at least five legal principles have emerged.

1. *Appropriate use of competency tests is constitutional.* All of the courts reviewing tests acknowledge the usefulness of testing as an educational tool. The courts have recognized that educators need the authority to use appropriate tests to aid in the diagnosis of a child's education needs. Legal problems with competency testing have been more "procedural" than substantive. In the leading case, *Debra P. v. Turlington,* the U.S. Court of Appeals for the Fifth Circuit found that the state's interest in establishing a functional literacy examination was legitimate, so long as the implementation procedure and the test instrument were fair. The court held that the state could require passage of a fair test as a diploma requirement. 644 F.2d 397, 406 (5th Cir. 1981).

2. *There must be adequate notice.* This is perhaps the most well established, as well as the most straight-forward principle to emerge from the judicial decisions thus far. Fair warning and opportunity to prepare for a competency test must be given to students. The Fifth Circuit in *Debra P.,* affirming the district court's ruling on the point, held that Florida's rapidly paced schedule for implementing a test requirement for graduation violated due process of law. Students had only 13 months notice that they would have to pass the State Student Assessment Test in order to get a high school diploma. This was not enough time to permit students to prepare for such a test, in the opinion of the Fifth Circuit. The opinions are reported at 474 F.Supp. 244 (M.D. Fla. 1979), *affirmed in part, vacated and remanded in part,* 644 F.2d 397 (5th Cir. 1981). Other courts have also followed the lead set by *Debra P.* on this point. *Board of Education v. Ambach,* 436 N.Y.S.2d 564 (S.Ct. Albany County 1981). And, in *Anderson v. Banks,* 520 F.Supp. 472 (S.D.Ga. 1981), the court also relied on *Debra P.* for the notice requirement, but distinguished the facts of inadequate notice in *Debra P.* and held sufficient the "twenty-four months [which] passed between the notice and the implementation of the diploma sanction. Remedial courses were provided during the period." 520 F.Supp. at 506.

From *ECS Footnotes* (January 1982). Reprinted with permission of the author.

3. *Competency tests may not carry forward the effects of past racial discrimination.* The Fifth Circuit in *Debra P.* also held that where there is a past history of purposeful discrimination (such as a dual school system), testing must not have a racially discriminatory impact unless the defendants can show that the disproportionate failure rate was due to some factor other than "educational deprivation" stemming from past wrongful policies. 644 F.2d at 408. The trial court in *Debra P.* must now review the evidence and determine whether "vestiges" of past discrimination remain and taint the test. Likewise relying on *Debra P.* as to the vestigial effects of the earlier dual school system, the court in *Anderson* prohibited the imposition of the test until the class of 1983, the first group to begin their schooling after the abolition of the dual system.

In another case concerning discriminatory school policies, the Fifth Circuit recently explained some of the legal principles governing so-called "ability grouping," that is, class placements made on the basis of test scores and school grades—a practice that sometimes also yields racially disparate results. In *Castaneda v. Pickard*, 648 F.2d 989, 994–998 (5th Cir. 1981) the court observed that this kind of "grouping" is "not, per se, unconstitutional." 648 F.2d at 996. The court noted, however, that whenever such practices are questioned, the history of the school system must be considered. Where there has been no prior history of discrimination, or where a sufficient period of time has passed, then ability grouping is permissible "despite segregative effects." 648 F.2d at 996.

The use of standardized test scores for student placement purposes has recently also figured in *Wright v. County School Board of Greensville County,* Civil Action No. 4263 (E.D. Va. 1981), a school desegregation case. Pursuant to a court approved settlement, the school system agreed to eliminate consideration of allegedly nonvalidated standardized test scores in assigning students to classes. However, the settlement agreement also affirmed the school system's right to base class promotion upon demonstrated achievement.

4. *A graduation test must reflect material taught.* Finally, in *Debra P.* the Fifth Circuit ruled that the state must demonstrate that the material on the test was actually taught in the state's classrooms in order to establish the requisite "content validity." This ruling was based on principles of constitutional fairness derived from both the due process and equal protection clauses of the Constitution. This burden of showing content validity exists irrespective of any claims of racial discrimination. The district court must now receive evidence and determine whether the state is able to provide proof of such validity. Unfortunately, the appellate decision offers no advice on how a state is to prove what material was in school curricula. Worse, *Debra P.* seems to require the state to show what was *actually* taught in classrooms.

This part of *Debra P.* appears to have generated considerable controversy even (or, especially) among the judges of the Fifth Circuit. In an unusual development, the panel of three judges who decided *Debra P.* on appeal issued a subsequent opinion clarifying their decision, in response to other Fifth Circuit judges' "concern about the ramifications of the panel opinion," expressed when the full court decided not to review the panel decision. 654 F.2d 1079, 1079 (5th Cir. 1981). Two judges wished to rehear the panel's decision, and dissented from the court's denial of the request for a full court review, heatedly criticizing the decision as intruding on the traditional role of state educators in making academic decisions. The dissenters relied on a principle articulated in an earlier Fifth Circuit decision barring courts from interfering with academic decisions. *Mahavongsanan v. Hall,* 529 F.2d 448 (5th Cir. 1976). The dissenters vehemently objected to the imposition on the state of the burden of proof on the test's academic validity. On this point Judge James C. Hill cited Charles Dickens: "'If the law supposes that,' said Mr. Bumble . . . 'the law is an ass, a idiot.'" 654 F.2d at 1088 n.3 (Hill, J., dissenting).

The judge in *Anderson,* the second competency testing case, seemed obviously reluctant to apply this principle of *Debra P.* In response to *Debra P.,* Judge B. Avant Edenfield reopened the case for further hearings and required Tatnall County school authorities to show that the test covered only material actually taught. Nonetheless, the court indicated its discomfort with *Debra P.'s* imposition on school authorities of the burden of proof of test validity:

> The Court is curious as to whether the ruling in *Debra P.* will mean that in the future any diploma determinative test, perhaps a final exam in senior English, will require this justification by school authorities. (520 F.Supp. at 509 n.11.)

Hearings took place in October 1981 and await further decision by the court.

5. *Section 504 does not prohibit requiring handicapped students to meet valid test requirements in order to receive a regular diploma.* The *Anderson* court also examined the application of Section 504 of the Rehabilitation Act of 1973, and ruled that schools are not required to lower their academic standards in order to accommodate properly classified handicapped students who cannot meet those standards because of their handicap. 520 F.Supp. at 511. *Anderson's* holding concerning the Section 504 claim is consistent with the earlier New York decision in *Board of Education v. Ambach*, cited above. The New York court found no Section 504 violation because students who could not pass the test were therefore not "otherwise qualified." (Persons must be "otherwise qualified" in order to make a Section 504 claim of discrimination on the basis of handicap under *Southeastern Community College v. Davis*, 442 U.S. 397 (1979).) In nevertheless finding inadequate notice had been given to the handicapped children, the *Ambach* court noted that "the time frame for notice to them is much more crucial than that for nonhandicapped students in conventional programs." 436 N.Y.S.2d at 574. The case is currently on appeal.

Although special students do not have an entitlement to a *regular* diploma under Section 504, those who complete their agreed-upon individualized education programs are entitled to some form of certification. Judge Gesell, on the federal court for the District of Columbia, last year ordered the district's board of education to award a "special education diploma" to a handicapped child who had completed her individualized course of study prescribed by the board of education. The basis for the decision was the Education for All Handicapped Children Act (P.L. 94–142). Judge Gesell at the same time held that the student was not "entitled to an ordinary diploma" because she had not met "the entire standards" required for the ordinary diploma. The case is *Lenfant v. District of Columbia Board of Education*, 3 E.H.L.R. 552:272 (D.D.C. 1980).

This issue is still being litigated elsewhere. For example, in *Deborah B. v. Illinois State Board of Education*, No. 81-3089 (C.D. Ill. 1981), handicapped children are challenging the Peoria schools' requirement that they pass a competency test in order to receive a diploma. Briefs have been submitted.

Norm-Referenced Versus Criterion-Referenced Measurements

Interpreting a score by comparing it to other scores is called *norm referencing*. Interpreting a person's performance by comparing it to some specified behavioral standards is called *criterion referencing*. Test construction procedures may vary somewhat from tests with criterion-referenced scores to tests with norm-referenced scores; although, the scores from many tests could be interpreted in both manners.

Depending on the decision to be made, one of these two ways of interpreting the score will, most likely, be more useful than the other. The views of educational psychologists differ regarding the kinds and number of decisions that would best profit from each method of referencing. At the 1978 annual meeting of the American Educational Research Association there was a debate between the then current president of the organization (Popham) and a previous president (Ebel) regarding the relative merits of the two approaches to referencing. The two readings that follow are an outgrowth of that debate.

In the first reading Ebel builds the case for norm-referenced measurement. He recognizes some uses for criterion-referenced tests but lists eight major advantages to norm-referenced testing. In the second reading Popham makes the case for criterion-referenced measurement, concentrating mainly on achievement tests. Although it may not be completely clear to those who are unfamiliar with other Popham writings, he is not really opposed to normative referencing but, rather, to some test construction approaches and uses. He has, for example, written another article (Popham, 1976) in which he urges the gathering of normative data for criterion-referenced tests.

Thought Questions

For which types of decisions would norm-referenced data be most useful? For which types would they be least useful?

For which types of decisions would criterion-referenced measurement be most useful? For which types would they be least useful?

Explain Angoff's statement, "Scratch a criterion and you will find a norm." Do you agree with this statement? Why or why not?

Does it seem to you that Popham is comparing existing norm-referenced tests with theoretically ideal, but nonexistent criterion-referenced tests? Is this a fair comparison? Explain your answer.

Are there some educational decisions that absolutely require one type of measurement? Are there some that require both?

Are criterion-referenced tests less culturally biased against minority groups than norm-referenced tests? Defend your answer.

Evaluate the assertion that norm-referenced tests are more suitable for diagnostic purposes, but less suitable for instructional (treatment) purposes.

The Case for Norm-Referenced Measurements

Robert L. Ebel

To build the case for norm-referenced tests and for the measurements they yield on a firm foundation, we need to begin by making clear precisely what we are talking about. In some respects, the term "norm-referenced" is unfortunate. It focuses on only one aspect, and not the most important aspect, of a large and diverse category of tests. Until Glaser referred to these tests as "norm-referenced," to distinguish them from the kinds of tests specially designed to meet the needs of programmed instruction and mastery learning which he called "criterion-referenced," they used to be referred to simply as achievement tests.

This large and diverse category includes the survey tests of spelling used by Rice in 1894, the Regent's examinations in New York State, the Iowa academic tests and tests of basic skills and of educational development, the tests developed by the Board of Examiners at the University of Chicago and at Michigan State University, and practically all published standardized tests and teacher-made classroom tests. In fact, most of the achievement tests

From *Educational Researcher* (December 1978):3–5. Copyright 1978 American Educational Research Association, Washington, D.C. Reprinted with permission.

used in the past and those currently in use belong in this category.

No sooner had the distinction between norm-referenced and criterion-referenced tests been made than we began to hear that the old-style achievement tests were really not much good, and ought to be replaced by criterion-referenced tests as quickly as possible. Had this intelligence reached the ears of the elder Thorndike, Kelley, McCall, Ruch, Brigham, Lorge and others who did so much to lay the foundations and give initial direction to the science and technology of educational measurement, no doubt they would have been surprised, and quite possibly annoyed. I will not venture to speak for our contemporaries—Linquist, Lennon, Anastasi, Cronbach, Stanley and Bob Thorndike—but if any of them has rushed to jump on the criterion-referenced bandwagon, the notice has escaped me.

Some Differences Between Norm- and Criterion-Referenced Tests

The tests called norm-referenced differ from criterion-referenced tests in a number of ways. They are considerably older, for one thing. This means that norm-referenced tests, and the technologies associated with them, have been more fully developed. Their virtues as well as their limitations are better known. The problems associated with their use have been identified and, on the whole, solved.

The two kinds of tests yield somewhat different indications of achievement. The single score that is the most important result of a norm-referenced test provides a concise summary of the examinee's general level of achievement in some area of learning. A criterion-referenced test, on the other hand, can, and often does, provide a fairly detailed and specific listing of what the examinee has or has not learned to do. This distinction can be blurred, if on a norm-referenced test the items an examinee answered correctly or incorrectly are reported, or if on a criterion-referenced test the report simply indicates how many objectives were achieved. But these kinds of accommodations do not erase the essential difference.

Related to this difference in the information to be provided is a difference in the sampling of tasks or items included in the test. In a norm-referenced test, each item provides a separate and independent indication of some aspect of achievement in the domain of learning encompassed by the test. The items in a criterion-referenced test are written in clusters, each cluster focusing on a particular objective of instruction or aspect of achievement. As a result of its more extensive and more widely distributed sampling of achievements, the norm-referenced test yields a more reliable measure of a pupil's general level of achievement in a subject of study. The criterion-referenced test provides more reliable indications of whether or not some particularly important objectives have been attained.

Related also to differences in information provided and to patterns of item sampling are differences in the educational purposes to be served by the test. Norm-referenced tests are well adapted to summative evaluation, to the measurement of the results of efforts to learn. Criterion-referenced tests are more useful in formative evaluation, to guidance of the process of learning. Here again the distinction is easy to overemphasize. Deficiencies revealed by a norm-referenced test can be remedied in

subsequent instruction and learning, and the number of objectives attained can be used to indicate the effectiveness of prior instruction and learning. But a difference remains in how well each kind of test can serve each educational purpose.

There is a difference in the levels of attainment that each test form is best adapted to measure. Norm-referenced tests are intended to indicate a wide range of achievement levels from outstanding excellence to serious deficiency. Criterion-referenced tests set a single standard of achievement for all. A pupil either meets or fails to meet it. To put the standard within reach of all, it tends to be set rather low. The objectives whose attainments are to be indicated by a criterion-referenced test are often only minimums.

Proponents of criterion-referenced tests sometimes criticize the attainments tested in norm-referenced standardized tests for their lack of relevance to particular local instructional objectives. Locally designed and built criterion-referenced tests are offered as better measures than published standardized tests for the assessment of particular local instructional programs, and the success in learning of pupils in a particular local school. Of course, norm-referenced tests can be tailored to fit local instructional objectives, and criterion-referenced tests can be designed to assess the common objectives of learning in a state or a nation, but that there is some difference in emphasis between the two types of tests in this respect can hardly be denied.

Finally, and most importantly, there is a difference in the conception of learning implied by the two tests. If the primary goals of learning are to acquire a series of essential abilities, distinct enough from each other, few enough in number, and important enough individually to be specified separately, studied separately, and mastered separately, then a criterion-referenced test is clearly the test that ought to be used. But if the substance of learning is an infinity of particulars, too numerous to be specified separately, too inter-dependent to be studied or mastered separately; if the goal of learning lies beyond acquisition to understanding; and if understanding results from coming to know the multitude of relationships among these particulars, then a test that probes for these relationships at as many different points and from as many different angles as possible is the kind of test that ought to be used. Such a test is now commonly referred to as a norm-referenced test.

Thus, there are important differences between norm-referenced and criterion-referenced tests, differences in the age and development of the two test forms, in the kind of information they provide, in their sampling of tasks, in the educational purposes they serve, in the range of achievement levels they measure, in the range of schools for which they are appropriate and in the conceptions of learning they imply. But there are substantial similarities, too.

Similarities of Norm- and Criterion-Referenced Tests

Looked at individually, the items used in the two tests are indistinguishable. Both are intended to assess achievement in learning. The kind of tasks to be included in each can be specified precisely. The territory and the boundaries of the domain of achievements from which particular tasks are to be selected can be defined with all the precision that is necessary for either type of test.

In actual use, both kinds of tests yield scores that differ from pupil to pupil. Of course, a test of either kind might be built so as to show no score variance, but it is difficult to understand what educational value such a test would have. For since individual differences in background for learning, efforts to learn, and success in learning cannot be abolished, the only way to build a test on which all pupils would make the same score is to include tasks so simple that virtually no background for learning and no effort to learn is required for success.

Critics of norm-referenced tests sometimes claim that score variance is irrelevant to the quality of a criterion-referenced test of educational achievement. Since these critics seldom

assert that differences among pupils in achievement do not exist, a proposition that would be exceedingly difficult to sustain in the face of overwhelming evidence to the contrary in all fields of human endeavor, the claim of irrelevance implies that such differences are of no concern to them. If that is so, then why test at all? The only reason to test for an achievement is that it may or may not be there. If some pupils have an achievement and others lack it, scores will vary. Score variance is not irrelevant to *any* test of achievement. Unless a criterion-referenced test of achievement is sensitive to differences in achievement, it is worthless as a test. And in general, the more sensitive a test is to such differences, the higher its quality.

Those who construct norm-referenced tests are sometimes accused of seeking score variance at any cost, of accepting it gratefully, whether or not it is related to the achievement being measured. That accusation is false. Of course, not all the variance of any test score, norm-referenced or criterion-referenced, is true score variance. There is sampling error variance. There is score variance due to bias. Test constructors are well aware of these sources of irrelevant variance. They know how to estimate their magnitudes and to minimize their effects. To do so, they pay attention to score variance, instead of claiming that it is irrelevant. Constructors of criterion-referenced tests would be well advised to follow their example.

Another point of similarity between norm- and criterion-referenced tests has to do with norms. Because criterion-referenced tests were offered in their inception as an alternative to norm-referenced tests, there was a natural tendency for the advocates of criterion-referenced tests to express disapproval of norms and of the comparisons they inevitably involved and encouraged. But when teachers and school systems began to use criterion-referenced tests, the value of norms and the need for them quickly became apparent. Norms for criterion-referenced tests are not only possible, they are essential for effective test interpretation and use. If one is interested in excellence in education, comparisons are unavoidable, for excellence can only be determined by making comparisons.

A related point, sometimes overlooked, is that norms are involved in establishing the criteria of achievement on which criterion-referenced tests are based. On what basis are standards for pupil learning set? Is it not on the basis of what pupils can learn because many of them have learned it? As Angoff has said, "Scratch a criterion and you will find a norm."

The Case Against Easy Items

Advocates of criterion-referenced tests criticize those who make norm-referenced tests for rejecting items that are extremely easy, particularly those that are answered correctly by all examinees. Such items, they say, are likely to test the most important outcomes of instruction. To reject them, they claim, leads to underestimation of the true achievements of pupils and schools.

The argument that the easiest items test the most important outcomes goes like this. What is most important, the school will spend the most teaching time. What it spends the most time teaching, pupils will learn the most thoroughly. If they learn it thoroughly, they will do well on items testing for it.

That is a valid argument as far as it goes, but it does not go far enough. It suggests that all pupils should learn perfectly all that their teachers try to teach. But only if the teachers were perfect teachers, and the pupils were perfect students, would it be reasonable to expect perfection in learning. Nor do we find that kind of perfection in practice. There are no 100 percent success items in the criterion-referenced tests used in the Michigan State Assessment. These items are designed to test the achievement of minimum competency on the most important objectives of instruction. On none of them do pupils in Michigan display anything approaching 100 percent success.

Note also that this argument mentions only how hard teachers try to teach something. It does not consider how hard that thing may be

to learn. Some of the most important things may be difficult to learn. As Goethe said, "All distinguished things are difficult." Hence, there probably is no high correlation between the importance of an educational outcome and the degree of success pupils show in attaining it. That the easiest items are also the most important is most unlikely.

Granting all this, why throw out items on which all pupils succeed? The answer, I think, is that we should not, provided that the two requirements are met. The *first* is that the item unquestionably tests an achievement of unquestionable importance. Experience has taught test constructors to be suspicious of any item that all examinees answer correctly. Perhaps what it tests is common knowledge, not related at all to specific instruction. Perhaps the item includes an irrelevant give-away clue. For all or most pupils in a class, a school, a state, or a nation, to master any ability appropriate for them is a most unlikely event. An item that says they have all learned it may be suspected of lying. The *second* requirement to be met before retaining an item that all examinees answer correctly is that the absolute value of the test score, that is the number of items answered correctly, or the number of objectives mastered, is more important than its relative value, that is its percentile rank, stanine or z-score. This requirement focuses on one of the major differences between criterion-referenced and norm-referenced tests.

The trouble with the absolute standards of the criterion-referenced test constructor is that they are absolute only in a relative sense—relative to the standards of that particular test constructor or test scorer. And as Starch, Elliott, Ruch, and many others have shown, the standards of different test constructors and test scorers are highly personal, highly subjective, and hence highly undependable.

Suppose constructors of a criterion-referenced test define carefully the achievements the test is intended to measure. It is still their prerogative to aim high or low to pursue difficult or easy achievements. If they aim low enough, they may find a number of items that most pupils can answer correctly. The pupils and the school will look good, until someone compares what they can do with what pupils in other schools can do; that is, until the criterion-referenced test constructors' absolute standards are checked against the world's relative standards.

If pupil achievements are going to be judged ultimately in relative terms, why not judge them in relative terms immediately? And if the judgments are to be relative, items that most pupils answer correctly have little to say about relative amounts of achievement.

Some Advantages of Norm-Referenced Tests

The question before us, as I see it, is not either/or. It is which/when. As a youth, I advanced part way up the ladder of classes and merit badges in the Boy Scouts by passing some criterion-referenced tests. In Michigan, criterion-referenced tests are being used effectively to focus attention on some of the most serious deficiencies in learning of pupils in our elementary schools. There is a place, an important place, for criterion-referenced tests in the improvement of educational achievement.

But I disagree most strongly with those who contend that criterion-referenced tests are a generally superior alternative to the more familiar and widely-used tests of achievement that have come to be called norm-referenced. Here are some advantages I see in norm-referenced tests.

1. They assess pupils' broad general level of knowledge and understanding of a subject, not their mastery of a few particulars.

2. They reflect common nationwide goals for learning, not unique local goals.

3. They assess achievements at all levels of excellence and mediocrity. They do not focus primarily on minimum essentials.

4. Because each item can test a different aspect of achievement, they provide a broader and more representative sampling of achievements.

5. They are consistent with the view that achievement in learning is a matter of more or less, not of everything (mastery) or nothing.

6. They provide a single score that concisely summarizes pupils' general level of achievement, not an extended inventory of things learned or not learned.

7. They are primarily useful for summative, not formative evaluation. They indicate how successful the pupils' efforts to learn have been; how successful the teachers' efforts to foster that learning have been.

8. They imply that the primary responsibility for successful learning rests with the pupil, not with the instructional delivery system.

It seems unfortunate to me that the advocates of criterion-referenced tests have joined the advocates of no testing at all in wholesale condemnation of conventional achievement tests. For the new effect of their combined efforts, if those efforts were to succeed, would be to discredit a good and useful tool for improving the effectiveness of education, without establishing anything nearly so good in its place. I sincerely hope that good sense will prevail and they they will not succeed.

The Case for Criterion-Referenced Measurements

W. James Popham*

Proposition One: For purposes of instruction or evaluation, norm-referenced achievement tests are essentially worthless. This indictment extends not only to poorly constructed norm-referenced achievement tests, but also to the very best members of this well-established measurement genre. *Proposition Two: Criterion-referenced achievement tests, if they are properly fashioned, can be of enormous utility to instructors and evaluators.* The issues at stake in this dispute are far more profound than is sometimes evident in theoretical disagreements between academicians. Indeed, the decisions resulting from the application of educational tests are of paramount human import.

In well over half of our fifty states, students are not obliged to display minimum competence prior to receiving a high school diploma. In most of these states, this means that high school graduates must pass a test of some sort. In instances where the wrong tests are used,

and incorrect decisions are made, the self-esteem of thousands of young people will be seriously damaged, perhaps irreparably. There are also scores of decisions currently being made regarding whether to retain, revise, or scrap particular educational programs. In many instances these decisions are reached, in part, on the basis of test results. If the wrong tests are used and the wrong programs are scrapped, then countless pupils will be robbed of an effective instructional program. Clearly, the issue under analysis is more than theoretical.

But before trotting out the arguments and evidence that I hope will convince you of the soundness of my two major propositions, it is necessary to engage in a bit of stage-setting. We need to define a few terms and to retrospect briefly in order to see why this debate with my good friend and esteemed colleague, Robert L. Ebel, is even necessary.

From *Educational Researcher* (December 1978): 6–10. Copyright 1978 American Educational Research Association, Washington, D.C. Reprinted with permission.
*I am indebted to Louis Sinopoli and Joan Taylor for their assistance in assembling a variety of data needed for this analysis.

Term-Tightening

Fortunately, there's not much disagreement about what a norm-referenced test is. They've been around for so long that almost everyone concurs in viewing a norm-referenced test as a measuring device which is used to ascertain an examinee's performance in relationship to the performance of other examinees on the same measuring device.

Unfortunately, with respect to criterion-referenced tests, there's no unanimity regarding meaning. Much of the current ambiguity shrouding the phrase, criterion-referenced test, stems from Glaser's classic 1963 treatise.[1] In that essay Glaser contrasted traditional norm-referenced tests with the kinds of tests needed to assess learner performance when highly effective instruction was present, for example, such as was then being produced by programmed instructional sequences.

Yet, despite its decisively positive overall impact on educational measurement practice, Glaser's 1963 piece allowed readers to draw two substantially different conclusions regarding what he meant by the expression criterion-referenced test. Some people picked upon the traditional psychometric meaning of the term *criterion* and concluded that a criterion-referenced test was one which related examinee's scores to a well-defined cut-off score or *level* or performance. Glaser's 1963 analysis included numerous phraes, e.g., "criterion levels" and "level of proficiency," which could lead one to such an interpretation. Other readers were more attentive to Glaser's emphasis on the fact that a criterion-referenced test "provides explicit information as to what the individual can or cannot do." Such readers, noting Glaser's assertion that a criterion referenced test can describe a student's achievement of "specific behaviors," inferred that a criterion-referenced test is used to ascertain an individual's status with respect to a well-defined behavioral domain.

It is the second of these two interpretations which I shall be using throughout this debate. The former interpretation, that is, referencing an examinee's performance on tasks (no matter how poorly defined) to a *level* of proficiency, offers little improvement over norm-referenced measurement srategies. On the other hand, conceiving of a criterion-referenced test as a measure of a well-defined class of behav-

iors offers all sorts of advantages to evaluators and instructors.

Finally, throughout this analysis I shall be focusing on achievement rather than aptitude measures. Norm-referenced aptitude measures can prove most helpful to educators, for instance, in fixed quota instructional settings where one must choose among individuals on the basis of their relative likelihood of subsequent success. My current quarrel is not with such aptitude measures but, rather, with norm-referenced achievement tests and the manner in which they have been used.

What Hath WWI Wrought?

Norm-referenced testing received its biggest boost during World War I when the Army Alpha, the first widely used norm-referenced aptitude test for groups of examinees, was administered to over 1,725,000 men. In brief, the purpose of this Herculean measurement effort was to sort out individuals according to their *relative* intellectual aptitude in order to make military personnel decisions. This major excursion into testing by the Army was an unparalleled success. As Du Bois observed, "It was the widespread appreciation of the Army program which greatly stimulated the making and standardizing of a wide variety of new measures and accelerated their application."[2]

The impact of the Army's testing program was particularly discernible in the exponential expansion of the norm-referenced achievement tests copyrighted in the United States after 1920. Almost without exception, these achievement tests were constructed along the lines of the mental testing model so effectively employed by the military. These post-World War I norm-referenced achievement tests were *widely misapplied*, since they were employed in situations where they ought not to have been used. They were employed, for example, to appraise the quality of instructional programs, a mission not consonant with the original mental testing model of providing information for making relative contrasts among individuals.

Norm-referenced achievement tests have also been touted as useful diagnostic tools, that is, instruments to aid teachers in deciding which skills to emphasize for which pupils. As most teachers will tell you, however, norm-referenced achievement tests provide little if any, useful information for instructional diagnosis.

Why shouldn't educators have been seduced into using norm-referenced achievement tests for just about every purpose under the sun? The tests came to us professionally printed and beautifully packaged, accompanied by resplendent technical manuals loaded with enough reliability and validity coefficients to secure deference from all but the psychometrically seasoned. Moreover, norm-referenced achievement tests were born in such centers of cerebral excellence as Princeton, New Jersey. And to clinch matters, norm-referenced achievements tests became known as "nationally standardized achievement tests." To criticize them clearly bordered on latent un-Americanism.

When norm-referenced achievement tests have been used in connection with instructional design or program evaluation, it is my belief that they have typically yielded data which are either meaningless or misleading. I shall decribe three defects of norm-referenced achievement tests, arguing that it is the *nature* of norm-referenced acheivement tests to possess liabilities which render them unsuitable for purposes of instruction or evaluation.

Deficit One: Teaching-Testing Mismatches

One deficit of norm-referenced achievement tests flows from the profit-making imperatives of commercial test-publishing firms.

In skeletal form, the argument runs as follows:

1. Commercial test publishers must sell large numbers of their tests to stay in business.
2. But America's historic local control of education has resulted in great curricular diversity throughout the land.
3. If test publishers spelled out explicitly what their achievement tests were measuring, many educators would see that a test was not congruent with local curricular emphases, hence would not buy the test.
4. To promote wider acceptance of their tests, commercial test publishers describe what's being measured in very general terms, thereby making the test more appealing to a larger group of would-be purchasers.
5. The result of such imprecise descriptions is that when such tests are purchased there are often mismatches between what is taught and what is tested, such mismatches frequently being unrecognized by local educators.
6. Mismatches between what is taught and what is tested yield spurious data, resulting in misleading conclusions.

Let's spend a moment or two with the key features of this argument. First off, is it true that there is great curricular diversity in the land? Commercial test publishers often deny it, as do proponents of norm-referenced tests.[3] Yet careful analysis of curricular patterns by DeVault, Harnischfeger, and Wiley[4] reveal enormous disparities in the amount of emphasis given even basic subjects. Of course most school districts have curricula which include such main-line subjects as reading, mathematics, and social studies.[5] But it is necessary to dig beneath these superficial similarities to see that, *substantial differences in curricular emphases exist at the level of detail where pupils answer test items.*

Yet why is it that advocates of norm-referenced tests go through such gyrations in efforts to convince us that curriculum emphases throughout America are identical? The answer is simple. The more divergence there is in *local* curriculum patterns, the less suitable a *nationally* produced achievement test can ever be.

But in spite of all these protestations, the fact remains that our historic local control of schooling has resulted in great curricular diversity. Although commercial test publishers may attempt to mask this problem by fuzzing up their descriptive information, the problem persists.

Here, for example, are some representative examples of the level of descriptive detail supplied by most publishers of norm-referenced achievement tests.[6]

- *Mathematics:* Includes items measuring numeration, sets, and logic; geometry; measurement; problem-solving and operations; whole numbers
- *Reading Comprehension:* Graded reading passages with test items based on the following objectives: literal, inferential, evaluative, and word meaning in context
- *Language:* Includes items measuring listening comprehensions; grammar and syntax; spelling; study skills; punctuation and capitalization, and usage

Even Professor Ebel ends up engaging in verbal cartwheels when he tries to defend the descriptive quality of norm-referenced tests. He points out, quite properly, that a good norm-referenced test must have more than mere relative meaning, it must also have *content* meaning. He then drives home his point about content meaning as follows: *"These meanings and understandings are seldom wholly absent when norm-referenced measures are used."*[7] (italics added) Since content meanings are "seldom wholly absent" in norm-referenced tests, we can rest comfortably with the assurance that such explicit meanings are *almost never totally not there.*

Is it any wonder that given such loose, fuzzy descriptions of what these tests measure, more than a few educators assume that the national tests match their local curricula? But those assumptions may or may not be warranted. Often, they're not. The resulting *unrecognized* mismatch between what's being taught and what's being tested can have serious, deleterious consequences.

Deficit Two: Imprecise Instructional Targets

A related but distinct problem arising from the generality with which standardized tests are described is that they provide inadequate cues for instructional design. This is true with respect to the original organization of an instructional sequence as well as formative evaluation attempts to remedy sickly instructional programs.

In shorthand form, here's how the argument goes:

1. For economic purposes, norm-referenced achievement test publishers describe their tests very generally and also attempt to measure many skills with only a few items per skill.
2. The imprecision of these descriptions offers insufficient targets for instructional designers or formative evaluators.
3. Moreover, the inadequate number of items per measured behavior precludes reliable assessment for purposes of diagnosing the nature of an individual learner's accomplishments.

Recent large-scale investigators[8] have confirmed the common sense notion that *time-on-task* is one of the most potent variables for predicting the success of an instructional program. But if the descriptive information available with a norm-referenced achievement test is at near-Rorschach level, who can tell what kinds of behaviors should be practiced? The following descriptions of a history subtest from a widely used social studies achievement test illustrates that point. This subset:

> . . . emphasizes (1) the effects of man's increasing control over the forces of nature including conflicts with natural environment, influences of technological development, and historical change and (2) the ways in which man attempts to understand and adjust to his environment including the

influences of magic, superstition, mythology, religion, philosophy, and science.[9]

Even worse, in most norm-referenced achievement tests there are insufficient numbers of items available for the skills being measured to yield any reliable estimate of an examinee's true mastery of that skill. Who would be willing to claim, for example, that a one- or two-item test should be used for diagnostic instructional purposes? Some norm-referenced testing devotees are even more open about the point, defending with rapture the exotic statistical manipulations that can be performed to help teachers make use of *one-item subtests*.[10]

This severe deficit of norm-referenced achievement tests is more closely associated with the needs of instructional specialists rather than educational evaluators, but certainly evaluators will find themselves in a similar quandary if they try to revive a defective instructional program on the basis of norm-referenced achievement test results.

Deficit Three: Psychometric Tendencies to Eliminate Important Test Items

The third deficiency of norm-referenced tests for purposes of instruction and evaluation stems from the desire of norm-referenced test developers to construct tests that result in considerable response variance among examinees, that is, considerable differences in examinees' test performances. Without substantial response variance it is impossible to make the fine-grained comparisons among examinees which are at the core of a norm-referenced measurement model. Furthermore, if the response variance is small, there is far less likelihood of securing the high reliability coefficients which often prove instrumental in promoting satisfactory sales of such tests.

Unfortunately, this practice has resulted in another whopping deficit for norm-referenced tests if we try to use them for instruction or evaluation. Here's how this situation comes about:

1. Developers of norm-referenced achievement tests strive to create tests that yield substantial response variance.
2. Test items that maximize response variance possess difficulty levels of .50, thus items which are answered correctly by large proportions of the examinees must be eliminated.
3. But items which large numbers of students answer correctly often deal with topics and skills that teachers thought important, hence have stressed during instruction.
4. Therefore, particularly with oft-revised norm-referenced achievement tests, items covering important topics or skills tend over time to be excised from the tests.

Now this doesn't mean that *all* important items will be removed from achievement tests, but the *tendency* of traditional psychometric procedures to result in the elimination of important test items is clearly present.

This is surely a classic instance of Catch 22 from the teacher's perspective. The more effectively that teachers promote a particular skill, the better their student will do on the test items measuring that skill. But the better that students do on those items, the more likely the items are to be discarded from future revisions of the test. In time, is it any surprise that frequently revised achievement tests begin to resemble aptitude tests?

When items have very low or very high difficulty levels, it is impossible to make the items discriminate effectively. In such instances, what should a test constructor do? No less an authority on norm-referenced test construction than Ebel has an answer:

> If the low discrimination is due to the extreme ease or extreme difficulty of the items, they should, if possible, be revised to make them more appropriate in difficulty. If such attempts prove unsuccessful or seem certain to fail, the items should be dropped. *However defensible their inclusion may be in principle*, they will make little prac-

tical difference in the relative scores of the students[11] (Italics added)

Let's be clear about what is meant by difficulty of an item. A well-instructed student should find test items easy. That doesn't render such items intrinsically easy. It is just that after decent instruction, kids should answer test questions correctly. But the mentality of norm-referenced test developers often matches Ebel's, when, irrespective of curricular defensibility, they discard items that fail to garner the requisite discrimination indices. This third and final deficit of norm-referenced achievement tests tends to make these measures instructionally insensitive,[12] and thus valueless for both instructors and evaluators.

Criterion-Referenced Tests as an Antidote

Before turning to the potential advantages of criterion-referenced tests for purposes of instruction and evaluation, let's dismiss a couple of straw person allegations that almost invariably rise when norm-referenced test proponents take out after criterion-referenced measurement strategies.[13]

The first of these unwarranted assumptions is that educators are opting for criterion-referenced tests instead of norm-referenced tests merely because they are reluctant to be held accountable.[14] One could cogently argue that it is not the fear of accountability that terrifies educators, but the fear of *inappropriately conceived accountability*. Accountability schemes which center on the use of instructionally insensitive and curricularly off-target norm-referenced tests are decisively inappropriate. Educators are not turning to criterion-referenced tests because they see them as less stringent. On the contrary, criterion-referenced tests can conceivably be far more demanding than traditional norm-referenced measures. However an equitable accountability system which features the use of criteron-referenced tests will give educators at least a reasonable chance to

succeed. With norm-referenced measures they have no chance at all.

A second allegation which peppers the writings of those who share Professor Ebel's dim view of criterion-referenced tests is that such tests must necessarily deal with trivial instructional outcomes, while norm-referenced tests can measure higher level outcomes. Ebel is willing, for example, to assign criterion-referenced tests to the assessment of "a limited number of specifically defined goals."[15] But when it's necessary to tap a student's mastery of more profound learnings, then he implies that it's time to roll out our heavy testing artillery, that is, norm-referenced tests.

But before we start dismissing criterion-referenced tests merely because they may currently deal with the puerile rather than the profound, let's remember that in contrast to the measurement tradition of norm-referenced tests, criterion-referenced tests are still in their infancy. I readily concede that there aren't many exemplary criterion-referenced tests around these days. That doesn't mean that high quality criterion-referenced tests, tests that tap truly high import behaviors, cannot be created. In the embryonic field of criterion-referenced measurement, what *is* clearly does not reflect what *can be*.

Deficit Reducing

Earlier in this analysis three key deficits of norm-referenced tests were isolated. Let's see now how criterion-referenced tests can take care of those problems.[16]

The initial deficit of norm-referenced tests arose from their inadequate descriptive power, eventuating in unrecognized mismatches between what is tested and what is taught. Since the major strength of a well-constructed criterion-referenced test is its sharpened descriptive quality, this problem is eliminated. It is eliminated, of course, assuming that the developers of the criterion-referenced test have the courage to spell out precisely what's being measured. And it takes *economic* courage, since the more explicitly a testing firm spells out what's being measured, the less likelihood that the test will be widely purchased. Many of the so-called criterion-referenced tests being peddled these days carry with them descriptive literature which is only a shade more explicit than that found with norm-referenced tests. By demanding high quality descriptions from criterion-referenced test publishers, educators will surely be able to reduce the degree of teaching-testing mismatches, and to eliminate altogether any *unrecognized* mismatches of that sort.

The second deficit of norm-referenced achievement tests was that they failed to provide adequate instructional targets because of imprecise descriptions and an insufficient number of items per measured behavior. Both of these deficiencies can be rectified in short order by criterion-referenced test developers. To include a substantial number of test items per measured behavior, criterion-referenced test developers must eschew the assessment of small-scale skills, attempting instead to measure truly high import competencies that subsume lesser, en route skills. By focusing on such high level skills, creating detailed descriptions of the behavior being measured, and providing an adequate number of items per measured behavior, criterion-referenced test designers can take care of deficit two with dispatch.

The third deficit of norm-referenced tests stemmed from the all-consuming need of norm-referenced test developers to produce response variance. The psychometric procedures employed to pull this off, as we saw, often resulted in the elimination of test items covering important concepts and skills. Fortunately, there is no intrinsic need to spread examinees out on criterion-referenced tests. This allows us to retain test items that many students

might, after decent instruction, answer correctly. If an item is a valid index of an important skill, and many students are answering the item correctly, then we should rejoice, not despair. On all three counts, then, criterion-referenced tests can correct the inadequacies of norm-referenced tests for purposes of instruction and evaluation.

But beyond merely correcting for the deficits of norm-referenced tests when used for instruction or evaluation, high quality criterion-referenced tests provide a number of bonuses when used for such purposes. Most of these dividends flow directly from the greater clarity with which criterion-referenced tests spell out what they're measuring. Moreover, this descriptive clarity does not evaporate when we gather examinee performance data on criterion-referenced tests for comparative purposes. When using criterion-referenced tests accompanied by comparative performance data, we can engage in a simultaneous orgy of simultaneous cake-having and cake-eating.

As noted before, because of the recency of their introduction on the educational scene, there aren't currently all that many outstanding criterion-referenced tests which can be wheeled out to show how really first rate they are. The technical base on which criterion-referenced tests are being constructed today is admittedly primitive.

But we are not debating the defects of poorly constructed criterion-referenced or norm-referenced tests. We are debating the adequacy of the underlying rationale associated with norm- and criterion-referenced measurement. It basically comes down to a choice between a measurement strategy which compares people versus a measurement strategy that lets us know what it is that people can or can't do. For purposes of instruction and educational evaluation, that choice is easy.

ENDNOTES

1. Glaser, R. Instructional technology and the measurement of learning outcomes: Some questions. *American Psychologist*, 1963, 18: 519–21.

2. Du Bois, P. H. *A history of psychological testing.* Boston, Mass.: Allyn and Bacon, 1970.

3. Kelsey, K. and Munday, L. *By the numbers.* Special Report No. 2. Iowa City, Iowa: Houghton Mifflin Co., Test Department, N.D., 5.

4. De Vault, M. L.; Harnischfeger, A.; and Wiley, D. E. *Curricula, personnel resources, and grouping strategies.* M.L. Group for Policy Studies in Education, CEMREL, Chicago: March, 1977. See also Harnischefeger, A., and Wiley, D. E., *Time allocations in fifth grade reading.* Paper presented at the Annual Meeting of the American Educational Research Association, New York, April 1977.

5. Rudman, H. C. The standardized test flap. *Phi Delta Kappan,* 1977, 59, 3: 179–185.

6. *Metropolitan Achievement Tests.* 1978 editions. The Psychological Corporation, New York, 1978.

7. Ebel, R. L., *Essentials of educational measurement.* Englewood Cliffs, N.J.: Prentice-Hall, 1972, 86.

8. See the recent work of David Berliner and his associate, e.g., Marliave, R. S.; Fisher, C. W.; and Dishaw, M. N., Academic Learning Time and Student Achievement in the A-B Period. December 1977. *Technical Note* VIA, Beginning Teacher Evaluation Study. San Francisco Far West Laboratory for Educational Research and Development.

9. *Handbook, sequential tests of educational progress, STEP series II,* Princeton, N.J.: Educational Testing Service, 1971, 117.

10. Rudman, H. C., op. cit.

11. Ebel, R. L. *Essentials of educational measurement.* Englewood Cliffs, N.J.: Prentice-Hall, Inc., 1972, 394.

12. See Carver, R. P. The Coleman Report. Using inappropriately designed achievement tests. *American Journal of Educational Research,* 1973, 12, 1: 77–86.

13. See, for example, Ebel, R. L. The uses of standardized testing. *Phi Delta Kappan,* 1977, Fastback No. 93.

14. Ebel, R. L. Education tests: Valid? Biased? Useful? *Phi Delta Kappan,* October 1975.

15. Ibid., 85.

16. For a more elaborate treatment of these points, see Popham, W. J. *Criterion-referenced measurement.* Englewood Cliffs, N.J.: Prentice-Hall, 1978.

The Computer Revolution

"Snoopy said it years ago: There's no greater burden than a great potential. Today everyone seems to agree that the potential of educational computing is very great indeed" (Komoski, 1984, p. 244). But, as Komoski goes on to point out, "it is not at all clear just who is up to bearing the burden of fulfilling that potential."

Actually, it is an exaggeration to suggest that *everyone* agrees about the great potential, but it probably is *not* an exaggeration to suggest that all those who do believe in the *potential* recognize the burden of fulfilling it, and many of those believers are quite concerned about some dangers in the computer revolution.

Predictions regarding the actualization of either the potential or the dangers are difficult to make. Indeed it turns out that the predictions regarding the number of computers available to schools, let alone their educational value, have frequently been wrong. Brzezinski (1984) reported that

> In 1950, the RAND Corporation predicted that because computers were so large and expensive, no more than 12 corporations in the United States would ever need or be able to afford one" (p. 7). That prediction turned out to be a little conservative! Bork reported that "by April 1984 U.S. schools had approximately 350,000 computers available to students in grades 1 through 12—an average of about four computers per school. In the past few years, the number of computers in the schools has roughly *doubled* each year (1984, p. 240).

Thus, by the time you read this introduction, there may well be over 1,000,000 computers in the schools. While the recent growth is quite amazing, Papert, writing in 1984, put it all in a different perspective,

> . . . there's a lot of balihoo in the press about this computer revolution—that computers are everywhere in the schools. But, in fact, there is scarcely one for every 100 children—which is like no computer at all if you average it out. A very small number of schools are thinking in terms of one for every 30 children because that means each child can get an hour a week at the computer—which is a little better. But think of one hour a week for the pencil, and it's obvious that this is still absurd (Papert, 1984, p. 423).

To stimulate your mind regarding the advancement of computers we provide you with one more quote:

> Had improvements in efficiency and reductions in the cost of automobiles followed patterns similar to the computer industry, each of us would be able to buy a Rolls-Royce today for roughly $2.75; it would get nearly 3,000,000 miles to the gallon and would deliver enough power to tow an aircraft carrier. In short, recent changes in the power and cost of computer technology have been truly astonishing, and we

seem to be on the edge of a period of rapidly increasing and widespread distribution of this technology (Lepper, 1985, pp 1–2).

The two articles we have chosen for this section present quite different perspectives regarding the computer revolution. Small, in "The Microchip Revolution: Implications for Education," takes an optimistic stance regarding the revolution. While mentioning the fact that limitations exist, Small chides some educators who seem to view the new computer technologies "either as nearly diabolical instruments for depriving them of their jobs and livelihood, or as simply irrelevant to their own professional concerns." Later in the paper there is presented what many may feel is an implied threat. "Teachers and future teachers who want to remain competitive and save their jobs will have to retrain themselves in the use and understanding of the new technologies through courses, seminars, and workshops."

O'Brien, in "Waiting for Godot: The Great Ed Tech Dream," takes a more pessimistic view of the revolution. O'Brien explains reasons for teachers' lack of enthusiasm rather than chiding them. Further, he suggests that high costs and poor software still present serious problems.

The two articles presented here are excellent in terms of presenting points of view about the computer revolution. However, they are quite general in nature. For those of you interested in further reading, several references are given at the end of this unit. Leonard (1984) provides an interesting description of what an "Interactive Learning School" will be like in 1994. For his vision to come to pass, some of the problems with inadequate software must be solved. Sardello (1984) "stands frimly opposed to the introduction of the computer as a technological device oriented toward changing the very tradition of education" (1984, p. 621). Walker (1983) discussed seven ways that microcomputers can contribute to education, and seven problems or severe limitations of microcomputers. Lepper (1985) focused on motivational and social issues. He suggests that "technological changes frequently have important social and psychological consequences" (1985, p. 1). In the summary of his article he points out that there is considerable debate about the effects of computer technology:

> To advocates, this technology offers possibilities for enhancing children's intellectual abilities and their intrinsic motivation for learning; for increasing children's perceptions of personal competence and self-esteem; and for promoting an internal locus of control, increased persistence in problem solving, and heightened feelings of independence. To critics, this technology is viewed instead as likely to produce impulsive and distractible children; to stifle creativity and undermine intrinsic motivation outside of the computer context; and to promote social isolation, dehumanization, and decreased social interaction skills among frequent users (Lepper, 1985, pp. 15–16).

Thought Questions

What ratio of computers to children do you feel is necessary for there to truly be a computer revolution in education?

What is your definition of "computer literacy?" Is it that one knows how to do computer programming in at least one language? Is it simply that one knows about computers and how to use available programs for various purposes?

Should computers be used in schools primarily to assist in students' learning about computers and computer programming; or should they primarily be used to facilitate the teaching of other material?

If students were to spend much of their time in school working in front of a computer terminal, what do you think would happen to their social skills?

The Microchip Revolution: Implications for Education

Michele Geslin Small

Just as the triangular sail, the rudder, and the compass fostered increased commerce among the Mediterranean countries and initiated voyages to new worlds; just as the longbow and gunpowder led to the collapse of the medieval feudal system; just so, many innovations or seemingly singular discoveries in the centuries before ours launched irrevocable waves of change. Certain discoveries and innovations have altered our environment forever and led to now taken-for-granted amenities such as electricity and the telephone or to terrifying and potentially destructive forces such as nuclear missiles.

We find ourselves today in the early dawn of the silicon chip era, which has already made and will unquestionably continue to produce unprecedented changes in our lives. It is difficult to imagine the full variety of social impacts that the microcomputer revolution will generate. It has already begun to affect our family life and recreation, transportation, government, and international relations, for ex-

ample. One of the greatest areas of impact is in the realm of education.

Implications for Educators

As futurists review contemporary eduction in America, they perceive a tremendous discrepancy between the information explosion outside the walls of our schools and the resistance to it inside. While information technology has progressed by leaps and bounds in the last five years, the reaction it has caused in education circles is cause for some concern.

Instead of perceiving the new technologies as liberating and exciting, some educators seem to view them either as nearly diabolical instruments for depriving them of their jobs and livelihood, or as simply irrelevant to their own professional concerns. In every technology, there is always potential for abuse, but there is also potential for good. The defensive reactions of educators are simply a matter of perception, a symptom of what Arthur Clarke calls "failure of nerves and failure of imagination." They are expressions of fear of the unknown, often exacerbated by feelings of per-

From *Curriculum Review* (February 1984). Reprinted with permission.

sonal insecurity and inadequacy in the face of a still shaky economy and demographic forecasts of declining enrollments and massive employment cutbacks in education.

Certain trends are clear, however. Within a decade we will have fewer fiscal resources at our disposal for salaries, facilities, equipment, and maintenance. And the taxpayers' revolts indicate that people are not willing to increase their contributions to education. The new information technologies (home TV programs, calculators, videodiscs, and home computers) can and must provide an educational support system as we search for new solutions.

Unless educators alter radically their viewpoints in the face of the inevitable, and decide to seek the opportunities embedded in what they consider a crisis, their fears of losing their jobs might be well-founded and turn into self-fulfilling prophecies. The microcomputer like any other technology will eliminate jobs, but then any teacher who can be replaced by a machine deserves to be. There will always be a place for those who look upon their work as a creative, problem-solving opportunity to benefit society.

Once educators fully recognize the potential as well as the limitations of these new machines, they will be able to forget their earlier prejudices and start thinking about how to take advantage of new options. Some will see the machines as a means to reduce the most mechanical chores of pedagogy (drills, information delivery, grading, tutoring) and will dedicate their time and energy to the higher and more exciting tasks: to foster critical thinking, creativity, open-mindedness, and the joy of learning.

Others, more far-sighted perhaps, will recognize the new opportunities which reside in the making and packaging of educational software in a burgeoning new market. Or they may become involved in advocating the exercise of rigorous quality control which must accompany any standardized, widely distributed instructional material; one critical mistake in a program could mean that millions would learn the same error.

Students and the Chip

The chip revolution will profoundly affect students in markedly different ways, and the new technology holds both promises and perils. On one hand, the new technology can provide infinite storage and easy retrieval of information across the arbitrary boundaries established by nation-states all over the world. The chip can make everything there is to know universally accessible, in effect bypassing the time-consuming, elitist, and affluent concepts of education based on the ability to read, write, and do arithmetic.

Peter Wagschal reminds us that "only a minority of the globe's population can afford the time and resources required to learn the 3 R's." Any attempt on our part to preserve the status quo would simply mean that, like the medieval scholars who feared the newly printed books, we want to preserve our professional advantages locally and the supremacy of our Western culture globally.

On the other hand, the darker side of the coin is still very evident. Information is power in the sense that the more we possess, the wider the variety of options and choices we have. This fact alone raises the specter of the ultimate discrimination—beyond those of race, sex, age, and religion—that of access. Unless we proceed with extreme caution and think of the long-range consequences of our actions, we might well have to face a new generation of "haves" and "have nots," locally as well as globally—those who have access to the control over information and those who do not. As computers become increasingly indispensable to the sciences, government, business, education and everyday life, those educated in their use will have a tremendous advantage over the rest of the population. Computer illiteracy may well become the major handicap of those who will live in the 21st century.

Fortunately, current trends seem to be going in the direction of wide dissemination and lower prices, if one can judge by the proliferation of pocket calculators, digital watches, video games, home computers, and the mushrooming of private electronic cottage industries and do-it-yourself kits. Together they allay the nightmarish vision of an Orwellian, highly centralized, computerized, elitist, totalitarian global regime.

As they become cheaper, the new electronic technologies have the potential to become the private tutors of a new Renaissance, transcending the constraints imposed by socioeconomic factors which, as recent research has indicated, seem to play such an important and detrimental part in the education of our children. All students will be able to learn at their own pace with the mode which is most appropriate for them.

"Slow" students could find in a robot-like machine a private tutor, kind, considerate, and patient. The computer could be programmed to know individual backgrounds, levels of achievement, strengths and weaknesses, personal temperament, and even tastes and hobbies. Such "robots" already exist and are in use in some classrooms. They can wait for an answer, give immediate positive reinforcement, or go back a few steps and reiterate information which the student has not properly assimilated. They can also establish a change of pace or even tell a joke. This process can do much to teach children what they need to know without the negative pressures imposed by a competitive classroom atmosphere. Students thus feel more at ease, more confident, and more successful, qualities which in themselves are self-reinforcing and self-generating.

For "bright" students, the only limits will be their own individual talent and imagination. A student might listen to a lecture delivered at Harvard, plug into countless data bases, use computer conferencing facilities to discuss and share ideas, or converse wtih another student in another part of the world. In short, the chip revolution can contribute to making education a truly democratic process in which students can realize their full potential. This highly individualized instruction, in conjunction with a truly synergistic regular classroom where students can discuss, debate and share ideas, hone and refine their own perceptions by exposure to others' views, and enjoy much-needed human and social contacts, will foster tremendous diversity, heterogeneity, and true learning.

Breaking Down Barriers

Finally, the chip revolution in education will lead the way in breaking down the factitious barriers which have been erected between the school and society. When all—adults as well as children, workers as well as students—can learn through home TV programs delivered on multiple cable channels, play simulation games together, and increase their knowledge in whatever area they may choose, learning will become a truly lifelong experience. Thus, we shall finally be able to reduce the fundamental age segregation which has plagued all educational systems in contemporary highly industrialized nations.

Once again, some thinkers are raising grave concerns about the political implications of such a major transformation. The Dutch physicist Ilya Prigogine, for example, wonders if a technology permitting every individual to respond immediately and directly to the central government on every issue in a truly democratic fashion would not result in a stable, but ultimately conservative order. The so-called Silent Majority would no longer be silent.

Perhaps, but could we not also argue that this new order would itself be subjected to new fluctuations? With such a variety of electronic tools in their hands, would men, women, and children of the 21st century tolerate any particular nationalistic values and commitments? Would they not also transcend the manmade geographical and political boundaries and come to the realization that we are all citizens of one planet, a world which we must share and whose survival we must preserve, ensure, and cherish?

What Do We Do Now?

This brief look at some of the possible direct impacts of the silicon chip revolution on education shows us that this innovation, albeit tiny in size, will be powerful in effect. If we invoke one of the cardinal principles of biology, that "one can never do merely one thing," or, put in systems terms, "everything is connected to everything else," the chip revolution by virtue of its complexity poses formidable challenges.

We can expect many different impacts on other sectors of society, directly or indirectly connected with the school. Will the book survive? Could we not save tons of paper, when all there is to know can be contained in a few information centers and made available to the public? What effect would this have on loggers, paper manufacturers, publishing companies, and others whose livelihood depends on books and paper?

The lessons are clear. Microcomputers are here and here to stay. What we must do now is establish some control over the development of the new technologies: how much and how soon? Aware that major fluctuations do lead to new order in complex social and biological systems, we must chart a transitional course guided by three key principles: anticipation, design and planning.

Anticipation   With global coordination, we need to conduct studies of technological assessment and social impact assessment and disseminate the results worldwide. Since we are rushing headlong toward what Marshall McLuhan has called the "global village," we cannot afford selfish isolation in our efforts, which could lead to disastrous political, economic, social, and cultural side-effects.

Design   We must develop and consider basic concepts to direct our progress. To manage the information and electronic age, we must be educated about information and electronics.

Participative Planning   In such a rapid and pervasive transformation, planning cannot be left exclusively in the hands of so-called experts. We must inform and involve all, so that each individual can understand better the new technologies and organize his or her life to maximize its benefits and minimize its dangers.

In the educational sphere, this will mean preparing the younger generations for the massive changes which are going to occur within their lifetime. Three curricular directions are desirable: future studies, systems thinking and global learning at all levels, and the study and use of computers from kindergarten on. Children raised with the new technology must be in an adequate position to understand its limits, appraise its potential, and control its development.

Teachers and future teachers who want to remain competitive and save their jobs will have to retrain themselves in the use and understanding of the new technologies through courses, seminars, and workshops. They might seek the help of private enterprise, which is already quite competent at training its own recruits and is decades ahead of academia in accepting and using micro-technology.

But schooling is only a tiny fraction of what education really is. Broadly conceived, education is life, in the sense that we are doomed to learn by the very fact that we are alive. Education occurs in the world of work, the family, the community, the church. We should not discount those major spheres of influence. Moreover, the school is already suffering from the burden of everyone's expectations for solving society's problems. (Not only does it have to teach conceptual skills but it is also supposed to form character, teach values, foster equality, and even babysit.) The school itself will be subjected to major transformations in the years ahead. We must, therefore, take another tack and, on a parallel course, make massive efforts to educate the population at large through the media, radio, print and—why not?—the electronic gadgetry already on the market.

In recent years, magazines like *Science News, Science 84,* and *Omni* as well as TV programs such as *Nova, Connections,* and *Cosmos* have attempted to convey to the masses some of the awesome and sometimes frightening frontiers of science and technology. While these efforts are most commendable, they are not enough and are still restricted to an educated and interested minority. Since familiarity breeds confidence and information is power, we must find ways (and find them fast) to inform, educate, and prepare our societies for the major changes already in progress. Then, and only then, can we look forward to the exciting promises of what has been called "the Second Industrial Revolution."

REFERENCES

Clarke, Arthur C. *Profiles of the Future*. New York: Harper and Row, 1973.

Coleman, J. S. et al. *Equality of Educational Opportunity*. Washington, DC: U.S. Government Printing Office, 1966.

Freeman, Michael and Gary P. Mulkowski, "Advanced Interactive Technology—Robots in the Home and Classroom." In *Education and the Future*. Edited by Lane Jennings and Sarry Cornish. Washington, DC: The World Future Society, 1980, pp. 41–45.

Jencks, Christopher, *Inequality*. Hardmonworth, England: Penguin Books, 1975.

Maruyama, Mogoroh. "Toward Cultural Symbiosis." In *Evolution and Consciousness: Human Systems in Transition*. Edited by Erich Jantsch and Conrad H. Waddington. Reading, MA: Addison-Wesley, 1976, pp. 198–211.

Prigogine, Ilya and Isabelle Stengers. *La Nouvelle Alliance: Metamorphose de la Science*. Paris: Editions Gallimard, 1979.

Prigogine, Ilya., "Order Through Fluctuation: Self Organization and Social Systems." In *Evolution and Consciousness: Human Systems in Transition*. Edited by Erich Jantsch and Conrad H. Waddington. Reading, MA: Addison-Wesley, 1976, pp. 93–126.

Wagschal, Peter H. "Illiterates with Doctorates: The Future of Educaton in an Electronic Age." In *Education and the Future*. Edited by Lane Jennings and Sally Cornish. Washington, DC: The World Future Society, 1980, pp. 39–40.

READING 36

Waiting for Godot: The Great Ed Tech Dream

Steven O'Brien

During the mid-1960s it seemed likely that technology was about to solve the problems of public education in America. Technology would finally make it possible to achieve the American dream of equal educational opportunity for all—black and white, gifted and handicapped, rich and poor, male and female, motivated and unmotivated. All of these and every other conceivable group would find intellectual fulfillment in school through machines. Audiovisual materials would explain and motivate, and the computer would provide instruction to students when and as they needed it.

Teaching quality would become standardized because the curriculums would be standardized, and the machines would make up for any on-location teacher deficiencies. The classroom teacher's occupation would change from being primarily that of an instructor to that of a resource and classroom management facilitator.

The anticipated educational technological revolution has not happened. As far as the secondary level teacher is concerned, teaching today is not much different than it was 20 years ago. The reasons for this, with the benefit of hindsight, are not difficult to discern. The effort

to revolutionize public education through technology was not a success because too much was claimed, too little research and development had been done, institutional and human dynamics were overlooked, and economic conditions were unfavorable.

Now, in the 1980s, technology proponents are convinced that the revolution prophesied for the 1960s is about to happen at last. The micros are coming. By the end of this decade the new mass-produced microcomputers will have completely altered the public school experience.

What About Today?

The problem for classroom teachers is not with the dreams of the technologists. We share their frustration over the lack of time teachers have for students and the goal of individualized instruction. In the long run we may indeed see technology revolutionize the classroom. The classroom teacher's dilemma is that dreaming about how teaching might be different tomorrow because of computer technology does not necessarily improve the teaching environment today.

Indeed, the frenzy with which school systems are rushing to climb on the computer bandwagon may actually have a negative effect.

From *Curriculum Review* (April 1984). Reprinted with permission.

Precious funds are being spent for equipment acquisition today under the premise that there will be a beneficial result tomorrow. In the meantime, actions which could improve contemporary conditions, such as lower student-teacher ratios or sabbaticals, have fallen by the wayside.

From the classroom teacher's perspective, the computer revolution has been coming for so long that the operation and planning of educational administrators for its arrival has taken on a strange resemblance to Samuel Becket's *Waiting for Godot*. The gap for the classroom teacher between what we've claimed the microcomputer will do versus what it's currently doing is tremendous.

Tomorrow, the story goes, the computer is going to make life much easier for the classroom instructor. Not only will true individualized instruction be possible, but the mundane chores of grading papers, recording marks, and maintaining student records will all be done by machine. So far, however, the introduction of the microcomputer has meant more, not less, work and pressure for the teacher.

Teachers hear that if the technological revolution does not take place this time, a large part of the blame will be theirs. They will have failed to embark on an intensive retraining program quickly enough to meet the instructional needs of their computer-eager students. In the worst scenarios, classroom teachers' failure to retrain might result in not only their obsolescence, but the obsolescence of the public school system.

The Teachers' Burden

Computer proponents talk despairingly of teachers' lack of enthusiasm to embrace the future and its hardware. However, to classroom teachers, even those who heartily endorse the new technology, the lack of teacher cooperation with industry proponents is no mystery at all, and it cannot be laid at the door of ignorance or indolence.

The contemporary secondary classroom teacher is simply too exhausted, after teaching five periods a day and dealing with the tremendous energy levels of adolescents, to be capable of serious intellectual effort—which is what computer training sesssions require for those of us who were never proficient in algebra. It takes a truly Herculean effort to force oneself to endure after-school inservice sessions, or (even worse) evening school, in order to become computer literate.

For those with the stamina and ambition to pursue the computer literacy route, the structure of the present public school salary system provides little, if any, financial remuneration. Most teachers who have been teaching for over 10 years—and this category includes the majority of secondary level teachers in America—are already at their top salary step.

In addition, teachers quickly realize that the systems for which they work, public schools, are not really ready to implement microcomputers on a wide scale. The result is that newly computer-proficient classroom teachers look to the burgeoning computer industry for positons which will financially reward them for their extra effort and offer career advancement. Computer proficiency training for teachers is turning out to be not a way to improve classroom teaching performance, but a step in the process of getting out of classroom teaching.

High Costs, Poor Software

The cost of providing one microcomputer system for each student is still prohibitive, even for affluent school systems. Proponents propose that costs will continue to drop at the same rate that they have in the past, so that systems which cost a thousand dollars today will cost only a hundred dollars in eight years. Perhaps.

But in the meantime, school systems are investing ever-increasing amounts of limited funds to purchase equipment which is going to be used primarily by a minority of the school's population—the very students who already receive a large share of the school's resources—the bright, college-bound, mathematically talented, usually upper middle and middle class students who may even have a computer at home. The classroom teacher sees the gap between the "have" and "have-not" students widening, not narrowing, as a result of the new technologies that are supposed to equalize educational opportunity.

Even if we found the means to provide microcomputers for every child in our secondary schools, unless we also provide programs which meet students' needs, they will be of limited usefulness. Proponents of computers dismiss the contemporary lack of educational software as a short-term phenomenon which we will quickly overcome, just as soon as a sufficient market is created by the wide distribution of hardware throughout our nation's schools.

To a classroom teacher, however, software shortage means a lack of curriculum, and that translates into the most serious problem possible: no lessons. Without lesson plans you cannot teach very much, no matter how enticing the machine is, or how well trained the teacher may be. Teachers will not, as proponents claim, simply create their own programs. With the exception of a few subject areas, such as mathematics, it is simply impractical. Social studies teachers, for instance, simply do not have enough time to develop and work the bugs out of their own simulation programs and continue to teach at the same time. Curriculum software must be provided for the hardware to be properly and cost-efficiently utilized.

At the present time there are no basal software packages available for high school use. Most programs currently available are drill-and-practice applications for supplementary classroom use. Ninety-five percent of the large computer packages which do exist are arithmetic programs, and although all programs contain teacher's manuals, few provide lesson plans or specific activities to integrate them into a curriculum. The major emphasis of contemporary programs is on the recall of previously learned facts.

Where to Turn?

The marketplace is not likely to be much help in solving the lack of educational software because the greatest profit lies in the development of games and software for industry. Profits draw talent. Unless federal funding is provided, software development for secondary level schools is likely to be slow. If federal funding were provided, this scenario could change dramatically, but the likelihood of that development is not good under the Reagan administration.

Are computers being oversold? Since the 1960s, a wide variety of instructional technologies have appeared with great fanfare, only to eventually disappear into the compelxity that is the public education system in America. The programmed text was followed by the teaching machine, which preceded typewriter-oriented computer-assisted instruction (CAI) and computer-managed instruction (CMI), which were replaced by display-oriented CAI and CMI and their equivalents on microcomputers. The next system to join the line is the intelligent video-disc currently being developed.

Through it all, only one educational medium has continued to offer ease of use, portability, durability, programmability, and cost benefit ratio—the book.

REFERENCES AND ADDITIONAL READINGS FOR UNIT 3

Stricter Standards for the Nation's Schools

Albrecht, J. E. (1984). A Nation at Risk: Another View. *Phi Delta Kappan, 65,* 10, 684–685.

Cross, K. P. (1984). The Rising Tide of School Reform Reports. *Phi Delta Kappan, 66,* 3, 167–172.

Currence, C. (1985, October 16). Reforms Could Increase Dropouts, Dilute Curriculum, Study Says. *Education Week, 5,* 7, 5.

Glaser, N. (1984, May). Review Symposium: The Problem with Competence. *American Journal of Education.* 306–313.

Ohanian, S. (1985). Huffing and Puffing and Blowing Schools Excellent. *Phi Delta Kappan, 66,* 5, 316–321.

Passow, A. H. (1984). Tackling the Reform Reports of the 1980s. *Phi Delta Kappan, 65,* 10, 674–683.

The National Commission on Excellence in Education. (1983). *A Nation at Risk: The Imperative for Educational Reform.* Washington, DC: U.S. Government Printing Office.

Competency (Certification) Testing for Teachers.

Associated Press. (1985, July 4). Teachers Support Dismissal Resolution. *Lansing State Journal, 3A.*

Gallup, G. H. (1984). The 16th Annual Gallup Poll of the Public's Attitudes Toward the Public Schools. *Phi Delta Kappan, 66,* 1, 23–38.

Hackley, L. V. (1985). The Decline in the Number of Black Teachers Can Be Reversed. *Educational Measurement: Issues and Practice, 4,* 3, 17–19.

Hodgkins, R. & McKenna B. (1982). Testing and Teacher Certification: An Explosive Combination. *Educational Measurement: Issues and Practice, 1,* 2, 10–12 & 26.

Lehmann, I. J. & Phillips, S. E. (1985). *Teacher Competency Examination Programs: A National Survey.* Paper presented at the annual meeting of the National Council on Measurement in Education, Chicago, IL.

Lines, P. M. (1985). Testing the Teacher: Are There Legal Pitfalls? *Phi Delta Kappan, 66,* 9, 618–622.

Popham, W. J. (1985). Recertification Tests for Teachers. *Educational Measurement: Issues and Practice, 4,* 3, 23–25.

Shanker, A. & Ward, J. G. (1982). Teacher Competency and Testing: A Natural Affinity. *Educational Measurement: Issues and Practice, 1,* 2, 6–9 & 26.

Vold, D. J. (1985). The Roots of Teacher Testing in America. *Educational Measurement: Issues and Practice, 4,* 3, 5–7.

Minimum Competency Testing

Anderson, B. & Pipho, C. (1984). State-Mandated Testing and the Fate of Local Control. *Phi Delta Kappan, 66,* 3, 209–212.

Bracey, G. W. (1978) Some Reservations About Minimum Competency Testing. *Phi Delta Kappan, 59,* 549–552.

Citron, C. H. (1983). Courts Provide Insight on Content Validity Requirements. *Educational Measurement: Issues and Practice, 2,* 4, 6–7.

Debra, P. vs. Turlington. (1983). Case 78–892. Memorandum Opinion and Order (M.D. Florida, May 4).

Ebel, R. L. (1978). The Case for Minimum Competency Testing. *Phi Delta Kappan, 59,* 546–549.

Mehrens, W. A. (1979). The Technology of Competency Measurement. In Robert Ingle, Mary Carroll, and William Gephart, eds. *Assessment of Student Competence.* Bloomington, Ind.: Phi Delta Kappa.

Mitzman, B. (1978, November). Is Minimum Competency Flunking Its Test? *Learning ,* 98–101.

Mottl, R. M. vs. Cawelti, G. (1978, February). Point/Counterpoint: Are You in Favor of a National Competency Test? *Instructor, 32.*

Newman, W. B. (1979, May). Competency Testing: A Response to Arthur Wise. *Educational Leadership, 36,* 549–551.

Pipho, C. (1979). Involving Yourself in the Minimum Competency Testing Movement. *Teacher 97,* 3, 62–63.

Pipho, C. (1979, May). Competency Testing: A response to Arthur Wise. *Educational Leadership, 36,* 551–554.

Thurstone, P. & House, E. R. (1981). The NIE Adversary Hearing on Minimum Competency Testing. *Phi Delta Kappan, 63,* 2, 87–89.

Wise, A. (1979). Why Minimum Competency Testing Will Not Improve Education. *Educational Leadership, 36, 546 –549.*

Norm-Referenced Versus Criterion-Referenced Measurements

Airasian, Peter W., and Madaus, George F. "Criterion-Referenced Testing in the Classroom." *Measurement in Education* 3, no. 4 (1972): 1–8.

Carroll, John B. "Problems of Measurement Related to the Concept of Learning for Mastery." In *Mastery Learning: Theory and Practice,* ed. James H. Block. New York: Holt, Rinehart, and Winston, 1971, p. 152.

Carver, Ronald P. "Two Dimensions of Tests: Psychometric and Edumetric." *American Psychologist* 29 (1974): 512–518.

Glaser, Robert, and Nitko, Anthony J. "Measurement in Learning and Instruction." In *Educational Measurement,* 2nd ed. ed. Robert L. Thorndike, Washington, D.C.: American Council on Education, 1971, pp. 625–670.

Jackson, Rex. *Developing Criterion-Referenced Tests.* Princeton, N.J.: ERIC Clearinghouse on Tests, Measurement and Evaluation, June 1970.

Klein, Stephen P., and Kosecoff, Jacqueline. *Issues and Procedures in the Development of Criterion-Referenced Tests.* Princeton, N.J.: ERIC Clearinghouse on Tests, Measurement, and Evaluation, Educational Testing Service, TM Report 26, Sept. 1973.

Lyman, Howard B. "Criterion-Referenced Testing." *Measurement News* 15, no. 3 (1972): 3.

Mehrens, William A., and Ebel, Robert L. "Some Comments on Criterion-Referenced and Norm-Referenced Achievement Tests." *Measurement in Education* 10, no. 1 (1979): 1–8.

Popham, W. James. "Normative Data for Criterion-Referenced Tests." *Phi Delta Kappan* 57 (1976): 593–594.

Popham, W. James. "An Approaching Peril: Cloud-Referenced Tests." *Phi Delta Kappan* 55 (1974): 614–615.

Popham, W. James, and Husek, T. R. "Implications of Criterion-Referenced Measurement." *Journal of Educational Measurement* 6, no. 1 (1969): 1–10.

The Computer Revolution

Bork, A. (1984). Computers in Education Today—and Some Possible Futures. *Phi Delta Kappan, 66, 4* 239–243.

Brzezinski, E. J. (1984). Microcomputers and Testing: Where Are We and How Did We Get There? *Educational Measurement: Issues and Practice, 3,* 2, 7–10.

Hassett, J. (1984). Computers in the Classroom. *Psychology today, 18,* 9, 22–28.

Judd, W. (1983). A Teacher's Place in the Computer Curriculum. *Phi Delta Kappan, 65,* 2, 120–122.

Komoski, P. K. (1984). Educational Computing: The Burden of Insuring Quality. *Phi Delta Kappan, 66,* 4, 244–248.

Leonard, G. (1984, April). The Great School Reform Hoax. *Esquire, 101,* 4, 47–56.

Lepper, M. R. (1985). Microcomputers in Education: Motivational and Social Issues. *American Psychologist, 40,* 1, 1–18.

Papert, S. (1984). New Theories for New Learnings. *School Psychology Review, 13,* 4, 422–428.

Railsback, C. E. (1983). Microcomputers: Solutions in Search of Problems? *Phi Delta Kappan, 65,* 2, 118–120.

Sardello, R. J. (1984). The Technological Threat to Education. *Teachers College Record, 85,* 4, 631–639.

Snider, R. C. (1984). Terminal Time in the Classroom. *Phi Delta Kappan, 65,* 2, 115–118.

Walker, D. F. (1983). Reflections on the Educational Potential and Limitatons of Microcomputers. *Phi Delta Kappan, 65,* 2, 103–107.

Classroom Dynamics

Regular Versus Special Education:
Is This Dual System Justified?

Teacher Expectancies: Teacher Expectations
as Self-Fulfilling Prophecies

Motivation: Intrinsic and Cognitive
Versus Extrinsic and Social Factors

Discipline: Self-Guidance Versus External Control

Regular Versus Special Education: Is This Dual System Justified?

Developments presently occurring in the education of exceptional children differ drastically from patterns established during the past twenty-five years. The consequences of these changes are so extensive that they affect not only the education of handicapped children and youth, but the future of all children. Whereas the self-contained special class was historically the most popular model for educating handicapped children, mainstreaming has become a well established educational practice as a result of recent federal legislation that guarantees the handicapped child's right to equal educational opportunity.

More than a decade has elapsed since Public Law 94–142 (the Education for All Handicapped Children Act of 1975) was passed, and it is instructive to review the major criticisms being leveled at special education programs today. Four significant charges have been made against special education programs for students with mild learning and behavior problems (Pugach and Lilly, 1984).

1. Special education programs have grown indiscriminately, resulting in an over-identification of students as handicapped. The primary determinant of whether a student receives special education services appears to be the act of referral by a classroom teacher.

2. Special education resources or pull-out services are not the most effective alternative if the goal is to support regular education teachers and to help students succeed in the regular classroom. Given a period of no-growth budgets in education, the very growth of special education services has prevented the growth of quality education by smaller class sizes in regular education.

3. Special education has often become the only means of providing supportive services to teachers and students. In many instances, growth of learning disability services has brought about the demise of regular remedial services.

4. The notion of differentness is a myth in which the presumed differences between students have been overstressed.

As a result of these criticisms, educators on both sides have recognized the need to establish a mutual ground that focuses on defining the common elements of regular and special education. In the opening article, William and Susan Stainback argue that a dual system of education is no longer necessary.

They contend that sorting students into "normal" and "mildly handicapped" represents an arbitrary decision and that all students are unique. Furthermore they postulate that individualized instructional programs and services are important for all students and that such services should not be designed solely for exceptional students. The instructional needs of the mildly handicapped, they say, do not warrant two educational systems. Instead of duplicating services unnecessarily and competing with each other, educators should cooperate and share their expertise and resources to benefit all children.

Mesinger contends that the Stainbacks' views represent a minority positon. He suspects that more specialized personnel would be needed under a unified system but that the needed funding would not be forthcoming. He is reluctant to ban special education until regular education training and practice improve dramatically.

Thought Questions

Is there evidence to suggest the superiority of merger over dichotomous placement, or is the merger movement based primarily on social and political values?

Does evidence on mainstreaming *attitudes* indicate that regular educators are indeed willing to enter into a marriage with special education? If regular education and special education were divorced initially because of regular education's unwillingness or inability to individualize instruction for children who are "mildly handicapped," what has changed to suggest that a second marriage will be any more effective?

Are the educational goals of a regular class well suited to the needs of exceptional children? Does the use of the normalization principle ignore the fact that, by definiton, normalization procedures work best with normal children?

What special training and supportive services are needed to enhance a regular class teacher's willingness and readiness to cope with difficult children?

If a merger becomes a reality, what will be the fate of other children in the regular class? For example, will the greater individualization of instruction result in an improved quality of education for all members of the class, or will the non-handicapped peers suffer because the teacher has to spend undue amounts of time with the special learners?

Is there a danger that in reconceptualizing services the resources necessary to provide relevant assistance to teachers and students may be lost rather than redistributed? For example, can and will state departments of special education allow reimbursement for handicapped students who are mainstreamed on a full-time basis?

What can be done to facilitate the social acceptance of handicapped children in a regular class setting?

What implications would merger have for teacher training?

Do you think that parents of handicapped children would be supportive of the merger movement?

A Rationale for the Merger of Special and Regular Education

William Stainback and Susan Stainback

Special education was developed over a century ago to meet the instructional needs of students considered exceptional or special. Since that time, there have been two types of education, special and regular. Although special education is technically a subsystem of regular education, as noted by Reynolds and Birch (1982), in effect, a dual system of education has operated, each with its own pupils, teachers, supervisory staff, and funding system. While there have been attempts in recent years to reduce the sharp dichotomy between special and regular education (Dunn, 1968; Hobbs, 1975; Lilly, 1979), the dual system basically remains intact. There are still special and regular school personnel, students, and funding.

The purpose of this article is to propose that this dual system, while initially a positive step for education, is no longer needed. The authors take the position that the time has arrived for special and regular education to merge into one unified system structured to meet the unique needs of all students. To justify this position, a rationale for the merger of regular and special education is presented. The implica-

tions of such a position for meeting the instructional needs of all students are also considered.

Rationale for Merger

The rationale for merger is based on two premises. The first is that the instructional needs of students do not warrant the operation of a dual system. There are several reasons for this premise.

"Special" and "Regular" Students

There are not two distinct types of students—special and regular. According to Martin (1976), "One of the ways in which many of us concerned with education have been incorrect is in our conceptualization of children as dichotomized into normal and exceptional" (p. 5). All students differ along continuums of intellectual, physical, and psychological characteristics. Individual differences are universal and thus the study of deviant people is really a study of all humankind (Telford & Sawrey, 1981).

The idea that some students are distinctly different from the "normal" population of students, and are therefore "special," has been

From *Exceptional Children* 51 (1984): 102–111. Reprinted with permisison.

justified on the basis that some students deviate to an extreme from the "norm" or "average" on one or more characteristics (Schulz & Turnbull, 1983). Designation of what is extreme has been cited for a wide range of characteristics deemed pertinent to educational success, from achievement and intellectual to emotional, auditory, and visual characteristics.

However, regardless of any designated cutoffs, all students still differ to varying degrees from one another along the same continuums of differences. The designation of arbitrary cutoffs does not make students any more different between the special and regular groups than within these groups. This may be one reason why so many researchers have resorted to complex clusters and interactions of behaviors in their definitions and sophisticated statistical analyses in their attempts to differentiate "special" students from those who are "normal" or "regular." As noted by Algozzine and Ysseldyke (1983), when these definitions and "statistical concoctions are deemed most impressive they have included every imaginable human characteristic and scores on a myriad of tests" (p. 246).

In short, there are not—as implied by a dual system—two distinctly different types of students, that is, those who are special and those who are regular. Rather, all students are unique individuals, each with his/her own set of physical, intellectual, and psychological characteristics.

Individualized Services

There is not a separate group of students requiring special individualized services to meet their instructional needs. Special education, and the dual system, is largely based on the assumption that there is a special group of students who need individualized educational programs tailored to their unique needs and characteristics. Such a position is educationally discriminatory. As noted above, *all* students are unique individuals and their individual differences can influence their instructional needs (Blankenship & Lilly, 1981). Thus, individual-

ized educational programming and services are important for all students and, as stated by Jordan (1980), there is nothing to warrant that individualized programming should be a privilege provided only to "exceptional" students. Tailor-made instructional programs should be provided for all students, whether considered bright, handicapped, minority, or average (Ellis, 1980; Shane 1979).

It should be noted that while individualization in basic educational programming (e.g., pacing, materials) is important for all students, there is increasing recognition in both special (Lloyd, 1984) and regular (Goodlad, 1983) education that individual differences among students do not necessarily imply that students should be given different educational "treatments." On the contrary, the "aptitude-treatment interaction" research casts considerable doubt on the practice of individualizing or assigning students according to the remedial, compensatory, or preferred learning style training models (Lloyd, 1984). However, if it is found in future research that individualization can be made profitable in regard to, for example, learning styles, then this type of individualization should occur for *all* students who need it, not just "special" or "regular" students.

Instructional Methods

There are now two discrete sets of instructional methods—one set for use with "special" students and another set for use with "regular" students. As used here, instructional methods refer to basic instructional processes, such as the development of behavioral objectives, curricular-based assessment procedures, task analysis, the arrangement of antecedents and consequences, and open education/discovery learning methods. While such methods need to be tailored to individual characteristics and needs, few, if any, can be clearly dichotomized into those applicable only for special students or only for regular students. As stated by Gardner (1977) "There are no unique methods for use with exceptional children that differ in kind from those used with normal children"

(p. 74). Fortunately, the longstanding assumption that there are two methodologies or psychologies of learning—one for "special" people and one for "regular" people—is beginning to erode (Bogdan & Taylor, 1976; Sarason, 1982). While basic instructional methods are emphasized here, it is discussed later in this article why a dual system is not necessary in order to offer instruction in what some people consider "unique" curricular areas such as self-care/community living skills, braille, sign language, mobility trainings, and speech-reading.

In general, the instructional needs of students do not warrant the operation of a dual system. On the contrary, the instructional needs of students would support the merger of the two systems into a comprehensive, unified system designed to meet the unique needs of every student.

The second premise on which the rationale for merger is based centers on inefficiency of operation. There are a number of reasons why maintaining two systems is inefficient.

Classification

The dual system creates an unnecessary and expensive need to classify students. Stainback and Stainback (1980) have noted that the existence of special education encourages categorization and the subsequent stereotyping of students. It works against viewing all students as individuals, each with his/her own profile of strengths and weaknesses.

Categorization is encouraged since it becomes necessary with a dual system to determine who belongs in which system. A great deal of time, money, and effort are currently expended trying to determine who is regular and who is special and what "type" or category of exceptionality each special student fits. This continues to be done in spite of the fact that a combination of professional opinion and research indicates that classification is often done unreliably, it stereotypes students, and is of little instructional value (Biklen, in press; Blatt, Biklen, & Bogdan, 1977; Gables, Hen-

drickson, Shores, & Young, 1983; Gardner, 1982; Sailor & Guess, 1983; Potter, Ysseldyke, Regan, & Algozzine, 1983).

While most of the criticisms, research, and recommendations related to classification practices have been directed toward the "soft" categories (e.g., learning disabilities), there is little evidence that classification of students with severe limitations in intellectual ability, vision, hearing, or movement of body parts is educationally useful for comprehensive educational planning. A student who has little or no vision, for example, is a whole human being with many intellectual, social, psychological, and physical characteristics. Classification according to one or a few characteristics is minimally useful in planning a total educational program. Similarly, while it may be worth while from a medical perspective to classify students as having Down's syndrome, or autism, there is little educational value to such classifications. The educational needs of students classified Down's syndrome or autistic can be distorted by not viewing them individually and as whole persons. In short, there is much more to a child classified autistic than the characteristics that define him/her as having autism.

Competition and Duplication

The dual system has fostered competition and, in some cases, unnecessary duplication rather than cooperation among professionals. Educators should share their expertise and pool their resources in order to get maximal "mileage" from their instructional efforts. However, the dual system approach has interfered with such cooperative efforts. As Lortie (1978) has explained:

> The historical separation of special and regular educators has taken its toll in the relations between them; shared viewpoints and mutual understanding, it appears, are not the rule. Educators outside special education are often perceived as either indifferent to, or even prejudiced against, the needs of children considered handi-

capped. Special educators, on the other hand, sometimes project the attitudes of an embattled group with its "them versus us" mentality. (p. 236)

This breakdown of professional relationships, and the resulting inefficiency, occurs on multiple levels. On an educational research level, the special/regular education dichotomy often interferes with widespread use of research findings, since potentially useful information may be overlooked by special or regular educators because of its affiliation with the other system. In addition, colleges and universities often organize parallel special and regular education departments and programs to train teachers without coordinating or consolidating their efforts. This inefficiency also occurs in direct service programs. At the local, state, and federal levels there are generally divisions or offices of special and regular education that tend not to cooperate or share in the use of personnel, materials, equipment, or the development and operation of accounting, monitoring, and funding mechanisms. Recent indepth field investigations have documented the widespread existence of this separateness and lack of cooperation between special and regular educators (Bogdan, 1983a, 1983b).

The poor professional relationships noted above not only reduce the potential benefits of pooling expertise and resources, but also encourage detrimental, counterproductive advocacy attempts. Factions within education, perpetuated by the dual system, limit advocacy potential for the education of all students. By factioning out lobbying efforts for educational resources designated for subgroups of children, there is a resulting divided effort. These divided efforts cause advocates for education to compete with one another rather than work together to gain greater educational resources for all students. As pointed out by Moran (1984), when interest groups are divided, all lose in the long run. By joining forces in a unified educational system, a larger, more powerful working and lobbying group could be organized.

In short, a dual system creates artificial barriers between people and divides resources, personnel, and advocacy potential. As noted by Martin (1978):

> We need to examine the assumptions that have led us to think of regular education and special education as dichotomous constructs. This kind of thinking has led to the treatment of common problems by separate groups who use different language constructs, publish in different journals, and in general, cannot communicate. We need to find a way to share and to work together, rather than to continue to divide our tasks. (p. iv)

Eligibility by Category

In the dual system, eligibility for instructional and related services is based on category affiliation, interfering with attention to the specific learning needs and interests of each student. In the dual system an elaborate procedure for classifying/categorizing students is used to determine who is and who is not eligible for a variety of educational and related services. Services such as occupational therapy, instruction in self-care skills, social interaction skills, and creative thinking; access to instructional materials such as large print, talking or braille books, and adapted seating or communication devices are generally determined on the basis of the category to which a student is assigned.

However, these categories often do not reflect the specific educational needs and interests of students in relation to such services. For example, some students categorized as visually handicapped may not need large print books, while others who are not labeled visually impaired and thus are ineligible for large print books could benefit from their use. Similarly, not all students labeled behaviorally disordered may need self-control training, while some students not so labeled may need self-control training as a part of their educational experience. Such categories—perpetuated by the dual system—actually interfere with providing some students with the services they require to progress toward their individual educational goals. Eligibility for educational and related services, as pointed out by Gardner (1977) and Meyen (1983), should be based on the abilities, interests, and needs of each student as they relate to instructional options and services, rather than on the student's inclusion in a categorical group.

In regard to eligibility, it should be noted that some professionals have argued that categorization of students is essential in order to make them eligible for special assistance. However, as noted by Telford and Sawrey (1981), people in need of assistance can be given help without categorization. All human beings in need of assistance should be entitled to help, whether or not they fall within prescribed categorical limits. Providing special assistance only to special categories of people results in the multiplication of categories and the assigning of people to these groups, rather than focusing on their circumstances and needs.

The only reason for eligibility criteria is if some people are entitled to assistance and others are not. However, in education, *all* students are (or should be) entitled to assistance if they need it (Moran, 1983). The only criteria should be that their assessment profile indicates that they need assistance. For instance, if a student needs assistance because of a letter reversal problem, a self-control problem, or a mobility problem, the student should receive the best assistance available regardless of whether the criteria for inclusion in a categorical group is met. To do otherwise is to blatantly discriminate against some students.

Curricular Options

The dual system unnecessarily reduces the range of curricular options available to students. In the dual system, a number of curricular offerings have generally been designated as the domain of either special or regular education. For example, most regular education students are not provided access to social interaction skill training or instruction in creative thinking, whereas special education students do not always have access to many regular education curricular offerings such as typing or band. Although there has been an increasing involvement of special education students in regular education course offerings, there does

not appear to be a reciprocal trend to involve regular education students in special education offerings that could benefit them. Furthermore, duplication of offerings in the basic skill areas such as math and reading unnecessarily drains resources. By consolidating all curricular offerings in one unified system, all students could be provided a broader range of curricular options with less wasted effort.

With consolidation, the individual needs of students would have a better chance of being accommodated. Not only would all students be provided more diverse curricular options, but also selection of learning experiences could be based more directly on what each student needs, rather than on category affiliation. For example, if a student's assessment profile indicated a need for rudimentary language development and/or self-care skills, the student could be included in classes or courses appropriate for his/her age range which are designed to teach those skills without the necessity of being labeled. Similarly, if a student needed front row seating or instruction in speechreading to comprehend what the teachers were saying, the student could receive it. In short, by consolidating all curricular offerings into one unified system, any one student would have access to any of the classes, individualized tutoring, support personnel, and material adaptations now offered in special and regular education.

The "Deviant" Label

The dual system requires students to fit the available regular education program or be labeled as deviant. With the dual system, if a student exhibits learning or behavior characteristics which do not match the demands of the regular education program, the student is typically referred for assessment and, in many cases, is labeled "deviant," "different," "special," or "exceptional." Once labeled, an attempt is then made to provide the student an appropriate program through special education in the regular classroom, resource room, or special class. The premise is that the student does not fit the program and should change to a "special" program, rather than modify or adjust the regular program to meet the needs of the student. Also, this sytem does not allow for addressing the unique learning needs and characteristics of the large numbers of nonlabeled students who can adjust only marginally to the demands of the regular program. An underlying tenet of American education is that the education program should fit the needs of the student rather than that the student should fit the needs of the education program. Inherent in the dual system is a contradiction of this basic tenet; the student must fit the regular program or be labeled deviant or special. A unified system could alleviate this contradiction. By special and regular educators uniting in their advocacy attempts and pooling their resources, modifications and adjustments could be made in regular education to meet the unique learning needs and characteristics of all students. As noted by Reynolds and Birch (1982), for years the rhetoric of both regular and special educators has centered on achieving individualization of instruction for all students. Merger could set the stage for achievement of that goal.

In conclusion, it is inefficient to operate two systems. This inefficiency, coupled with the lack of need for two systems, supports the merger of special and regular education. Table 1 presents a summary and comparison of the characteristics of the current dual system and the proposed unified system. The rationale for merger is based on the more advantageous characteristics of the unified system as compared to the dual system.

Implications

Obviously merger would have numerous implications. Several of the most salient are discussed here.

Personnel Preparation and Assignment

Without the special/regular education dichotomy, the training and assignment of personnel such as teachers, consultants, and resource specialists would need to be refocused. Similar to the need for teachers with expertise in reading or social studies, there would be a need in a unified system for teachers with specialization in self-care and community living skills for example. Also needed would be resource specialists and consultants in areas such as behavior management, material adaptation, and alternative communication systems, including expertise in various communication boards and equipment, sign language, and speechreading.

The major difference between what is currently practiced and what would be needed in a merged system is the reorganization of personnel preparation and assignment according to instructional categories rather than by categories of students. This would require special and regular education departments in universities and colleges to pool their resources to ensure that all educators obtain a strong base in the teaching/learning process. Some teachers, resource specialists, and consultants would also need to have specialization in instructional areas traditionally covered by special education. For example, while many teachers and consultants would continue to specialize in traditional regular education areas such as reading and language arts, or math and science, others might specialize in basic motor and self-care skills or alternative communication systems.

Classification

Merger would provide an opportunity to reduce much of the current emphasis on classification, homogeneous grouping, and "tracking" of students. Instead, students of similar ages could be *heterogeneously* grouped in the same school programs and activities whenever possible. The reasons for, and benefits of, heterogeneous educational arrangements have been repeatedly discussed in the professional literature (Biklen, in press; Bogdan, 1983a; Goodlad, 1983; Moran, 1983; Oakes, 1983; Stainback & Stainback, in press; Taylor, 1982). There is also substantial research evidence that most students can be academically and socially successful in heterogeneous groupings if adaptive, in-

Table 1
Comparison of Dual and Unified Systems

Concern	Dual System	Unified System
1. Student characteristics	Dichotomizes student into special and regular	Recognizes among all students continuum of intellectual, physical, and psychological characteristics
2. Individualization	Stresses individualization for students labeled special	Stresses individualization for all students
3. Instructional strategies	Seeks to use special strategies for special students	Selects from range of available strategies according to each student's learning needs
4. Type of educational services	Eligibility generally based on category affiliation	Eligibility based on each student's individual learning needs
5. Diagnostics	Large expenditures on identification of categorical affiliation	Emphasis on identifying the specific instructional needs of all students.
6. Professional relationships	Establishes artificial barriers among educators that promote competition and alienation	Promotes cooperation through sharing resources, expertise, and advocacy responsibilities
7. Curriculum	Options available to each student are limited by categorical affiliation	All options available to every student as needed
8. Focus	Student must fit regular education program or be referred to special education	Regular education program is adjusted to meet all students' needs

dividualized, and cooperative learning programs are established (Biklen, in press; Johnson & Johnson, 1980; Madden & Slavin, 1983; Slavin, 1983; Wang, 1981; Wang & Birch, 1984; Want and Walberg, 1983; Taylor, 1982).

While heterogeneous educational arrangements should be encouraged wherever possible, students would still need to be grouped, in some instances, into specific courses or classes according to their instructional needs. For example, not all students would need to learn basic self-care/community living skills. Similarly, some students may not be able to profit from advanced physics. It has been recommended, however, that when such groupings occur, they be kept flexible and fluid to avoid the development of a tracking system and to allow students to move in and out and across the groupings as their individual needs and interests dictate (Stainback & Stainback, 1980). With increased computer capabilities in the schools, flexible scheduling based on individual student needs could be more easily accomplished than might be initially envisioned.

Support Personnel

Support personnel now spend a great deal of time classifying and making eligibility decisions. This would not be necessary in a merged system. If a request for help was received, help could be given regardless of who the student or teacher happen to be. No one would have to "qualify" for assistance. As a result, the enormous amount of time currently spent by support personnel in classifying and making eligibility decisions could be used in more productive ways, such as going into classrooms on request and working directly with teachers and students on specific problems. The emphasis could be on instructional assessment and program planning as opposed to classification and eligibility.

Funding

In special education, funding is now based largely on categories of exceptionality. A different funding approach would be needed in a merged system. Hobbs (1980) has proposed that funding be related to service or program elements. For example, categorical funds might be disbursed for individual tutoring or lessons in social skill training, total communication, or speech therapy. The purpose would be to get away from "child-in-category" as the funding unit (i.e., number of students in a category as indicative of number of students requiring a particular training option) and, instead, move to a service unit.

If, for instance, a given number of students required instruction in an alternative communication system, self-care skills, or advanced physics, the cost estimates to operate such services would constitute the justification for monetary appropriations, rather than categories of labeled students. Or, if it is documented that there is a deficiency of research, personnel preparation, or other resources in an area traditionally covered by special education (e.g., sign language and speechreading), it may be necessary to earmark monies for the particular deficient area. This could be done without "child-in-category" funding. It could be done in a manner similar to what is done now when there is an identified lack of research, personnel, or resources in areas such as math and science. State and federal legislators could ear-

mark funds to facilitate research, training, and the accumulation of resources in the deficient instructional areas.

It should be stressed that it would be critical to move cautiously toward a reorganization of funding patterns. An initial step might be for federal and state agencies involved in the facilitation of research to earmark some support for studying funding options. A second step might be for federal and state agencies involved in funding service delivery to devise options or alternatives wherein a few states or school systems could submit plans to receive funding, on an experimental basis, to meet the needs of all students, without the necessity of categorizing and labeling some students. Such plans should include monitoring and accountability procedures to assure that *all* students are, in fact, having their needs met. With such an approach, it would be possible to slowly and cautiously move toward merger, without the threat of a radical reduction in funding and resources for students unserved or ill-served in the past.

While labels have created a wellspring of pity and sympathy that has resulted in strong federal and state support for special education (Deno, 1970), no student should have to be categorized, labeled, and pitied in order to receive a free and appropriate education. All students should be entitled to a free and appropriate education without any student being subjected to the de-individualizing and stereotyping impact of a pity-evoking label.

Perception of Individual Differences

Merger could alter the way in which individual student characteristics are viewed. No longer would there be a need to approach differences in human capabilities or characteristics as disabilities on which to base categorical groupings. This is important because individual differences in auditory or visual ability, rate of intellectual development, or degree and type of body movements do not represent the entire person. This is often implied when individuals are referred to as deaf, blind, retarded, or orthopedically impaired persons. As mentioned earlier, people are complex and possess a variety of intellectual, physical, psychological, and social characteristics. The policy of using one or a few characteristics to classify students seldom reflects, and may tend to distort, the educational needs of the person as a whole.

In a merged system, an individual difference in visual ability, for example, could be viewed as only one of numerous characteristics of a student, rather than the overriding educational focus of a student's life (i.e., a blind student should receive an "education for the blind"). This individual characteristic, along with the other characteristics of a student, may assist educators in selecting supplemental instruction or types of materials (e.g., Braille readers) that could help foster the students' educational achievements. However, it would not dictate differential placement and treatment according to a categorical affiliation which is often inherent in the disabilities approach to education.

Conclusion

Dichotomizing students into two basic types (special and regular), maintaining a dual system of education, separate professional organizations, separate personnel preparation programs, and separate funding patterns does very little to foster the values inherent in the mainstreaming and integration movement of the past decade. In essence, during the past decade we have been attempting to integrate students while separating them into two kinds and without integrating programs, personnel and resources (Taylor & Ferguson, in press).

The issue is not whether there are differences among students. There obviously are differences, even extreme differences. It is also clear that because of these differences some students may need adaptations or modifications in their educational experiences. However, this should not be used as a justification to label, segregate, or maintain a dual system of education. With careful planning, it should be possible to meet the unique needs of *all* stu-dents within one unified system of education—a system that does not deny differences, but rather a system that recognizes and accommodates for differences.

As stated by Ysseldyke and Algozzine (1982):

> The challenge that faces special educators is formidable and goes beyond the development of manuals for writing IEPs or the question of whether our research should be basic or applied. We are faced with decisions greater than the appropriate content and form of inservice or preservice training. In fact, we must question the basis for the existence of special education. (p. 254)

Although merger is proposed here, it is not intended to imply that special education has failed to fulfill its purpose. Quite to the contrary, special education has a long and rich tradition of accomplishing its purpose. Largely because of special education advocacy, recent legislation and litigation have mandated that all students must now receive a free and appropriate education. However, with this mandate, special education has reached its major goal: the right to a free and appropriate education for all students. It is now time in the historical evolution of special education to consider merging with regular education. This move could help ensure that all students not only receive an appropriate education, but that they receive it as an inherent right and not as a "special" provision. It also could help us overcome the popular notion that some students (those labeled special) are *given* appropriate, individualized educational programs and services because of their needy or "special" condition, rather than because they, just as any other student, should receive an education geared to their capabilities and needs (Voeltz, 1984).

The possibility of merging special and regular education into one unified system has been fermenting for several years. Gilhool (1976) alluded to the possibility of merger when he noted:

> We are approaching the day when, for each child, the law will require that the schooling fit the

child, his needs, his capacities, and his wishes; not the child fit the school. Thus, special education may become general and general education, special. (p. 13)

Meyen (1978) stated that the most significant change that could occur in the future would be for public education to individualize instruction and "to eliminate the dichotomy between serving exceptional and nonexceptional students" (p. 53). A review of the history of special education indicates the trend is in the direction of eventually eliminating the dichotomy. This has been reflected in the past several decades by the emergence of concepts such as deinstitutionalization, normalization, integration, mainstreaming, and zero rejection. Reynolds and Birch (1982) pointed out that "the whole history of education for exceptional students can be told in terms of one steady trend that can be described as progressive inclusion" (p. 27). At this point in the progressive inclusion trend, it is time to stop developing criteria for who does or does not belong in the mainstream and instead turn the spotlight to increasing the capabilities of the regular school environment, the mainstream, to meet the needs of *all* students.

Reform of general education will not be accomplished quickly or easily. Regular education has a history of being reluctant to meet the needs of all students. That is the primary reason special education was developed in the first place. Further, as Deno stated (1978), categorization is

deeply entrenched in the social commitments of categorically defined special-interest advocacy groups; in the structure of health, education, and welfare programs at direct service levels; in the staffing of teacher training institutions; in other professional training programs; and in general public thinking. (p. 39)

Despite these realities, there is a need to move toward merger to whatever degree possible. A dual system of education can serve to legitimize exclusion of some students from regular education, reduce opportunity for equal participation by other students, and sanction other forms of discrimination. As Hobbs (1980) noted, by placing a person in a separate category or system of education, it becomes possible to treat the person in ways that would not be tolerated were he or she a fully accepted member of the "normal" or "regular" group. Thus, it is important to explore, suggest, and attempt change.

The authors wish to acknowledge Maynard Reynolds, Lee Courtnage and Patti Swatta for their contributions to this article.

REFERENCES

Algozzine, B., & Ysseldyke, J. (1983). Learning disabilities as a subset of school failure: The oversophistication of a concept. *Exceptional Children, 50,* 242–246.

Biklen, D. (in press). (Ed.) *The complete school: Integrating special and regular education.* Columbia University: Teacher's College Press.

Blankenship, C., & Lilly, S. (1981). *Mainstreaming students with learning and behavior problems.* New York: Holt, Rinehart and Winston.

Blatt, B., Biklen, D., & Bogdan, R. (1977). *An alternative textbook in special education.* Denver: Love Publishing.

Bogdan, R. (1983a). A closer look at mainstreaming. *Educational Forum, 47,* 25–434.

Bogdan, R. (1983b). Does mainstreaming work? is a silly question. *Phi Delta Kappan, 47,* 425–434.

Bogden, R., & Taylor, S. (1976). The judged, not the judges: An insider's view of mental retardation. *American Psychologist, 31,* 47–52.

Deno, E. (1970). Special education as developmental capital. *Exceptional Children, 37,* 229–237.

Deno, E. (1978). *Educating children with emotional, learning, and behavior problems.* Minneapolis: University of Minnesota, College of Education, National Support Systems Project.

Dunn, L. M. (1968). Special education for the mildly retarded—Is much of it justifiable? *Exceptional Children 35,* 5–22.

Ellis, J. (1980). Individualized education in the 1980's. *The Serrculator, 9,* 7–8.

Gable, R., Hendrickson, J., Shores, R., & Young, C. (1983). Teacher-handicapped child classroom interactions. *Teacher Education and Special Education, 6,* 88–95.

Gardner, W. (1977). *Learning and behavior characteristics of exceptional children and youth.* Boston: Allyn & Bacon.

Gardner, W. (1982). Why do we persist? *Education and Treatment of Children, 5,* 369–378.

Gilhool, T. (1976). Changing public policies: Roots and forces. In M. Reynolds (Ed.), *Mainstreaming: Origins and implications* (pp. 8–13). Reston VA: The Council for Exceptional Children.

Goodlad, J. (1983). Individuality, commonality, and curricular practice. In G. Fenstermacher & J. Goodlad (Eds.). *Individual differences and the common curriculum,* (pp. 300–318). Chicago: The University of Chicago Press.

Hobbs, N. (1975). *The futures of children.* San Francisco: Jossey-Bass.

Hobbs, N. (1980). An ecologically oriented service-based system for the classification of handicapped children. In E. Salzinger, J. Antrobus, & Glick (Eds.), *The ecosystem of the "risk" child* (pp. 271–290). New York: Academic Press.

Johnson, D., & Johnson, R. (1980). Integrating handicapped students into the mainstream. *Exceptional Children, 47,* 90–98.

Jordan, K. F. (1980). Individual plans for all children. *The Serrculator, 9,* 7–8.

Lilly, S. (1979). *Children with exceptional needs.* New York: Holt, Rinehart and Winston.

Lloyd, J. (1984). How shall we individualize instruction—Or should we? *Remedial and Special Education, 5,* 7–15.

Lortie, D. (1978). Some reflections on renegotiation. In M. Reynolds (Ed.), *Futures of education for exceptional students* (pp. 235–244). Reston VA: The Council for Exceptional Children.

Madden, N., & Slavin, R. A. (1983). Mainstreaming students with mild handicaps: Academic and social outcomes. *Review of Educational Research, 53,* 519–569.

Martin, E. (1976). Integration of the handicapped child into regular schools. In M. Reynolds (Ed.), *Mainstreaming: Origins and implications* (pp. 5–7). Reston VA: The Council for Exceptional Children.

Martin, E. (1978). Preface. In M. Reynolds (Ed.), *Futures of education for exceptional students* (pp. iii–vi). Reston VA: The Council for Exceptional Children.

Meyen, E. (1978). An introductory prospective. In E. Meyen (Ed.), *Exceptional children and youth* (pp. 2–84). Denver: Love Publishing.

Meyen, E. (1983). Special education: The influence of yesterday on tomorrow. *Journal for Special Educators, 19,* 37–43.

Moran, M. (1983). Inventing a future for special education: A cautionary tale. *Journal for Special Educators, 19,* 28–36.

Moran, M. (1984). Excellence at the cost of instructional equity? The potential impact of recommended reforms upon low achieving students. *Focus on Exceptional Children, 16,* 1–11.

Oakes, J. (1983). Tracking and ability grouping in American schools: Some constitutional questions. *Teachers College Record, 84,* 801–819.

Potter, M., Ysseldyke, J., Regan, R., & Algozzine, B. (1983). Eligibility and classification decisions in educational settings: Issuing "passports" in a state of confusion. *Contemporary Educational Psychology, 8,* 146–157.

Reynolds, M., & Birch, J. (1982). *Teaching exceptional children in all America's schools* (2nd ed.). Reston VA: The Council for Exceptional Children.

Sailor, W., & Guess, D. (1983). *Severely handicapped students.* Boston: Houghton Mifflin.

Sarason, S. (1982). *The culture of the school and the problem of change.* Boston: Allyn & Bacon.

Schulz, J., & Turnbull, A. (1983). *Mainstreaming handicapped students.* Boston: Allyn & Bacon.

Shane, H., (1979). *Forecast for the 80's. Today's Education, 68,* 62–65.

Slavin, R. (1983). *Cooperative learning.* New York: Longman.

Slavin, R., Madden, N., & Leavey, M. (1984). Effects of cooperative learning and individualized instruction on mainstreamed students. *Exceptional Children, 50,* 434–443.

Stainback, S., & Stainback, W. (1980). *Educating children with severe maladaptive behaviors.* New York: Grune & Stratton.

Stainback, S., & Stainback, W. (in press). (Eds.) *Integration of students with severe handicaps in regular schools.* Reston VA: The Council for Exceptional Children.

Taylor, S. (1982). From segregation to integration: Strategies for integrating severely handicapped students in normal school and community settings. *Journal of the Association for the Severely Handicapped, 8,* 42–49.

Taylor, S., & Ferguson, D. (in press). A summary of strategies utilized in model programs and resource materials. In W. Stainback & S. Stainback (Eds.), *Integration of students with severe handicaps into regular schools,* Reston VA: The Council for Exceptional Children.

Telford, C., & Sawrey, J. (1981). *The exceptional individual* (4th ed.). Englewood Cliffs NJ: Prentice-Hall.

Voeltz, L. (1984). Program and curricula innovations to prepare children for integration. In N. Certo, N. Haring, & R. York (Eds.), *Public school integration of severely handicapped students,* (pp. 155–184). Baltimore: Paul Brookes Publishing.

Wang, M. (1981). Mainstreaming exceptional children: Some instructional design and implementation considerations. *Elementary School Journal, 81,* 195–221.

Wang, M., & Birch, J. (1984). Effective special education in regular classes. *Exceptional Children, 50,* 391–398.

Wang, M., & Walberg, H. (1983). Adaptive instruction and classroom time. *American Educational Research Journal, 20,* 601–626.

Ysseldyke, J. E., & Algozzine, B. (1982). *Critical issues in special and remedial education.* Boston: Houghton Mifflin.

Commentary on "A Rationale for the Merger of Special and Regular Education" or, Is It Now Time for the Lamb to Lie Down with the Lion?

John F. Mesinger

I began reading the Stainbacks' article in the October issue of *Exceptional Children* with enthusiasm which quickly turned to puzzlement as I saw the trend they were developing. Then I recalled the story of the blind wise men and the elephant. It appears from the article that the Stainbacks are exploring a side of the beast other than mine.

They assert that "an underlying tenet of American education is that the education program should fit the needs of the students rather than that the student should fit the needs of the education program." The literature I read on practices in other countries indicates that such a statement would not be supported elsewhere. In America, the literature on alternative education, the failure to fund programs for the gifted, the movement toward fundamentalist schools seem to me to be a reflection of a widespread belief in John Goodlad's observation (1969):

> But the lack of fit between school and client extends in other realms until one is forced to ask

From *Exceptional Children* 51 (1985) 510–512. Reprinted with permission.

whether our educational system serves even 50% of its clientele in reasonably satisfying ways. (p. 61)

I conclude that the Stainbacks' assertion is a distinctly minority viewpoint even in America, although it may be given more lip service than practice.

Under their unified system I suspect there would still be a need for far more specialized personnel than we now have (Smith-Davis, Burke, & Noel, 1984). This year in one state, when over 700 waivers of credentials were requested to staff special needs children, for whom no fully endorsed teachers could be employed, more than 500 were for teachers with from 1 to 10 credits in specialized instructional techniques. Last year I saw an unpublished survey which indicated that only one state appeared to be serving an expected incidence of handicapped youth. That state was not Virginia (Virginia Department of Education, 1983) where 0.7% ED (emotionally disturbed), 4.2% LD (learning disabled), and 1.4% MR (mentally retarded) were being served. (No multihandicapped were reported. The reader may speculate on reasons for this in a multicategory endorsement state.) In the youth corrections schools of that state (Virginia Department of Corrections, 1984), in 1983, 38.3% of the youth were diagnosed as handicapped (the U.S. average was reported as 41.4% [National Association of State Directors of Special Education, 1984]). Of 454 handicapped adolescents in corrections, only 179 were diagnosed as such prior to their commitment. Of the total, 245 were ED, 93 LD, 68 EMR (educably mentally retarded), and 38 multiple handicapped. This hardly supports the assertion that "special education has reached its major goal."

It is true that "State and federal legislators could earmark funds to facilitate research, training. . . . " They always *could*. They usually have not, do not, and will not vote funds for adequate longitudinal research. Nor will the executive departments see to it that all the funds noted are actually spent, particularly in R & D.

My reading of commentaries on the Rowley case (Tucker, 1983; Yudof, 1984), indicates that the U.S. Supreme Court is unlikely to require that schools live up to the mandate the Stainbacks' assert P.L. 94–142 requires. Rowley is fortunate in having parents who are well above average in educating themselves to encourage, motivate, and help their daughter with homework and other developmental tasks which involve her hearing loss. It appears to me that the parents make up for some school omissions and, since the child receives average grades, the court has ruled that the efforts taken by the schools are sufficient. Nowhere in the commentaries have I read that this point was raised in court by briefs filed in support of Rowley.

Without strong advocacy by well connected special groups, few advances for the handicapped have ever occurred. The reason blind and deaf children received educational support earlier than others is the obvious nature of their handicaps, the small numbers involved (cost factor), the existence of dedicated support groups and the empathy developed in the public for such handicapped children. Can the same really be said about the emotionally disturbed? I observe an equation: No strong advocacy group equals no funds for the handicapped.

The statement, "With this mandate, special education has reached its major goal: the right to a free and appropriate education for all students," seems to me to be far from true. As many minorities can attest, the legal right is not enough if it is not accorded in practice. The authors show that they have apparently touched my side of the beast when they state "Regular education has a history of being reluctant to meet the needs of all students." Agreeing with them on this statement about the nature of the beast, I do not believe it is time to place our handicapped children in the cage with it.

What really seems to be missing from their plot development? Teacher qualities! What can an average teacher do? What youth needs more than this? The "Nation at Risk" report (National Commission on Excellence in Education, 1983) indicates that not enough academically proficient persons are entering teacher training.

Recent critiques of public education have been severe in condemning professional preparation, the faculties, and the products (Peterson, 1983). Many teacher training programs begun in the 1970s were profit makers for their colleges at the time because of low faculty costs and high FTEs. Now, nearly devoid of standards, they should be closed. In the last decade, 113 new preservice programs were added while there was a 53% decline in graduates. Many excellent teachers are leaving and fewer talented people are entering the profession (Feistritzer, 1984). In some states some colleges are responding to declines in high talent teacher trainees by enrolling more low scoring students (Schlechty & Vance, 1983).

I don't know what vital teacher qualities the National Teacher Examination really measures, but I get nervous when some educational professionals claim that cutoff scores ranging from the 14th to the 10th percentile will be discriminatory against some entering the profession.

Clinical observation indicates that one educational problem relating to the diversity of human behavior is that adults, including teachers, vary in their abilities to cope with, manage, and teach groups of differing ranges and intensity of diversity. Some adults can cope well with larger numbers of youths behaving in more widely divergent ways than others can. The high attrition rate of ED teachers testifies to this.

Special education preservice training programs have not always produced a good product (Cruickshank, 1971; Dunn, 1968; Johnson, 1962; Mesinger & Hanvik, 1966). Although we are probably doing a better job in the 1980s with instructional methodologies, we generally do not adequately prepare students during preservice to cope with violent and recalcitrant youths (especially adolescents) and those handicapped adolescents who need vocational preparation for the world of work.

Since the literature to date seems to deny the hope that there will be a good match between students' learning problems and specific instructional methods, then at least part of the so-lution would appear to require more than just skill-training teachers at a level low enough to get all of them to a 90% competency level. Perhaps we had better take a more careful look at who we recruit into the field of preservice training and what we do (or fail to do) to help them grow into mature, competent, adult professionals.

I do not think we have to abandon a dual system in order to meet Hobbs's idea of funding services (provided by skilled specialists). I am reluctant to abandon special education as a system until I see *evidence* of a drastic improvement in regular educational teacher training and professional practice in the public schools. A true negotiation of new relationships should involve positions of comparable power or we will end up with acquiescence. I judge it is not yet time for lambs to lie down with lions in the absence of lion tamers; the Stainbacks' proposal seems premature by years.

REFERENCES

Cruickshank, W. M. (1971). Special education, the community and constitutional issues. In D. L. Walker & D. P. Howard (Eds.), *Special education: Instrument of changes in education for the 70s.* Selected papers from the University of Virginia Lecture Series, 1970–71, 5–21.

Dunn, L. M. (1968). Special education for the mildly retarded—Is much of it justifiable? *Exceptional Children, 35*(1), 5–22.

Feistritzer, E. (1984). *The making of a teacher: A report on teacher education and certification.* Washington, DC: National Center for Educational Information.

Goodlad, J. I. (1969). The schools vs. education. *Saturday Review, 52*(16), 59–61, 80–82.

Johnson, G. O. (1962). Special education for the mentally handicapped: A paradox. *Exceptional Children, 29*(10), 62–69.

Mesinger, J. F., & Hanvik, L. J. (1966). And the beanstalk grows. *Exceptional Children, 32*(6), 577–580.

National Association of State Directors of Special Education (1984). Problems in youth correctional fa-cilities. Washington, DC: *Liaison Bulletin, 10*(3).

National Commission on Excellence in Education (1983). *A nation at risk: The imperative for educational reform.* Washington, DC: U.S. Government Printing Office.

Peterson, P. E. (1983). *Making the grade.* Report of the Twentieth Century Fund Task Force on Federal Elementary and Secondary Education Policy. New York: The Fund.

Schlechty, P. C., & Vance, U.S. (1983). Institutional response to the quality/quantity issue in teacher training. *Phi Delta Kappan, 65*(2), 94–101.

Smith-Davis, J., Burke, P., & Noel, M. (1984). Personnel to educate the handicapped in America: Supply and demand from a programmatic viewpoint. Reviewed in *Phi Delta Kappan, 64*(9), 652.

Stainback, W., & Stainback, S. (1984). A rationale for the merger of special and regular education. *Exceptional Children, 51*, 102–111.

Tucker, B. P. (1983). Board of Education of the Henrick Hudson Central School District v. Rowley:

Utter chaos. *Journal of Law and Education, 12*(2), 235–245.

Virginia Department of Education, Division of Special Education Programs and Pupil Personnel Services (1983). *Program description request for FY 1984–86 Under Part B Virginia* from IX Comprehensive System of Personnel Development (20 U.S.C. 1413(a)(s); 34 CFR 300.139 (p. 101).

Virginia Department of Corrections (1984). *Characteristics of children committed to the Virginia Department of Corrections in FY 1983.* Division of Program Development and Evaluation. Research and Reporting Unit, Report #83206.

Yudof, M. G. (1984). Education for the handicapped: *Rowley* in perspective. *American Journal of Education, 92*(2), 163–177.

Grade Retention or Social Promotion?

Retention and social promotion are practices that come into play when a student does not complete a year's work satisfactorily: Retention is the practice of having the student repeat the entire grade; social promotion is the practice of promoting the student to the next grade. Both practices have their advocates, but the literature on the topic "remains atheoretical, virtually non-experimental, and highly opinionated" (Carstens, 1985, p. 48).

The issue of retention versus social promotion is not a new one. In the early 19th century, grade retention was common. One estimate was that every other child was retained at least once during the first eight years of school (Larson, 1955). This practice remained common until the 1930s when social promotion came to be seen as a more enlightened practice. By the 1960s educators noted a decline in student achievement and began to doubt the wisdom of social promotion. Many felt that the reinstatement of stricter promotion standards would improve public school education and ensure that at least all graduates had a minimal mastery of the basics. The minimum competency testing movement (see the related issue in this book) primarily was a movement to require all high school graduates to pass a test on basic skills, but it also served as a catalyst for stricter grade-to-grade promotion standards; nineteen states have now specified standards for grade promotion (Adler, 1978).

There are arguments for and against both the practices of retention and social promotion. Carstens (1985) summarizes these as follows:

The following is a condensation of views which are posited for retention and against social promotion:

1. A socially promoted child falls to the bottom of his or her class and is forced to participate in academic tasks which are too difficult.

2. Retention provides more time with nonmastered skills and is a more effective educational intervention than social promotion.

3. Social promotion leads to frustration, apathy, poor self-esteem, unhappiness and discipline problems.

4. Retention makes instruction easier to manage by creating a more homogeneous class.

5. Social promotion degrades the meaning of a high school diploma.

The arguments for social promotion and against retention are:

1. A retained student is stigmatized because he or she is older and larger than other children in the classroom, leading to poor social adjustment.

2. Retention is ineffective as an academic intervention.

3. Retention lowers motivation and self-esteem. It leads to frustration, apathy, unhappiness and discipline problems.

4. Retention is costly.

5. Retention policies discriminate against minority and poor children (p. 49).

Of course advocates of each position can critique the arguments for the opposite position.

As the article by Cooke and Stammer reprinted here points out, research has not shown retention to be the preferred approach. However, much of the research has suffered from severe design flaws (see Rose, et al., 1983). Further, even if research showed that social promotion in general was better than retention, it would not follow that it was better for all students. There may well be a subset of children that would be better off if they were retained in their current grade for another year. In general, both research and educators' beliefs suggest that if retention is to occur, the earlier the better.

Cooke and Stammer discuss models proposed by Light and Lieberman to assist in the promotion and retention decision making. However, you should be aware that other professionals are somewhat leery of such models. Vasa, Wendel, and Steckelberg investigated the content validity of Light's Retention Scale and concluded that its use was not warranted either as a psychometric instrument or as a nonpsychometric counseling tool. They concluded that "caution should be employed in using the scale for any purposes directly related to predictions or decisions about student performance and retention" (1984, p. 449).

While we believe that grade retention is useful for some students (particularly in kindergarten or first grade for students who are immature) we agree with Cooke and Stammer that neither retention nor social promotion necessarily "solves the academic difficulties of low-achieving students." Other solutions need to be tried, such as those briefly described in the article.

Thought Questions

What variables would you consider in deciding whether to retain a first grade student? Why are those variables important?

Some have argued that stricter standards for grade-to-grade promotion will result in students being more motivated and working harder in school. What are your views concerning this argument?

A study by Schuyler (1985) found that 77 percent of the teachers and 71 percent of the parents thought retainees had been successful. How persuasive are such opinions in answering the question of what is best for the children?

Grade Retention and Social Promotion Practices

Gary Cooke and John Stammer

There is no reliable body of evidence that indicates that grade retention is more beneficial than grade promotion for students with serious academic or adjustment difficulties.

Gregg Jackson

Introduction

According to Department of Health, Education and Welfare statistics, over one million students were retained in American schools during 1972. Nothing has transpired over the past decade that indicates a decline in this number. To the contrary, the "back-to-basics" movement and the more recent pronouncements about "excellence in education" have intensified concerns about student shortcomings. (The report of the National Commission on Excellence in Education in April of 1983 has put additional pressures on classroom teachers to maintain stringent academic standards. The commission report and others like it will result in a new epidemic of student retentions at all grade levels.)

From *Childhood Education* 4(1985): 302–310. Reprinted with permission from the authors and publisher.

Failing, retained, "socially promoted" or inappropriately placed students are symptoms of an educational system that is suffering from serious malfunctions. It is a system where retention practices habitually focus on the child as the problem rather than looking at the shortcomings of the system as a possible contributing factor in the problem.

The purpose of this article is to remind educators that " . . . schools should be made to fit the student, not the students made to fit the schools" (Koons, 1977, p. 701).

Without an awareness of and responsiveness to this reality, the losers will be those children who, for whatever reasons, do not meet arbitrary standards and are retained, often to spend another 40 weeks redoing the same work, or moved ahead to spend another year in ego-reducing failure experiences. One teacher expressed it this way: "They'll (the students) stay there until they get it right."

This means that school systems, and especially classroom teachers who are closest to the children, must resist getting caught up in the contest to maintain standards and "look good" to the public by retaining low-achieving students year after year. As increased pressure is applied for accountability in classrooms, it is imperative that teachers familiarize themselves with research regarding the effects of retention and promotion. With this research knowledge, thoughtful and intelligent decisions can be initiated about appropriate placement policies and procedures, and effective choices made about student placement which address all elements of the learning environment. Common sense tells us that students having difficulty learning in school need special attention through carefully designed and individualized programs. When students are failing, educators should examine teaching (effective methodology), curriculum (its appropriateness) and learning (the progress of the child toward goals) as a source of the problem instead of automatically blaming student "shortcomings."

The foundation for decisive educational change must be built on what research tells us. In examining promotion and retention, a number of questions must be asked: What do we know about the effectiveness of grade retention and so-called social promotion? Does an extra year to complete work automatically help a low-achieving student? Do social promotions really bolster children's self-esteem by keeping them with their age and peer group? Do social promotions just result in another year of continued failing experiences? Does the extra year really let children catch up?

Research Findings

These and other questions have been the concern of teachers since schools began the practice of grading in the mid-1800s. The following research section encapsulates retention and promotion practices within schools over the past 65 years.

Major Reviews

The most impressive summary of research on retention and promotion practices appeared in the *Review of Educational Research* (Jackson, 1975). The author surveyed over 100 studies related to retention and promotion. From this extensive analysis 44 studies were scrutinized

closely, since they met the primary criterion of having been original research.

Among Jackson's conclusions was the suggestion that " . . . those educators who retain pupils in a grade do so without valid research evidence to indicate that such treatment will provide greater benefits to students with academic or adjustment difficulties than will promotion to the next grade" (p. 627).

Jackson further concluded that there were four weaknesses commonly found among the 44 studies which reduced both their validity and reliability:

1. Failing to sample from varied populations of students, severely limiting the researcher's ability to generalize.
2. Failing to carefully define the treatments or procedures for children in retained or socially promoted classrooms.
3. Failing to conduct longitudinal research, thus severely limiting statements about long-term effects of retention and promotion practices.
4. Failing to investigate the interactive effects between treatments, the general characteristics of students, the conditions for which they were considered for retention, and the nature of their schools.

A 1977 review (Bocks) discussed the results of 20 studies and suggested the following conclusions:

1. Grade retention was not an effective device to ensure greater mastery of elementary school subject matter.
2. Grade repetition produced many harmful consequences.
3. Social promotion did not create a wider range of abilities for upper-grade teachers to deal with.

Reiter (1973) in another extensive research review reported that retention appeared to produce long-term damaging effects and did not help schools maintain high achievement standards.

Individual Studies

In addition to confusing or contradictory results, other studies suffer from what might best be termed "fuzzy" definitions and questionable comparisons. Reinherz and Griffin (1970) followed 57 boys of normal intelligence who were repeating for the first time in grades 1 to 3. They found that children who were judged to be "immature" made the most significant gains in the retained year. In addition, they found that children with good peer relationships and good emotional adjustment also did well in the retained year. But we are forced to ask just what *is* "immature"? And how would these children have done had they been socially promoted? These imponderables raise serious questions about the authors' findings.

Not all studies, however, reveal negative or necessarily ambiguous outcomes regarding retention. Two studies frequently quoted in the literature, Owen and Ranick (1977) and Finlayson (1977), lend support to the notion that retention can be an effective educational decision for some students. The difficulty is finding out which students could benefit most from such a decision to retain. Studies by Strigner (1960) and Sandoval and Hughes (1981) have attempted to isolate and define more carefully the characteristics of students which would help teachers, parents and administrators decide whether retaining or promoting a marginal student would be most appropriate. By making decisions based on more specific learner and environmental characteristics, educators hope to accomplish a higher rate of success and more positive outcomes for retained students. Some guidelines for making these decisions are discussed in the literature.

Decision-Making Models

Light (1977) and Lieberman (1980) constructed models to assist teachers and administrators in the task of making promotion and retention decisions. The Decision-Making Model for In-Grade Retention (Nonpromotion) by Lieberman uses a rational, problem-solving approach. The model asks the decision-maker (e.g., teacher, counselor, principal) to consider characteristics within three important categories.

Examples of elements within these categories are as follow:

Child Factors	Family Factors
physical disability	geographical moves
academic potential	attitude toward retention
chronological age	age of siblings

School Factors
System attitude on retention
teacher attitude on retention
program services

There are a total of 16 child factors, 5 family factors and 7 school factors. Each of the elements can be rated in one of four categories: for retention, against retention, undecided and not applicable.

Light's Retention Scale uses a numerical scale applied to 19 criteria. These criteria include factors such as school attendance, intelligence, age, emotional background, physical size and sex. Each criterion has a point system and a child is assigned points depending on the evaluation. In the "physical size" category, for example, the child may receive 0, 2, 4 or 5 points depending on the child's size in relationship to grade and age peers. The sum of the 19 categories provides a figure that helps place a student in one of five classifications for retention: excellent, good, fair, marginal, poor, or as a student who should not be retained.

Light cautions the user of the instrument that the score is only an indication (of what is best for the child), and should not—by itself—be used as the final word in regard to retention decisions. It appears that the value of both the Light and Lieberman approaches lies in the careful and systematic posture that forces decision-makers into attempting to determine what is most appropriate for a child.

Implications and Recommendations

Research studies have accomplished little toward providing data that would lead to a foolproof formula for teachers and administrators in making decisions about retention or promotion of marginal children. From Cook (1941) to Dobbs and Neville (1967) and Lehr (1982), a central theme is reiterated:

> The crucial issue appears to be not whether the slow-learning pupil is passed or failed but how adequately his needs are met wherever he is placed (Cook, 1941).
>
> Low achievers continue to experience failure whether promoted or retained unless classroom activities are adjusted to the ability of the individual child (Dobbs and Neville, 1967).
>
> The reason for imposing or changing school policy (regarding retention and promotion practices) should be that it benefits students, not that it quiets criticism (Lehr, 1982).

It appears that neither grade retention nor social promotion necessarily solves the academic difficulties of the low-achieving students. We believe that the retention versus social promotion debate be considered as only one aspect of resolving the larger issue: the child's successful education. Teachers, administrators and parents should concentrate more energy and resources on positive approaches to solving each child's problem. The most important consideration is not to pass or fail the student but to meet that child's needs *in whatever environment that child is placed*. This means carefully considering the other elements in an instructional model such as the curriculum, the teaching and the learning. We seriously question that "recycling" children through the same or similar curriculum has substantive value to either the child or society. Alternatives to retention and social promotion should be considered. Some of the possibilities that permit alteration of curriculum, teaching and learning are:

- *Transitional Classrooms* that offer the child in the kindergarten or 1st grade (traditionally) a move to a new classroom environment—and teacher—while getting an opportunity to mature both socially and intellectually in a less-advanced and specially designed curriculum. Under such circumstances, the child generally meets the requirements of kindergarten and 1st grade in three years instead of two, but under positive environmental and learning conditions.

- *Continuous Progress/Ungraded Classes* that allow the child to acquire skills according to his or her own timetable. In such a program, the curriculum is clearly designed to meet the needs of the child.

- *Intensive Remedial Instruction*, where teaching is based on specific learner characteristics. The child with a specific modality strength receives instruction that is best suited to his/her learning style.

- *Individual Tutoring Programs* that occur on a year-round basis. Such programs offer content-specific instruction beyond that normally occurring in the school.

- *Home Assistance Programs* that offer help to parents in learning to build positive psychological climates. A major thrust of such programs is to provide opportunities for parents to help foster improved self-images in children.

Beyond formal program structures, three other considerations come to mind. First, smaller class size, particularly in the primary grades, seems crucial to improved learning climates. An accurate measure of pupil-teacher ratios must be based on calculations using classroom teachers and pupils only. Second, it seems important that specialized inservice and professional growth programs for personnel be an ongoing part of any school system to lend both vitality and improved functioning to such a system. Finally, better funding is crucial to permit the development of more lively, positive and relevant learning environments.

In addition to seeking alternatives to help children be more successful in school, we seek successes that evolve naturally from the improvement of curriculum and teaching. We believe that each school district should develop and institute policies that articulate promotion and retention standards. It is critical that systems establish guidelines for making decisions which address both the needs of teachers and parents in coming to grips with questions of effective promotion or retention and the eventual appropriate placement of the child.

When one attempts to answer the questions posed at the beginning of this article, two things are clear. First, there are no definitive or unambiguous answers. Second, and more important, the questions traditionally asked manage to avoid the real issues—analyzing the effect—instead of examining the roots of the problem. There really is only one question in regard to the problem of promotion, retention and pupil placement: How may this child's needs best be served?

REFERENCES

"A Nation at Risk: The Imperative for Educational Reform" *The Chronicle of Higher Education* (May 1983): 11–16.

Bloom, Benjamin S. "Affective Outcomes of School Learning," *Phi Delta Kappan* (Nov. 1977): 193–98.

Bocks, William. "Non-promotion. A Year to Grow?" *Educational Leadership* (Feb. 1977): 379–83.

Cook, Walter. *Grouping and Promotion in the Elementary School,* Minneapolis: Univeristy of Minnesota Press, 1941.

Dobbs, V., and D. Neville. "The Effect of Nonpromotion on the Achievement of Groups Matched from Retained First Graders and Promoted Second Graders." *The Journal of Educational Research* (July/Aug. 1967).

Farley, E. "Regarding Repeaters—Sad Effects of Failure upon the Child." *Nation's Schools* 18,4 (1936): 37–38.

Finlayson, Harry. "Nonpromotion and Self-concept Development." *Phi Delta Kappan* (Nov. 1977).

Jackson, Gregg. "The Research Evidence on Effects of Grade Retention." *Review of Educational Research* (Fall 1975):613–35.

Klene, V., and E. Branson. Reported in *The Elementary School Journal* 29 (1929):564–66.

Koons, C. I., "Nonpromotion: A Dead End Road." *Phi Delta Kappan* (May 1977): 701–02.

Lehr, Fran. "Grade Repetition vs. Social Promotion." *The Reading Teacher* (Nov. 1982).

Lieberman, Laurence M. "A Decision-making Model for In-grade Retention (Nonpromotion)." *Journal of Learning Disabilities* 13 (May 1980): 268–72.

Light, Wayne. *Light's Retention Scale and Recording Form.* Novato, CA: Academic Therapy Publications, 1977.

Lindvig, Elise Kay. "Grade Retention: Evolving Expectations and Individual Differences." *The Clearing House* (Feb. 1983): 253–56.

Owen, Samuel, and Deborah Ranick. "The Greenville Program: A Common Sense Approach to Basics." *Phi Delta Kappan* (Mar. 1977): 213–18.

Reinherz, Helen, and Carol Griffin. "The Second Time Around: Achievement and Progress of Boys Who Repeated One of the First Three Grades," *The School Counselor* (Jan. 1970): 213–18.

Reiter, Robert. *The Promotion/Retention Dilemma: What Research Tells Us.* Report #7416, Philadelphia: Philadelphia School District Office of Research and Evaluation, 1973 (ED 099 412).

Sandoval, J., and G. P. Hughes. *Success in Non-promoted First Grade Children: A Final Report.* Davis, CA: University of California, Department of Education, 1981 (E1) 212–371).

Stringer, Lorene. "Report on Retentions Program." *The Elementary School Journal* (Apr. 1960): 370–75.

Teacher Expectancies

How much should teachers know about their students? No one seriously argues that complete ignorance is bliss. Teachers do need to have some information about their pupils in order to provide appropriate learning experiences, but are there some types of data that teachers should not obtain because they are so apt to misuse them? If teachers are not provided with data, will they form expectations based on preconceived biases or stereotypes? These questions are important to consider if teacher expectations function as self-fulfilling prophecies. If teachers' expectations affect how they treat their students, and this differential treatment affects how (or how much) students learn, then the topic is of considerable importance in education.

As Good and Brophy point out in their reading, wide interest and controversy about this topic was created with the publication of *Pygmalion in the Classroom* in 1968. Good and Brophy suggest that subsequent evidence supports the idea that teacher expectations are *sometimes* self-fulfilling. In their well-thought-out presentation they make a distinction between *induced* teacher expectations and *natural* teacher expectations. The former do not seem to produce self-fulfilling prophecies. The authors go on to discuss how the process of self-fulfilling prophecies works, what appropriate teacher expectations are, and how one can form and change expectations.

Thought Questions

Does the Good and Brophy reading suggest that it would be effective to systematically dupe teachers by presenting them with inaccurately high data regarding their students' abilities?

How can we determine whether or not the predictive value of test data is due to self-fulfilling prophecies?

What steps could you take as a teacher to avoid the negative aspects of self-fulfilling prophecies?

What steps could you take as a teacher to translate positive expectations into a form of intervention to benefit children?

Evaluate the attitude of the teacher, who is genuinely committed to fairness and to treating all children exactly the same, in relation to the effects of self-fulfilling prophecies.

Identify the elements of a self-fulfilling prophecy in the following example from Good and Brophy's book. A junior education major tells her roommate that she bets her boyfriend will buy her roses for their pinning anniversary. On her next date with her boyfriend, Ralph, she laughs about the funny sweater her friend knitted for her pin-mate on their pinning anniversary. Later the same evening, she mentions the lovely sorority initiation and how she particularly loved the flowers, especially the roses. "They are so special. They make me feel warm and happy." When Ralph arrives Saturday night for their anniversary date he presents her with a lovely bouquet of roses.

Teacher Expectations as Self-Fulfilling Prophecies

Thomas Good and Jere Brophy

Robert Rosenthal and Lenore Jacobson's *Pygmalion in the Classroom* (1968) created wide interest and controversy about self-fulfilling prophecies. Their book described research in which they tried to manipulate teacher expectations for student achievement to see if these expectations would be fulfilled. The study involved several classes in each of the first six grades of school. Teacher expectations were created by claiming that a test (actually a general achievement test) had been developed to identify late intellectual bloomers. The teachers were told that this test would identify children who were about to bloom intellectually and, therefore, could be expected to show unusually large achievement gains during the coming school year. A few children in each classroom were identified to the teachers as late bloomers. They actually had been selected randomly, not on the basis of any test. Thus, there was no real reason to expect unusual gains from them, and no factual basis existed for the expectations induced in the teachers.

From T. L. Good and J. Brophy, *Looking in Classrooms*, 3rd ed. (Harper & Row, 1984) pp 94–95, 96–99, 109–112. Reprinted with permission.

However, achievement test data from the end of the school year indicated that these children did show better performance (although the effects were confined primarily to the first two grades). Rosenthal and Jacobson explained their results in terms of the self-fulfilling prophecy effects of teacher expectations. They reasoned that the expectations they created about these special children somehow caused the teachers to treat them differently, so that they really did achieve more by the end of the year.

Controversy has raged over this topic ever since. The findings of *Pygmalion in the Classroom* were widely publicized and discussed, and for a time were accepted enthusiastically. Later, after critics had attacked the Rosenthal and Jacobson study (Snow, 1969; Taylor, 1970) and after a replication failed to produce the same results (Claiborn, 1969), the idea that teacher expectations necessarily function as self-fulfilling prophecies began to be rejected. For a critical analysis of teacher expectation research, see Dusek (1975). More recent analyses of research on teacher expectations are contained in Weinstein (1982) and Cooper and Good (1983). We think the evidence now available indicates that teacher expectations are sometimes self-fulfilling (see Braun, 1976, and Brophy and Good, 1974). However, this statement requires some explanation, both of the research available and of the way the expectation process is defined and described.

Regarding research, one must make a distinction betweeen two types of studies in this area. The first type, which includes Rosenthal and Jacobson's work as well as research by others who have tried to replicate the study, involves attempts to *manipulate* or induce teacher expectations. That is, the investigators tried to create expectations by identifying "late bloomers," using phony IQ scores or providing some other fictitious information about students' abilities. The second type of study uses teacher expectations as they exist naturally. No attempt is made to induce expectations. Instead, teachers are simply asked to make predictions or to rank or group students according to achievement or ability. Below we will present examples of naturalistic and induced expectation studies.

Studies involving induced expectations have produced mixed, but mostly negative, results. In some of these studies, teacher expectations failed to affect teaching behavior because the teachers did not acquire the expectations that the experimenters wanted them to. The most obvious case is one in which teachers knew that the expectation was not true, as in Schrank's (1970) adaptation of his earlier study of Air Force mathematics courses. For this second study, Schrank merely simulated the manipulation of teacher expectations; the teachers actually knew that the students had been grouped randomly rather than by ability levels. Under these conditions, even with instructions to teach the groups as if they had been tracked by ability, no expectation effects were observed. Similar results were obtained by Fleming and Anttonen (1971), who tried to falsify children's IQs. They found that teachers did not accept the phony IQs and therefore did not allow the scores to affect their treatment of students.

These results suggest that attempts to induce expectations in teachers will fail if the expectations are too discrepant from students' observable characteristics. Credibility of the source is probably another important factor. Teachers are much more likely to accept the opinions of a principal or a teacher who has worked with students the previous year than the opinions of a researcher.

The negative results in studies using induced teacher expectations should not necessarily be taken as disproof of the self-fulfilling prophecy idea. Negative findings are more likely due to failure to induce the desired expectations in teachers than to failure of teachers' expectations to affect their behavior. Naturalistic studies using teachers' real expectations about their students have often shown that high and low teacher expectations are related to differential teacher behavior (Cornbleth, Davis, and Button, 1972; Jeter and Davis, 1973; Brophy and Good, 1974; Cooper, 1976; Good, Cooper, and Blakey, 1980). These studies suggest that teacher expectations may have self-fulfilling prophecy effects, causing teachers to behave in ways that tend to make their expectations come true.

Expectation Effects Are Real but Not Universal

It is likely that students in some classrooms are not reaching their potential because their teachers do not expect much from them and are satisfied with poor or mediocre performance when they could obtain something better. For instance, one of the few attitudes that differentiated teachers who were obtaining good student gains from those who were not was the belief that students could and would learn (Brophy and Evertson, 1976).

Overenthusiastic, popular accounts of *Pygmalion in the Classroom* have sometimes misled people about the self-fulfilling prophecy phenomenon. They often imply that the mere existence of an expectation will automatically guarantee its fulfillment or that a magical and mysterious process is involved (just make a prediction and it will come true). Most teachers rightfully reject this idea as utter nonsense, and this is not what we mean when we say that teacher expectations can act as self-fulfilling prophecies. Rather, we refer here to something resulting naturally from a chain of observable causes.

In the original *Pygmalion* study, Rosenthal and Jacobson (1968) compared a positive expectation group with students who had not had positive information about them conveyed to the teacher. Many studies have followed in the spirit of Rosenthal and Jacobson (e.g., Beez, 1968); however, many other researchers have studied negative expectation effects. Because for obvious reasons researchers do not want to create negative expectations for teachers, behavioral scientists have developed a variety of research strategies that enable them to study negative expectations (e.g., examining teachers' natural expectations, using hypothetical students—Brophy and Good, 1970b; Babad, 1980).

Recent research definitely shows that both positive and negative expectations can be found in classrooms (Rosenthal and Rubin, 1978; Smith, 1980). However, we agree with Babad, Inbar, and Rosenthal (1982), that though it is clear that expectations exist, all teachers will not become Pygmalions nor will all students be affected by teacher expectations. As we noted sometime ago, teacher expectations are general but far from universal (Brophy and Good, 1974). However, Babad, Inbar, and Rosenthal have made an important contribution in noting that teachers may vary not only in their general susceptibility to expectation effects, but also in their susceptibility to positive or negative information.

How Expectations Become Self-Fulfilling

The fact that teacher expectations can be self-fulfilling is simply a special case of the more general principle that any expectation can be self-fulfilling (see Jones, 1977, for a discussion of expectation effects outside classroom settings). The process is not confined to classrooms. Although it is not true that "wishing can

make it so," *our expectations do affect the way we behave, and the way we behave affects how other people respond.* In some instances, our expectations about people cause us to treat them in a way that makes them respond just as we expected they would.

For example, look ahead to the time when you accept your first teaching job and receive notice about which school you are being assigned to (or look back on this experience if you are teaching now). Unless they already have information, most teachers in this situation want to find out as much as possible about the school and the principal with whom they will be working. Information can often be obtained from a friend already teaching at the school. Suppose the friend said, "Mr. Jackson is a wonderful man. You'll love working for him. He's very warm and pleasant, and he really takes an interest in you. Feel free to come to him with your problems; he's always glad to help." If you heard this about Mr. Jackson, how do you think you would respond to him when you met him? Think about this situation for a few moments, then consider a different situation. Suppose your friend said, "Mr. Jackson? Well, uh, he's sort of hard to describe. I guess he's all right, but I don't feel comfortable around him; he makes me nervous. I don't know what it is exactly, it's just that I get the feeling that he doesn't want to talk to me, that I'm wasting his time or irritating him." How do you think you would act when meeting Mr. Jackson after you had heard this?

If you are like most people, your behavior would be quite different depending on which of these contrasting descriptions you heard. If you received the positive information, you would look forward to meeting Mr. Jackson and would approach him with confidence and a friendly smile. Among other things, you would likely tell him that you have heard good things about him and that you are happy to be working with him and are looking forward to getting started. Having heard the other description, however, you would probably behave quite differently. You would be unlikely to look forward to the meeting, and you might well become nervous, inhibited, or overly concerned about making a good impression. You would likely approach him with hesitation, wearing a serious expression or a forced smile, and speak to him in rather reserved, formal tones. Even if you said the same words to him, the chances are that they would sound more like a prepared speech than a genuine personal reaction.

Now, put yourself in Mr. Jackson's place. Assume he knows nothing about you as a person. Take a few moments to think about how he might respond to these two disparate approaches. Mr. Jackson would likely respond quite differently. In the first instance, faced with warmth, friendliness, and genuine-sounding compliments, he would likely respond in kind. Your behavior would put him at ease and cause him to see you as a likable, attractive person. When he smiled and said he would be looking forward to working with you, too, he would really mean it.

What if Mr. Jackson were faced with a new teacher who approached him somewhat nervously and formally? Again, he would likely respond in kind. Such behavior would likely make him nervous and formal, if he were not already. He would respond in an equally bland and formal manner. This would probably be followed by an awkward silence that would make both of you increasingly nervous. As the authority figure and host, the principal would probably feel compelled to make the next move. In view of your behavior, attempts at small talk would be risky, so he would get down to business and begin to speak in his capacity as principal, talking to you in your capacity as a teacher.

The examples show that it is not just the existence of an expectation that causes self-fulfillment; it is the behavior that this expectation produces. This behavior then affects other people, making them more likely to act in the expected ways. In the classroom, the process works like this:

1. The teacher expects specific behavior and achievement from particular students.
2. Because of these different expectations, the teacher behaves differently toward various students.

3. This treatment tells students what behavior and achievement the teacher expects from them and affects their self-concepts, achievement motivation, and levels of aspiration.
4. If this treatment is consistent over time, and if students do not resist or change it in some way, it will shape their achievement and behavior. High-expectation students will be led to achieve at high levels, while the achievement of low-expectation students will decline.
5. With time, students' achievement and behavior will conform more and more closely to that originally expected of them.

The model clearly shows that teacher expectations are not automatically self-fulfilling. To become so, they must be translated into behavior that will communicate expectations to students and will shape their behavior toward expected patterns. This does *not* always happen. A teacher may not have clear-cut expectations about every student, or those expectations may continually change. Even when the expectations remain consistent, the teacher may not necessarily communicate them to the student through consistent behavior. In this case, the expectation would not be self-fulfilling even if it turned out to be correct. Finally, a student might prevent expectations from becoming self-fulfilling by overcoming them or by resisting them in a way that makes the teacher change them.

The work of Rhona Weinstein and her colleagues has been very valuable in demonstrating the potential importance of students' perceptions of the communication of expectations. Weinstein (1983) argues that students' perceptions of teacher behavior help to determine what significance they attribute to it and how they respond.

Appropriate Teacher Expectations

We have suggested that teachers' low performance beliefs about individual students and/ or groups of students may lead these students to receive less serious and less interesting instruction. In this section, we discuss some of the ways in which teachers may attempt to reduce undesirable expectation effects.

Some authors have suggested that teachers should avoid self-fulfilling prophecy effects by not forming any expectations. This means refusing to discuss students with their previous teachers and ignoring cumulative records or test information. This is *not* a good suggestion, for two reasons. First, expectations cannot be suppressed or avoided. We remember experiences that make an impression on us. When events occur repeatedly, they gradually are seen as expected and normal, and expectations are reinforced every time repetition occurs. Thus, teachers form expectations simply from interacting with students, even if they try to avoid other sources of information. Second, whether other sources of information are examined is not as important as *how* information is used. Information about students will create expectations about them, but it can also be useful in planning individualized instruction to meet their specific needs. A teacher should try to get information and use it in this way, rather than avoid obtaining information.

Others too have commented on the need for teachers to make decisions and to rely on their own judgments, even though classroom evidence is limited. Teachers' judgments will be subjective to some extent, but we agree with Anderson-Levitt (in press), who argues that there is no reason to close student files simply because teachers cannot process information more logically than do other professionals (e.g., all professionals have to rely upon subjective interpretations to some extent)! Information about a student's past behavior and performance is helpful if teachers use that information to form hypotheses about where to start with the student. To consider information definitive or unchangeable is a dangerous practice.

The suggestion that teachers should have only positive expectations is superficially appealing. Confidence and determination are important teacher qualities, and a "can do" attitude helps reduce large problems to workable size. However, this attitude must not be carried to the point of distorting reality. Students show large individual differences in learning abilities and interests, and these cannot be eliminated through wishful thinking. Teachers will only frustrate both themselves and their students if they set unrealistically high standards that students cannot reach.

Expectations should be appropriate rather than necessarily high, and they must be followed by appropriate instructional behavior; that is, planned learning experiences that move students through the curriculum at a pace they can handle. An appropriate pace allows continued success and improvement and varies for different students. Teachers should not feel guilt or feel that they are stigmatizing slower learners by moving them along at a slower pace. As long as students are working up to their potential and progressing at a steady rate, a teacher has reason to be satisifed.

Regular repetition of student behavior will build up strong expectations in all teachers, including (and perhaps especially) teachers who try to deny or suppress expectations. Inevitably, some of these expectations will be pessimistic. However, teachers can avoid undesirable self-fulfilling prophecy effects if they remain alert to the formation of, and changes in, their own expectations and if they monitor their own behavior to see that negative expectations are not communicated. To the extent that such expectations do exist, they should be of the helpful variety that encourages teachers to combine expressions of concern with behavior designed to remediate difficulties. Saying that a student needs help is bad only if the teacher does not provide that help in a positive, supportive way.

Forming and Changing Expectations

Teachers form expectations about their students before they even see them. Individual cumulative record files provide IQ data, achievement scores, grades, and teacher comments that create expectations about achievement and conduct. Other expectations are gained from conversations with colleagues who taught the students in earlier grades. The reputation of the family or the teacher's prior experience with an older brother or sister may also condition what he or she expects from a particular student. For example, Seaver (1973) conducted a natural, quasi-experiment to see if the achievement of 79 students in first grade was affected by the previous achievement patterns of older siblings. The hypothesis tested was that students would achieve better when taught by the same teacher if their older siblings had been good students and worse when older siblings had been poor students (in contrast to control students, who had a different teacher than their older siblings). It was found that following a sibling who was a good student had positive consequences upon achievement for younger siblings, especially males. It is not entirely clear how teachers' perceptions of home conditions influence their actual behavior, but it does seem possible that some teachers may inadequately assess the potential of students by emphasizing "status" factors (home background, sex, older siblings, etc.).

Some teachers deliberately try to avoid being influenced by the past. They do not look at records or seek information about their students until they have had a chance to see them and form their own impressions. This is not necessarily an improvement, however, since a lack of such data does not prevent most teachers from forming strong, general impressions very quickly. In one study, for example, first-grade teachers were able to rank their students in order of expected achievement after the first week of school (Willis, 1972). Furthermore, these rankings, made without benefit of any test data, were highly correlated with achievement ranks from tests given at the end of the year. Thus, first impressions can lead to specific and largely accurate expectations about students, even in teachers who are aware of the expectation phenomenon. Rather than trying to eliminate expectations, teachers must remain aware of them and see that they do not lead to inappropriate treatment of certain students.

Expectations created as a result of recurring classroom behavior can be very compelling. If Susan frequently fails to do homework assignments, a teacher may gradually change his or her behavior from attempting to change Susan's work habits to accepting poor performance as "what is to be expected." To avoid falling into this rut, teachers need to keep their expectations flexible and bear in mind their role as instructors. If expectations are allowed to become too strong or too fixed, they can distort perception and behavior. Teachers may notice only those behaviors that fit their expectations and as a result may deviate from good teaching practice.

Once formed, expectations tend to be self-perpetuating for students as well as teachers, because expectations guide both perceptions and behavior. When we expect to find something, we are much more likely to see it than when we are not looking for it. For example, most people do not notice counterfeit money or slight irregularities in clothing patterns. However, treasury department officials and inspectors for clothing manufacturers, who have been trained to look for such deviations, will notice them. Similarly, valuable rare coins and unusual abilities and aptitudes usually are not noticed except by those who are on the lookout for them. This is part of the reason why teachers often fail to notice good behavior in students who are frequent discipline problems in the classroom. With expectations for misbehavior, teachers miss much of these students' good behavior that someone else might have noticed and reinforced.

Expectations not only cause us to notice some things and fail to notice others, but they also affect the way we *interpret* what we do notice. The optimist, for example, notices that the glass is half full, while the pessimist observes that it is half empty. Mistaken beliefs and attitudes about other people are self-perpetuating and difficult to correct because of their tendency to influence how we interpret what we see. If we are convinced that a person has particular qualities, we often see these qualities when we observe this individual.

Consider the teacher who asks a difficult question and then gives students some time to think about the answer. After a while he calls on Johnny Bright, whom he sees as an intelligent and well-motivated student. Johnny remains silent, pursing his lips, knitting his brow, and scratching his head. The teacher knows that he is working out the problem, so he patiently gives him more time. Finally, Johnny responds with a question, "Would you repeat that last part again?" The teacher is happy to do so, because this indicates that Johnny has partially solved the problem and may be able to do it by himself with a little more time. He asks Johnny what part he wants repeated and then obliges. He then waits eagerly, but patiently, for Johnny to respond again. If someone interrupted the teacher at this point to ask him what he was doing, he might respond that he was "challenging the class to use creativity and logical thinking to solve problems."

Suppose, however, that the teacher had called on Sammy Slow instead. The teacher knows that Sammy is a low achiever, and he does not think Sammy is very well-motivated, either. When called on, Sammy remains silent, although the teacher notes his pursed lips, his furrowed brow, and the fact that he is scratching his head. This probably means that Sammy is hopelessly lost, although it may mean that he is merely acting, trying to give the impression that he is thinking about the problem. After a few seconds, the teacher says, "Well, Sammy?" Now Sammy responds, but with a question instead of an answer, "Would you repeat that last part again?" This confirms the teacher's suspicions, making it clear that any more time spent with Sammy on this question would be wasted. After admonishing Sammy to listen more carefully, he calls on someone else. If interrupted at this point and asked what he was doing, the teacher might respond that he was "making it clear that the class is expected to pay close at-tention to the discussion, so that they can respond intelligently when questioned."

In this example, the teacher's expectations for these two students caused him to make different inferences about the students' behavior than a more neutral observer would have made. Although the behavior of the two boys was the same, and they made the same response to the initial question, the teacher interpreted the behavior quite differently by reading additional meaning into it. His interpretations about the two boys may have been correct, but we (and he) cannot tell for certain because he did not verify them. Instead, he acted as if his interpretations were observable facts, so that his treatment of Sammy may have been grossly inappropriate.

Although the need to continually review and adjust expectations may seem obvious, it can be difficult to do in everyday life as well as in the classroom. (For example, the widely advertised brand is not always better than the unknown brand, the more expensive item is not necessarily better than the cheaper one, nor is the large economy size always a better bargain than the regular size. Yet every day, most people automatically accept such things without verifying them.)

Similarly, the fact that a student could not do something yesterday does not mean that he or she cannot do it today, but the teacher will not find out unless the student is given a chance. Expectations stress the stable or unchanging aspects of the world. The teacher, however, is a change agent who is trying to make students into something different from what they are. Teachers, therefore, must keep their expectations in perspective. To the extent that they are negative, expectations represent problems to be solved, not definitions of reality to which a teacher must adapt.

REFERENCES

Anderson-Levitt, K., "Teachers' Interpretations of Student Behavior: A Case Study and a Model." *Elementary School Journal* (in press).

Babad, E., "Expectancy Bias in Scoring as a Function of Ability and Ethnic Labels." *Psychological Reports*, 46 (1980), 625–626.

Babad, E. & Inbar, J., "Teachers' Judgment of Students' Potential as a Function of Teachers' Susceptibility to Biasing Information." *Journal of Personality and Social Psychology*, 42 (1982), 541–547.

Beez, W., "Influence of Biased Psychological Reports on Teacher Behavior and Pupil Performance." *Proceedings of the 76th Annual Convention of the American Psychological Association*, 1968, 605–606.

Braun, C., "Teacher expectation: Socio-Psychological Dynamics." *Review of Educational Research*, 46 (1976), 185–213.

Brophy, J. & Evertson, C., *Learning from Teaching: A Developmental Perspective*. Boston: Allyn & Bacon, 1976.

Brophy, J. & Good, T., "Teachers' Communication of Differential Expectations for Children's Classroom Performance: Some Behavioral Data." *Journal of Educational Psychology*, 61 (1970b), 365–374.

Brophy, J. & Good, T., *Teacher-Student Relationships: Causes and Consequences*. New York: Holt, Rinehart and Winston, 1974.

Claiborn, W., "Expectancy Effects in the Classroom: A Failure to Replicate." *Journal of Educational Psychology*, 60 (1969), 377–383.

Cooper, H. *Intervening and Expectation Communication: A Follow-up Study to the "Personal Control" Study*. Hamilton, New York: Colgate University, 1976.

Cooper, H. & Good, T., *Pygmalion Grows Up: Studies in the Expectation Communication Process*. New York: Longman, 1983.

Cornbleth, C., Davis, O., & Button, C., "Teacher-Pupil Interaction and Teacher Expectations for Pupil Achievement in Secondary Social Studies Classes." Paper presented at the annual meeting of the American Educational Research Association, 1972.

Dusek, J., "Do Teachers Bias Children's Learning?" *Review of Educational Research*, 45 (1975), 661–684.

Fleming, E. & Anttonen, R., "Teacher Expectancy or My Fair Lady." *American Educational Research Journal*, 8 (1971), 214–252.

Good, T., Cooper, H. & Blakey, S., "Classroom Interaction as a Function of Teacher Expectations, Student Sex, and Time of Year." *Journal of Educational Psychology*, 72 (1980), 378–385.

Jeter, J. & Davis, O., "Elementary School Teachers' Differential Classroom Interaction with Children as a Function of Differential Expectations of Pupil Achievements." Paper presented at the annual meeting of the American Educational Research Association, 1973.

Jones, R. *Self-Fulfilling Prophecies: Social, Psychological, and Physiological Effects of Expectancies*. Hillsdale, New Jersey, Erlbaum, 1977.

Rosenthal, R. & Jacobson, L., *Pygmalion in the Classroom: Teacher Expectation and Pupil's Intellectual Development*. New York: Holt, Rinehart and Winston, 1968.

Rosenthal, R. & Rubin, D. "Interpersonal Expectancy Affects: The First 345 Studies." *The Behavioral and Brain Sciences*, 3 (1978), 377–415.

Schrank, W., "A Further Study of the Labeling Effect of Ability Grouping." *Journal of Educational Research*, 63 (1970), 358–360.

Seaver, W., "Effect of Naturally Induced Teacher Expectancies." *Journal of Personality and Social Psychology*, 28 (1973), 333–342.

Smith, M., "Meta-Analysis of Research on Teacher Expectation." *Evaluation in Education*, 4 (1980), 53–55.

Snow, R., "Unfinished Pygmalion." *Contemporary Psychology*, 14 (1969), 197–199.

Taylor, C. "The Expectations of Pygmalion's Creators." *Educational Leadership*, 28, (1970), 161–164.

Weinstein, R., "Expectations in the Classroom: The Student Perspective," Paper presented at the annual meeting of the American Educational Research Association, New York City, April 1982.

Weinstein, R., "Student Perceptions of Schooling." *Elementary School Journal*, 83 (1983), 287–312.

Willis, S., *Formation of Teachers' Expectations of Students' Academic Performance*. Unpublished doctoral dissertation, University of Texas at Austin, 1972.

Motivation: Intrinsic and Cognitive Versus Extrinsic and Social Factors

Motivation is a very general term for factors and conditions which cause a person to begin an activity and pursue it with vigor and persistence. In everyday terms, motivation refers to the *whys* of behavior, just as ability means the *cans*. When we question students' motivation for learning, we assume they can try to learn but ask, "Why do they?"; "Why don't they?; or perhaps, "How do we get them to?" The authors of the readings on this issue suggest somewhat different answers to these questions. Whereas Brophy stresses intrinsic cognitive factors, Robert Slavin prefers to rely on extrinsic, social factors to enhance student achievement.

In the first reading, Jere Brophy, noting that classrooms are work settings stressing compulsory activities of an intellectual nature, argues that more attention should be paid to the cognitive aspects of motivation and the value that students place on academic activity. Brophy offers suggestions as to how teachers can help their students become more motivated, not just to get work done, but to acquire the knowledge or skills that an academic pursuit is designed to develop. He defines classroom motivation as motivation to *learn* rather than merely to perform, that is, to value the actual processes of learning and the natural consequences of these processes, increases in knowledge or skill. He sees his views as distinct from most social learning theory approaches, which stress reinforcement extrinsic to the task itself.

Robert Slavin, while recognizing such motivational factors as intrinsic interest of the task at hand, parental interest in educational pursuits, and the students' own perceptions of their abilities and chances for success, favors the use of classroom incentives to affect student motivation as these are under the control of the teacher. Of the various incentives available to teachers, Slavin emphasizes the importance of cooperative incentives to influence peer norms and possibly peer sanctions favoring high achievement. He presents evidence to show that, instead of changing the content or delivery of instruction, a relatively simple change in the classroom incentive system can increase student achievement.

Thought Questions

What evidence of the reality and importance of intrinsic or self-motivating activities have you observed? Does children's play appear self-sustaining and self-motivating, or are external rewards needed? Is it intrinsic or extrinsic motivation that keeps the artist in the garret and the scientist in the laboratory?

Albert Bandura, a social learning theorist, points out that most of the things people enjoy doing, because they are self-reinforcing, were not always self-reinforcing. They became that way through the influence of extrinsic rewards. He argues that human experience and psychological research both show that human behavior is established and maintained by anticipated consequences, that is, by rewards. What is your point of view?

How might Brophy counter the arguments of behavioral psychologists, who point out that in the real educational world students must perform tasks chosen by teachers who claim it absurd to expect that every student will find every important task intrinsically attractive? Aren't teachers responsible for stating objectives for student learning and establishing a reward system to ensure that the desired behavior occurs?

Do you think it significant that teacher activities related to intrinsic motivation, such as the provision of desirable models or intriguing situations, come before the learner acts or responds, whereas external rewards come after the response? How many teachers use this difference in timing to combine intrinsic and extrinsic motivation effectively?

In a reading in Unit I, Benbow, Stanley, and Leder discuss sex differences in mathematical achievement. After reviewing the views of Brophy and Slavin on motivational differences, how do you think girls could be helped to compete more effectively? Do you think Brophy's or Slavin's approach would be more effective in accomplishing this end?

Is the distinction between extrinsic and intrinsic motivation really a false dichotomy? Do not real life examples of achievement motivation often consist of at least three components—a cognitive component concerned with knowledge acquisition and problem-solving as ends in themselves, an ego-enhancement component concerned with the achievement of status, and an affiliative component concerned with securing the approval of others?

What role, if any, do you see for external rewards? Under what circumstances would a teacher be most likely to use them?

Conceptualizing Student Motivation

Jere Brophy

Stimulating Student Motivation through Socialization

Much of the literature on motivation is of limited value to teachers, because it concerns free choice play situations rather than work situations and because it concentrates on the affective aspects of motivation to the relative neglect of the cognitive aspects. Another problem is its concentration on motivational states or traits as predictors of differential behavior, to the relative neglect of study of how those motivational states or traits were developed in the first place.

When attention is confined to students' existing motivational systems, individual differences do seem to present formidable problems to teachers. We know, for example, that anx-ious and dependent students respond well to teacher praise and encouragement but not to teacher challenge or criticism, but that confident, independent students have the opposite pattern. Some students prefer material rewards, others prefer symbolic rewards, and still others prefer special privileges. It is not yet clear how powerful these individual differences in response to teacher motivation efforts may be (relative to common responses). It is possible that teachers' motivational activities (unlike their instructional activities) typically may have more powerful interaction effects than main effects and that the interactions involved typically would be disordinal rather than merely ordinal. Thus, instead of facing a situation in which the same basic set of motivation strategies works for all students but must be used more often or intensively with some students rather than others, teachers may be facing a more complex situation in which different students need different motivational strategies, and application of a strategy that increases motivation in some students may decrease motivation in others.

Eden (1975) has suggested a general theory of motivation that incorporates this idea. He assumes that, for a given person in a given situ-

This work is sponsored in part by the Institute for Research on Teaching, College of Education, Michigan State University. The Institute for Research on Teaching is funded primarily by the Program for Teaching and Instruction of the National Institute of Education, United States Department of Health, Education, and Welfare. The opinions expressed in this publication do not necessarily reflect the position, policy, or endorsement of the National Institute of Education. (Contract No 400–81–0014)

ation, certain motives are relevant and others are not, so that the effect of tying performance of a particular task to a motive will depend on the relevance of that motive to that person at the time. If task performance results in the delivery of some relevant motivational consequence, there is likely to be a (probably substantial) increase in motivation to perform the task. However, if task performance results in delivery of some irrelevant motivational outcome, there is likely to be a small but real decrease in motivation to perform the task. Eden's article presents evidence in support of this theory (although it does not refer specifically to student behavior in classrooms).

Such theorizing leads to the suggestion that, where possible, teachers should provide students with choices of what assignments to do, or when and how to do them. The notion of a "reinforcement menu" that allows students to apply their "earnings" toward the "purchase" of reinforcers that are most personally appealing to them follows from the same principles. These ideas are useful as far as they go, but there are inherent limitations in what teachers can accomplish if they confine themselves to catering to students' existing motivational systems. If feasible, the strategy of choice would appear to be to develop desirable motivation systems in students through systematic socialization. Since motivation systems are learned, it is certainly possible to do this in theory. It remains to be seen whether teachers can do it in a reasonable time, within the constraints under which they work. My own thinking is presented in the following sections.

Qualitative Aspects of Motivation

In addition to its quantitative aspects (level of arousal), motivation has several qualitative aspects that should be considered when socializing students. As shown in Table 1, students' attitudes toward particular classroom tasks can be construed as lying on a continuum from negative through neutral to positive. They also can be characterized as concerned with factors endogenous to the task itself (the processes involved in engaging in the task and the learning it engenders), vs. exogenous to the task (focused on the self rather than the task, or on the anticipated consequences of task performance), and as concerned either with the value that the student places on the task or with the expectations that the student has for succeeding on the task or being rewarded for performance.

Theory and research on classroom motivation have focused much more on manipulation of task-exogenous factors to control student behavior than on attempts to develop intrinsic motivation by focusing student attention on task-endogenous factors, and much more on motivating students to perform than on motivating them to learn. Such an emphasis appears to imply that school learning is necessarily unappealing to students, and thus must be motivated through reward and punishment. In fact, although there does not seem to be anything inherent in school activities to support this expectation (especially in this age of enlightened teachers and attractive school curricula and materials), it may have *become* true through self-fulfilling prophecy effects of the near-universal tendency to view classroom motivation as a matter of finding ways to manipulate students to engage in (presumably unappealing) tasks, rather than a matter of teaching students to find meaning and satisfaction in tasks that are appealing (or at least potentially appealing, if initially neutral). An analogy with classroom management may be apropos here. Historically, most approaches to that topic treated it, in effect, as if it were a matter of "discipline" in which knowledgeable but uncooperative students were to be pressured into doing what they were not inclined to do naturally. In recent years, however, research has shown that effective classroom management is much more a matter of instructing willing but ignorant students in classroom rules and routines, with much more emphasis on instruction, modeling, cueing, and feedback, than on manipulation through reward and punishment. It seems likely that parallel findings

Table 1
Qualitative Aspects of Students' Motivation Related to Specific Academic Tasks

Direction	Task Endogenous Motivation		Task Exogenous Motivation	
	PERFORMANCE OUTCOME FOCUS	**TASK VALUE FOCUS**	**TASK VALUE FOCUS**	**PERFORMANCE OUTCOME FOCUS**
	Affect: Anxiety, embarrassment, fear of failure. *Cognition:* Task focus is "invaded" by perception of confusion, failure, helplessness. Attribution of (poor) performance to insufficient ability.	*Affect:* Anger or dread. Student dislikes the task, which is in effect a punishment. *Cognition:* Task focus is "invaded" by resentment, awareness of being coerced into unpleasant or pointless activity.	*Affect:* Alienation, resistance. Student doesn't want to acquire this knowledge or skill. *Cognition:* Perceptions of conflict between what this task represents and one's self concept, sex role identification, etc. Anticipation of undesirable consequences to involvement in such tasks.	*Affect:* Apathy, resignation, resentment. *Cognition:* Perception that one cannot "win," that one has no realistic chance to earn desired rewards, satisfactory grades, etc.
NEGATIVE				
NEUTRAL	No particular expectatons; neither success nor failure are salient concerns.	Neutral attitude toward task; open minded (if new) or indifferent (if familiar).	Neutral; the knowledge or skills developed by the task elicit neither avoidance nor excitement.	No extrinsic consequences are expected; performance will neither be rewarded nor punished.

POSITIVE	*Affect:* Enjoyment, pleasure. Engagement in this task is a reward in its own right. *Cognition:* Relaxed concentration on the processes involved in doing the task. "Flow." Metacognitive awareness of what the task requires and how one is responding to it. Focus on the academic content when learning, and on the quality of the product when performing.	*Affect:* Satisfaction (perhaps occasional excitement) as skills or insights develop. Pride in craftsmanship, successful performance. *Cognition:* Perception of progress toward goals, achieved with relative ease. Attribution of (successful) performance to (sufficient) ability plus (reasonable) effort. Focus on one's developing knowledge and skills.	*Affect:* Energized, eager to learn this knowledge or skill (for its instrumental value). *Cognition:* Recognition that the task is a subgoal related to attainment of important future goals (often as a "ticket" to social advancement). Focus on the "relevant" aspects of the learning.	*Affect:* Excitement, happy anticipation of reward. *Cognition:* Recognition that one can attain desired rewards with relative ease. Focus on meeting stated performance criteria.

might emerge in the area of classroom motivation, if research can be designed to allow such discoveries (particularly research on teachers who seem to be highly successful in motivating their students).

In any case, as shown in Table 1, attempts to improve student motivation can address task endogenous as well as task exogenous factors, and can address the value placed on learning in addition to expectations concerning level of performance. It should be noted that although Table 1 refers to student motivation with respect to particular tasks in particular situations (motivational states), similar considerations apply to more general motivational traits. Thus, students can be construed as generally negative through neutral to positive in their attitudes toward school tasks and their expectations for successful performance. For simplicity, I will concentrate on Table 1 and task-specific motivational states, although occasional reference to motivational traits will appear in the subsequent discussion.

Counteracting Negative Motivation

The types of positive task described in the bottom of Table 1 cannot reasonably be expected to develop in students who are burdened by negative attitudes, anxiety, fear of failure, and the other types of negative motivation also described in the top of Table 1. Thus, for these students, the process of socializing positive motivation to learn must begin with attempts to eliminate negative motivation.

Conventional approaches to this task focus on fear of failure, learned helplessness, and related problems associated with expected failure outcomes attributed to low ability. For these problems, social learning theorists would program for continuous progess and consistent success, achievement motivation theorists would train students to set challenging but achievable goals, and attribution theorists would train students to attribute poor performance to insufficient effort rather than to lack of ability. I would expect each of these approaches to have some positive effects, but I see

the need for two caveats in using the goal setting or attribution retraining approaches.

First, the task must be appropriate to the student. "Appropriate" is taken here to mean "offering the prospect of success with reasonable effort." If the task is too difficult for the student, it will not be possible to set goals that are reasonably achievable, and it will not be valid to attribute failure to lack of effort rather than ability. This may seem obvious and not worth mentioning, but classroom researchers who have examined the assignments given to students have concluded that it is very common for students to be given assignments that are much too difficult for them (Fisher, Berliner, Filby, Marliave, Cahen, & Dishaw, 1980; Jorgenson, 1977). Without appropriate assignments, there appears to be no hope of creating positive student attitudes toward classroom tasks.

A second caveat concerns the focus on effort, to the exclusion of ability, in attribution training approaches. It is clear that students must perceive effort-outcome covariation (i.e., perceive that levels of outcome depend on levels of effort, such that increases in effort are likely to produce increases in outcome) if they are to put forth serious efforts on classroom tasks. It is also clear that "helpless" students attribute their failures primarily to low ability rather than to low effort. One should not conclude from these facts, however, that motivation (or performance, for that matter) will be maximized when successful outcomes are attributed entirely to effort. Harter (1978) has shown that motivation is higher when students achieve success with what they perceive as reasonable effort than when they achieve success only with what they perceive as sustained maximal effort, and Covington and Omelich (1979) have shown that students much prefer to be seen as both able and hard working than merely as hard working. Thus, in training students to make *success* attributions, there should be emphasis on ability as well as effort—the students should be led to conclude that they have the ability to meet the demands made on them if they make reasonable efforts to do so. This is quite different from training them to expect success only if they consistently extend themselves to their limits.

Assuming appropriate tasks, and with these caveats in mind, it appears that recently developed approaches to reversing failure expectation and related "helpless" behaviors can be effective in improving both motivation and performance. Diener and Dweck (1978) have shown this in their attribution retraining efforts, as have Bandura and Schunk (1981) in their program for developing perceptions of efficacy through proximal goal setting. Various techniques of cognitive behavior modification (Meichenbaum, 1977) designed to "innoculate" students against anxiety or stress and train them to persist in the face of confusion or frustration also seem applicable here.

In addition to these approaches concerned with changing performance expectations, however, we could use approaches concerned with changing task values. Many students simply do not enjoy the process of working on school tasks. Often, of course, this is because the tasks they are given are too difficult for them, and the problem can be eliminated by prescribing more appropriate tasks and preparing them more effectively to handle the tasks they are assigned. Assuming that the problem is not task difficulty but something about the task itself, however, what can be done to improve the situation? Lepper and Gilovich (1982) provide some suggestions about how uninteresting tasks can be made more interesting by making them more game-like by inducing children to set personal goals or to "enrich" the task with fantasy (such as pretending to be an astronaut collecting rock samples on the moon when picking up objects from the floor). Other possibilities are suggested in the following sections.

Probably more common than the problem of dislike for the actual processes involved in the task is the problem of resistance to involvement in a task (even when "success" could be achieved with ease) because the perceived consequences of such involvement are unacceptable. This is often seen in connection with sex-typed tasks (Parsons & Goff, 1980). Certain boys may resist artistic or poetic activities, for example, and certain girls may resist mathematics or science activities. At a more sophisticated level, certain career oriented individuals may avoid learning typing or computer programming for fear of being pigeon holed into jobs that they do not desire. This root problem in these situations (i.e., when a person could do well at a task but chooses not to) usually is some kind of conflict between the task (or whatever the task represents to the person) and the person's self-concept. Pep talks and the like probably will not help here, although "active listening" (Gordon, 1974) and related counseling techniques might. Modeling of task participation by indiviudals with whom the person identifies is likely to be even more effective.

Developing Positive Motivation

Various sources of negative motivation must be eliminated if what I have called "motivation to learn" is to develop. However, eliminating negative motivation merely sets the stage for development of positive motivation; it is a necessary but not sufficient condition.

Nor is it sufficient to be merely neutral. A neutral stance toward classroom tasks is in effect a slightly negative stance given the realities of classroom life. That is, if students simply do not care about the processes involved in an academic task, or about its outcome, there is no positive motivation to counteract the probable negative motivation associated with the fact that the task will involve some effort (it will be work, not play), done under some form of accountability pressure with the prospect of evaluation and consequation of outcome.

Just as workers who do not derive intrinsic satisfaction from their work will put forth reasonable effort when the work is not too demanding and the boss is well liked (or at least respected), students who lack enthusiasm for their school work will "go along to get along" with a teacher who is seen as making reasonable demands and having the characteristics of a "good boss." Teachers who want more than this minimal level and quality of task engagement, however, will have to take more direct action to motivate their students to learn. A variety of strategies has been suggested.

Task-Exogenous, Performance-Focused Strategies

To date, most approaches to classroom motivation have stressed manipulation of student behavior through offering incentives or rewards for successful task performance. This is an effective way of motivating students to perform (assuming that the students expect to be successful and thus gain access to the rewards), but by itself, it does nothing to develop student motivation to learn. In fact, to the extent that the rewards are salient and attractive, and to the extent that task performance is seen merely as instrumental behavior engaged in, in order to get the rewards rather than for its own sake, students are likely to concentrate on whatever will maximize their rewards rather than on acquiring the knowledge or skills that the task was designed to develop. The result may be a piecework mentality, in which students concentrate on efficiently doing the minimun necessary to obtain rewards, without valuing the activity itself or aspiring to gain understanding or produce a high quality product.

The likelihood of these undesirable effects of rewards can be minimized by tying their delivery to quality rather than mere quantity of output, and by seeing that the task itself, and not just the expected reward, is significant to the student.

Task-Exogenous, Value-Focused Strategies

After controlling student performance through rewards, the next most common approach to classroom motivation is to try to stimulate students to value a task because the knowledge or skills that it teaches will be needed in their present or future lives outside of school. This is still a task-exogenous approach, because it portrays whatever the task teaches as a tool or ticket to social advancement, rather than something useful in its own right. Still, it moves closer to what I have been calling "motivation to learn," because it focuses on the learning developed by the task, rather than merely on the consequences of performance outcome. Also, this approach links the knowledge or skills taught by the task to motives and goals developed naturalistically by the student, rather than to situationally bound and artificially applied consequences. This should provide for more continuity between in-school performance of the task and the rest of the student's life.

This approach to motivation is probably effective, at least when tasks are portrayed as subgoals leading toward long range goals that students have adopted and expect to be able to attain. However, I suspect that it is not used as often as it could be, and that when it is used, it is often used in self-defeating ways. Rather than stress the positive by identifying the present or future application value of what is being learned, many teachers stress personal embarrassment ("You don't want people to think that you are ignorant") or future educational or occupational disasters ("You'll never get through sixth grade," "How are you going to get a job if you can't do basic math?"). Other teachers use variations that cast the student in a more positive light but portray society as a hostile environment (Learn to count so that merchants don't cheat you; learn to read so that you don't get taken when signing a contract). Rather than stir up such fears, teachers would do better to help students to appreciate their developing knowledge and skills and to come to value these for their own sake in addition to whatever application value they may have. Also, unless handled carefully, attempts to stress a task's instrumental value for future activities can have the effect of devaluing the task itself (by making it seem to be just a hurdle in one's path rather than an intrinsically worthwhile activity).

Task-Endogenous, Performance-Focused Strategies

In order to stimulate true motivation to learn, teachers will have to supplant (or at least supplement) the task-exogenous approaches described above with task-endogenous approaches designed to foster student appreciation for learning itself, and for its outcomes as represented by gains in knowledge and skill. Task-endogenous, performance-focused approaches attempt to help students to become more aware and appreciative of the knowledge and skills that they develop as a result of their learning efforts, and to take pride in what they are able to accomplish when they apply what they have learned.

It is not clear from the literature how this can be accomplished most effectively, but provision of relevant concepts and labels seems important (you can't appreciate what you don't see or understand). Students need concepts and language to help them articulate situational goals and think about end products in terms of understanding, skills, or accomplishment (not merely task completion or compliance with minimal requirements). Such concepts and labels are useful both for stating the objectives of learning activities (thus helping students to formulate specific goals) and for evaluating performance and giving feedback later. This is especially important for repetitive practice activities in such subjects as grammar, computation, or penmanship. To begin with, students should be aware that such practice is important because the ultimate goals—writing and problem solving in life situations—cannot be accomplished efficiently until their relevant subskills are mastered to levels of smooth, accurate performance, such that they can be integrated with other relevant subskills and applied "effortlessly" as needed (analogies to the importance of isolated skill practice in developing integrated athletic performance might be useful here).

In addition, though, students need concepts and labels to describe the immediate outcomes of their learning efforts. It is probably more meaningful and motivating to think about a reading assignment in terms of "understanding why slavery flourished in the South but not in the North" rather than "studying history"; to "learn to divide when there is both a decimal point and a remainder" rather than merely to "do your math problems"; or to "learn to adjust your writing position so that you stay on the line and maintain the same slant as you move across the page" rather than merely to "practice your penmanship." Similarly, feedback phrased with reference to such goals should be more meaningful and motivating than grades or general evaluative comments that do not mention specific, qualitative aspects of performance.

Task-Endogenous, Value-Focused Approaches

Motivational attempts in this category would be geared toward stimulating students to value or enjoy the actual process of working on academic tasks, hopefully to the point that they would frequently experience something like Csikszentmihalyi's "flow" when doing so. Here again, this is unlikely to occur unless teachers are able to provide students with relevant concepts and labels to use in learning to monitor and appreciate their learning efforts. Recent work on stimulating students' general metacognition seems relevant here, as well as approaches that have been developed to accomplish more specific goals, such as stimulating students to develop an active learning set in approaching academic content, to notice content outlines and headings that show how material has been organized, to identify main ideas in paragraphs, to check for understanding by summarizing content in their own words, or to generate their own questions about content for followup discussion or research. In addition to teaching curriculum content per se, teachers could be coaching their students in learning to learn skills, self-regulation, independent problem solving, etc.

These suggestions are not radical departures from existing approaches to classroom motivation, but they differ in focus or orientation. They involve cueing or goal setting, but with respect to task processes rather than just to task outcomes. They involve attributions, but focus on attributions concerning the specific reasons for engaging in tasks rather than attributions of performance outcomes to causes. They suggest ways that teachers might make academic tasks more meaningful and intrinsically motivating to students, but go beyond appeals to existing affect or personal interests by calling for socialization of the more cognitive aspects of task engagement—helping students to recognize the opportunity that academic tasks provide for exercising or extending knowledge and skills.

These suggestions about presenting specific tasks to students can be extended to include general modeling and socialization designed to stimulate students to value learning (both in its own right as a satisfying, mind expanding activity and as a means of equipping one to succeed in society and to live a richer, more stimulating life). Also important here is socialization designed to develop appreciation for accomplishments and pride in craftsmanship. Teacher modeling of these motivational traits is probably essential here, in that teachers who do not possess such traits themselves seem unlikely to develop them in their students. It also seems likely, however, that such modeling will not be sufficient by itself, and that teachers will also have to be able to provide students with the concepts and labels that they will need to sustain task-endogenous orientations toward academic activities. Thus, it is not enough to urge students to work carefully or do their best; in addition, it is necessary to *show* them how to approach tasks with an orientation toward gaining the potential benefits inherent in them, and how to monitor their progress. That socializing motivation to learn as a general trait is a viable possibility is suggested by Graef, Csikszentmihalyi, and Gianinno (1981), who found that the tendency to find intrinsic value in work is more a personal trait or individual difference variable than a task or situation variable in the everyday lives of the people they studied.

In any case, references to task-endogenous reasons for engaging in academic tasks appear to be rare in the classrooms, and those that are observed tend to focus on the affective rather than the cognitive aspects of motivation.

None of the teachers ever even mentioned the possibility that students might derive cognitive benefit or satisfaction from engaging in the tasks, let alone conducted anything like the systematic socialization of task endogenous, value-focused motivation to learn described above. Given what is said about classroom motivation in most sources of advice to teachers, perhaps this should not be surprising.

Evidence of motivation to learn is also lacking in students. Anderson (1981), for example, found that students who were questioned about their seatwork assignments talked mostly in terms of getting them done and showed little awareness of or interest in the knowledge they were supposed to be developing. Rohrkemper and Bershon (1984) found that, of 49 students questioned, two were concerned only about getting finished, 45 were concerned about getting the correct answers, and only two mentioned trying to understand what was being taught. Corno and Mandinach (1983) and Blumenfeld, Hamilton, Wessels, and Meece (1983) have also expressed concern about the low quality of students' engagement in classroom tasks. The situation seems unlikely to improve until teachers begin to use task-endogenous, value-focused motivational strategies much more often than they do now.

Conclusion

Most of the literature on motivation has been developed from the study of free choice behavior in play situations, but school is a work situation in which students engage in compulsory activities that require primarily mental rather than physical effort. Under these circumstances, although the more overt aspects of task performance can be manipulated through reward and punishment, development of motivation to learn (not merely to meet minimal requirements) will require attention to the more qualitative and cognitive aspects of academic task engagement. Freedom from anxiety, fear of failure, and other types of negative motivation, as well as opportunities to work on tasks at an appropriate difficulty level appear to be necessary (but not sufficient) conditions to allow motivation to learn to develop. Assuming the presence of those necessary conditions, the degree to which it does develop would appear to depend on the degree to which students are socialized to value learning opportunities for their own sake, enjoy the actual processes of learning, recognize and appreciate advances in knowledge and skill, and take pride in craftsmanship as they work on assignments. More attention to these aspects of classroom motivation is needed in conceptualizing the topic, designing research, and communicating with teachers.

REFERENCES

Anderson, L. Short-Term Student Responses to Classroom Instruction. *Elementary School Journal,* 1981, *82,* 97–108.

Bandura, A., & Schunk, D. Cultivating Competence, Self-Efficacy, and Intrinsic Interest Through Proximal Self-Motivation. *Journal of Personality and Social Psychology,* 1981, *41,* 586–598.

Blumenfeld, P.; Hamilton, V.; Wessels, K.; & Meece, J. Teacher Talk and Student Thought: Socialization into the Student Role. In J. Levine & M. Wang (Eds.), *Teacher and student perceptions: Implications for learning.* Hillsdale, New Jersey: Erlbaum, 1982.

Corno, L., & Mandinach, E. Student Interpretive Processes in Classroom Motivation. *Educational Psychologist,* in press.

Covington, M., & Omelich, C. It's Best to Be Able and Virtuous, Too: Student and Teacher Evaluative Responses to Successful Effort. *Journal of Educational Psychology,* 1979, *71,* 688–700.

Diener, C., & Dweck, C. An Analysis of Learned Helplessness: Continuous Changes in Performance, Strategy, and Achievement Cognitions Following Failure. *Journal of Personality and Social Psychology,* 1978, *36,* 451–462.

Eden, D. Intrinsic and Extrinsic Rewards and Motives: Replication and Extension with Kibbutz Workers. *Journal of Applied Social Psychology,* 1975, *5,* 348–361.

Fisher, C.; Berliner, D.; Filby, N.; Marliave, R.; Cahen, L.; & Dishaw, M. Teaching Behaviors, Academic Learning Time, and Student Achievement: An Overview. In C. Denham & A. Lieberman (Eds.), *Time to Learn.* Washington, D.C.: National Institute of Education, 1980.

Gordon, T. *T.E.T. Teacher Effectiveness Training.* New York: David McKay, 1974.

Graef, R.; Csikszentmihalyi, M.; and Gianinno, S. Measuring Intrinsic Motivation in Everyday Life. Paper presented at the annual meeting of the American Psychological Association, Los Angeles, 1981.

Harter, S. Effectance Motivation Reconsidered: Toward a Developmental Model. *Human Development,* 1978, *21,* 34–64.

Jorgenson, G. Relationship of Classroom Behavior to the Accuracy of the Match Between Material Difficulty and Student Ability. *Journal of Educational Psychology,* 1977, *69,* 24–32.

Lepper, M., & Gilovich, T. Accentuating the Positive: Eliciting Generalized Compliance Through Activity-Oriented Requests. *Journal of Personality and Social Psychology,* 1982, *42,* 248–259.

Meichenbaum, D. *Cognitive-Behavior Modification.* Morristown, N.J.: Plenum, 1977.

Parsons, J., & Goff, S. Achievement Motivation and Values: An Alternative Perspective. In L. Fyans (Ed.), *Achievement Motivation: Recent Trends in Theory and Research.* New York: Plenum, 1980.

Rohrkemper, M., & Bershon, B. The Quality of Student Task Engagement: Elementary School Students' Reports of the Causes and Effects of Problem Difficulty. *Elementary School Journal,* 1984, *85,* 127–147.

Students Motivating Students to Excel: Cooperative Incentives, Cooperative Tasks, and Student Achievement

Robert E. Slavin

Students who are unmotivated to learn do not learn. This is virtually a truism, certainly known to every teacher and researcher interested in increasing student learning. Yet research over the past decade has largely avoided consideration of means of motivating students to do academic work and to want to learn. The principal exception to this is the behavior modification tradition, which generally lies outside of the mainstream of educational research (see Brophy 1983; Greer 1983). Most motivational research in education focuses on understanding rather than increasing student motivation.

It is important to distinguish between "student motivation" and "classroom incentives." "Student motivation" is used here to refer to students' interest in doing academic work and learning academic material. "Classroom incentives" refer to methods teachers use to mo-

tivate students to do academic work and learn academic material. Typical classroom incentives are grading systems, provision of stars, tokens, or rewards for doing academic work, praise or recognition for correct responses or academic efforts, and so on. Student motivation is influenced in part by classroom incentives, but also by such factors as intrinsic interest in the task at hand, parents' interest in achievement, and students' perceptions of their abilities and chances of success. However, given tasks of a certain level of intrinsic interest and difficulty, classroom incentives are the primary means under the control of the teacher to affect student motivation.

One substantial line of research on alternative classroom incentives in regular elementary and secondary classrooms involves methods generally referred to as "cooperative learning" (see Slavin 1980a, 1983a). In cooperative learning methods students work in small learning groups (four to six members) and are rewarded for doing well as a group. For

From *Elementary School Journal* 85 (1984): 53–64. Reprinted with the permission of the author and the University of Chicago Press.

example, groups of students whose average score exceeds a certain level might receive certificates or recognition in a class newsletter, or might even receive grades on the basis of their group's performance.

The principal idea behind the cooperative learning methods is that by rewarding groups as well as individuals for their academic achievement, peer norms will come to favor rather than oppose high achievement. Coleman (1961) points out that students do not value their peers who do well academically, while they do value their peers who excel in sports. He hypothesizes that this is so because sports success brings benefits to groups (the team, the school, the town), while academic success benefits only the individual. In fact, in a class using grading on the curve or any competitive grading or incentive system, any individual's success reduces the chances that any other individual will succeed. We can hardly expect Sue to be happy when Mary gets an "A," because this may make it harder for Sue to get an "A." Because of this, students develop norms that oppose doing well academically. Students tell one another that academic success is not an important goal, that those who work too hard are "grinds," "teacher's pets," or worse. The most able students, or those with parents who communicate strong proacademic norms, may not care about antiacademic norms among their peers or may participate in smaller peer groups that do value academic achievement. However, for many or perhaps most students, striving to achieve is a sucker's game. As the peer group becomes increasingly important to students in upper elementary and especially in middle or junior high school, peer pressures against achievement may overwhelm parental or school pressure in favor of achievement.

Norms against achievement are probably inevitable products of incentive systems in which individuals are in competition with one another. Alternatively, incentive systems based on *group* performance create norms in favor of achievement (see Slavin 1981). The reason for this is not difficult to see; individuals who are

working together toward a common goal are likely to encourage one another to do whatever helps the group to be rewarded (see, e.g., Thomas 1957).

Cooperative learning methods used in elementary and secondary classrooms change more than the classroom incentive structure. They also change classroom tasks, as students work in small learning groups. Because cooperative incentives and cooperative tasks are usually seen together (when they are seen at all), it is difficult to disentangle the effects of each on student achievement. Yet determining the separate effects of cooperative incentives and cooperative tasks on student achievement is important. If cooperative tasks are found to increase student achievement, we might then investigate the peer interaction processes that operate within cooperating groups to find out why they did work, so that we could find principles of learning that might apply beyond group learning situations (see, e.g., Webb 1982). If cooperative incentives are found to have an independent positive effect on student achievement, then we might direct further efforts toward understanding and experimenting with classroom incentive systems, and we might focus on student motivation as a critical determinant of student achievement.

There are several reasons that one might expect cooperative tasks to improve student achievement. It has long been known from research on peer tutoring that teaching a fellow student helps tutors learn the material (see Devin-Sheehan, Feldman, & Allen 1976). Discussion of reading matter improves comprehension more than isolated study (Slavin & Tanner 1979), and controversy increases comprehension of social studies materials (Smith, Johnson, & Johnson 1981). On the other hand, research by Webb (1982) indicates that effects of cooperative learning tasks on achievement depend on behaviors within the learning group, characteristics of students, and other factors and are thus beneficial in some circumstances and harmful in others.

The purpose of this paper is to review the research evidence from studies of cooperative learning methods in elementary and secondary classrooms in an attempt to discover the separate effects of cooperative incentives and cooperative tasks on student achievement.

Cooperative Learning Methods

As noted above, there are two primary components of cooperative learning methods: a cooperative incentive structure and a cooperative task structure. Cooperative incentive structure is what most theorists mean when they refer to cooperation (see, e.g., Deutsch 1949). The critical feature of a cooperative incentive structure is that two or more individuals are interdependent for a reward they will share if they are successful as a group. For example, if three people traveling in a car help push the car out of the mud, all of them benefit from each other's efforts by being able to continue their trip. Either all of them will be rewarded or none of them will be, depending on their combined efforts and external factors, such as how deeply the car is stuck. Group competition, as in team sports, is also a cooperative incentive structure, because the group's success depends on the efforts of the group members, and all group members share the same reward (winning or losing).

Cooperative task structures are situations in which two or more individuals are allowed, encouraged, or required to work together on some task, coordinating their efforts to complete the task. Cooperative incentive structures usually involve cooperative tasks, but the two are conceptually distinct. For example, suppose a school district decides to give bonuses to teachers in schools that increase their students' achievement the most. The teachers in each school are under a cooperative incentive structure (they all benefit if the school does well) even if they cannot directly help each other teach (i.e., they are not under a cooperative task structure).

Cooperative learning methods used in classrooms always involve cooperative tasks, although not all of them involve cooperative incentives. The forms of the tasks and incentives vary considerably across different methods. The task structures used in cooperative learning methods can be divided into two categories: task specialization and group study. In methods that use task specialization, each group member is responsible for a unique part of the group activity; in group study methods, all group members study together and do not have separate tasks.

The incentive structures used in cooperative learning methods can be summarized in three categories, depending on whether or not rewards are given on the basis of individual learning or a single group product. In methods that use group rewards for individual learning, rewards such as recognition (e.g., newsletters, certificates), grades, praise, or tangible rewards are given to students in groups that achieve some standard, such as making one of the highest group scores in the class or exceeding a preset criterion. The group score is the average score received by group members on an assessment of individual learning, such as a quiz. In methods that use group rewards for group products, similar group rewards are provided, but they are given based on the quality of a single group work sheet or report to which all group members contributed, rather than individual learning. Cooperative learning methods that use individual rewards have students work together and instruct them to help one another but provide only individual grades to students based on their own performance.

Thus, all of the cooperative learning methods can be located in a 3 × 2 table produced by the two factors: incentive structure and task structure. This is depicted in Table 1. The methods categorized in the six resulting cells are described below.

Group Study/Group Reward for Individual Learning

Methods in this cell typically involve students working in small groups to master work sheets

Table 1
Categorization of Cooperative Learning Methods by Incentive and Task Structures

	INCENTIVE STRUCTURE		
TASK STRUCTURE	*Group Reward for Individual Learning*	*Group Reward for Group Product*	*Individual Reward*
GROUP STUDY (no task specialization)	STAD TGT TAI		Peterson & Janicki (1979) methods Huber et al. (1981) methods
		Learning Together Wheeler & Ryan (1973) methods	
	Humpreys et al. (1982) methods Hamblin et al. (1971) methods Lew & Bryant (1981) methods		Starr & Schuerman (1974) methods Webb & Kenderski (1982) methods
TASK SPECIALIZATION	Jigsaw II	Group Investigation Wheeler (1977) methods	Jigsaw

SOURCE: Adapted from Figure 1 in Slavin (1983c).

or other information initially presented by the teacher. Following the group study time, the students are individually assessed, and the group members' scores are summed to form group scores. These are recognized in class newsletters, or qualify the groups for certificates, grades, or other rewards. Cooperative learning methods categorized in this cell include three developed at Johns Hopkins University: Student Teams-Achievement Divisions, or STAD (Slavin 1978); Teams-Games-Tournament, or TGT (DeVries & Slavin 1978); and Team Assisted Individualization, or TAI (Slavin, Leavey, & Madden 1984). In STAD, the teacher presents a lesson (one to two class periods), and then students study work sheets in four-member teams that are heterogeneous on student ability, gender, and ethnicity. Students quiz each other, compare answers and discuss problems within their groups. Following this, students take individual quizzes, and team scores are computed based on the degree to which each student improved over his or her own past record. The team scores are recognized in class newsletters. TGT is the same as

STAD, except that, instead of taking quizzes, students compete against members of other teams who are similar in past performance to add points to their team scores. In TAI, students work in heterogeneous teams, but they work on individualized curriculum materials at their own levels and rates. Teams receive certificates based on the number of units completed and the accuracy of their members' final tests. Figure 1 from Slavin (1983b), illustrates the primary features of STAD and TGT. Additional methods in the group study, group reward for individual learning category are listed in Table 1.

Group Study/Group Reward for Group Product

In these methods, students are asked to work or study together, and the group produces a single work sheet or test, which is the basis for evaluation of the group. The largest number of such studies involve methods developed by David and Roger Johnson, called "Learning Together" methods (from the title of their book, *Learning Together and Alone* [1975]). In most of the Learning Together studies, students in small, heterogeneous groups worked together to complete a single work sheet and were praised and rewarded as a group.

Group Study/Individual Reward

The group study method most commonly seen in practice simply involves students working or studying in small groups, with no group rewards. Students are graded solely on the basis of their own work.

Task Specialization/Group Reward for Individual Learning

Only one study (Ziegler 1981) appears in this cell. This study used Jigsaw II (Slavin 1980b), an adaptation of Aronson's (1978) Jigsaw method (see below). In Jigsaw II, each student in a heterogeneous team is given a unique topic on which to become an "expert." The students from different teams with the same topics meet in "expert groups" to discuss their topics and then return to their teams to teach their teammates what they have learned. Finally, all students are tested on a quiz that covers all topics, and the quiz scores are summed to form team scores. In the Ziegler (1981) study, students received grades based in part on their team scores.

Task Specialization/Group Reward for Group Product

Several cooperative learning studies have evaluated methods that use task specialization, but give group rewards or evaluations based on a single group product or report rather than on individual learning. The primary method in this category is called Group Investigation (Sharan & Sharan 1976), a method in which small groups choose subtopics from a unit being studied by the entire class, and then students within the group choose subtasks within the group topic. The groups then prepare reports on their topics and present them to the rest of the class. Students are evaluated in large part based on the quality of their group presentations or other group products.

Task Specialization/Individual Reward

This cell contains only Aronson's (1978) original Jigsaw model. This method is essentially the same as Jigsaw II (described above), except that, instead of receiving grades based in part on the average of group members' quiz scores as in Jigsaw II, students in the original Jigsaw method receive only individual grades based on their own test scores.

Achievement Outcomes of Cooperative Learning Studies

Slavin (1983c) identifies 46 field experiments on cooperative learning that were conducted in elementary and secondary classes (mostly Grades 3–9). To be included in this review, these studies had to include a control group (usually with random assignment of classes or students to treatments) and had to have evaluated a cooperative learning method in regular elementary or secondary classes for at least 2 weeks (more typically 6–12 weeks).

The achievement outcomes of these studies are summarized in Table 2. In the table "positive" means that the students in the cooperative learning classes learned significantly, $p < .05$, more than those in the control group, "negative" means that they learned significantly less, and "no effect" means that there were no significant differences.

Taken together, the effects of cooperative learning methods on student achievement are clearly positive. Of the 46 studies, 29 (63%) showed cooperative learning methods to have significantly positive (or, in one case, marginally positive) effects on student achievement. Fifteen (33%) found no differences, and two (4%) found significantly higher achievement for a control group than for a cooperative treatment.

However, the overall results mask important differences among studies. Table 2 illustrates these differences by categorizing the

Table 2
Achievement Outcomes of Cooperative Learning Studies by Categories of Incentive and Task Structures

TASK STRUCTURE AND EFFECT FOUND IN STUDY	INCENTIVE STRUCTURE							
	Group Reward for Individual Learning		Group Reward for Group Product		Individual Reward		All Rewards	
	N	%	N	%	N	%	N	%
Group study (no task specialization):								
Positive	24	89	0	0	0	0	24	67
No effect	3	11	3	75	5	100	11	31
Negative	0	0	1	25	0	0	1	3
Total studies	27		4		5		36	
Task specialization:								
Positive	1	100	3	75	1	20	5	50
No effect	0	0	1	25	3	60	4	40
Negative	0	0	0	0	1	20	1	10
Total studies	1		4		5		10	
All incentive structures:								
Positive	25	89	3	38	1	10	29	63
No effect	3	11	4	50	8	80	15	33
Negative	0	0	1	13	1	10	2	4
Total studies	28		8		10		46	

SOURCE: Adapted from table 3 in Slavin (1983*c*).
NOTE: Some percentages total more than 100% because of rounding.

achievement results by type of incentive and type of task (group study vs. task specialization). As can be seen in the top half of Table 2, there is a dramatic difference in achievement outcomes among the group study methods, depending on their use of rewards. Of 27 studies that used group study and group rewards for individual learning, 24 (89%) found positive effects on student achievement, while three (11%) found no differences. In contrast, none of the nine studies of group study methods that did not use group rewards for individual learning found positive effects on student achievement.

The results for studies that used task specialization are less clear because of the much smaller number of studies (10) that used this task structure. However, there is an interesting

pattern to the findings. The only study to use task specialization and group rewards for individual learning (Ziegler 1981) found strong effects on student achievement, which were maintained in a 5-month follow-up. Three of the four task specialization studies in which students were rewarded on the basis of a group product found positive achievement results. In contrast, there is little evidence that the original Jigsaw method (which uses no group rewards) increases student achievement more than control methods. The one Jigsaw study to find positive achievement effects (Lucker, Rosenfield, Sikes, & Aronson 1976) obtained them only for a small subsample of minority students in a very brief study (2 weeks). No positive effects were found for Anglos in that study, or for Anglo or minority students in the other

Jigsaw studies. Thus, this evidence suggests that the effects of task specialization methods on achievement depend on the use of group rewards, regardless of whether the rewards are based on individual learning or group performance.

The evidence summarized in Table 2 presents strong support for the observation that group rewards for individual learning are critical to the effectiveness of cooperative learning methods. Restricting attention to the group study methods, the presence or absence of group rewards for individual learning clearly discriminates methods that increase student achievement from those that do no better than control methods. Component analyses and comparisons of similar methods further bear out the importance of this factor. Slavin (1980c) varied rewards (team vs. individual) and tasks (group vs. individual) in a study of STAD. The results of this study indicated that providing recognition based on team scores (the mean of the members' improvement scores) increased student achievement, regardless of whether or not the students were allowed to study together. The students who could study in groups but received no group rewards learned *less* than all other students, including those who studied individually and received only individual rewards. This study also found that, when students in interacting groups were working toward a team reward, they helped each other substantially more than when they could work together but received no team rewards. Huber, Bogatzki, and Winter (1981) also compared STAD with group study without group rewards and to individual study. They found that STAD students learned more than the group study and individual work students, but there were no differences between the group study and individual study conditions. Finally, a study of TGT (Hulten & DeVries 1976) found that providing recognition based on team scores (the mean of the members' game scores in the TGT tournaments) improved achievement whether or not students were permitted to study together. Group study itself had no effects on student achievement. Thus, these component analyses add three

more evaluations of methods that use group study but not group rewards. In no case did students in the group study conditions learn more than those in control conditions, and in one case (Slavin 1980c) they learned less. However, in all three studies, the addition of specific group rewards based on members' learning made the methods instructionally effective.

The pattern of results for the studies that used a group study task, both across the different methods and within the component analyses, supports an unexpected conclusion: the opportunity for students to study together makes little or no contribution to the effects of cooperative learning on achievement. Providing an opportunity for group study without providing further structure in the form of individual assessment and group reward has not been found (among the studies that meet the criteria for inclusion applied in this paper) to increase student achievement more than having students work separately. On the other hand, studies of group study methods in which cooperative learning students could earn group rewards based on group members' individual academic performance were relatively consistent in showing the superiority of these methods to individualistic, competitive, or traditional control methods.

Why Do Group Rewards for Individual Learning Increase Student Achievement?

The causal mechanism linking use of group rewards for individual learning and increased student achievement in cooperative learning that has the greatest empirical as well as theoretical support is that provision of rewards based on group performance creates group member norms supporting performance. That is, group members try to make the group successful by encouraging each other to excel. Even though rewards given to groups are likely to be less closely related to individual performance than rewards given to individuals (see Slavin 1983a), group members are hypothesized to create a very sensitive and effective reward system for each other, in which they pay a great deal of attention to one another's efforts and socially reinforce efforts that help the group achieve its goal (see Deutsch 1949). By the same token, group members are likely to apply social disapproval to group mates who are goldbricking or clowning instead of learning.

The occurrence of peer norms supporting classmates' achievement has been documented in several of the STAD and TGT studies, in which students who have experienced cooperative learning are much more likely than control students to agree with such statements as, "Other children in my class want me to work hard" (e.g., Hulten & DeVries 1976; Madden & Slavin 1983). Students' perceptions that their classmates want them to excel probably have a strong effect on their own motivations to do so and contrast sharply with the situation in classrooms in which individual competition for grades leads students to express norms *against* academic excellence (see Coleman 1961; Slavin 1981). As noted earlier, peer norms for or against academic efforts may be more important for many students than teacher or parent pressure to achieve. In such cases, changing peer norms to favor academic efforts may be especially important.

In theory, group rewards based on *group* performance, however defined, should create group norms favoring performance. However, this theory only applies to group member behaviors that are actually critical for the group to be successful. For example, on various tests Hamblin, Hathaway, and Wodarski (1971) reinforced groups based on the performance of (*a*) the highest three scores, (*b*) the lowest three scores, or (*c*) the average group score. They found that, when the group was rewarded based on the highest scores, high achievers learned the most, while low achievers learned the most when the group depended on their scores. Therefore, it is hypothesized that in cooperative learning only if the group reward is based on the sum of individual learning performances will interpersonal sanctions be directed at increasing the academic performance of *all* group members. If, for example, groups are judged based on a single work sheet or test produced by the group, pro-performance

norms may be produced, but they should apply only to the performance of those group members deemed by the group to have the most to contribute to the group product (such as the most able or energetic group members), since all group members are unlikely to be able to contribute equally to the group product.

Conclusions

The results of the field experimental research on cooperative learning methods indicate that the positive effects of these methods on student achievement result from the use of cooperative incentives, not cooperative tasks. This result appears to be because of an effect of cooperative incentives on peer norms and possibly peer sanctions favoring high achievement.

This conclusion highlights the importance of incentives in general. The most successful cooperative learning methods do little to alter the content or delivery of instruction. They do change how students study work sheets (in groups rather than individually), but the group study aspect of the cooperative learning methods has not been found to contribute to the achievement effects. The evidence indicates that a simple change in the classroom incentive system produces relatively consistent changes in student achievement. This evidence suggests that incentive systems in traditional classrooms are not optimal and that their deficiencies may have important consequences for student achievement. That is, attempts to create more effective instruction by improving the quality of instruction, student time on task, and so on may fall short without a consideration of incentives directed at increasing student motivation to learn.

For practitioners, the research summarized in this paper clearly suggests that student achievement can be enhanced by use of cooperative learning methods that use group study and group rewards for individual learning, and possibly by other cooperative learning methods than maintain high individual accountability for students. It should be noted that cooperative learning methods have also been found to have positive effects on a wide range of social-emotional outcomes, such as student self-esteem, race relations, and acceptance of mainstreamed academically handicapped students (see Slavin, 1983a). These noncognitive outcomes do not appear to depend to the same extent on particular incentive or task structures, and for many practical applications these outcomes might justify use of cooperative learning methods as long as they do not reduce student achievement.

The challenge for future research on cooperative learning and student achievement will be to understand more about how cooperative incentives function as motivators and to understand how cooperative incentives interact with variously constructed tasks to enhance student achievement. There is also a continuing need for development and evaluation of cooperative learning methods, both to solve practical problems of instruction and to expand the range of operationalizations of cooperative learning.

Furthermore, the effects of cooperative incentive structures on student achievement point to the classroom incentive structure as a potential focus for instructional improvement. If, as hypothesized in this paper, increasing student motivation to learn (by means of cooperative incentives) increases student learning, then it is probable that *any* means of increasing motivation to learn might have the same effect. The search for simple, practical, and effective means of improving classroom incentives must continue.

Note: This paper is based on research at the Center for Social Organization of Schools funded by the National Institute of Education grant NIE-G-80-0113 and Office of Special Education grant G-80-01494. However, the opinions expressed are those of the author and do not represent official policy.

REFERENCES

Aronson, E. (1978). *The Jigsaw classroom.* Beverly Hills, CA: Sage.

Brophy, J. (1983). If only it were true: a response to Greer. *Educational Researcher,* **12**(1), 10–12.

Coleman, J. S. (1961). *The adolescent society.* New York: Free Press of Glencoe.

Deutsch, M. (1949). A theory of cooperation and competition. *Human Relations,* **2**, 129–152.

Devin-Sheehan, L.; Feldman, R.; & Allen, V. (1976). Research on children tutoring children: a critical review. *Review of Educational Research,* **46**, 355–385.

DeVries, D. L., & Slavin, R. E. (1978). Teams-Games-Tournament (TGT): review of ten classroom experiments. *Journal of Research and Development in Education,* **12**, 28–38.

Greer, R. D. (1983). Contingencies of the science and technology of teaching and prebehavioristic research practices in education. *Educational Researcher,* **12**(1), 3–9.

Hamblin, R. L.; Hathaway, C.; & Wodarski, J. S. (1971). Group contingencies, peer tutoring, and accelerating academic achievement. In E. Ramp & W. Hopkins (Eds.), *A new direction for education: behavior analysis.* Lawrence: University of Kansas, Department of Human Development.

Huber, G.; Bogatzki, W.; & Winter, M. (1981). Cooperation: condition and goal of teaching and learning in classrooms. Unpublished manuscript, University of Tübingen, West Germany.

Hulten, R. H., & DeVries, D. L. (1976). Team competition and group practice: effects on student achievement and attitudes (Report No. 212). Baltimore: Johns Hopkins University, Center for Social Organization of Schools.

Humphreys, B.; Johnson, R.; & Johnson, D. W. (1982). Effects of cooperative, competitive, and individualistic learning on students' achievement in science class. *Journal of Research in Science Teaching,* **19**, 351–356.

Johnson, D. W., & Johnson, R. T. (1975). *Learning together and alone.* Englewood Cliffs, NJ: Prentice-Hall.

Lew, M., & Bryant, R. (1981). The use of cooperative groups to improve spelling achievement for all children in the regular classroom. Paper presented at the Massachusetts Council for Exceptional Children, Boston.

Lucker, G.; Rosenfield, D.; Sikes, J.; & Aronson, E. (1976). Performance in the interdependent classroom: a field study. *American Educational Research Journal,* **13,** 115–123.

Madden, N. A., & Slavin, R. F., (1983). Cooperative learning and social acceptance of mainstreamed academically handicapped students. *Journal of Special Education,* **53,** 519–569.

Peterson, P. L., & Janicki, T. C. (1979). Individual characteristics and children's learning in large-group and small-group approaches, *Journal of Educational Psychology,* **71,** 677–687.

Sharan, S., & Sharan, Y. (1976). *Small-group teaching.* Englewood Cliffs, NJ: Educational Technology Publications.

Slavin, R. E. (1978). Student teams and achievement divisions. *Journal of Research and Development in Education,* **12,** 39–49.

Slavin, R. E. (1980a). Cooperative learning. *Review of Educational Research,* **50,** 315–342.

Slavin, R. E. (1980b). *Using Student Team Learning,* rev. ed. Baltimore: Johns Hopkins University, Center for Social Organization of Schools.

Slavin, R. E. (1980c). Effects of student teams and peer tutoring on academic achievement and time on-task. *Journal of Experimental Education,* **48,** 252–257.

Slavin, R. E. (1981). Cooperative learning: changing the normative climate of the classroom. Paper presented at the annual convention of the American Educational Research Association, Los Angeles.

Slavin, R. E. (1983a). *Cooperative learning.* New York: Longman.

Slavin, R. E. (1983b). *Student Team Learning; an overview and practical guide.* Washington, DC: National Education Association.

Slavin, R. E. (1983c). When does cooperative learning increase student achievement: *Psychological Bulletin,* **94,** 429–445.

Slavin, R. E., & Tanner, A. M. (1979). Effects of cooperative reward structures and individual accountability on productivity and learning. *Journal of Educational Research,* **72,** 294–298.

Slavin, R. E.; Leavey, M.; & Madden, N. A. (1984). Combining cooperative learning and individualized instruction: effects on student mathematics achievement, attitudes, and behaviors. *Elementary School Journal,* **84,** 409–422.

Smith, K.; Johnson, D. W.; & Johnson, R. (1981). Can conflict be constructive? Controversy versus concurrence seeking in learning groups. *Journal of Educational Psychology,* **73,** 651–663.

Starr, R., & Schuerman, C. (1974). An experiment in small-group learning. *American Biology Teacher,* **36,** 173–175.

Thomas, E. J. (1957). Effects of facilitative role interdependence on group functioning. *Human Relations,* **10,** 347–366.

Webb, N. (1982). Student interaction and learning in small groups. *Review of Educational Research,* **52,** 421–445.

Webb, N., & Kenderski, C. (1982, May). Student interaction and learning in small group and whole class settings. Paper presented at the Conference on Student Diversity and the Organization, Processes, and Use of Instructional Groups in the Classroom, University of Wisconsin—Madison.

Wheeler, R. (1977). Predisposition toward cooperation and competition: cooperative and competitive classroom effects. Paper presented at the annual convention of the American Psychological Association, San Francisco.

Wheeler, R., & Ryan, F. L. (1973). Effects of cooperative and competitive classroom environments on the attitudes and achievement of elementary school students engaged in social studies inquiry activities. *Journal of Educational Psychology,* **65,** 402–407.

Ziegler, S. (1981). The effectiveness of cooperative learning teams for increasing cross-ethnic friendship: additional evidence. *Human Organization,* **40,** 264–268.

Discipline: Self Guidance Versus External Control

Classroom discipline has always been one of the foremost problems for teachers. Indeed, the adequate control of a classroom is a prerequisite to achieving instructional objectives and to safeguarding the psychological and physical well being of students. Control techniques are of vital concern to students and parents. Students' attitudes towards school as well as the extent to which they learn are influenced to an appreciable degree by the disciplinary factors used by the teacher. Parents also express considerable interest about the kinds of disciplinary practices employed by schools. Although some people believe that schools are already too severe and restrictive in their handling of students, Gallup polls over the last 10 years have shown that the large majority of Americans believe lack of discipline constitutes the major problem confronting our public schools. Not only are parents concerned about classroom discipline, but teachers report that students who flout discipline can and do disrupt a positive classroom atmosphere. Even experienced teachers are often at a loss how to cope with deviate behavior. The passage of Public Law 94-142, the Education for all Handicapped Act of 1975, has increased the number of "hard to manage" children in regular education classes. Moreover, the de-institutionalization movement has shifted severely disturbed children from residential settings to special classroom settings. Thus, whether you are in regular education or special education, teachers have more difficult children to teach and manage today than they once had.

In the opening article Jere Brophy views classroom management as primarily a matter of telling and showing willing but ignorant students what to do rather than enforcing compliance. Moreover, he notes that such development does not occur on its own but that it must be stimulated through socialization by parents, teachers, and others important in the child's life. Finally, he stresses the notion that classroom management is a form of instruction rather than a form of discipline or control. In a sharply contrasting approach, Lee and Marilyn Canter have advocated a take charge approach for today's educators. Assertive discipline provides the means for interacting with students in calm yet forceful ways that result in more compliant behavior. This approach is based on principles from assertion training and behavior modification. Assertive discipline combines clear expectations, insistence on appropriate behavior, consistent follow through, and warmth and support so that students can be provided with a climate appropriate to maximum learning and student development.

Thought Questions

Which style of discipline is more consistent with the teacher's role, Brophy's or Canters'?

Is it better to impose rules on students or to let them arrive at the rules for classroom behavior on their own? Could you use assertive discipline with emotionally impaired children as the Canters suggest?

What is your reaction to Brophy's statement that students are generally willing and potentially cooperative rather than alienated or predisposed to misbehavior?

Discuss the proposition that effective classroom managers are successful because they are good at preventing problems, that is, good at maximizing the time that students spend on lessons.

What methods might Brophy recommend to teachers when the child's socialization in self-guidance is deficient, resulting in continual misbehavior?

Does assertive discipline promote self-management or reliance on external control?

Are some students likely to become more hostile under the use of assertive discipline techniques?

Is a shy, anxious, withdrawn student likely to be frightened simply by observing a teacher use assertive disciplinary techniques with his or her classmates?

Does assertive discipline with its "all kids can behave" philosophy overlook the fact that some students do not have the skills to behave? That is, can all discipline problems be reduced to motivational problems?

Classroom Management as Instruction: Socializing Self-Guidance in Students

Jere Brophy

The title of this article touches on three basic themes that underlie its approach to the topic, teaching self-discipline. First, it refers to self-guidance rather than self-control. This subtle but important difference reflects basic assumptions about what students are like and what they need from their teachers. Students are seen as generally willing and potentially cooperative rather than alienated or predisposed to misbehavior. Thus, classroom management is seen as primarily a matter of telling and showing willing but ignorant students what to do, rather than enforcing compliance from students who know what to do but tend not to do it on their own.

Second, the title refers to "socializing" self-guidance in students. This is a reminder that although students have the potential to develop self-guidance, such development does not occur automatically. Instead, it must be stimulated through socialization by parents, teachers, and significant others. Third, the title is a reminder that classroom management may be

thought of as a form of instruction, instead of a form of discipline or control. In particular, most of the things teachers do to develop self-guidance in their students involve modeling and instruction rather than, or at least in addition to, propounding and enforcing rules.

This article shows how these themes keep appearing in research on child rearing in the home and classroom management at school, and draws upon research and related theory to suggest approaches teachers can use to socialize self-guidance in their students.

Socialization in the Home

Mature forms of self-guidance do not suddenly appear full blown in children. Instead, they develop gradually (if at all) following passage through a series of less mature forms determined in part by children's levels of cognitive development and in part by the nature of the socialization they receive (especially in the home). This development occurs within a context of dependency on adults, not only for basic survival necessities, but also for concepts with

From *Theory Into Practice* 24(1985):233–240. Reprinted with permission.

which to understand the meanings of experience and guidance about how to respond to it.

In infancy, the connections between language, thought, and behavior are loose and the child's potential for achieving cognitive control over behavior is very limited. Over the next several years, during what Piaget calls the preoperational period, cognitive abilities become both more differentiated and more integrated with one another and with behavior. Gradually, the child becomes able to use thought, particularly thought mediated by speech and expressed as inner speech or self-talk (Vygotsky, 1962), to plan and regulate behavior. Such cognitive regulation begins with a child's physical responses to the immediate environment but gradually extends to include social interactions as well. Cognitive mediation is perhaps especially crucial in the social sphere where relatively little of what occurs can be understood merely by observing people's physical movements. In order to understand and participate in human social interaction, one must understand the language and associated concepts and referents that form the core of such activities and provide the context for meaning.

Even as their cognitive and linguistic abilities develop throughout the preoperational years (ages 2 through 6 or 7) and into the concrete operational years (ages 6 or 7 through adolescence), children remain heavily dependent on adult guidance in learning to interpret and respond to their social environments. Preschool and early elementary school students tend to identify with and seek to please their parents and teachers, developing what Kohlberg (1969) has called a "good boy" or "good girl" level of moral thinking. They tend to accept (even if they do not always follow) the conduct norms propounded by these adult authority figures because they want to please them by "being good," and being good means following these conduct norms.

Because they are so dependent on adults for information and predisposed to accept what adults tell them (at least if what adults tell them is consistent), young children tend to accept what they are told about behavioral norms without much reflection or attempt at evalua-

tion. In Freud's terms, they "introject" moral concepts and behavioral norms—acquire them directly from statements by adults, retain them in the concrete form in which they were originally learned, and reproduce them in similar contexts in the future. Typically, children come to think of these norms as their own (that is, as something they always knew or they figured out for themselves), losing sight of the fact that the norms were originally taught to them by adult authority figures.

Introjected moral norms do not contribute much to effective self-regulation of behavior because they tend to be isolated verbal responses—conditioned reactions to particular situations—rather than "words to live by" that have been consciously adopted and function as part of a general philosophy that provides guidance to one's behavior (Brophy, 1977). Typically, children do not begin to actively question the moral norms to which they have been exposed and seek to develop a moral philosophy of their own until they reach adolescence and enter Piaget's stage of formal operational thinking. Even then, great individual differences exist in the degree to which previously introjected norms are consciously examined and a more mature and functional set of norms is adopted, internalized, and developed into a consistent system. These individual differences are closely related to the degree and nature of moral socialization to which the individuals have been exposed.

Characteristics of Successful Socialization

Research on child rearing suggests that successful socialization has two noteworthy characteristics. First, such socialization is extensive in volume and rich in cognitive content. Effective parents spend a great deal of time interacting with their children in ways that stimulate the children's cognitive development (Hess, 1970). In particular, such parents socialize the children's beliefs, attitudes, and expectations about morality, social interaction, politics, and related social realities. They supply their children not merely with norms, but with concepts, labels, principles, rationales, and related cognitive input that provide a basis for understanding cognitive realities and a context of meaning within which to interpret norms and prescriptions. In short, such parents provide their children with a great deal of instruction, and not merely with a brief list of do's and don'ts.

Second, effective socialization is what Baumrind (1971) calls "authoritative" rather than "authoritarian" or "laissez-faire." Authoritative parents accept their roles as authority figures responsible for socializing their children and therefore place demands and limits on the children. However, they routinely explain the rationales underlying these demands and help the children appreciate that demands are appropriate and motivated by a concern for people's (including the children's) rights and best interests.

Contrasting patterns of parenting lack the balance and effectiveness of this authoritative pattern. Laissez-faire parents make few demands on their children. They tend to ignore them and let them do as they please, so long as they do not become destructive or annoying. This pattern is often a form of apathy or rejection, and may lead to feelings of insecurity and low self-esteem in the children. In any case, it involves requiring the children to make decisions about how to behave without first having equipped them with the principles and concepts needed for making such decisions. At best, this leads to a great deal of unnecessary and sometimes painful trial and error learning, and it also is likely to lead to traits such as insecurity, anxiety, or fear of failure.

Authoritarian parents make constant demands on their children with little attempt to explain these demands or help the children understand the reasons for them. Instead, they "boss the children around" with a "you'll do it because I said so" attitude and a readiness to punish failure to comply. This sets up the issue of regulation of behavior as a contest of wills and a matter of power exertion rather than as self-regulation based on concepts of rights and responsibilities.

The authoritative approach is the most likely to give children both the cognitive tools and the emotional freedom to think about and evaluate behavioral norms, to consciously adopt the norms that make sense and use them to guide behavior, and to integrate them into a systematic and internally consistent moral philosophy (Brophy, 1977). In contrast to laissez-faire parents, authoritative parents provide their children with a well-articulated model of such a systematic moral philosophy, which the children can learn and use as a base from which to develop their own moral thinking. It is easier to first master and then work from such a base than to try to develop an integrated system of moral principles by working from scratch.

Authoritative parents provide their children not only with the cognitive tools for evaluating behavioral norms but also with the modeling and emotional freedom that will encourage them to do so. They consistently present behavioral norms as means toward ends rather than as ends in themselves. Ultimately, the justification for rules and demands lies in the golden rule or associated concepts of justice, fairness, or morality, rather than in the authority of the parent over the child. The children are encouraged to think about why they behave as they do and to evaluate their behavior in terms of its effectiveness in attaining the goals toward which it is ostensibly directed.

In contrast, authoritarian parents discourage such thinking by demanding conformity and submission to their authority and focusing on threat of punishment rather than moral justification in presenting their demands. If they succeed in breaking the child's will, the result will be a docile individual who rigidly follows prescribed norms and is essentially externally controlled rather than self-guided. If they fail, the result will be an individual who resents and resists authority and is prone to delinquency and crime. The docile, intimidated child lacks the emotional freedom to evaluate behavioral prescriptions because he or she has learned to equate this with rebellion against powerful authority figures; the oppositional child lacks the motivation to do so because he or she has learned to equate behavioral prescriptions with arbitrary and oppressive exertion of power by authority figures.

Classroom Management

Theory and research on classroom management have concentrated mostly on how teachers can control student behavior rather than on how teachers can develop self-guidance in their students. This is largely understandable because of the bureaucratic nature of schools, the unfavorable student/teacher ratio, the competition for grades, the public nature of classroom instruction, and all of the other factors that make it difficult to establish the classroom as an effective learning environment. Even so, appropriate student self-guidance is an implicit ideal. The teachers who are most admired as classroom managers are those whose classes run smoothly without a great deal of cueing or direction giving, whose students are actively engaged in academic activities, and who can leave the room or turn the class over to a substitute without fear of disruption or inappropriate behavior.

Prior to the seminal work of Kounin (1970), little systematic research had been done on effective classroom management. Advice to teachers was of the "Don't smile until Christmas" variety, in which the emphasis was on control or discipline and the advice consisted of an ill-assorted "bag of tricks" based on experience rather than an integrated set of principles developed from systematic research.

Kounin (1970) approached this problem by comparing the behaviors of effective and ineffective classroom managers. He videotaped activities in ideal classrooms such as those described above and also in poorly managed classrooms in which the teachers were fighting to keep the lid on the students who were regularly inattentive and frequently disruptive. His initial approach, following the "discipline" orientation dominant at the time, was to compare the two groups of teachers' handling of disruptive incidents. Surprisingly, in view of the clear differences in effectiveness between these two

groups of teachers, the analyses failed to produce consistent results. Effective classroom managers did not differ in systematic ways from ineffective classroom managers when they were responding to student misbehavior.

However, Kounin and his colleagues noticed that effective managers differed from ineffective managers in other ways that they eventually were able to define and measure systematically through reanalyses. Some of the key behaviors shown by the effective managers were the following:

Withitness. Remaining "with it" (aware of what is happening in all parts of the classroom at all times) by continuously scanning the classroom, even when working with small groups or individuals; demonstrating this withitness to the students by intervening promptly and accurately when inappropriate behavior threatens to become disruptive, thus avoiding both timing errors (failing to notice and intervene until an incident has already become disruptive) and target errors (confusion or mistakes concerning which students were responsible for the problem).

Overlapping. Doing more than one thing at a time. In particular, responding to the needs of individuals while sustaining a group activity (using eye contact or physical proximity to restore inattentive students' attention to a lesson while continuing the lesson itself without interruption).

Signal continuity and momentum during lessons. Teaching well-prepared and briskly paced lessons that focus students' attention by providing them with a continuous academic signal which is more compelling than the noise of competing distractions in the classroom, and by sustaining the momentum of this academic signal throughout the duration of the lesson.

Challenge and variety in assignments. Encouraging student engagement in seatwork by providing assignments pitched at the right level of difficulty (easy enough to insure success with reasonable effort but new or difficult enough to provide challenge) and varied enough to sustain interest.

These and other principles discovered by Kounin indicate that effective classroom managers succeed not so much because they are good at handling disruption when it occurs, but because they are good at maximizing the time students spend attending to lessons and engaging in assignments. They are good at preventing disruption from occurring in the first place. Their focus is not on prevention of disruption as such but on establishing the classroom as an effective learning environment, preparing and teaching good lessons, and selecting and monitoring student performance on good follow-up assignments.

Evertson and Emmer (1982) and their colleagues have replicated and extended Kounin's findings in a series of studies of how teachers establish effective classroom management at the beginning of the year and sustain it thereafter. These studies have replicated and reinforced Kounin's findings and have demonstrated the importance of showing and telling students what to do. Teacher clarity about rules and routines is crucial, as is the ability to explain and, if necessary, demonstrate the desired behavior to the students.

Especially in the lower grades, effective classroom managers spend a great deal of time in the early weeks of school explaining expectations and conducting lessons not only in the formal curriculum but in the routines and procedures to be used in the classroom. Their students are given detailed explanations and modeling (and, if necessary, opportunities to practice and receive feedback) concerning such matters as when and how to use the pencil sharpener or how to manage the transitions between reading groups.

In the upper grades it is less important for teachers to model or provide formal lessons in desired routines (the students are already familiar with most of these routines or can understand them sufficiently from verbal explanation) but it is just as important for them to be clear and detailed in describing what behavior

they expect. At all grade levels, teachers need to insure that the students follow the desired procedures, providing additional reminders or feedback as needed.

Effective managers consistently monitor compliance with rules and demands, enforce accountability procedures and associated penalties for late or unacceptable work, and are prepared to punish students for repeated misconduct if necessary. But their emphasis is positive and prescriptive rather than threatening or punitive. This and other work on classroom management (reviewed by Brophy, 1983, and Doyle, in press) shows clearly that effective classroom management goes hand in hand with effective instruction and that it primarily involves teaching willing students what to do before the fact rather than applying "discipline" following misconduct.

Strategies for Problem Students

No comparable set of research findings exists regarding strategies teachers should use with students who present chronic personality or behavior problems and require something more than what is effective with the group, and few teachers have had training in such techniques (Brophy & Rohrkemper, 1981). However, writers interested in applications by teachers of techniques developed in psychotherapy and mental health settings have begun to suggest principles that complement those known to be effective for group management. Gordon (1974), Glasser (1977), and Good and Brophy (1984) are representative of these contemporary sources of advice to teachers about counseling problem students. Gordon's approach begins with analysis of problem ownership. A problem is owned by the teacher if the teacher's needs are being frustrated (as when a student persistently disrupts the class by socializing with friends). The student owns the problem when the student's needs are being frustrated (such as when the student is being rejected by the peer group). The teacher and the student share a problem when each is frustrating the needs of the other (the teacher gives the student work that is too difficult and the student responds by giving up and becoming disruptive).

For student-owned problems Gordon recommends "active listening," in which the teacher not only listens to the student's point of view, but attempts to reflect it back accurately to the student, with attention to the student's feelings and personal reaction in addition to behaviors and events. For teacher-owned problems he recommends "I" messages in which the teacher states explicitly the linkages between the student's objectionable behavior, the problem that this behavior causes the teacher (how it frustrates the teacher's needs), and the effects of these events on the teacher's feelings (discouragement, frustration). Shared problems would call for combinations of active listening and "I" messages.

Such communications should help teachers and students achieve shared rational views of problems and assume cooperative, problem-solving attitudes. Together they can work to resolve conflicts using what Gordon calls the "no lose" method of finding the solution that will work best for all concerned. The process involves six steps: Define the problem; generate possible solutions; evaluate those solutions; decide which is best; determine how to implement this decision; and assess how well the solution is working (a new solution will have to be negotiated if the first one does not work satisfactorily).

Glasser stresses the need to develop appropriate classroom rules (preferably in collaboration with the students) and to enforce those rules and refer to them when correcting student misbehavior. His "ten steps to good discipline" (Glasser, 1977) are designed to focus students' attention on their behavior in order to make sure that they realize and accept responsibility for what they are doing (often this alone is sufficient to change the behavior). In some cases he suggests requiring the student to develop a plan that includes a commitment to changing problem behavior and a description

of steps to be taken to insure that such change occurs.

Good and Brophy (1984) suggest ways that teachers can observe and interview problem students in order to develop an understanding of why they behave as they do, as well as strategies for developing productive personal relationships with such students and counseling them individually. They stress the importance of supporting the positive elements of the student's self-concept, projecting positive expectations about the student's willingness and ability to change behavior, setting realistic goals and monitoring progress toward attaining them, and emphasizing the teacher's role as a helper rather than as an authority figure (while still exerting that authority and making demands on the student).

Beyond Management: Promoting Self-Guidance

In combination, the approaches to classroom management reviewed above will allow teachers to establish their classrooms as effective learning environments and themselves as effective leaders for the group and counselors for individuals. In order to develop self-guidance in students, however, additional strategies are needed.

In setting limits and prescribing procedures, teachers should use an informational rather than a controlling style (Koestner, Ryan, Bernieri, & Holt, in press). They should stress the reasons for the limits and procedures, implying that these are reasonable and useful guidelines students will want to follow because they help insure the attainment of important academic or social goals. Even though acting as an authority figure, the teacher uses a tone and manner that suggests soliciting students' cooperation rather than issuing orders. The emphasis is on what to do and how this will yield desirable benefits rather than on the consequences for failure to comply. The idea is to induce students to consciously adopt the desired procedures for themselves and thus begin to use them as internal guides to behavior, minimizing the degree to which they see the guidelines as externally imposed and enforced.

As a way to insure student commitment to the guidelines, some teachers prefer to develop them in collaboration with students during classroom meetings held for this purpose. This method can be effective, but it takes time and the teacher needs to set a positive tone and provide guidance and structure to the meetings. If left on their own, students will tend to make up large numbers of overly specific rules rather than smaller numbers of general ones, to stress "don'ts" rather than "do's," and to focus on prescribing punishment for violators. Furthermore, even with this level of student involvement in rule making, the teacher remains the ultimate authority figure in the classroom. As Baumrind (1971) has shown, the form of socialization of children and youth that best fosters the development of self-guidance abilities is "authoritative," not "democratic."

The degree to which a guideline becomes functional in regulating student behavior will be determined not so much by whether the students participate in establishing the guidelines as by whether they see it as reasonable and choose to adopt it for themselves. Presenting guidelines in an informative rather than a controlling style encourages students to make this choice. The following are aspects of an informational style of presenting guidelines.

First, teachers should always give the reasons for the guideline in addition to the guideline itself. If it is not easy to show that the guideline is intended as a means toward a desirable end, something is probably wrong with the guideline.

Second, guidelines should be presented with positive expectations and attributions. Teachers should assume that students will want to follow reasonable guidelines because the students themselves are reasonable and prosocially oriented individuals who want to cooperate and pursue the common good.

Third, when it becomes necessary to correct misbehavior, such corrections should empha-

size the desired positive behavior ("Talk quietly so as not to disturb those who are still working."). As much as possible, such corrections should be phrased as friendly reminders rather than as power assertive direct orders, and should encourage students to see themselves as regulating their own behavior rather than being controlled externally ("You only have a few more minutes to finish your assignment" is better than "If you don't get back to work and finish that assignment before the bell, you will have to stay in during recess").

Fourth, if it becomes necessary to punish students who have not responded to more positive approaches, the punishment should be announced with a tone of sadness and disappointment rather than vengefulness or righteous indignation. The student should understand that the teacher does not want to have to punish but feels it necessary to do so because of the student's own repeated misbehavior and failure to respond to more positive approaches. The punishment is not an arbitrary exertion of power by the teacher; rather, it is an unfortunate but necessary and appropriate consequence of the student's repeated misbehavior, and one the student can avoid in the future if he or she chooses to do so.

Underlying this is the implication that students can and are expected to behave appropriately, and it is primarily their own responsibility to regulate their behavior rather than the teacher's responsibility to control them externally. The teacher is a facilitator, not a prison warden, and the student is a well-intentioned, reasonable human being, not a wild animal in need of training or a weak individual dominated by emotions or compulsions that he or she cannot control.

Finally, some students will need individualized counseling and assistance in developing effective self-regulation. Often this can be accomplished simply through conversations designed to develop personal relationships with such students, establish the teacher as a helper and resource person, and develop the students' insights into their own behavior. The suggestions of Glasser (1977), Gordon (1974), and

Good and Brophy (1984) are useful in this regard. Some students, however, may need not only general guidance but explicit instruction in methods of self-regulation of behavior. Recent developments in theory and research provide teachers interested in self-guidance with some exciting new approaches in this regard.

One set of sources has been developed through an approach called cognitive behavior modification (Meichenbaum, 1977). In this approach teachers go beyond merely telling students what to do in a general way. Instead they model the process by verbalizing aloud the self-talk that is generated and used to regulate behavior while carrying out the activity (generation of goal statements, review of strategies to be used in pursuing the goals, self-instructions produced at each step, monitoring and evaluation of performance, methods of responding effectively to failure or unexpected events, self-reinforcement for progress and success). Such modeling shows students how to regulate their own behavior by making visible the perceptions, thoughts, and other self-talk that regulate effective coping behavior but usually remain invisible to the observer.

The cognitive behavior modification approach has been used to teach students to respond reflectively rather than impulsively to multiple choice tasks (Meichenbaum & Goodman, 1971), to "innoculate" aggression-prone individuals against overreaction to provocation and help them to control their anger (Novaco, 1975), and to help hyperactive and disruptive students learn to control their behavior more effectively (Kendall & Braswell, 1982). More recently, this approach has been adapted for use in helping students cope with academic tasks and manage their learning more effectively, in addition to applications to control of classroom conduct and social interaction (Meichenbaum & Asarnow, 1979).

Other approaches to what is becoming known as "strategy training" have been developed by theorists working outside the cognitive behavior modification tradition, although their approaches are similar to and compatible with cognitive behavior modification approaches.

One such approach involves modeling coupled with role playing or other simulation exercises (Good & Brophy, 1984; Sarason & Sarason, 1981). Other strategy training approaches have been developed by individuals interested in teaching students strategies for reading with comprehension or for learning and problem solving with clarity of purpose and metacognitive awareness of the strategies being applied (Brown, Bransford, Ferrara, & Campione, 1983; Palincsar & Brown, 1984).

Conclusion

Even though schooling is compulsory and teachers must prescribe and control student behavior in order to establish the classroom as an effective learning environment, teachers can still stimulate self-guidance, and not merely compliance, in their students. This is done by deemphasizing the authority figure aspects of the teacher's role and emphasizing the rationales that justify the demands made on students, projecting positive expectations concerning students' ability to foster the common good, and encouraging students to view behavioral guidelines as reasonable and adopt them as their own.

Most students develop effective self-guidance mechanisms on their own, even though the self-talk involved in such self-guidance ordinarily is covert and cannot be observed directly. Students who have not developed effective self-guidance procedures will need direct assistance in doing so, however, and recently developed procedures for strategy training and cognitive behavior modification are suggested for this purpose.

Note: This work is sponsored in part by the Institute for Research on Teaching, College of Education, Michigan State University. The Institute for Research on Teaching is funded primarily by the Program for Teaching and Instruction of the National Institute of Education, United States Department of Education. The opinions expressed in this article do not necessarily reflect the position, policy, or endorsement of the National Institute of Education. (Contract No. 400-81-0014)

REFERENCES

Baumrind, D. (1971). Current patterns of parental authority. *Developmental Psychology Monograph, 4* (1), part 2.

Brophy, J. (1977). *Child development and socialization.* Chicago: Science Research Associates.

Brophy, J. (1983). Classroom organization and management. *Elementary School Journal, 83,* 265–285.

Brophy, J., & Rohrkemper, M. (1981). The influence of problem ownership on teachers' perceptions of and strategies for coping with problem students. *Journal of Educational Psychology, 73,* 295–311.

Brown, A., Bransford, J., Ferrara, R., & Campione, J. (1983). Learning, remembering, and understanding. In J. Flavell and E. Markman (Eds.), *Handbook of child psychology* (4th ed.)—*Cognitive development* (Vol. 3) (pp 77–166). New York: Wiley.

Doyle, W. (in press). Classroom organization and management. In M. Wittrock (Ed.), *Handbook of research on teaching* (3rd ed.). New York: Macmillan.

Evertson, C., & Emmer, E. (1982). Preventive classroom management. In D. Duke (Ed.), *Helping teachers manage classrooms.* Alexandria, VA: Association for Supervision and Curriculum Development.

Glasser, W. (1977, November-December). Ten steps to good discipline. *Today's Education, 66* (4), 61–63.

Good, T., & Brophy, J. (1984). *Looking in classrooms* (3rd ed.). New York: Harper and Row.

Gordon, T. (1974). *T.E.T. teacher effectiveness training.* New York: David McKay.

Hess, R. (1970). Social class and ethnic influences upon socialization. In P. Mussen (Ed.), *Carmichael's manual of child psychology,* (Vol. 2, 3rd ed.) (pp. 457–557). New York: Wiley.

Kendall, P., & Braswell, L. (1982). Cognitive-behavioral self-control therapy for children: A components analysis. *Journal of Consulting and Clinical Psychology, 50,* 672–689.

Koestner, R., Ryan, R., Bernieri, F., & Holt, K. (in press). Setting limits on children's behavior: The differential effects of controlling versus informational styles on intrinsic motivation and creativity. *Journal of Personality.*

Kohlberg, L. (1969). Stage and sequence: The cognitive-developmental approach to socialization. In D. Goslin (Ed.), *Handbook of socialization theory and research* (pp. 347–480). Chicago: Rand McNally.

Kounin, J. (1970). *Discipline and group management in classrooms.* New York: Holt, Rinehart, & Winston.

Meichenbaum, D. (1977). *Cognitive-behavior modification.* New York: Plenum.

Meichenbaum, D., & Asarnow, J. (1979). Cognitive-behavioral modification and metacognitive development: Implications for the classroom. In P. Kendall & S. Hollon (Eds.), *Cognitive-behavioral interventions: Theory, research, and procedures* (pp. 11–35). New York: Academic Press.

Meichenbaum, D., & Goodman, J. (1971). Training impulsive children to talk to themselves. *Journal of Abnormal Psychology, 77,* 115–126.

Novaco, R. (1975). *Anger control: A development and evaluation of an experimental treatment.* Lexington, MA: Heath.

Palincsar, A., & Brown, A. (1984). Reciprocal teaching of comprehension-fostering and comprehension-monitoring activities. *Cognition and Instruction, 1,* 117–175.

Sarason, I., & Sarason, B. (1981). Teaching cognitive and social skills to high school students. *Journal of Consulting and Clinical Psychology, 49,* 908–918.

Vygotsky, L. (1962). *Thought and Language.* Cambridge, MA: MIT Press.

The Canter Model: Assertively Taking Charge

C. M. Charles

The Canters' Key Ideas

The following list presents the key ideas that form the core of assertive discipline. It provides a summary of the assertive model of discipline. These ideas are explained in greater detail in subsequent sections of this chapter.

1. Teachers should insist on decent, responsible behavior from their students. Students need this type of behavior, parents want it, the community at large expects it, and the educational process is crippled without it.

2. Teacher failure, for all practical purposes, is synonymous with failure to maintain adequate classroom discipline.

3. Many teachers labor under false assumptions about discipline. They believe that firm control is stifling and inhumane. It is not. Firm control maintained correctly is humane and liberating.

4. Teachers have basic educational rights in their classrooms including:

   a. The right to establish optimal learning environments.

   b. The right to determine, request, and expect appropriate behavior from students.

   c. The right to receive help from administrators and parents when it is needed.

5. Students have basic rights in the classroom, too, including:

   a. The right to have teachers who help them limit their inappropriate, self-destructive behavior.

   b. The right to have teachers who provide positive support for their appropriate behavior.

   c. The right to choose how to behave, with full understanding of the consequences that automatically follow their choices.

6. These needs, rights, and conditions are best met through assertive discipline, in which the teacher clearly communicates expectations to students and consistently follows up with appropriate actions but never violates the best interests of the students.

7. This assertive discipline consists of the following elements:

   a. Identifying expectations clearly.

From C. M. Charles, *Building Classroom Discipline From Models to Practice* (2nd ed.), New York: Longman, 1985. Reprinted with permission.

b. Willingness to say, "I like that," and "I don't like that."

c. Persistence in stating expectations and feelings.

d. Use of firm tone of voice.

e. Maintenance of eye contact.

f. Use of nonverbal gestures in support of verbal statements.

8. Assertive discipline enables teachers to do such things as:

a. Say no, without feeling guilty.

b. Give and receive compliments genuinely and gracefully.

c. Express thoughts and feelings that others might find intimidating.

d. Stand up for feelings and rights when under fire from others.

e. Place demands comfortably on others.

f. Influence students' behavior firmly without yelling and threatening.

g. Work more successfully with chronic behavior problems.

9. Teachers who use assertive discipline do the following:

a. Employ assertive response styles, as opposed to nonassertive or hostile response styles.

b. Eliminate negative expectations about student behavior.

c. Establish and communicate clear expectations for positive student behavior.

d. Use hints, questions, and I-messages rather than demands for requesting student behavior.

e. Use eye contact, gestures, and touches to supplement verbal messages.

f. Follow through with promises (reasonable consequences, previously established) rather than with threats.

g. Be assertive in confrontations with students, including using statements of expectations, indicating consequences that will occur, and noting why the action is necessary.

10. To become more assertive in discipline, teachers should do the following:

a. Practice assertive response styles.

b. Set clear limits and consequences.

c. Follow through consistently.

d. Make specific assertive discipline plans and rehearse them mentally.

e. Write things down; do not trust the memory.

f. Practice the broken record technique for repeating expectations.

g. Ask school principals and parents for support in the efforts to help students.

The Need for Assertive Discipline

Discipline is a matter of great concern in schools; it remains so year after year. Teachers hold it as their greatest concern in teaching. It is the overwhelming cause of teacher failure, burn out, and resignation. Parents and the community name school discipline far more than any other factor as the area in which they would like to see improvement. Discipline remains a source of sore concern for several reasons. Among those reasons are a general decline in our society's respect for authority, a decline in parents' insistence that their children behave acceptably in school and elsewhere, and a leniency within law enforcement and legal circles in dealing with juvenile offenders. But teachers and school administrators have to share some of the blame, too. The societal conditions just mentioned make discipline more difficult, yet much of the control problem can be placed at the feet of teachers and administrators who hold such mistaken ideas about discipline as:

1. Good teachers can handle discipline problems on their own without help.

2. Firm discipline causes psychological trauma in students.

3. Discipline problems disappear when students are given activities that meet their needs.

4. Misbehavior results from deep-seated causes, which are beyond the influence of the teacher.

These mistaken ideas about discipline cause teachers to be hesitant about controlling misbehavior. They are afraid they will do ethical or psychological harm, and become reluctant to confront misbehaving students. Teachers hesitate to take action, and by the time they realize that action is necessary, the situation in the classroom is out of hand.

We must supplant these thoughts with correct ideas about discipline including:

1. We all need discipline for psychological security.
2. We need discipline as a suppressant to acts that we would not be proud of later.
3. We need discipline as a liberating influence that allows us to build and expand our best traits and abilities.
4. Discipline is necessary to maintain an effective and efficient learning environment.

The Basis of Assertive Discipline

Canter and Canter (1976) say that an assertive teacher is one who clearly and firmly communicates needs and requirements to students, follows those words with appropriate actions, responds to students in ways that maximize compliance, but in no way violates the best interests of the students.

The basis of this assertive posture is *caring* about oneself to the point of not allowing others (students) to take advantage, and caring about students to the point of not allowing them to behave in ways that are damaging to themselves. Such care can only be shown when the teacher takes charge in the classroom. The manner must be positive, firm, and consistent. It must be composed. It cannot be wishy-washy, hostile, loudly abusive, or threatening. These negative postures are doomed to failure. The calm, positive manner shows students that teachers do care about them, their needs, and their proper behavior. It provides the climate of support that best assists students' own self-control.

A climate of care and support rises up from what Canter and Canter (p.2) call basic teacher rights in working with students.

1. The right to establish optimal learning environments for students, consistent with the teacher's strengths and weaknesses.
2. The right to expect behavior from students that contributes to their optimal growth, while also meeting the special needs of the teacher.
3. The right to ask and receive help and backing from administrators and parents.

The climate of care also has origins in what Canter and Canter (p.8) call rights of students, when under the teacher's guidance.

1. The right to have a teacher who will limit inappropriate and self-destructive behavior.
2. The right to have a teacher who will provide positive support for appropriate behavior.
3. The right to choose one's own behavior, with full knowledge of the natural consequences that follow that behavior.

The climate of positive support and care is best provided, Canter and Canter believe, through the careful application of principles of assertion training to classroom discipline. Such application produces assertive discipline. It replaces teacher inertia and hostility with firm positive insistence. While certainly not a cure-all for problems that occur in the classroom, assertive discipline greatly helps teachers establish and maintain the sort of working climate that meets students' needs as well as their own. Canter and Canter (p.12) say that assertive discipline provides the following helps for teachers:

1. Identify situations where assertiveness will help both teacher and students;
2. Develop more consistent and effective communication with students;
3. Gain confidence and skills for making

firmer and more consistent demands on students;

4. Reduce hostile teacher behavior, replacing it with the more effective positive, firm, composed insistence;

5. Gain confidence and skills for working more

effectively with chronic behavior problems in the classroom.

Canter, L. and Canter, M. *Assertive Discipline: A Take-Charge Approach for Today's Educator*. Seal Beach, CA: Canter and Associaties, 1976.

REFERENCES AND ADDITIONAL READINGS FOR UNIT 4

Special Versus Regular Education: Is This Dual System Justified?

Lieberman, L. Special Education and Regular Education: A Merger Made in Heaven? *Exceptional Children,* 1985, *51,* 513–516.

Messick, S. Assessment in Context: Appraising Student Performance in Relation to Instructional Quality. *Educational Researcher,* 1984, *13,* 3–11.

Pugach, M. & Lilly, N. Reconceptualizing Support Services for Classroom Teachers: Implications for Teacher Education. *Journal of Teacher Education,* 1984, *35,* 48–55.

Stainback, S. & Stainback, W. The Merger of Special and Regular Education: Can It Be Done? A Response to Lieberman and Mesinger. *Exceptional Children,* 1985, *51,* 517–521.

Wang, M. & Reynolds, M. Avoiding the "Catch 22" in Special Education Reform. *Exceptional Children,* 1985, *51,* 497–502.

Grade Retention or Social Promotion

Adler, R. (1978, November). State-by-State Roundup of Minimum Competency Testing. *Learning,* p.99.

Carstens, A. A. (1985). Retention and Social Promotion for the Exceptional Child. *School Psychology Review,* 14, 1, 48–63.

Holmes, C. T. & Matthews, K. M. (1984). The Effects of Nonpromotion on Elementary and Junior High School Pupils: A Meta-Analysis. *Review of Educational Research,* 54, 2, 225–236.

Larson, R. E. (1955). *Age-Grade Status of Iowa Elementary School Pupils.* Unpublished doctoral dissertation, State University of Iowa.

Rose, J. S. et al. (1983). A Fresh Look at the Retention-Promotion Controversy. *Journal of School Psychology,* 21, 3, 201–211.

Schuyler, N. B. (1985). *Does Retention Help? Perspectives After Three Years.* Paper presented at the annual meeting of the American Educational Research Association, Chicago.

Vasa, S. F.; Wendel, F. C.; & Steckelberg, A. L. (1984). Light's Retention Scale: Does It Have Content Validity? *Psychology in the Schools,* 21, 4, 447–449.

Teacher Expectancies

Cooper, H. & Tom, D. Teacher Expectation Research: A Review with Implications for Classroom Instruction. *The Elementary School Journal,* 1984, *85,* 77–89.

Dusek, J.; Hall, V.; & Meyer, W. (Eds.). *Teacher Expectations.* Hillsdale, NJ: Lawrence Erlbaum, 1985.

Proctor, C. Teacher Expectations: A Model for School Improvement. *The Elementary School Journal,* 1984, *85,* 468–481.

Raudenbusch, S. Magnitude of Teacher Expectancy Effects on Pupil IQ as a Function of the Credibility of Expectancy Induction: A Synthesis of Findings of Eighteen Experiments. *Journal of Educational Psychology,* 1984, 76, 85–97.

Motivation: Intrinsic and Cognitive Versus Extrinsic and Social

Connell, J. P. & Ryan, R. M. A Developmental Theory of Motivation in the Classroom. *Teacher Education Quarterly,* 1985, *11,* No. 4, 64–77.

Covington, M. The Self-Worth Theory of Achievement Motivation: Findings and Implications. *The Elementary School Journal,* 1984, *85,* 5–20.

Deci, E. The Well Tempered Classroom. How Not to Motivate Teachers and Students: Impose Stricter Standards, More Controls and Greater Conformity. *Psychology Today,* 1985, *19,* 52–54.

McClelland, D. How Motives, Skills and Values Determine What People Do. *American Psychologist,* 1985, *40,* 812–825.

McCombs, B. L. Processes and Skills Underlying Continuing Intrinsic Motivation to Learn: Toward a Definition of Motivational Skills Training Interventions. *Educational Psychologist,* Fall, 1984, *19,* No. 4, 199–218.

Morgan, M. Reward-Induced Decrements and Increments in Intrinsic Motivation. *Review of Educational Research,* 1984, 54, 5–30.

Pearl, R. Cognitive Behavioral Interventions for Increasing Motivation. *The Journal of Abnormal Child Psychology*, 1985, *13*, 443–454.

Schunk, D. H. Enhancing Self-Efficacy and Achievement Through Rewards and Goals: Motivational and Informational Effects. *Journal of Educational Research*, 78, No. 1 (September/October 1984), 29–34.

Discipline: Self Guidance Versus External Control

Combs, A. Achieving Self-Discipline: Some Basic Principles. *Theory into Practice*, 1985, *24*, 260–263.

Canter, L. & Canter, M. *Assertive Discipline: A Take-Charge Approach for Today's Educator*. Seal Beach, CA: Canter & Associates, 1976.

Matson, J. & DiLorenzo, T. *Punishment and Its Alternatives*. New York: Springer, 1984.

Pepper, F. & Henry, S. Using Developmental and Democratic Practices to Teach Self-Discipline. *Theory into Practice*, 1985, *24*, 264–270.

Whalen, C.; Henker, B.; & Hinshaw, S. Cognitive-Behavioral Therapies for Hyperactive Children: Premises, Promises and Prospects. *Journal of Abnormal Child Psychology*, 1985, *13*, 391–410.

Wong, B. Issues in Cognitive Behavioral Intervention and Academic Skill Areas. *Journal of Abnormal Child Psychology*, 1985, *13*, 425–442.

SUBJECT INDEX

AUTHOR INDEX